ACTION
KNOWLEDGE
AND
REALITY

ACTION
KNOWLEDGE
AND
REALITY

Critical Studies
in Honor of Wilfrid Sellars

Edited by
Hector-Neri Castañeda
Mahlon Powell Professor of Philosophy
Indiana University
1975

THE BOBBS-MERRILL COMPANY, INC.

INDIANAPOLIS

Copyright © 1975 by The Bobbs-Merrill Company, Inc.
Printed in the United States of America
All rights reserved. No part of this book shall be reproduced or
transmitted in any form or by any means, electronic or mechanical,
including photocopying, recording, or by any information or re-
trieval system, without written permission from the Publisher:

The Bobbs-Merrill Company, Inc.
4300 West 62nd Street
Indianapolis, Indiana 46268

First Edition
First Printing 1975

Library of Congress Cataloging in Publication Data

Main entry under title:

Action, knowledge, and reality.

CONTENTS: Studies in Wilfrid Sellars' philosophy: Aune,
B. Sellars on practical reason.—Castañeda, H.-N. Some
reflections on Wilfrid Sellars' theory of intentions.—Donagan, A.
Determinism and freedom: Sellars and the reconciliationist thesis.
[etc.]
1. Sellars, Wilfrid—Addresses, essays, lectures. I. Sellars,
Wilfrid.   II. Castañeda Calderón, Héctor Neri, ed.
B945.S444A25   191   74-8419
ISBN 0-672-61213-5

CONTENTS

Preface

PART TWO

SELLARSIANA

PREFACE

This collection of previously unpublished essays aims to advance both the scholarship on Wilfrid Sellars and the understanding of some philosophical problems.

Wilfrid Sellars is a rare philosopher who combines a profound sensitivity to all philosophical problems with an apparently unlimited gift for appreciating the most diverse philosophical positions. Thus, in an array of studies spanning more than three decades, he has worked steadily at building an all-encompassing system of philosophy and has also offered masterful exegeses of historical views.

Sellars' philosophical investigations have ranged over all the fields of philosophy. They have yielded: beautiful phenomenological analyses of the structures—both practical and theoretical—of human experience; careful distillations of the categories of entities, whether encountered in ordinary experience or postulated by scientific theories; challenging metaphysical views about the reality underlying the world of experience, and about the interconnections of mind, language, and reality. A glance at Sellars' bibliography at the end of this volume will give an idea of the variety and number of philosophical problems to which he has contributed something important.

Sellars' expertise in the history of philosophy has stood him in excellent stead. He has used it to illuminate the classical systems of great philosophers. He has also made admirable use of it to do justice to, and to build upon, the opposing insights of great historical controversies. One of the most important lessons I remember learning from him is to view the history of philosophy as somehow a criterion of adequacy for philosophy, so that good philosophizing has to illuminate one or another of the classical disputes.

The essays in Part I are critical studies on different aspects of Sellars' philosophical views. They each show something of the depth and intensity of his insights. They examine some of his views, clarify some of his arguments, demarcate obscure areas, stake challenges, and suggest corrections and further developments. Thus, this anthology is composed of papers that not only represent their authors' tributes to Sellars but also bring the understanding of the problems which they discuss one notch further.

As a grateful and admiring student of Wilfrid Sellars, I hoped to prepare a *Festschrift* which would be published in celebration of his sixtieth birthday in May 1972. Editorial complications have delayed the appearance but have not dampened the spirit of the *Festschrift*.

I apologize to those whose essays are absent from this collection—the many students, friends, admirers, and opponents of Sellars whose contributions would fill several interesting volumes.*

I am grateful to the various publishers, listed in the bibliographies at the end of each article, who have kindly granted permission to reprint fragments of their copyrighted materials. Finally I thank Mrs. Anita Baugh, Mrs. Elizabeth Myers, Miss Deborah Pettry, Mr. Michael McKinsey, and Mr. William Rapaport for valuable assistance in the preparation of the *Festschrift*.

H-N. C.

*A complementary mini-*Festschrift* for Sellars appears in *Noûs,* 7 (May 1973). It contains studies on some of Sellars' philosophical views by Keith Lehrer, Murray Kiteley, James W. Cornman, Robert Ackermann, Ausonio Marras, and James McGilvray, as well as a previously unpublished paper by Sellars himself.

ACTION
KNOWLEDGE
AND
REALITY

Sellars on Practical Reason

BRUCE AUNE
University of Massachusetts at Amherst

OVER the past twenty years, Sellars has worked out the most detailed theory of practical reason in the recent philosophical literature.[1] Although this subject is now very popular with philosophers, Sellars' theory has provoked little critical comment. The aim of this paper is to call attention to Sellars' achievement by offering a critical exposition of his fundamental ideas on purposive thought and its relation to intelligent action.

1. *Reasoning and Action*

According to Sellars, the key to understanding intelligent, nonhabitual human action is to appreciate the practical reasoning lying behind it. Consider the behavior of a boy wandering through the woods on a moonlit night holding open a large cloth bag. What exactly is he doing, and why is he doing it? If we ask him what he is doing, he might say "Snipe hunting." As a first-year visitor at a summer camp, he has been asked to join the annual snipe hunt. As a joke he has been told that snipe are crafty birds that can barely see at night, and that if he keeps walking through the woods, the birds, frightened by the other boys, will fly into his bag. Since he wishes to succeed at the new activity of snipe hunting,

1. Sellars' views on practical reason are developed in five essays: "Imperatives, Intentions, and the Logic of 'Ought'," *Methodos* 8 (1956): 227-68; revised version in [7]: 159-218; "Thought and Action," in [13]: 105-39; "Fatalism and Determinism," in [13]: 140-74; "Objectivity, Intersubjectivity, and the Moral Point of View," in [17]: 175-229; and "Metaphysics and the Concept of a Person," in [12]: 219-52. I shall refer to these essays as, respectively, *IILO, TA, FD, SM,* and *MCP*; my references to *IILO* will be to the reprint in [7].

he finds a large bag, goes into the woods, and behaves as instructed.

Like the boy's actions in hunting snipe, the behavior we consider intelligent and nonhabitual is purposive. To understand why it is done in the way it is done we must normally know (1) what the agent intended to accomplish, (2) what he believed about the means of realizing his intentions, and (3) how his beliefs and intentions gave rise to the actions in question. To understand point (3) we must understand something about the logic of practical reasoning and about the relation of such reasoning to intelligent action.

As a preliminary to discussing the logic of practical reasoning, we might consider how such reasoning results in overt action. Sellars' view, in outline, is this. (See esp. *TA,* pp. 105-10; *FD,* pp. 150-57; and *SM,* pp. 177ff.) Successful practical reasoning terminates, or at least finds its rational terminus, in a volition to bring something about by doing something that the agent believes is in his power there and then. If the agent is not mistaken about his powers, a volition to do something results in his doing it. Consequently, what we may call the "material terminus" of his reasoning (if it has one) is an action on his part. For Sellars, an action is the immediate result of a volition when it is explainable by reference to the agent's practical reasoning.

Sellars calls the action immediately resulting from a volition a "minimal act" (*FD,* pp. 157ff). Such an act need not be a mere muscle movement or bodily gesture; it may be highly complicated, requiring considerable skill. When a child is learning to play the piano, a minimal act for him may consist of pressing middle C with his right thumb; but years later a minimal act may consist of playing an entire passage with both hands. In general, we can be trained to perform extremely complicated minimal acts. An act is minimal for a given person just in case he can perform it successfully without consciously intending to bring about some component of the act. To put it in another way, if the mere thought "I will do *A* here and now" can result in the agent's doing *A* without any other practical thinking being involved, then and only then his doing *A* is a minimal act.

2. *The Concept of Volition*

The concept of volition has been unpopular with English-speaking philosophers for nearly twenty years. This unpopularity is due to a number of causes, outstanding among which, in my opinion, is a serious misunderstanding of what a volition (or "act" of will) is best understood to be. Since Sellars has recently defended the concept of volition in a very clear way against standard lines of criticism (*MCP*, pp. 243-47), I shall restrict myself for the most part to explaining what Sellars' view of volition is, commenting only incidentally on a couple of familiar objections.

Sellars conceives of a volition somewhat as Kant did, and it will be useful to recall Kant's definition of the will: it is, he says, the faculty of bringing forth objects corresponding to conceptions or of determining itself to do so whether the physical power is present or not ([11]:15). Although noticeably obscure, this is an improvement over Hume's definition ([10], Bk. II, Pt. III, Sect. I, p. 399), for when we will to do something, we do not merely have a peculiar internal "impression;" we are consciously aware of what we are going to do. It is, in fact, the thought of what we are going to do that, occurring in a special way, brings about our action. A willed action is not, in other words, a spontaneous movement or series of movements that could conceivably surprise the agent; it is an item of behavior that somehow results from his consciousness of what he is going to do. When we do something voluntarily or willfully, we bring about an object (an action) corresponding to our conception (our awareness) of what we are going to do.

If a man intends to do a thing A in circumstances C, then if he believes he is in C, is able to do A, and has no conflicting intentions, then he will do A. This holds by virtue of the meaning of "intending to do A in C." Now, a man's doing A as the result of his intention to do A in C is apt to be the outcome of practical reasoning. This reasoning, made fully explicit, would have the following form:

> I will do A in circumstances C.
> I am now in circumstances C.
> Therefore, I will do A (here and now).

If the doing of A is not, for the agent, a minimal action, further reasoning may be required; it might be necessary to reason:

> I will do A.
> I can do A by doing B, which is open to me here and now.
> In addition to realizing A, B has no undesirable consequences.
> Therefore, I will do B (here and now).

If the action A is a minimal one, however, the intention to do A here and now can be regarded as a volition, for this occurrent intention is the last conscious step that leads the agent to act.

For Sellars, a volition is a "here and now" occurrent intention (*TA*, p. 109; *FD*, pp. 155f; *SM*, p. 177). Although the action immediately resulting from the volition is, for the agent, a minimal one, Sellars does not require that the idea involved in the volition be limited to the minimal act. For reasons that emerge in his treatment of certain forms of practical reasoning, he insists that a volition may have a form as complicated as "I will now do *A* in order to bring about *G* in spite of preventing *C*" (*TA*, p. 109).

As I have described them, volitions occur as the rational termini of lines of practical reasoning. But it is clear that not all volitions have such a rational source; we frequently will to do things on impulse. Sellars offers several other important points about volitions in a short paragraph:

> Notice that volitions are not *tryings*. To try to do *A* is to do one or more things which one thinks likely in the circumstances to constitute doing *A*. Nor are volitions *choosings*. One can will to do *A* without choosing to do *A* rather than something else—even refraining from doing *A*. Nor are volitions *decisions*: a volition need not be the *culmination of a process* of deliberation or practical reasoning. (*FD*, p. 156.)

Although Sellars' conception of volition is novel in the present philosophical climate, similar conceptions have been defended by traditional philosophers concerned with the relation of thought to action. R. G. Collingwood, in his important but neglected book *The New Leviathan*, spoke of the will as follows:

> A will, as distinct from the corresponding deed, is an example of *practical thinking*. So far as it is thinking, it expresses itself (like all thinking) in words; thus the intention to shut the door is expressed as a thought by saying "I will shut the door."
>
> But in addition to being a thought, it is also practical; and as practical it expresses itself by the initial stage of the action of shutting the door; for example lifting my hand in the appropriate way. ([8]:97.)

The idea of a volition as a practical thought is not, therefore, peculiar to Sellars; it has a long history in philosophy, being defended even by Kant. It is this conception of a volition, not the anomalous and useless conception of, say, Hume, that should be the target of thoughtful philosophers wishing to prove that volitions are fictions.

Although Sellars' conception of volition is well rooted in philosophical tradition, it is not merely the copy of an old idea. The peculiarity of his conception stands out when we consider his view of the *relation* between volition and action. For Sellars, the following is a conceptual (or analytic) truth:

If *x* wills to do *A* at *t* and has the ability and opportunity to do it, then *x* does *A* forthwith.

In view of this conceptual truth, some philosophers might conclude that the relation between volition and action is logical or conceptual. But this way of describing the relation is inaccurate or confused. Strictly speaking, it is only concepts or statements that are logically related, not volitions and actions or riders and horses. The conceptual truth of the statement above does not imply that the relation between volition and action is anything other than causal.

According to Sellars, the relation between volition and action is to be understood in stimulus-response terms. His idea is this (*TA*, pp. 109f; *FD*, p. 158; *SM*, pp. 177f). One has to learn to use a conceptual scheme and thus learn to think of oneself as doing this or that. To understand locutions of the kind ''I will do *A* here and now,'' one must not only come to understand something about time, space, and speaker identity, but one must develop a habit of relating such locutions to one's own behavior. In particular, one must gain the propensity to do *A* when one says ''I will do *A* .'' A child who says this but makes no effort to do *A* is likely to be criticized: ''You *said* you were going to do *A* , but you didn't do it!'' It is only when this propensity is fully developed that the thought or covert response ''I will do *A* here and now'' can be considered a full-fledged volition.

Sellars' view of the relation between volition and action may be summarized as follows. If a certain kind of mental act—namely, one of thinking ''I will now do *A* ''—tends to result in appropriate behavior, then, and only then, it is correctly regarded as a volition. The relation between volition and overt behavior is therefore causal—and necessarily so. If the thought did not *result* in the behavior (given ability and opportunity), then the thought would not be a volition. If we wish to express this fact by saying, with some philosophers, that a volition is conceptually related to appropriate behavior, we may certainly do so, but we must not forget that this is a loose, inaccurate way of speaking that can generate needless perplexity. The frequent question ''How could a cause be conceptually related to its effect?'' is fundamentally confused and should never be asked.

To say that a volition causes certain behavior is not to imply that a volition *causes a man* to behave in a certain way (*FD*, p. 156). Tom's volition may cause Tom's behavior, but it does not cause Tom to do anything. Tom's volition is Tom's willing; and when Tom wills to do something, *he* (given ability and opportunity) is the so-called agent cause of his behavior. He brings about his behavior by willing it. Contrary to the views of Chisholm and others, so-called agent causation makes sense, at least in connection with voluntary action, only by reference to the causal efficacy of an agent's volitions. To make something happen willfully is to bring it about by willing it. As Davidson has recently insisted ([9]), causal claims imply causal regularities; and for Sellars, at least, the regularities appropriate to agent causation (when it is voluntary) pertain to volitions and their resulting actions. Since one cannot directly will to will, one cannot be said to cause oneself directly to will; a man may cause his actions by willing them, but he cannot directly cause himself to will them.[2] Sellars' conception of a volition does not, therefore, invite an infinite regress.

To round out this discussion, I want to say something about a standard objection to volitions—namely, that we are not always conscious of any distinctive mental episode when we do something voluntarily. Although I am not certain what Sellars would say in answer to this objection, three responses consistent with his position are easily given.

First, it is a plain fact that we are not always in a frame of mind to monitor our thoughts. When we are thinking about football, we are not generally concerned with our active thought about football. Similarly, when we will to do something, we are aware of what we are going to do, but we are not likely to be concerned with our awareness of what we are going to do. Since willing is an act of thought and not some mental object or impression, our failure to discern a distinctive mental object when we will to do something is not at all surprising.

Second, although we characterize a volition by reference to such words as "I will now do *A*." it does not follow that a volition so characterized requires verbal imagery to run through our heads. For Sellars, thoughts of all kinds are characterized by their conceptual structure, which is *formally* analogous to the conceptual structure of a statement ([15]:127-96; and *SM*, 151-74). But a formal or functional

2. One can indirectly will to will something *A* by directly willing a course of action that leads one to will *A*. Thus, although I could not directly will to perform certain brutal actions, I could, if I thought it sufficiently important to do them, will to enter a course of training that would render me so brutal that I would be certain to will them.

analogy does not imply material or empirical similarity. As far as the nonformal aspects of thought are concerned, it is entirely possible, on Sellars' view, that they are describable in neurophysiological terms ([15]:35). I have discussed this possibility elsewhere and shall not therefore elaborate on it here (see [1]:236). Suffice it to say that, since on Sellars' view verbal imagery is not essential to the volition "I will now do A," our failure to discern such imagery when we perform a voluntary action does not imply that we do not *will* to perform that action.

A third response to the objection is based on what Quine has called "the transitivity of conditioning" ([14]: 12). Although the practical reasoning that explains a man's doing A by reference to the premises "I will do A if P" and "P" requires a rational terminus of "I will do A (here and now)," this practical conclusion may not actually be drawn by agents trained to reason in accordance with the pattern. The behavior naturally elicited by the volition "I will do A (here and now)" may, by transitivity of conditioning, be elicited by the premises that normally prompt that volition. In such a case, the volition to do A may be called "implicit." A man's doing of A may, in other words, occur merely "in accordance with a volition" as the conclusion of a deductive argument may be drawn in accordance with a missing premise. Although I do not know what Sellars would say about this possibility, I myself regard it as indisputable. If I am right about this, another objection can, in a sense, be granted: we do not explicitly will to do everything that we do voluntarily. On the other hand, the notion of voluntary action can be understood as such only by reference to a volition. To explain fully why an intention and a belief might result in a certain action we must refer to the volition that may have been eliminated by the transitivity of conditioning.

3. *Desire and Preference*

Even with the qualification that some voluntary action may occur without explicit volition, it might seem that Sellars' account of voluntary action is excessively intellectualized. For philosophers like Hume, it is, in fact, a mistake to suppose that reason can ever move a man to act; for them, he is prompted to act because of a "passion," such as desire. Reason can move a man to act only indirectly, either by exciting a passion that prompts his action or by showing him which action will satisfy some passion which he already has. If two or more passions conflict, the stronger will determine his action. In no case does reason itself have a "motive power" ([10], Bk. II, Sect. III, pp. 413-18).

Few philosophers today are likely to accept Hume's point of view without serious qualification, but there is undoubtedly some truth to it, and examining it briefly will serve to throw Sellars' view of action on desire into sharp focus. Sellars maintains that, in the case of conscious agents, the relation of desire or any other "passion" to rational action must be analyzed in terms of the relation of intention (and thus volition) to action (*TA*, pp. 117-26).

According to Hume, "when we have the prospect of pain or pleasure from any object, we feel a consequent emotion of aversion or propensity, and are carried to avoid or embrace what will give us this uneasiness or satisfaction" ([10]:414). An important question to ask is how we are to conceive of the emotion of aversion or propensity, which intervenes between the idea that something is pleasant or painful and the disposition to avoid or embrace it. Hume regards it as an impression, an "original existence" that must be experienced to be properly conceived of ([10]:399). It is this impression, and not the thought of the pleasant or painful object, that disposes us to pursue or avoid the object; it possesses the "motive force" that disposes us to act.

Since for Hume desire is a direct passion, immediately evoked by the prospect of pleasure, we may interpret him as holding that the prospect of gaining pleasure from some object excites a feeling of desire and that this feeling evokes, in turn, a disposition to pursue the desired object. There can be no doubt that Hume's view is partly correct: the thought that something is pleasant may well excite a desire for it, and the desire excited certainly prompts one, in some degree, to pursue the desired object. But it does not seem correct to characterize a desire as a mere feeling.

A desire may no doubt be accompanied by certain feelings, but no special feeling seems to be present whenever a desire is felt. Also, many desires seem to be far more intellectual than a mere feeling, involving the *idea* of a friend's happiness or the end of a brutal war. If one were to express such desires in words, one might say "Would that Tom were happy" or "I want the war to end." Finally, one may desire certain things for a lengthy period of time without either experiencing constant feelings of propensity or continually thinking of the things desired.

These points suggest that Hume's account of desire is radically defective. Far from being an occurrent feeling or impression, a desire seems to be a conscious tendency or propensity of some kind. It is tempting to say that a desire is nothing but the tendency to pursue the desired object—a tendency that Hume regarded as the mere effect of a desire. This tendency could not, of course, be understood wholly in terms of the overt behavior the agent might exhibit, for there is simply no pattern of overt behavior that is distinctive of a given desire. The actions, if any, that a man will perform when he desires something will depend not only on his many beliefs but also on his other desires, his moral commitments, his shrewdness or stupidity, and the like. The tendency to act which Hume speaks of must in fact be understood in relation to a more fundamental tendency—a tendency to direct one's practical reasoning toward certain goals.

This view concerning the nature of desire comes close to the position defended by Sellars. He grants that a desire is in part a complicated mental disposition, but he insists that desires are also the kind of thing that may be *satisfied* (*TA*, p. 119). The relevant notion of satisfaction adds to the intellectual character of a desire, because in a human being it is not properly the realization of a desire that brings satisfaction but the belief that it is realized. If I desire the war to end, my desire will be realized if the war does end, but it will be satisfied only if I believe it has ended. Since the notion of satisfaction is essential to that of desire, we must supplement the account of the last paragraph by saying that if S desires that E obtain, then S must be disposed to take satisfaction in the idea that E obtains.

To round out Sellars' conception of desire, we must be more explicit about the relation between desire and action. Since a man's beliefs, intentions, moral standards, and the like all bear upon his behavior, the most we can say until we have worked out a theory of practical reasoning is that if S desires that E obtain, then he will be disposed (have *some* tendency) to form the intention of doing things that will, as he believes, realize his desires (*TA*, pp. 117-26). We must speak of intentions here rather than overt behavior, because the rational terminus of practical reasoning is an intention (ultimately a volition) to act, and a specific desire is just one of the things that a man will consider when he tries to make up his mind about what to do on some specific occasion. Thus, a man may have a strong desire to do A but realize that A has morally objectionable consequences. He might accordingly be unwilling to satisfy his desire as matters stand, although he *would* conclude that A is worth doing (that is, form the intention of doing it), *if*, say, his moral beliefs were to change.[3]

Sellars' account of *preference* is also based on the concept of intention. Thus far I have spoken of the intention to *do* this or that, but it is clear that one may intend *that* something be the case or *that* a certain state of affairs obtain. Although the object of this latter kind of intention is not an action on one's part, it nevertheless involves the idea of such an action. According to Sellars, to intend that *E* obtain is to be disposed to perform actions that one believes necessary to bring about *E*.[4] Thus, to intend that one's children are properly educated is to intend to perform actions that one deems necessary for bringing it about that they are properly educated. Since the intention to do *A* in *C* may be construed as an intention *that* one does *A* in *C*, it is possible to express all intentions by a single canonical form.[5] Sellars represents this form by "Shall (*P*)", which may be read "It shall be the case that *P*". For purposes of my exposition, I shall abbreviate this canonical form by *"S(P)"* (*SM*, p. 180).

Sellars' concept of preference is, as he admits, a "thin" one, for it makes no reference to the notion of satisfaction. This omission is unimportant for Sellars' purposes, since he wishes to say just enough about preference to help clarify the logic of practical reasoning. His account is highly intellectualized, and it might accordingly be called "conscious preference." In general, if *S* prefers *A* to *B*, then assuming that *S* considers both *A* and *B* to be relevant to his interests but incapable of being jointly realized, he will intend *"S(A &~B)"* if the question arises: *"S(A &~B)* or *S(B &~A)*?"*. If, under these conditions, *S* does intend *"S(A &~B),"* we can say that *S* prefers *A* to *B*. To this Sellars adds that

3. Sellars' account of desire does not apply to all states covered by the vague word "want"; in particular, it does not apply to what might be called "appetites" or "hungers." On this, see *TA*, p. 30.

4. *SM*, p. 184. Note that Sellars' account of intending that *E* obtain is incomplete, since a person having such an intention will also be disposed to perform actions sufficient for *E*, provided at least that what is deemed sufficient is also viewed as necessary or as not undesirable in other respects.

5. In *SM*, p. 181, Sellars distinguishes two shall-operators, but I interpret him as having just one operator in his semi-formal "canonical" language. For a different interpretation, see Castañeda's essay in this volume. In a recent, unpublished manuscript, in which Sellars responds to criticisms which I have raised in this paper, he introduces two shall-operators into his canonical language. Note, however, that his basic axiom, from which he thinks that an adequate logic of intentions can be deduced, contains just one shall-operator. See my text corresponding to *SM*, pp. 179, 182.

"*S* prefers *A* to *B*" is nevertheless compatible with "*S* prefers *B* & *C* to *A* & *C*".[6]

4. *Sellars' Basic Practical Axiom*

According to Sellars, the logic of practical reasoning may be derived from a single axiom (*SM*, p. 179):

"*S(P)*" implies "*S(Q)*" *iff* "*P*" implies "*Q*".

Although I have expressed the axiom as a biconditional, it is more perspicuously expressed as a third-level principle telling us that the metalinguistic statement " '*S(P)*' implies '*S(Q)*' " implies and is implied by the metalinguistic statement " '*P*' implies '*Q*' ". Concerning this axiom Sellars says:

There is . . . no need for a special 'logic of intentions' other than that formulated by the third-level principle [just given] . . . together with certain conceptual truths about the function of 'shall'. (*SM*, p. 182.)

Since he also says "I am so using 'implies' that '*P* implies *Q*' is equivalent to '*Q* may be inferred from *P*'," his idea is that a statement of the form "*S(Q)*" may be inferred from one of the form "*S(P)*" just in case the corresponding indicative of the form "*Q*" may be inferred from the corresponding indicative of the form "*P*". Clearly, this is a philosophically exciting idea, for it implies that the logic of intentions is, as Sellars says, entirely "parasitical" on the logic of beliefs or indicatives ([16]:5).

Although Sellars' axiom is very exciting in its implications, we must be assured that it is really acceptable. Unfortunately, it is not easy to determine this, since Sellars uses "implies" or "may be inferred from" in a very broad sense. As far as indicatives are concerned, he uses these words to cover logical implication, causal or physical implication, and sometimes even related forms of dependent implication (*SM*, pp. 181f). As we shall see, this lack of clarity about the precise meaning he attaches to "implies" raises serious doubts about the soundness of his axiom and about its adequacy for a complete logic of intentions.

6. Sellars adds a qualification to his definition of "*S* prefers *A* to *B*," which I have not discussed. He also defines two additional concepts pertaining to preference. See *TA*, pp. 113-17.

Since Sellars wishes to include causal or physical implications within the scope of his axiom, it is natural to think of " 'P' implies$_i$ 'Q' " (where "implies$_i$" represents the relation between indicatives) as having the intuitive sense that, in any causally possible world, "Q" is true if "P" is true. As far as intentions are concerned, this would have the consequence that "$S(Q)$" is inferable from "$S(P)$" just in case "Q" is true whenever (causally speaking) "P" is true. Sellars says that S-statements, being canonical expressions of intention, are neither true nor false (*SM*, p. 188); but they must have some semantic values that, by virtue of his axiom, have a systematic relation to truth and falsity. If we interpret "implies$_i$" in the way I have suggested, this relation is easy to specify. Normally, we think of intentions as being realized or unrealized rather than as true or false. Since S-statements express intentions, it is thus natural to think of them as having the values R (for *realized*) and U (for *unrealized*). But these values have an obvious relation to truth and falsity: "S(I shall go skiing)" is realized just in case "I shall go skiing" is true; and it is unrealized just in case "I shall go skiing" is false. This suggests that "$S(P)$" implies$_n$ "$S(Q)$" (where "implies$_n$" refers to the implication-relation between intentions) just in case "$S(Q)$" is realized in any causally· possible world in which "$S(P)$" is realized. If this interpretation is accepted, then to say that one intention implies another is only to say that if the first intention is realized, the second is realized as well—it is not to say or even suggest that if someone *has* the first intention, he must also *have* the second intention.

But is this interpretation of " '$S(P)$' implies$_n$ '$S(Q)$' " really plausible? Is it an acceptable interpretation of the relation we have in mind when we say that one intention implies another? I think it is. If "$S(P)$" implies "$S(Q)$", then one who intended "$S(P)$" would be inconsistent if he intended anything incompatible with "$S(Q)$". Now, Sellars denies that S-statements may have external negations; he contends that the "denial" of "$S(P)$" is "$S(\sim P)$". To say that "$S(P)$" implies$_n$ "$S(Q)$" would then be to say that anyone who intended "$S(P)$" and "$S(\sim Q)$" would be inconsistent in the relevant sense: his intentions would at least be causally incompatible. But under what conditions, exactly, could two *intentions* be considered incompatible or inconsistent? The answer would seem to be that they have this property just in case they could not (causally or logically) be jointly realized. In other words, the set $\{$"$S(P)$", "$S(\sim Q)$"$\}$ is inconsistent just in case the set $\{$"P", "$\sim Q$"$\}$ is inconsistent. But this latter set is inconsistent just in case "P" implies$_i$

"Q". Thus, "P" implies$_i$ "Q" under precisely the same conditions as "$S(P)$" implies$_n$ "$S(Q)$", which is exactly as it should be if Sellars' axiom is really true.

It should be pointed out that Castañeda has long urged a semantical interpretation of practical inference in which intentions have specified values analogous to truth and falsity.[7] Though well aware of Castañeda's approach, Sellars has never suggested a semantical interpretation for his own system. Castañeda's system is more complicated than Sellars' and does not admit the simple interpretation I have just discussed. But since the logic of indicatives must ultimately be interpreted in relation to truth and falsity (whether it includes causal implications or not), Sellars' single axiom, which is supposed to reduce the logic of intentions to the logic of indicatives, calls for a semantic interpretation that is at least similar to the one I have suggested. Such an interpretation is not only plausible but (as I have indicated) it allows us to demonstrate that Sellars' axiom is in fact true.

Although Sellars' axiom is clearly acceptable on my interpretation, it does not seem adequate for a complete logic of intentions. For one thing, it merely allows us to deduce S-consequences from single premises. Obviously, however, inferences of the following sort are certainly valid:

$$\frac{\begin{array}{l}S(P)\\S(Q)\end{array}}{S(P\ \&\ Q)} \qquad \frac{\begin{array}{l}S(P \lor Q)\\S(\sim P)\end{array}}{S(Q)} \qquad \frac{\begin{array}{l}S(P)\\S(\sim[P\ \&\ Q])\end{array}}{S(\sim Q)}$$

To validate these inferences, we must reformulate Sellars' axiom so that an intention may be derived from arbitrarily many premises. We may do this as follows:

"$S(P_1)$", . . . , "$S(P_n)$" implies$_n$ "$S(C)$" *iff* "P_1", . . . , "P_n" implies$_i$ "C".

As reformulated, the axiom is capable of exactly the same kind of justification as before.

Another inadequacy in Sellars' axiom is that, even as reformulated, it does not seem adequate to validate inferences involving conditional intentions. A simple pattern of reasoning whose validity Sellars insists upon is this:

I *will* do A if P.

P.

So, I *will* do A.

7. See [6] for bibliographical details.

Sellars does not regard this simple inference as logically basic; he contends that it is derivable from his fundamental axiom. Yet that axiom (at least as I have interpreted it) makes no provision for practical inferences having mixed premises. It tells us that we can derive intentions from a set of premises consisting of intentions, but it does not tell us that we can derive an intention from a set of premises containing both S-statements and indicatives, where the indicatives are essential to the inference.

In spite of this, Sellars offers a derivation of the pattern above from his axiom (*IILO,* p. 190). His first step is to interpret the conditional intention "I *will* do A if P" as "$S(P \supset I$ shall do $A)$", which may be read "It shall be the case that if P, I shall do A". His aim is then to show that inferences of the canonical pattern

$S(P \supset I$ shall do $A)$
P
Therefore, $S(I$ shall do $A)$

can be validated by his axiom. His next step is to introduce the concept of dependent implication, or implication relative to an assumption. According to this concept,

X implies Y relative to A *iff* X & A implies Y.

With this concept in hand, Sellars then argues that since "$P \supset I$ shall do A" implies "I shall do A" (relative to "P"), we may conclude from his axiom that "$S(P \supset I$ shall do $A)$" implies "$S(I$ shall do $A)$" relative to "P". But this last relative implication is true just in case "P" and "$S(P \supset I$ shall do $A)$" independently imply "$S(I$ shall do $A)$". In view of Sellars' reading of "X implies Y" as "Y may be inferred from X", we must therefore agree that the pattern of practical inference in question is valid.

If this derivation is to be acceptable, the "implies" of Sellars' axiom must cover dependent implication as well as independent logical and causal implication. The justification I gave for his axiom is not applicable, however, when "implies" is interpreted so broadly. The question thus arises: "Is his axiom really acceptable when 'implies' is understood in this broad sense?" It seems to me that the answer to this question is far from obvious. To see this, note that his axiom will now allow us to derive the following questionable forms, where "Q" stands in place of an appropriate future-tense indicative[8]:

I $S(P)$ II P III $S(P)$

 $\dfrac{P \supset Q}{Q}$ $\dfrac{S(P \supset Q)}{Q}$ $\dfrac{P \supset Q}{S(Q)}$

If these forms are not regarded as valid (and they certainly do not look valid, at least *prima facie*), then Sellars' axiom cannot be regarded as acceptable when "implies" has the broad sense in question.

Since the form Sellars wishes to validate, namely,

IV P

 $\dfrac{S(P \supset Q)}{S(Q)}$

where "Q" is an appropriate indicative, cannot be derived from his axiom unless his "implies" covers dependent implication, it follows that Sellars is confronted with an important choice: he must either accept forms I, II, and III as valid, or he must restrict his "implies" to independent implication and then find some other means of validating form IV. It is not clear which choice he is prepared to make, since both alternatives can be supported by various things he has said.

Consider form III, for example. Although Sellars has not, to my knowledge, commented directly on this form, it would appear that he would want to reject it in view of his treatment of a class of arguments that might be taken as instances of it. The following schematic argument, which might have "Unless I do A, I can't bring about E", "If I am to bring about E, I must do A", or "A necessary condition of my bringing about E is that I do A" in place of premise (2), illustrates my point:

(1) I *will* bring about E.
(2) I can bring about E only by doing A.
(3) Therefore, I *will* do A.

8. The derivations for these forms follow the same strategy as Sellars' derivation. The derivations for I and II are based on the premiss that, since "P" and "$P \supset Q$" imply "Q", then "$S(P)$" and $S(P \supset Q)$" imply "$S(Q)$". We can therefore say that "$S(P \supset Q)$" implies "$S(Q)$" relative to "$S(P)$". From this we infer that "$(P \supset Q)$" implies "Q" relative to "$S(P)$", which validates form I. To validate form II, we use the premise above to conlude that "$S(P)$" implies "$S(Q)$" relative to "$S(P \supset Q)$" and then to conclude that "P" implies "Q" relative to "$S(P \supset Q)$". To validate form III, we simply note that "P" implies "Q" relative to "$P \supset Q$" and then infer that "$S(P)$" implies "$S(Q)$" relative to "$P \supset Q$".

To validate arguments of this kind, Sellars interprets premise (2) as a causal implication (*SM*, pp. 190f). Put in canonical form, the argument schema thus becomes:

(1′) S(I shall bring about E).
(2′)   "I shall bring about E" implies "I shall do A".
(3′)   Therefore, S(I shall do A).

Since, by virtue of premise (2), the indicative corresponding to (1′) causally implies the indicative corresponding to (3′), the argument may be validated by his original axiom. Evidently, it is because of arguments of this kind that he wishes his sense of "implies" to cover what he calls "causal implications."

Premise (2) as well as the related statements I mentioned above are, of course, modal statements that are logically stronger than mere material conditions. In applying truth-functional logic, however, we are frequently able to render such statements by material conditionals and thereby validate many familiar arguments containing them. If we could do the same for the arguments above, we could simplify our system of practical logic and define practical validity without reference to causal possibilities. Since Sellars does not interpret premise (2) as a material conditional and attempt to validate the inference as an instance of the form III, the presumption is that he does not think of this form as valid. If so, he should reject any interpretation of his axiom that validates this form.

Sellars has made remarks, however, that favor the other alternative—namely, that of accepting forms I, II, and III as valid. In one essay he said: ". . . an intending is *more than* but *includes* a thinking that something will be the case" and "that in the verbal expression of intentions which *makes* it an expression of intention *does not suspend this commitment* [to its being the case that . . .]" (*TA*, p. 128 and p. 127). Along with certain earlier remarks,[9] this makes it reasonably clear that he would accept the following inference as valid:

V $\dfrac{S(P)}{P}$.

9. *IILO*, p. 175, where Sellars says "it seems proper to stipulate that 'Shall [*my* shortly crossing the road]' implies 'I will shortly cross the road', i.e., that it contains the prediction, just as 'Necessary [Tom's shortly crossing the road]' contains 'Tom will shortly cross the road.'

He has also said that "shall" (where it serves to express intention) "can be said to be a *manner* rather than a *content* of thought" (*TA*, p. 129). Since the validity of an inference would appear to depend on the content of the relevant thoughts (or statements), it would appear that he would regard not only form V but form VI as valid:

VI $\dfrac{P}{S(P)}$.

Obviously, if both forms V and VI are valid, then forms I, II, III, and IV are valid as well, and his axiom would no doubt hold for dependent implication.

Although it might seem absurd to suppose that forms V and VI are valid, a reasonable case can be made in their favor. There is, first, the consideration that Sellars produced—namely, that the intention "I *will* do *A*" seems to differ from the indicative thought "I shall do *A*" not in content but in manner of affirmation. As far as the corresponding statements are concerned, the first differs from the second in expressing a volitional attitude toward a state of affairs that both affirm will obtain. This consideration seems to be supported by the observation that "I *will* do *A*" logically implies "I shall do *A*" just in case the set {"I *will* do *A*", "I shall not do *A*"} is inconsistent, and that "I shall do *A*" implies "I *will* do *A*" just in case the set {"I shall do *A*", "I *won't* do *A*"} is inconsistent. And these sets do seem inconsistent. Intuitively, it would appear that an intention is inconsistent with an indicative thought just in case the intention could not possibly be realized if the thought were true. This condition is clearly met for the intentions and indicative thoughts in question.

This conception of the conditions under which intentions and indicative thoughts are inconsistent suggests a semantical approach to mixed inferences that is related to the one which I introduced in attempting to justify Sellars' axiom. We simply postulate a positive semantic value 1 and a negative semantic value 0 defined as follows:

> *X* has the value 1 *iff* either (a) *X* is an indicative and has the value *T* or (b) *X* is an *S*-statement and has the value *R*. Otherwise, *X* has the value 0.

We can then say that an inference is valid just in case its conclusion has the value 1 whenever its premises have the value 1. This conception of validity not only validates inferences of the form IV, which Sellars wishes to validate, but it makes it unnecessary to have any special axiom for practical inference.

It may be objected, of course, that this conception of validity cannot really be acceptable for the logic of intentions, because it validates such questionable forms of inference as I, II, and III. But it is not really clear that there is anything wrong with these forms of inference. Take III, for example, which Sellars seems to reject. Exactly what is objectionable about this form of inference? One suggestion is that it has the consequence that an unfulfilled intention will imply anything at all, including inconsistent intentions. Thus, if "$S(P)$" is unrealized, "P" is false, "$P \supset Q$" is true for any "Q" whatever, and $S(Q)$ is true. I fail to see anything objectionable about this, however; it is merely an example of the so-called paradoxes of material "implication."

If a man has the premises "$S(P)$" and "$P \supset Q$", he should be willing to accept the conclusion "$S(Q)$" whether he happens to like it or not. premises "P" and "$P \supset Q$": if he accepts these premises, he should be willing to accept the conclusion whether he likes it or not. (Of course, if his dislike of the conclusion is strong enough in either case, he should pull in his horns and reject one of the premises.) On the other hand, if a man has the premise "$S(P)$" and knows that it will not be realized—that is, if he knows that $\sim P$—then, although he can then accept "$P \supset Q$" for any "Q" whatever, he should not be distressed, since two of his premises are presumably inconsistent—namely, "$S(P)$" and "$\sim P$". And it is a familiar principle of standard logic that anything may be derived from an inconsistency.

One thing shown by this last example is that the acceptability of form III actually rests on the acceptability of form V, which allows us to infer "P" from "$S(P)$". As we have seen, Sellars seems to accept this form of inference on the ground that "an intending is *more than* but *includes* a thinking that something will be the case." To accept this form of inference is not to claim that if a man has a certain intention, the corresponding thought or belief that something will be the case must be true. It is merely to claim that if his intention has an appropriate semantic value (which it seems natural to take as R), then the corresponding thought or belief will have an appropriate semantic value (namely, T). This seems to be a plausible basis for accepting V as a valid form of inference. If it is accepted, however, forms I and II should not appear objectionable, for each is easily validated by V.

Form III may still seem doubtful, but since it may be inferred from VI, I shall comment on the latter. In an unpublished manuscript, Sellars accepts the inference from *"P"* to *"S(P)"* in cases where *"P"* does not concern an action that the agent believes to be within his power (see note 5). Sellars calls the principle behind the inference "the So-be-it Principle," and he says that if a man believes that something will certainly be the case, it would be perfectly reasonable for him to conclude "So be it . . ." or "It shall be the case that . . ." Sellars evidently thinks, however, that the So-be-it Principle is not applicabale when the premise concerns something the agent believes is within his power. Yet it seems to me that, if the principle is applicable at all, it is applicable in both cases: after all, the principle is a purely formal one, and there is no *formal* test or mark by which to determine whether a premise concerns an action that an agent believes he can perform.

Consider that the simple indicative, "I shall raise my hand in two minutes." If I really believe that this premise is true—if I actually accept it—I might just as well accept the conclusion "I *will* raise my hand in two minutes." To adopt the principle in these cases is not to adopt a fatalistic attitude toward my future actions; at most, it is to adopt such an attitude toward what I believe will be the case. If I am an anti-fatalist who believes that no person's action can ever really be predicted, I shall find the So-be-it Principle useless in connection with voluntary actions: I shall deny that an appropriate premise can ever be well-founded.

Further support for the So-be-it Principle can be gathered from a source where Sellars has long disagreed with Castañeda. As Castañeda points out in his essay in this volume, Sellars holds that an *S*-statement cannot occur within the scope of a logical connective or quantifier. Sellars' grounds for this view are not entirely clear: presumably he thinks that such an occurrence is incompatible with the fact that *S*-statements lack truth-values. It seems clear to me, in any case, that Sellars is wrong about this point. Surely, statements like the following are perfectly familiar and perfectly unobjectionable:

(1) I *will* flunk that student—even though his father is a trustee.
(2) I *will* take on the job, provided that the pay is satisfactory.
(3) He doesn't need the job, but I *will* offer it to him anyway.

Yet these statements are naturally formalized with *S*-statements in the scope of connectives:

(1') S(I shall flunk that student) & (His father is a trustee).

(2') S(the pay is satisfactory $\supset$ I shall take the job) & S

(the pay is not satisfactory $\supset$ I shall not take the job).

(3') ~(He needs the job) & S(I shall offer the job to him).

It seems to me that any logic that does not allow for statements like these cannot be fully adequate for practical inference. Fortunately, the semantical approach I am recommending deals with such statements as a matter of course.

If, however, we do allow S-statements to appear within the scope of connectives (and, indeed, within the scope of quantifiers), what shall we say about the following?

(4) I *will* go tomorrow, but I shall not go tomorrow.

(5) I shall stay home tomorrow, but I *won't* stay home tomorrow.

It seems to me that both statements are best regarded as inconsistent. If this is right, then, since the inconsistency of (4) supports the validity of form V, and the inconsistency of (5) supports the validity of form VI, we have additional reason to accept the semantical interpretation according to which they are valid.

In pondering the apparently problematic argument forms which I have been discussing, we should keep in mind that the vernacular "shall" and "will" of volition do two distinct jobs: they serve to express the speaker's intention, and they indicate futurity. It is because of this that the canonical interpretation of "I *will* do A" is "S(I shall do A)" and the canonical interpretation of "Tom *shall* come" is "S(Tom will come)", where "shall" and "will" are used in the old-fashioned grammarian's sense. This point is worth keeping in mind, because the S-operator in the canonical counterparts to ordinary expressions of intention will always be applied to indicative statements in the future tense. When the formal machinery of Sellars' theory is put to work in formalizing practical discourse, anomalies can be expected to arise, for the S-operator will inevitably be applied to indicatives in the present or past tenses. Thus, since "I shall pay Jones the dollar I have owed him for years" implies "I have owed Jones a dollar for years", the statement "S(I shall pay Jones the dollar I have owed him for years)" implies "S(I have owed Jones a dollar for years)". Obviously, the last S-statement does not correspond to any vernacular expression of intention, and it is odd to think of it as expressing any intention at all. Oddities of this kind are not, as far as I can tell, really damaging to Sellars' theory, for his theory may be allowed its share of "don't care's," as Quine has called them. But it is possible to avoid all oddities of this kind by adopting a more informal approach to the logic of intentions.

If the semantical interpretation which I have suggested for Sellars' logic of intentions is accepted, and if it is permissible to join S-statements to other statements (whether S-statements or indicatives) by logical connectives, then there is really no need to introduce the apparatus of Sellars' S-operators. Given the validity of the argument forms which I have discussed, we can easily see that the volitional "shall" and "will" of everyday discourse are logically indistinguishable from the "shall" and "will" of mere futurity. Since arguments containing the latter words may be assessed for validity by the principles of ordinary "indicative" logic, the same will be true of arguments containing the volitional "shall's" and "will's" that Sellars formalizes with the use of his S-operator. If we take seriously Sellars' remark that the volitional "shall" represents "a *manner* rather than a *content* of thought," then this view is an entirely natural one to take.

Sellars might, of course, insist that expressions of intention are neither true nor false and that this fact requires us to provide a special logic for them. I agree that we do not think of intentions or their verbal expressions as true or false, but this does not seem worth insisting upon for systematic logical purposes. After all, if the obvious semantic values for S-statements are R and U, then the close relation of these values to T and F removes any formal or logical need for distinguishing them. It is, of course, obvious that "realized" is not synonymous with "true", but then "and" is not synonymous with "in spite of the fact that . . ."—even though they are properly regarded as logically indistinguishable. Another natural but ultimately unimportant point observed by Sellars is that S-statements or expressions of intention cannot have an external negation—that "~S(I shall go)" or "~(I *will* go)" do not really make sense. But from a semantical point of view, the position of the negation sign turns out to be insignificant. We can read "~S(P)" in the very same way as "S(~P)": both formulas have the value U (or F) just in case the formula "S(P)" has the value R (or T); and both have the value R (or T) just in case "S(P)" has the value U (or F). Furthermore, there is really no need to stipulate that S-operators cannot be iterated (though Sellars himself has not offered this stipulation). If the values R and T (or U and F) are not distinguished, then the value of "SS(P)" would be indistinguishable from the value of "*S(P)*"; the extra *S*-operator is mere decoration. These consequences may seem very surprising to anyone who has really struggled with the logic of intentions, but unless something is fundamentally wrong with the semantical approach which I have suggested in this essay, they are ultimately unavoidable.

It may be helpful to conclude this discussion with a concrete example of how a practical inference may be validated by ordinary indicative logic. The example may be set out schematically as follows:

(1) I *will* bring about *E*.
(2) Unless I do *A*, I can't bring about *E*.
(3) Therefore, I *will* do *A*.

If this argument is to be regarded as valid, premise (2) must be understood as implying

(4) I shall bring about $E \supset$ I shall do A,

where the "shall" represents mere futurity. Given my thesis that the volitional "will" is logically indistinguishable from the "shall" of mere futurity, the conclusion (3) follows from (1) and (4) by *modus ponens*.

Another example, which illustrates the advantages of this simplified approach to practical inference, was mentioned earlier. I remarked that in Sellars' system the conclusion "*S* (I have owed Jones a dollar for years)" is a logical consequence of the premises:

(1) *S*(I shall pay Jones the dollar I have owed him for years)
(2) "I shall pay Jones the dollar I have owed him for years" implies "I have owed Jones a dollar for years".

I admitted that, since the conclusion here does not, intuitively speaking, represent a genuine intention, Sellars could accept the inference as a "don't care" that, though awkward, is not logically unacceptable. Yet if we restrict ourselves to ordinary indicative logic, treating "will" and "shall" as logically indistinguishable in their first-person uses, we could simply say that the only relevant conclusion derivable from premise (2) and the expression of intention "I *will* pay Jones the dollar I have owed him for years" is the simple indicative, "I have owed Jones a dollar for years". It seems to me that this is a far more natural response to the premises in question.

5. *Inference and Decision*

Certain cases of practical inference raise problems that are quite distinct from those which I have thus far considered. One problem, which arises for Sellars' original system as well as for the alternative which I have proposed, concerns practical situations where we have an intention *S(Ei)*, where "*Ei*" means "I shall bring about *E*", and know only that doing something *A* is *sufficient* to bring it about that *E*. Is there any relevant practical conclusion that can be drawn in such a case?

The answer, of course, is "No"; to assume, for example, that one is entitled to the intention "*S*(I shall do *A*)" would be disastrous, since "I shall do *A*" provides a mere sufficient condition for "*Ei*", and this condition might, apart from bringing about *E*, have hideous consequences. Thus, if the action of doing *A* consisted in bringing about *E* while killing a neighbor, the intention "*S*(I shall do *A*)" would imply "*S*(I shall kill the neighbor)". In general, if a man intends "*S(Ei)*" and knows that "*B*" implies "*Ei*", he must at least consider whether he prefers the truth of "*B*" to the truth of "*~B*". If he prefers the former, then, given Sellars' account of preference, he will intend "*S*(*B* & *~~B*)", which means "*S*(*B*)". Of course, the man's grounds for intending "*S*(*B*)" need not, in a particular case, have anything to do with his intention "*S(Ei)*"; he may simply find the truth of "*B*" intrinsically preferable to that of "*~B*". The man's intention "*S*(*B*)" could, in fact, be purely irrational.

Although one may find some states of affairs intrinsically preferable to others, it is clear that many, if not most, preferences are extrinsic. I may prefer *A* to *B* because *A* is a means to *C*, which I value highly. Given my system of values, some of my momentary preferences may be shown to be positively irrational. If I prefer *B* to non-*B* on the mere ground that bringing about *B* will result in the satisfaction of an intention *S(Ei)*, then my preferences can be said to be irrational. Not only may non-*B* lead to the realization of intentions more important to me than *S(Ei)*, but doing *B* may, in addition to bringing about *E*, have numerous unwanted consequences. This would happen if doing *B* consisted in realizing *E* while killing a neighbor.

Sellars' account of preference does not include an account of rational preference, and it must for that reason be considered seriously incomplete. This gap in his account has significant consequences for his theory of practical reasoning, as the following example shows.

Suppose a man intends $S(Ei)$ and realizes that E can be brought about by doing either B or C. Suppose, further, that B and C are the only alternatives, so that realizing $S(Ei)$ implies doing B or doing C but not doing both together. The question therefore arises for the man: "$S(B$ & $\sim C)$ or $S(C$ & $\sim B)$?". If he prefers B to C, he will intend $S(B$ & $\sim C)$, in which case his practical reasoning will have the following form:

(1) $S(Ei)$.

(2) "B" implies "Ei".

(3) "C" implies "Ei".

(4) "Ei" implies "B or C".

(5) $S(B \vee C)$.   [From (1), (4), and Sellars' axiom]

(6) $\sim(B$ & $C)$.

(7) $S(B$ & $\sim C)$ or $S(C$ & $\sim B)$? [Practical question]

(8) $S(B$ & $\sim C)$.   [Expression of choice]

(9) Therefore, $S(B)$.   [From (8) & Sellars' axiom]

Given step (8), this is a valid form of practical reasoning. Step (8) is not, however, justified; there is no reason for thinking that the intention $S(B$ & $\sim C)$ is reasonable to have, given the leading intention $S(Ei)$. The transition from (7) to (8) represents a transition that the agent simply makes; it does not represent a transition that he is warranted in making by steps (1) through (6). A fully developed treatment of practical reasoning would include machinery for justifying such steps as (8). But this machinery is lacking in Sellars' account.[10]

10. This paper has undergone three radical revisions. I wish to thank Gareth Matthews, Hector-Neri Castañeda, and Wilfrid Sellars for their helpful comments on my first draft. The transition from the second to the third draft was largely owing to my sustained reflection on Castañeda's important work on the logic of imperatives and intentions. See in particular [4] and [5].

REFERENCES

[1] Bruce Aune, *Knowledge, Mind, and Nature* (New York: Random House, 1967).

[2] _____, *Rationalism, Empiricism, and Pragmatism* (New York: Random House, 1970).

[3] J. L. Austin, "Ifs and Cans," in J. O. Urmson and G. J. Warnock, eds., *Philosophical Papers by the Late J. L. Austin* (Oxford: Oxford University Press, 1961).

[4] Hector-Neri Castañeda, "On the Semantics of the Ought-to-do,"
    Synthese 21 (1970): 449-68.

[5] _____, "Intentions and Intending," *American Philosophical Quarterly*
    9 (1972).

[6] _____, "Some Reflections on Wilfrid Sellars' Theory of Intentions," in
    *Action, Knowledge, and Reality: Critical Studies in Honor of Wilfrid
    Sellars,* edited by H.-N. Castañeda (Indianapolis: Bobbs-Merrill, 1974).

[7] _____ and George Nakhnikian, eds., *Morality and the Language of
    Conduct* (Detroit: Wayne State University Press, 1965).

[8] R. G. Collingwood, *The New Leviathan* (Oxford: The Clarendon Press,
    1942).

[9] Donald Davidson, "Mental Events," in Lawrence Foster and J. W.
    Swanson, eds., *Experience and Theory* (Amherst, Mass.: University of
    Massachusetts Press, 1970).

[10] David Hume, *A Treatise of Human Nature,* L. A. Selby-Bigge, ed.
     (Oxford: The Clarendon Press, 1888).

[11] Immanuel Kant, *Critique of Practical Reason,* Lewis White Beck, tr.
     (New York: Library of Liberal Arts, 1956).

[12] Karel Lambert, ed., *The Logical Way of Doing Things* (New Haven: Yale
     University Press, 1969).

[13] Keith Lehrer, ed., *Freedom and Determinism* (New York: Random
     House, 1966).

[14] W. V. Quine, *Word and Object* (Cambridge, Mass.: MIT Press, 1960).

[15] Wilfrid Sellars, *Science, Perception and Reality* (London: Routledge &
     Kegan Paul, 1963).

[16] _____, "Form and Content in Ethical Theory," the Lindley Lecture for
     1967 (Department of Philosophy, University of Kansas).

[17] _____, *Science and Metaphysics* (London: Routledge & Kegan Paul,
     1967).

·～· 2 ·～·

Some Reflections on Wilfrid Sellars' Theory of Intentions

HECTOR-NERI CASTAÑEDA
Indiana University

Preface

IN A SERIES of fascinating essays Wilfrid Sellars has proposed one of the most profound and comprehensive meta-ethical theories. This has not been fully appreciated by our contemporaries. Not only is Sellars' style difficult, but his views are very wide-ranging and complex. He is one of the very few moral philosophers who has not tried to oversimplify but has attempted to deal with the full complexity of practical thinking. His views develop along the four fundamental philosophical dimensions: the ontological, the logical, the metapsychological, and the metaphysical.

To the *ontological* dimension belong, in general, the analysis and systematization of the categories and subcategories of the constituents of what appears to consciousness in thinking (as contrasted with what appears to consciousness in sensation). To the *logical* dimension pertain the schematization and modeling of the network of implication relationships between, and among, the basic units of the contents of thought consciousness. The *metapsychological* dimension includes, in this case, the study of the structuring of thinking and action that makes thinking practical. The *metaphysical* dimension involves the analysis of the contents of consciousness with the purpose of adjudicating degrees of ultimate (or primary) reality to the different aspects or constituents of such contents.

The first two dimensions belong to the phenomenological level which Sellars often refers to as the *Manifest Image*. On the other hand,

27

Sellars' conception of the *Scientific Image,* delivered by the totality of finished sciences as the quasi-noumenal reality, is a conception developed along the fourth, the metaphysical, dimension. Thus, while Sellars recognizes the role of Platonic and Fregean, as well as Cartesian, entities in the Manifest Image, his views along the fourth dimension are, in general, reductionistic, specifically, nominalistic and physicalistic. (See particularly [10]).

Sellars' meta-ethical theory is a complex four-dimensional edifice. Here, however, I shall concentrate on his meta-ethical theory at the phenomenological level of the Manifest Image. I will examine Sellars' ontological and logical views that pertain to practical consciousness. Given the complexity of the topic, in this essay I will limit myself to an examination of his views on intentions, which are for him the foundations of all practical and moral reasoning. This is a study of Sellars' fundamental practical philosophy.

Sellars' *Science and Metaphysics,* listed as [15], contains his latest discussion of intentions and ought-judgments. It will be my main text, but I will also search for clarification and development in his other writings on intentions, [11]-[13], and in [14], which contains a discussion of ought-judgments.

Conventions. In consonance with the Platonistic-Fregean character of the Manifest Image, we shall refer to the phenomenological entities or aspects of entities expressed or denoted by words, phrases, or sentences. We shall use asterisk-quotes around words, phrases, or sentences to refer to what they express or denote. In cases of ambiguity, we assume that a method of removing the ambiguity has been applied, and we also assume that some method for identifying propositions, intentions, actions, etc. has also been applied, so that the expressions within asterisks will be supposed to refer to a given entity or aspect. For instance,

the man next door, *loves*, and *Mary*

are constituents of the proposition

The man next door loves Mary.

We shall indent and display some examples, which will be preceded by a numeral within parentheses. Each of these numerals in parentheses will sometimes be used to refer to the sentence or expression which it precedes, but at other times it will be used to refer to what the expression which it precedes expresses. The context will make clear which one is meant.

I
Sellars' Theory of Intentions: Ontology

1. Intentions and propositions

In Sellars' theory of practical reasoning, the fundamental units of thought content are volitions. These are a special case of acts of intending to do something or other. A volition is a thought to the effect that one shall do some action *now* ([15]: 177; [12]: 109). In a slightly more generic sense, the fundamental units of practical thinking are for Sellars the contents of acts of intending. Such contents he calls *intentions*. They must be carefully distinguished from statements or propositions about a man's being in the state of *intending*, or performing an act of intending. For convenience I will refer to such statements as *intending* statements or propositions. One such statement is this:

(1) Now, in May, 1971, Richard Nixon intends to end the Vietnam war just before the 1972 presidential election.

On the other hand, Nixon's intention is what he would now express by saying:

(2) I shall end the Vietnam war just before the 1972 presidential election.

In one family of dialects of English, the word 'shall' is used to formulate or express intentions which the speaker has adopted. Sellars pays homage to such dialects by exalting the word 'shall' as a technical device expressive of intentions ([15]: 179; [12]: 111; [13]: 3; [11]: 168). Thus, on Sellars' notation (2) above contrasts with Nixon's statement:

(3) I will end the Vietnam war just before the 1972 presidential election.

Clearly, this contrast does not imply a comment on Nixon's dialect or idiolect. The point is that in the philosophically regimented Sellarsian dialect, Nixon can (at present) correctly utter (3) to express, not a decision or intention of his, but his resigned prediction of something the circumstances will make him do, in spite of anyone's intentions to the contrary. We shall adopt Sellars' terminological convention.

Now, what are intentions? What exactly is the contrast between (2) and (3)? For me this contrast is one between two copulae, i.e., two ways in which subjects (agents and patients and objects) are structured with properties (actions) into a logical and psychological unit which in the case of (3) is a proposition but in the case of (2) is a proposition-like intention. See my essays [2], [6], and [7]. Sellars, however, construes intention (2) as the non-propositional result of an operation on proposition (3). He puts this linguistically, rather than ontologically:

(S1) I shall reconstruct 'shall' to be an operator which turns indicative statements into statements of intention. Thus,

I shall do *A*

becomes

Shall [I will do *A*]. ([15]: 180; see also [12]: 127.)

We shall refer to both the linguistic thesis and the ontological thesis behind the former as (S1). The context should resolve any ambiguity.

Both Sellars' view and mine contrast with the view that makes intentions a special case of propositions. This latter view is simpler in that it distinguishes intending from believing merely by actual aspects of the two states of mind, since they both have contents of the same category. On the other hand, both Sellars' view and mine distinguish the states of believing and intending by their contents as well as by some actual features of the states themselves. But I will not go into this here.

Sellars' thesis (S1) is based on an important insight. He rejects Hare's view ([9]: 16f) that imperatives (and decisions) are composed of an imperative neustic and a gerundial core which is also the core of the corresponding sentences (or statements). Sellars notes that Hare's gerundial core by itself can be expressed without any commitment on the part of the speaker or thinker. He holds that if (my example) Nixon asserts (2), he not only thinks (3), but commits himself to (3) being the case:

. . . the context provided by that in the verbal expression of intention which *makes* it an expression of intention *does not suspend this commitment* [to its being the case that . . .] . . . we reconstruct "*S* shall be *P*: (and) "I shall soon do *A*" . . . as involving, *not* sterilized phrases such as "*S* going to be *P*" or "I doing *A* shortly", but *the corresponding full-blooded indicatives* [my italics]. On this interpretation, an intending is *more than* but *includes* a thinking that something will be the case, just as being under the visual impression that *S* is *P includes* but is *more than* a thinking that *S* is *P*. ([12]: 127f.)

Sellars, then, appears to support (S1) by an appeal to two theses:

(I.1)   "X occurrently intends (is rehearsing his intending) to do A" implies "X is thinking that he will do A."

(I.2)   "X intends to do A" implies "X is committed to its being the case that he will do A."

Furthermore, Sellars explicitly endorses the thesis:

(I.3)   "While intending to do A does not consist in believing that one will do A, it essentially includes it." ([12]: 126.)

In fact, Sellars presents the quotation from which I extracted (I.1) and (I.2) as an explanation or account of (I.3). Thus, the commitment mentioned in (I.2) may be construed as the commitment of believing.

Sellars is not correct in holding thesis (I.3); in any case, (I.1)-(I.3) do not imply (S1). Consider a man, Jones, who is under the visual impression that marble a is green. He is then also under the impression that a is also spread out in space in a certain way. Thus, in order for Jones to think that a is green while perceiving it he must also think that a is extended. Yet neither of the two latter propositions are *constituents* of the proposition *Marble a is green*. In general, there are propositions p and q such that believing p implies believing q, without q being a constituent of p. Similarly, intending to do A might, involve essentially, i.e., imply, believing that one will do A, even if the believed proposition is not a constituent of the intended intention. The non-discreteness of mental acts and mental states is compatible with the discrete differentiation of their contents.

2. Sellars' second thesis on intentions

Thesis (S1) seems to accord well with the generality that ordinary language bestows on the verb 'intend'. There are sentences of the form 'X intends to do A', as well as of the form 'X intends that such and such be the case'. We seem to have intending propositions that take as accusatives all kinds of intentions. This suggests that an intention can be produced by "applying" the operator expressed by 'shall' to any proposition whatever. Sellars recognizes this, but he also insists on some crucial distinctions. He formulates another structural thesis about intentions:

(S2)   A careful distinction must be drawn between 'shall' as an operator which operates on action verbs and 'shall' in the sense, roughly, of 'shall be the case' which operates on statements. ([15]: 181. The same distinction is drawn in [13]: 3.)

Again, there is an ontological thesis underlying this linguistic thesis, and we shall refer to it as (S2) for convenience.

According to thesis (S2), there are two kinds of intention because there are two kinds of intention-forming operators. To avoid confusions let 'SHALL' be the operator that operates on "action verbs," and '*shall*' the operator that operates on sentences. That is to say, ontologically, *SHALL* forms intentions by operating on actions, and *shall* forms intentions by operating on propositions.

Sellars speaks here of 'SHALL' operating on action verbs, but clearly neither 'SHALL [to go]' nor 'SHALL [go]' nor 'SHALL [going]' expresses an intention to do, for there is no agent. As I will document in section I.3, Sellars has in other papers characterized the operand of 'SHALL' as a gerundial clause ([11]: 174; [13]: 6), e.g., 'Jones going'.

In [14]: 309 ff, he defines *propositional action expressions* as expressions of the form '*x* to *A*', which are the operands of 'Ought'. One of his central views is that ought-statements are special cases of intentions. Thus, interpreting (S2) in the light of this, we construe 'SHALL' as operating on propositional action expressions, so that intentions to do are of the form *SHALL [I to *A*]*.

There is a conflict between (S1) and (S2), and the context of Sellars' discussion reinforces it. He introduces (S1) first, and then (S2). Since (S1) is a principle about intentions resulting from future statements, one natural way of reconciling (S1) and (S2) is to take (S1) as a principle about '*shall*'. Sellars' ensuing discussion ([15]: 185 ff) treats intentions expressible with sentences of the regimented form 'Shall [I will do *A*]' as formed by an operation on the corresponding sentence of the form 'I will do *A*', not by an operation on an action verb. Yet Sellars speaks of such intentions as intentions to do. It seems that Sellars' intention sentences of the form 'Shall [I will do *A*]' are really of the form 'SHALL [I to do *A*]'. Thus, the ontological contrast between the two operators is somewhat mysterious.

Sellars leaves it to the reader ([15]: 181) to determine from the context which operator he means in each case. It is, of course, easy to replace all of his illustrative future-tense sentences of the form 'I will do *A*' with the infinitive clause 'I to do *A*'. But what is important philosophically is to understand the semantics underlying these transformations. The question which Sellars has not discussed is this: What is the category expressed, denoted, represented (the word we use here is not important) by the action verbs on which 'SHALL' operates? I shall return to this question later on.

Sellars repeats, in [15]: 184 and [13]: 4, a brief discussion of the distinction between the two intention-forming operators. He appears to be analyzing *shall*-intentions into SHALL-intentions when he writes:

Roughly

　It shall be the case that-*p*

has the sense, when made explicit, of

　(Ceteris paribus) I shall do that which is necessary
　to make it the case that-*p*.

Sellars treats intentions that somebody else do something on a par with intentions that something be the case: He analyzes *Tom shall do *A** as:

　(Ceteris paribus) I shall do that which is necessary to make it the
　case that Tom does *A*. ([15]: 184; [13]: 4.)

He goes on to argue that *I shall do *A** "cannot, without the absurdity of an infinite regress, be supposed to have the form: *(Ceteris paribus)* I shall do that which is necessary to make it the case that I do *A*" ([15]: 184; [13]: 4).

This suggests that the difference between *SHALL* and *shall* is as follows: *SHALL* operates on first-person future-tense propositions, whereas *shall* operates on all other future-tense propositions. This suggestion does conform to a good deal of what Sellars says in his discussion. But it amounts to interpreting Sellars' "action verbs" as first-person future-tense sentences. Yet it seems audacious to suppose that Sellars really meant this and, nevertheless, opted for not saying it.

There is, however, one good reason for supposing that the preceding suggestion, whether Sellars meant it or not, is incorrect. Sellars is undoubtedly right in intimating that the analysis of intentions to do an action A in terms of intentions to make it the case that one does A involves a *vicious* infinite regress. But this does not imply that there are no intentions to make it the case that one does some given action. There are such intentions. A man who has lost his will power or lacks certain first-order abilities, and wants to do some action A, may do different things in order to make it the case that he does A. On the other hand, a man may intend to do some action A and may rehearse his intention to do A without any thought about its being necessary that for him to do A he must make it the case that he does A, and, hence, without intending to make it the case that he does A: the man may simply *take it for granted* that it will *just* happen that he does A as he is planning to do.

In short, besides intentions of the form *SHALL [I will do A]* or of the form *SHALL [I to do A]*, there appear to be intentions of the form *shall [I will do A]*. Therefore, we cannot reconcile theses (S1) and S2) by adding that *'shall'* applies to non-first-person future-tense sentences while 'SHALL' applies to first-person future-tense sentences. We must reckon with the fact that 'SHALL' and *'shall'* take different arguments: action verbs and sentences, respectively. Hence, the question about the category of what is expressed by action verbs is crucial.

There is another argument that shows that the difference between the operands of 'SHALL' and *'shall'* is not just the difference between first-person future-tense sentences and non-first-person future-tense sentences, respectively. This argument depends on Sellars' thesis that shall-operators are not in the scope of logical connectives. This thesis is discussed in section II.2 below. We will see that Sellars can adhere to it for the case of 'SHALL' precisely because, as in thesis (S2), he takes 'SHALL' to operate on something other than a sentence.

Consider my conditional SHALL-intention:

(1)   If I (will) finish this essay at time t, I shall visit Bruce Aune at time t'.

Evidently, the if-clause is a future-tense first-person sentence that expresses the proposition *I will finish this essay*, *not* the intention *I shall finish this essay*. Now, given Sellars' view that 'SHALL' is never in the scope of a connective, and as we will see further in section II.2, in accordance with thesis (S1), i.e., with the view that 'SHALL' operates on future-tense first-person sentences, Sellars would be committed to analyzing (1) as

(2)   SHALL [If I (will) finish this essay at time t, I will visit Bruce Aune at time t'].

Now, correctly on my view, Sellars insists that "the 'if . . ., then . . .' [of conditional intentions] is not 'implies' but the '→' of truth functional logic" ([15]: 181). Thus, we can write (2) more perspicuously as

(2a)   SHALL [I will finish this essay at time t → I will visit Bruce Aune at time t'].

Patently, (2a) is not even equivalent to (1). The different practical roles played by my finishing the essay and visiting Aune in (1) are lost in (2a). In (1) my finishing the paper is a condition and my visiting Aune is an intention. In (2a), neither future-tense first-person proposition plays either role. Indeed, (2a) is equivalent to the disjunctive intention

(2)   SHALL [I won't finish this essay at time t or I will visit Bruce Aune at time t'].

which is *not* equivalent to (1).

I can make my point in another way. In (2a) we can make the antecedent the condition, *or* we can make the consequent the condition. Thus, (2a) would have a serious ambiguity. If we take the antecedent of (2a) as the condition, we would have to consider (2a) as the analysis of (1). But if we take the consequent of (2a) as the condition, then (2a) turns out to be the analysis of

(3)   I shall finish this essay at time t, only if I visit Bruce Aune at time t'.

Evidently, (1) and (3) are *toto coelo* different.

In short, since among the conditions of one's intentions to do something are propositions about one's own doing of other future actions, *SHALL* has to operate on non-propositions, or *SHALL* has to be in the scope of logical connectives.[1] Sellars must hold the former, since he holds that (each) *shall* is "a *manner* rather than a *content* of thought" ([12]: 129).

Let us, therefore, set Sellars' thesis (S1) aside. Then, the picture that emerges from (S2) is this:

SH. 1.   *SHALL* is an operator that operates on propositional actions and yields intentions.

sh. 1.   *shall* is an operator that operates on future-tense propositions and yields intentions.

1. The preceding argument, based on the difference between the logical roles of antecedent-consequent and the pragmatical roles of conditioning-being conditioned, is an adaptation of an argument which I devised, in [3]: 227-28, against Hare's view, in [9]: 21-22, 189, that neustics are not in the scope of logical connectives.

3. Action operators

I have argued that, given Sellars' major thesis about intentions and
ought-statements, he may be construed as committed not to thesis (S1)
but to the thesis that *SHALL* operates on the propositional actions of
[14] to which, indeed, he refers the reader in [15]: 181 when he states
thesis (S2). Now, thesis (S1) is also incompatible with Sellars' related
view in [11]. But this view at first glance appears also to differ from (S2):

> ... one moves from an indicative statement to a shall-statement by
> turning the indicative statement into a gerund and prefixing it with
> the shall-operator. Thus, for example, we would go from
>> Tom will shortly cross the road
> to
>> Shall [Tom's shortly crossing the road]. ([11]: 174f; in [13]: 6,

Sellars also conceives of 'shall' as operating on gerunds.)

I conjecture that Sellars' gerunds of [11] are the same as his propositional action expressions of [14].

Let us, therefore, treat propositional action expressions and future-
tense sentences as non-synonymous. Let us say, with Sellars, that the
former express *propositional actions,* while the latter express future-
tense propositions. Thus, we must acknowledge the presence of a
propositional-actional operator that transforms a future-tense proposition into its corresponding propositional action. Let 'α' represent this
operator. Then as a first analysis of propositional actions we have:

> (A)   *X to do A*, which is the same as *X's doing A*, is
>   analyzable as *α (X will do A)*.

Now, one of Sellars' most important theses has been that ought-
statements are to be analyzed as shall-statements. (See, for instance,
[15]: 192, 211; [11]: 204.) Thus, 'ought' expresses, on a favorite view of
Sellars, an operator of some sort that applies precisely to what the
operator expressed by 'shall' applies to. Naturally, in accordance with
(S2), Sellars distinguishes an *Ought (to be)* and an *Ought (to do)*: the
former is a type of *shall*, and the latter a type of *SHALL*. Let us
concentrate on the latter.

In [14], Sellars studies with great patience numerous examples of
arguments for the operator *Ought (to do)*. On p. 316, he introduces the
operator *to bring it about that*, which forms concepts of actions from

propositions. Thus, the most general schema of an action concept is *to bring it about that p*. This makes it tempting both to reject (S1) together with (S2) and to adopt, instead, (S3) below and its linguistic counterpart:

(S3) *SHALL* is an operator that yields intentions by operating on propositional actions. The basic form of an intention is *SHALL [I to bring it about that p]*, i.e., *SHALL [α (I will bring it about that p)]*.

(S3) is a superficial thesis. Sellars has penetrated the matter much more deeply and has emphasized another distinction. Consider the following actions, described in Sellars' infinitive form:

(1) to bring it about that either he refrains from smoking or he uses the ashtray;

(2) to bring it about that if he smokes he uses the ashtray.

They yield ought-statements of the following forms:

(1a) Y ought (1);

(2a) Y ought (2).

As Sellars observes, in (1a) the agent Y is under the obligation to perform a disjunctive action. In (2a), Y is under the conditional obligation to use the ashtray, but the condition itself, namely, that Y smokes, is in no way demanded or obligatory: it is a mere circumstance, whose realization or non-realization is, from the perspective of statement (1a), ·just a brute fact. In my opinion, Sellars is *absolutely* correct in distinguishing between the *targets* and the *circumstances* of obligations. (See, e.g., [2] and [4].) Thus, he is correct when, on page 317 of [14], he introduces another operator that *seems* to apply to propositions in order to transform them into targets of obligation. He represents this operation by an accent placed to the right of an expression denoting the target. I shall, however, use 't' to represent this target operator. Now, given his claim that ought-statements are special shall-statements, or have a structural correspondence with intentions, we must construe Sellars' structural analysis of the arguments of *ought* as a constituent analysis of the arguments of *SHALL*. Thus, we are led to:

(S4) Intentions are the result of the operation of *SHALL* on a propositional action of the form *[I to bring it about that T]*, where *T* is a target of possible obligations, i.e., a complex of propositions and targets.

(S5)   An atomic target is the result of applying the target operator *t* to a proposition.

The simplest intentions are, hence, of the form *SHALL [I to bring
it about that *t(p)*]*, that is, *SHALL [α (I will bring it about that *t(p)*)]*.
Thus, the simplest intention involves four operators:

SHALL, *α*, *to bring it about that*, and *t*.

Sellars' theory of intentions is complex. But more perplexing than its
complexity is *t*. What sort of operator is it? What exactly are its results
(or values)? What are targets? To be sure, the expression 'target of
obligation' is, though metaphorical, rather clear in referring to an
important element in the above examples. But a general theory about the
phenomenological entity *t(p)* is in order.

II

Sellars' Theory of Intentions: Logic

1. The derivativeness of practical reasoning

One of the presuppositions that appears to undergird Sellars' conception of practical reasoning in general and of intentional implication in
particular is his contention that practical reasoning is derivative. This,
his latest statement, is much stronger than his earlier one:

Philosophically, the most important single feature of the logic of
intentions is that it is parasitical upon the logic of beliefs. ([13]: 5.)

Obviously, this latter claim is both correct and innocent. A simple reflection suffices to convince one that the implications between propositions are not only more basic than those between intentions, but are
also a model for them.

2. Compound intentions

Sellars insists throughout his papers that intentions lack the logical
properties of (external or total) negation and conjunction. That is to say,
there are for him no statements of the forms: *not-SHALL[...]*, and

SHALL[...] and SHALL[...]. Here are some important texts:

> . . . no meaning shall be given to "not shall[*P*]," as contrasted with "Shall[not-*P*]." Shall-sentences, unlike ought-sentences, do not have contradictories. ([12]: 112; similarly in [15]: 185ff.)
> Shall[*A*] · Shall[*B*]. No sense has been given to the latter, nor . . . has any sense been given to "Shall[*P*,*Q*]." ([12]: 115.)

It is apparent from Sellars' discussions that he means to endorse the general principle:

> (S.N)   *SHALL* (and *shall*, of course) are never in the scope of logical connectives.

There is at least one passage in Sellars' writings that strongly suggests that he also holds the principle:

> (S.Q)   Shall-operators are never in the scope of a quantifier.

The passage I have in mind is this:

> It shall$_{we}$ be the case that each of us does A_i in C_i which, on our analysis, is equivalent to the family of ought-statements
> If any of us is in C_i he ought to do A_i.

([15]: 219; Sellars' display.)

By (S.N), there are neither conjunctions nor disjunctions of intentions. At first sight this seems false, for there are intentions expressible with the following sentences:

> (1)   I shall work hard and I shall become rich.

> (2)   Either I shall succeed or I shall die young.

Sellars knows this, of course. He would, I am sure, insist that the repetition of the word 'shall' in each sentence is not a sign that there is a conjunction of intentions in (1) and a disjunction of them in (2).

However, the repetition of 'shall' both in (1) and in (2) is actually a good indication that two intentions are involved in each case. *The characteristic syntactical phenomenon is one of abbreviation of complex structures by elision of common constituents in the component substructures.* For example, 'John and (or) Mary came' abbreviates 'John came and (or) Mary came'. Thus, 'I shall work hard and become rich' looks and feels very much like an *abbreviation* of, rather than the original protracted to, 'I shall work hard and I shall become rich'. The suggestion, therefore, that the repetition of 'I shall' in both (1) and (2) is due to emphasis, which is the only one I can think of, is an uneasy one. At any rate, Sellars' view seems to be that intentions (1) and (2) are really, respectively, of the forms:

(1f)   SHALL[I to work hard and become rich].

(2f)   SHALL[I either to succeed or to die young].

Consider now the following two intentions:

(3)   I shall press button A, unless I press button B.

(4)   Unless I press button A, I shall press button B.

As far as I can see, intentions (3) and (4) are different. Both are disjunctions, but disjunctions of a proposition, the unless-component, and a simpler intention, the shall-disjunct. According to (3) my pressing button B is something that may happen, but it is something that I do not intend to do. My intention according to (3) is to press button A disjunctively dependent on my perhaps unintended pressing button B. On the other hand, the reverse is precisely the case with intention (4): my pressing button A is a circumstance, not something that I intend to do.

An additional way of bringing out the difference between (3) and (4) is this. Suppose that penalties are attached to the failure of carrying out simple intentions. Let the penalty attached to failing to fulfill the intention to press button A be $100, and let the penalty attached to not fulfilling the intention to press button B be $50. There is no penalty or reward for doing something not intended. Thus, if my intention is (3) and I fail to fulfill it, my penalty is $100; if my intention is (4) and I fail to carry it out, my penalty is only $50. They are, again, wholly different intentions and neither one implies the other.

At first glance it would seem that on Sellars' view intentions (3) and (4) have to be exactly the same intention, namely, the one constituted by an overall shall-operator in whose scope there is a disjunction:

(5)   SHALL [I either to press button A or to press button B].

But Sellars is not committed to this analysis of (3) and (4). For what (3) and (4) establish is that *SHALL* is not an overall operator that applies to propositions and never occurs in the scope of connectives. This argument is a variant of the one at the end of section I.2 showing that the operands of *SHALL* are not propositions.

Sellars can avoid (5) by insisting that *SHALL* applies to propositional actions, not to propositions, and that (3) and (4) are analyzable thus:

(3a)   SHALL [I to press button A unless I press button B].

(4a)   SHALL [unless I press button A, I to press button B].

In fact, given the many practical operators which Sellars has adopted, he can justify analyses (3a) and (4a) quite easily. Particularly, *t* stands ready to lend its services. Sellars may claim that inside the propositional actions in the scope of *SHALL* there is also a target, namely, the result of applying the operator *t* to an appropriate operand.

In general, for any sentence, however complicated, containing an occurrence of the word 'shall' not in indirect speech, Sellars can consistently claim that that occurrence of 'shall' represents *SHALL* and that *SHALL* applies to the propositional action expressed by the sentence in question.

A problem with Sellars' analysis of shall-sentences is raised by the following reasoning:

(6)   If it is raining, I shall come in;
      It is raining;
      Hence, I shall come in.

This reasoning seems to be a special case of modus ponens, but if Sellars is right about (S.N), then the first premise of (6) is

(7)   SHALL [if it is raining, I to come in],

and then (6) is not just a special case of modus ponens. Sellars is aware of the problem, and he offers an answer to it. In section II.3 I shall attempt to show that his answer needs some revision.

Prior to entering the topic of intentional implication, we must examine some rather complex intentions. Consider, for instance:

(8)   I shall do the following: if it rains, close the windows just in case the awnings are not up, provided that it does not hail, and turn circulator A on if circulator B is off and it hails, and not turn circulator A on only if circulator B is not off, in case it hails.

This is a straightforward intention with *SHALL* governing the whole complex propositional action composed of both propositions and simpler propositional actions. The latter are *I to close the windows*, *I to turn circulator *A* on*, and *I not to turn circulator *A* on*. The interesting thing is, however, that (8) is equivalent to:

> (9) If it rains, I *shall* close the windows just in case the awnings are not up, provided that it does not hail, and I *shall* turn circulator *A* on if circulator *B* is off and it hails, and I *shall* not turn circulator *A* on only if circulator *B* is not off, in case it hails.

On Sellars' view the equivalence between (8) and (9) cannot be accounted for by principles of distribution, or confinement, that allow shall-operators to move across the scope of logical connectives so as to apply directly to pure propositional actions. Since (9) cannot be denied to exist, on Sellars' view we must regard (9) and (8) as *exactly the same intention*. What are we to say, then, about the plurality of 'shall's in sentence (9) each having a different and small scope? Curiously enough, this multiplicity cannot be attributed to emphasis, for between sentences (8) and (9) it is (8), with its over-all and totalitarian 'shall', that appears emphatic. On what basis then can we identify intentions (8) and (9)?

As far as I can see, the only way in which we can identify intentions (8) and (9) is by regarding the expression 'shall' wherever it occurs in sentences (8) or (9) as *not* expressing a constituent of the intention in question. Otherwise, (8) would have one such constituent and (9) would have three, and hence (8) and (9) would not be identical. 'Shall' has nevertheless a meaning and has a function. Therefore, if (8) and (9) are the same intention, the role of 'shall' in sentences (8) and (9) is not to express a constituent of an intention, but to function as a *signal, external to intentions,* that a certain sentence expresses an intention. This has three consequences:

> (C.1) There is no intentional operator expressed by 'shall'.

> (C.2) An intention is a species of what Sellars calls propositional action, undoubtedly, a first-person species.

> (C.3) Intentions are linked to other intentions, or to propositions, by logical connectives.

These are all anti-Sellarsian theses. But I do not see now any way in which we can do justice to intentions like (9) that appear to have a complex structure within which both intentions and propositions appear as components. Patently, there are even much more complex patterns than the one (9) illustrates. I conclude, therefore, that such patterns do present a hurdle for Sellars' view that intentional or shall-operators are genuine operators and never appear in the scope of logical connectives.

3. Intentional implication

a. *Sellars' lone principle of intentional implication*

Sellars holds that "there is no need for a special 'logic of intentions' other than that formulated by the third-level principle [below] together with certain conceptual truths about the function of 'shall' " ([15]: 182):

(I.I) 'It is the case that-*P*' implies 'it is the case that-*Q*' ↔ 'It shall be the case that-*P*' implies 'it shall be the case that-*Q*' ([15]: 179; (I.I) also appears in [13]: 5 and in [12]: 111.)

Sellars means to express a relationship of co-implication by the symbol ' ↔'. He does not explain what sort of implication the symbol expresses, even though he is very emphatic that 'implies' is a generic term that includes several species of implication:

I shall further suppose that there are at least two species of implication in the ordinary sense: (a) logical, and (b) physical or natural; finally, that there is such a thing as derivative implication, where something implies something else, *relatively to a given assumption*. ([12]: 111, his italics; see also [15]: 179-182 and [13]: 6ff.)

Sellars' idea of working with a generic sense of implication is fascinating. It is a splendid thing to be able to contemplate several networks of implication as instances of one single system. His idea of unifying the whole formal system under the one principle (I.I) is also fascinating.

Principle (I.I) is somewhat perplexing. As we saw in section I.2, Sellars reduces *shall*-intentions to SHALL-intentions. Hence, the fundamental principle of intentional implication should be framed more generally in terms of SHALL-intentions. In fact, the typical example he discusses (to be examined soon) involves a mixed SHALL-intention. Presumably, then, the fundamental principle is:

(I.Ia) *[I to *A*]* implies$_k$ *[I to *B*]* ↔ *SHALL[I to *A*]* implies$_k$ *SHALL[I to *B*]*, where 'to A' is short for 'to bring it about that T_A' for some target T_A that determines the content of action A, and where the subscript 'k' stands for one of the types of implication: (i) non-relative and logical, (ii) logical but relative to assumption X, (iii) non-relative and causal, and (iv) causal and relative to assumption X. Note that species (ii) and (iii) are really general types themselves.

b. *Other principles seem to be needed*

Sellars seems to be justified in claiming that (I.I) does not presuppose any special logic. But (I.Ia) does presuppose a special logic, namely, the logic of *propositional actions*. Here we can see why Sellars was most interested in putting forward his first thesis on intentions (S1), examined in sections I.1-2. Clearly, if *SHALL* operates on future-tense first-person propositions, then we bypass the need for special principles governing propositional actions. But we saw in part I that (S1) conflicts with (S2) and other theses of Sellars.

To make sure that we get things right, recall the structure of intentions to which Sellars' discussion and cross-references led us in section I. Thus, (I.I) should perhaps be construed as:

> (I.Ib)   *P* implies$_k$ *Q* $\leftrightarrow$
> *SHALL[α(I will bring it about that $t(P)$)]* implies$_k$
> *SHALL[α(I will bring it about that $t(Q)$)]*.

Here we seem to be assuming nothing more than implications between propositions.

Yet on two counts we must assume other principles which specifically apply to the contents of practical thinking. First, the operators *α* and *bring it about that* must have some implicational properties of their own which are basic to the implicational properties of *SHALL*. Second, regardless of what happens to these two operators, the operator *t* must have its own logic. Recall, particularly, that *t* appears in the scope of logical connectives. In fact, in [14] Sellars discusses examples which show how some complex targets of obligation are mixed compounds, some components being atomic (so to speak) targets and some components being propositions. Here is one example:

> ... using the 'turnstile' to make the relevant proposition out of an action expression [where 'O' stands for 'it is obligatory that' and '$\rightarrow$' for conditionality]
> $O(x$ to $[A \cdot (\vdash A \rightarrow B)])$.

Let us call action expressions of the form

to $(p \rightarrow A)$

'conditional' action expressions, as contrasted with the 'implicative' action kinds [of the form 'to $(A \rightarrow B)$']. ([14]: 314f.)

Hence, we must simply have a *full logic of targets,* with rules of formation and of transformation, and with principles concerning the distribution of the operator *t* across logical connectives.

Let us return to Sellars' lone principle of intentional logic and consider first his own original formulation (I.I). If my argument in the preceding section to the effect that intentions do appear in the scope of connectives is sound, (I.I) needs the companionship of other principles. In particular, it needs a principle of the form:

> (I.C) Intention I implies intention $I' \rightarrow$ Intention $F(I)$, containing I as an extensional component, implies intention $F(I')$, containing I' instead of I.

But remember that our exegesis of Sellars' writings has revealed that shall-operators apply to compounds that have both targets and propositions as components. Thus, neither Sellars' original (I.I) nor (I.Ib) suffices to derive such intentions with hybrid contents. As (I.Ib) shows clearly, the target operator *t* makes out of the whole propositions that-P and that-Q the "atomic" targets *t(P)* and *t(Q)*.

If we are to preserve the overall dominant character of the shall-operators, we should have principles like (I.Ic) below, in addition to (I.I) or (I.Ib):

> (I.Ic) *F(P)* implies *G(Q)* $\leftrightarrow$
> *SHALL[α(I will bring it about that $F(t(P)))$]* implies$_k$
> *SHALL[α(I will bring it about that $G(t(Q)))$]*,

where *F(P)* and *G(Q)* are propositions having *P* and *Q* as components, respectively. Such principles must, however, have restrictions on the structure of *F(P)* and *G(Q)*. But I will not search for those restrictions here.

c. *The problem of mixed reasonings*

Sellars' view that his principle (I.I) is the only one required by intentional implication is well-entrenched. And he means 'only' literally:

(S11) . . . if we accept, as we have, the principle that intentions can *only* be derived from intentions . . . ([15]: 211, my italics; see also p. 180, and [12]: 111.)

This raises a question about perfectly ordinary reasonings having propositional premises, like:

    (r) (1) If it is raining, I shall come;
        (2) It is raining;
        Hence, (3) I shall come.

Sellars himself acknowledges that (r) is a "practical syllogism" ([15]: 181). Clearly, it is the derivation of an intention from *both* an intention and *a proposition*. Hence, it is a counter-example to (S11).

It must be noted that (S11) precludes the acceptance of (r) even as a *derived* or *derivative* inference.

Sellars sees this, of course, and tries to palliate the situation by offering what at first glance may seem like a derivation of (r), but which is instead an *analysis* of (2) as an *assumptive* inference, namely:

        Assumption: (2) It is raining.
(r′)   (1) If it is raining, I shall come;
               Hence, (3) I shall come.

Clearly, (r′) derives intention (3) from just intention (1). This derivation proceeds along the lines of implication$_k$, where k stands for "depending on the assumption *It is raining*." (See [15]: 181f, and [12]: 111.) This is a brilliant stroke of analysis.

Sellars' analysis of (r) shows how in general one can parse every intentional reasoning as having no propositional premises, but having always a set β of assumptions, all of which are propositions. Naturally, β is null in the case of non-relative implication. On the other hand, there is no clear indication that Sellars holds that intentional reasonings must have just one intentional premise. Nevertheless, he rejects a most plausible candidate for a valid intentional reasoning with two premises:

    . . . there is no logical move from

        Shall [A], Shall [B]

to

        Shall [$A.B$],

let alone

Shall[A]   . Shall[B]. ([12]: 114f.)

Now, although I admire the ingenuity of Sellars' analysis of ordinary intentional reasonings as assumptive reasonings, I prefer a theory of intentional logic that allows propositions and intentions to mix with one another, not only as components of complex intentions, but also as premises of hybrid reasonings. Naturally, I prefer a theory that acknowledges intentional reasonings with several intentional premises, whether such reasonings are assumptive or not, e.g.:

> (4) I shall go to Miami or to New Orleans.
> But I shan't go to Miami.
> Therefore, I shall go to New Orleans.

d. *Sellarsian implication*

Let us now consider the relation of implication which Sellars insists upon. Aside from the question of how many premises an intentional reasoning has on his view, it is clear that principle (I.I) or (I.Ib) can be refined as follows:

(S12) The basic schema of intentional implication is this:

If $X \mathrel{\underset{\to}{\beta}} {}_{j}Y$,

then $\mathrm{SHALL}[X] \mathrel{\underset{\to}{\beta}}_{j} \mathrm{SHALL}\ [Y]$,

where '$\underset{\to}{\llcorner}$' means implication, β is the set of assumptions, and 'j' stands for 'logically' or 'causally', and where we leave the asterisk quotes implicit.

For convenience we shall let X and Y be propositions when they stand by themselves, and propositional actions (or future-tense propositions, if you wish) when they are in the scope of *SHALL*. Sellars himself introduces the symbol '$\underset{\to|}{\llcorner}_{\beta_j}$' in [14], so that my generalization to '$\underset{\to}{\llcorner}_{\beta_j}$' is essentially a tightening up of his views.

The general conception of implication represented by '$\underset{\to}{\llcorner}_{\beta_j}$' is fascinating. Yet there is an initial perplexity about it. It is not clear how one intention can causally imply another intention. Strictly, causality seems to be a modality of propositions. Thus, the proposition that a man intends to A is certainly an ingredient of the causal network, but the content of this man's intending, his intention to A, does not seem itself to be subject to causal relationships. But I won't pursue this point.

Logical implication also raises an immediate difficulty for (S12). In a standard sense of logical implication, a contradiction implies any proposition whatsoever. Thus, representing negation by the sign '$\sim$':

(5) $\sim X, X \mathrel{\llcorner_{\rightarrow_L}} Y$, where '$L$' is 'logically'

Hence, (6) $X \mathrel{\llcorner \sim X_{\rightarrow_L}} Y$

Therefore, (7) SHALL$[X] \mathrel{\llcorner \sim X_L}$ SHALL $[Y]$.

That is, an intention that happens to be unrealized implies any other intention, so that an agent who believes one of his intentions to be unrealized would behave irrationally were he to reject any intention whatever.

The preceding difficulty can, however, be solved with the help of provisions which Sellars has stored in his papers, even though he is prone to formulate (I.I) with no qualifications. He states:

> . . . it is important not to suppose that if P strictly implies Q, then (Shall [P] implies Shall [Q]). Stronger requirements are necessary to avoid paradox. As far as I can see, something like A. R. Anderson's reconstruction of "entails" is necessary. ([11]: 216, footnote 15.)

One of the "paradoxes" of strict implication which Anderson wants to avoid is precisely that a pair of contradictory propositions implies any other proposition. Hence, the preceding difficulty for (S11) would be avoided if '$\mathrel{\llcorner_\rightarrow}$' expresses something like Anderson's 'entails'.

In fact, in [14] Sellars formulates some restrictions for the Ought-principle which are the counterpart of (I.I). Given that for Sellars ought-statements are at bottom intentions, we may suppose that some of those restrictions apply to (I.I) and to (S12):

> (β) . . . provided that the implication of Y by X has no assumption which either implies that X obtains or does not obtain, or . . . ([14]: 342.)

The other restriction cannot apply to intentions. These restrictions do apply to (7) above, since in (6) $\sim X$ implies that X does not obtain.

But other restrictions are needed. Thus, consider:

(8) $X, Y \mathrel{\llcorner_{\rightarrow_L}} Y$

(9) $X \mathrel{\llcorner Y_{\rightarrow_L}} Y$

(10) SHALL$[X] \mathrel{\llcorner Y_{\rightarrow_L}}$ SHALL$[Y]$.

That is, any intention is implied by any intention whatsoever on the assumption that it is realized. Thus, an agent who intends to do something or other is committed to intending to bring about the truth of any proposition which he believes to be true. The derivation of (10) from (8) is interesting in that (8) is no "paradox" of standard propositional logic.

Yet the derivation of (10) from (9) can be stopped by extending requirement (β) to the implicate, which seems natural enough.

In short, (S12) must be replaced with (S13):

> (S13) The basic schema of intentional implication is this:
> If $X \; \beta_j \; Y$,
> then $\text{SHALL}[X] \; \beta_j \; \text{SHALL}[Y]$
> provided that β implies neither X nor not-X nor Y nor not-Y.

Nevertheless, we have not reached the end of the restrictions to be added to (β). Just consider the following derivation:

> (11) $X,Y \; {}_{L \rightarrow L} \; X \& Y$
> (12) $X \; \underline{Y}_{\rightarrow L} \; X \& Y$
> (13) $\text{SHALL}[X] \; \underline{Y}_{\rightarrow L} \; \text{SHALL}[X \& Y]$.

Thus, each intention implies that every true proposition is part of some intention. The move from (12) to (13) does not violate (S13). Furthermore, we can presumably continue the derivation:

> (14) $X \& Y \; {}_{L \rightarrow L} \; Y$
> (15) $\text{SHALL}[X \& Y] \; {}_{L \rightarrow L} \; \text{SHALL}[Y]$
> (16) $\text{SHALL}[X] \; \underline{Y}_{\rightarrow L} \; \text{SHALL}[Y]$.

Step (16) issues from (13) and (15) by the transitivity of implication of a given species. Another perplexing result is derived as follows:

> (17) $X, \text{not-}(X \& Y) \; {}_{L \rightarrow L} \; \text{not-}Y$
> (18) $X \; \underline{\text{not-}(X \& Y)}_{\rightarrow L} \; \text{not-}Y$
> (19) $\text{SHALL}[X] \; \underline{\text{not-}(X \& Y)}_{\rightarrow L} \; \text{SHALL}[\text{not-}Y]$.

Clearly, (19) is derivable from (18) in full accordance with (S13). Thus, by (19), if a man believes a conjunctive proposition to be false and intends to bring about one conjunct of it, then it would be unreasonable for him not to intend to bring about the denial of the other conjunct. For instance, I believe that it won't happen that both President Nixon will win his unemployment fight and I will finish this paper in a week, and I intend to finish this paper in a week, hence, by (19), I am unreasonable because I do not intend to bring it about that Nixon does not win his unemployment fight. I am, in fact, most reasonably prepared to help Nixon try to win that losing fight—even if only to diminish the magnitude of the defeat.

Other counter-intuitive results can be derived from (S13). The natural diagnosis is this: Sellars' conception of relative or dependent implication commits a fallacy of exportation; it enthrones the move from *X*-and-*Y* implies *Z** to *Given *X*, *Y* implies *Z**, which exports implication illegitimately to the pair $\langle Y, Z \rangle$. There is something like this, but as I understand Sellars, since he refuses to detach the assumptions, there is no genuine full exportation.

In any case, it seems that Sellars' implication principle (I.I) or the revised (S13) needs overhauling. Since the sequence of restrictions to be imposed is rather impressive, perhaps a more basic alteration of his conception of intentional logic may be worth attempting.

III
An Alternative Kindred View

1. Development

I have examined Sellars' views on intentions at the level of the Manifest Image. Even though I have raised some problems and questions, and have suggested a few of my alternative preferences, I want to emphasize that Sellars' views are powerful and insightful. Undoubtedly, the overall plan is correct. The anatomy of intentions must be studied, their implicational relationships must be systematized, and their role in making thinking practical must be examined. Furthermore, Sellars' views about how intentions relate to propositions, and how intending relates to believing, are insightful. His view that intentions are not propositions, but contain propositions as components, possesses a substantial element of truth. His fundamental principle (I.I) of intentional implication also contains a true half. And many other claims of his are true or insightful, for instance, that intentions have only one negation. Perhaps my main criticism is only the esthetic one that by not having been developed into a full system, Sellars' views on intentions are as a whole both very complex and yet stand in need of more complexities.

In general, the direction in which Sellars' view should develop must include: (i) reduction of the operators involved in his separate discussions of intentions, or of ought-statements; (ii) recognition of the phenomenological datum that intentions do appear in the scope of connectives; and (iii) the recognition that other principles of implication are needed besides (I.I). The reduction envisaged in (i) should consist either of identifying intentions with *targets* and dropping the operator *α* or of combining the operators *t* and *α* into one basic operator. Of course, (ii) and (iii) must be satisfied by the precise formulation of the proper rules of formation and the principles of implication of intentional logic.

As said in section I.1, Sellars views intentions as the basic bricks from which the contents of practical thinking are built. This is, again, an insightful view. I accept a good deal of Sellars' analysis of ought-statements in terms of intentions. However, I find that the fundamental practical units of thought content are not only intentions, but also what I have sometimes called *prescriptions* (e.g., in [4]-[7]). Thus, I want to see Sellars' views developed so as to include prescriptions. Let me explain what these are.

Consider a man Jones and the action of going home. The two are involved in: (i) the proposition *Jones will go home*; (ii) the command *Jones, go home!*, which someone may, but need not, issue; (iii) the request *Jones, please go home*, and (iv) the piece of advice *Jones, you'd better go home*. The three practical units (ii)-(iv) have a common structure *Jones to go home*, which I call a *prescription*. So far, then, prescriptions are second-person contents, but it is easy to extend them to third-person contents. Let us do so. In some essays (e.g., [4] and [5]) I have used the word 'prescription' as a generic term to cover both the prescriptions just introduced and the corresponding first-person practical contents that are intentions. Since this use has led to misunderstandings, I have more recently introduced the term 'practition' as a generic term. Thus, *practitions* are either prescriptions (second- and third-person practical contents) or intentions (first-person contents). In my even earlier paper [2],[2] I spoke of *imperative-resolutives* to refer to sentential variables that in a formal, canonical, practical language were expressive of either prescriptions or intentions.

One of my earlier views has been that deontic sentences are declarative and that the atomic ones result from the application of a deontic opator to an imperative-resolutive. To put it ontologically, a deontic

2. Perhaps this is the place to clarify a matter which I am sometimes asked about. The book on practical discourse to which Sellars refers, in the Appendix to [11], as "forthcoming [and] important" will not be published. My [2] above contains part of Chapter IV of that unpublished manuscript. For a more developed formulation of the views expounded in that manuscript, see [8] or [4] and [5].

judgment is a proposition that results from the application of a deontic operator to a practition. This view is more general and differs from Sellars' view about ought-judgments in several respects. First, my deontic operators are mounted on a full logic of intentions and prescriptions that allows both to function in compound and mixed contents and in reasonings. Second, my deontic operators are connectives, so that intentions appear in the scope of connectives. Yet there is an important kinship between my view and Sellars': for both of us, intentions are more basic than deontic judgments. There are other important points in common, but since this is not an essay on Ought, I shall close this discussion here.

2. An alternative view

One, but *just* one, development of the views on intentions that Sellars has expounded in his essays culminates in a theory of intentions and prescriptions, i.e., practitions, that I very much like. It is significant that the results of Sellars' research can be pushed in a direction that converges on the theory which I prefer.

That preferred theory is very simple. It consists of the following ontological and logical theses:

Thesis 1. A simple practition (e.g., *I (=Jones) shall visit Mary* or *Jones, visit Mary*) differs from its corresponding performance proposition (*Jones will visit Mary*) in the *copula* that structures the subjects and the predicate action. In canonical notation, I have represented the propositional copula by means of a pair of parentheses and the practical copula by means of a pair of brackets. Thus:

I (=Jones) shall visit Mary = Will-visit $[$I(=Jones), Mary$]$

Jones, visit Mary = Will-visit $[$Jones, Mary$]$

Jones will visit Mary = Will-visit (Jones, Mary)

I (=Jones) will visit Mary = Will-visit $[$I(=Jones), Mary$]$.

Thesis 2. Standard propositional connectives yield compound thought contents by linking propositions and propositions, propositions and practitions, and practitions and practitions.

Thesis 3. Connective compounds having at least one practition as a component are practitions.

Thesis 4. Practitions are generally independent of their corresponding performance propositions.

Thesis 5. The logic of practitions, pure or mixed, is the same as the logic of pure propositions. More specifically, if the propositional variables of a standard propositional or quantificational calculus are interpreted as either propositions or practitions, that calculus is a systematization of the general connective and quantificational logic of practitions and propositions.

These five theses constitute a sub-system of the general theory of practical contents formulated in [1],-[2], [4] and [5]. The latter two contain defenses of Theses 3 and 5 for the case of prescriptions. My most general and detailed defense of Thesis 5 for prescriptions appears in [5]. Arguments for Theses 1, 2, and 3 for the case of intentions appear in [6] and [7]. In [7] there is a general argument for the parallelism between propositional and intentional logics. This argument is different from the argument for the prescriptional half of Thesis 5 in [5], and it has a prescriptional counterpart, which the reader can easily construct by himself.[3]

3. I am indebted to George Nakhnikian for some stylistic suggestions, and to Bruce Aune for a major stylistic overhauling of the paper.

REFERENCES

[1] Hector-Neri Castañeda, "The Logic of Obligation," *Philosophical Studies* 10 (1959): 17-23.

[2] _____, "Outline of a Theory on the General Logical Structure of the Language of Action," *Theoria* 26 (1960): 151-82.

[3] _____, "Imperatives, Decisions, and Oughts: A Logico-Metaphysical Investigation," in H.-N. Castañeda and G. Nakhnikian, eds., *Morality and the Language of Conduct* (Detroit: Wayne State University Press, 1963, 1965): 219-99.

[4] _____, "Actions, Imperatives, and Obligations," *Proceedings of the Aristotelian Society* 68 (1967-68): 25-48.

[5] _____, "On the Semantics of the Ought-to-do," *Synthese* 21 (1970): 449-68.

[6] _____, "Intentions and the Structure of Intending," *The Journal of Philosophy* 68(1971).

[7] _____, "Intentions and Intending," *American Philosophical Quarterly* 9(1972).

[8] _____, *The Structure of Morality* (Springfield, Illinois: Charles C. Thomas, Publisher, 1974).

[9] R. M. Hare, *The Language of Morals* (Oxford: Clarendon Press, 1952).

[10] Wilfrid Sellars, "Philosophy and the Scientific Image of Man," in Robert Colodny, ed., *Frontiers of Science and Philosophy* (Pittsburgh: University of Pittsburgh Press, 1962).

[11] _____, "Imperatives, Intentions, and the Logic of 'Ought'," in H.-N. Castañeda and G. Nakhnikian, eds., *Morality and the Language of Conduct* (Detroit: Wayne State University Press, 1963, paperback, 1965): 105-39.

[12] _____, "Thought and Action," in Keith Lehrer, ed., *Freedom and Determinism* (New York: Random House, 1966): 140-74.

[13] _____, *Form and Content in Ethical Theory* (Department of Philosophy, University of Kansas, the Lindley Lecture for 1967).

[14] _____, "Reflections on Contrary-to-Duty Imperatives," *Noûs* 1(1967): 303-44.

[15] _____, *Science and Metaphysics* (London: Routledge and Kegan Paul; New York: Humanities Press, 1967), especially Chapter VII entitled "Objectivity, Intersubjectivity, and the Moral Point of View," pp. 175-229.

·~· 3 ·~·

Determinism and Freedom: Sellars and the Reconciliationist Thesis

ALAN DONAGAN
University of Chicago

AMID a profusion of publications on its subject, Wilfrid Sellars' examination of "the reconcilability of the concept of 'action of one's own free will' with scientific determinism" ([11]: 141) has excited little comment. It is true that Sellars does not embroil himself in contemporary polemics: like R. M. Chisholm and Richard Taylor on the anti-reconciliationist side, his approach is classical. He sets out to show how, in view of recent fundamental work in philosophy of mind—including, of course, his own—the reconciliationist thesis of Hobbes, Hume, and J. S. Mill can be defensibly revised.

He does not share the late J. L. Austin's doubt as to whether determinism is a name for anything clear ([1]: 179). A deterministic system is a system of physical objects, a description of any temporal state of which is logically derivable, according to process laws, from a description of its state at any earlier time (cf. [11]: 143-44).[1] It is not implied that either the process laws of such a system, or any of its temporal state-descriptions, can be known by any observer within it. Indeed, if the system be the entire universe, it is improbable that either should be known to any observer within it. Hence the concept of a deterministic

---

1. This analysis is ultimately due to P. S. de Laplace, *Essai Philosophique sur les Probabilités* (Paris: 1814), tr. F. W. Truscott and F. L. Emory, *A Philosophical Essay on Probabilities* (New York: 1902). A mechanist, Laplace stated it in a mechanistic form, for which reason "Laplacean determinism" has been a bugbear to determinists and anti-determinists alike. However, Laplace's formulation may be generalized, as by Sellars, and freed from any implication of mechanism. I know of no coherent non-Laplacean analysis.

system is not exposed to Goedelian objections against implying that a scientific predictor could calculate its own future states.[2]

Determinism, as Sellars understands it, is the doctrine that man is "part and parcel" of a deterministic system, which is usually taken to be the entire universe (cf. [11]: 145). In view of his general characterization of a deterministic system, Sellars speaks of any temporal state of such a system, or any part of such a state, as "physically necessary" given any of the system's earlier states. This enables him to define determinism, with respect to human action, as follows. (I shall render Sellars' symbolic formulae into my own English, which I find easier to work with, although many readers may not.)

> For any arbitrarily chosen individual x, any arbitrarily chosen action A, and any arbitrarily chosen moment of time t:
>
> PD-I. x does A at t only if it is physically necessary, given the state of the universe (including that of x) immediately before t, that x does A at t. ([11]: 168.)

In subsequent renderings, I shall omit the parenthesis "including that of x", stipulating that the state of the universe in which an agent acts is always to be understood as including the state of the agent. According to Sellars, PD-I entails:

> PD-III'.[3] x does A at t only if there is no action incompatible with A, such that it is physically possible, given the state of the universe immediately before t, that x does *that* action at t. ([11]: 169.)

In other words, it follows from PD-I that there is no alternative to A which it is physically possible that x do at t, relative to the state of the universe immediately before t ([11]: 169).

What reasons are there for determinism, as Sellars defines it? Henry Sidgwick gave the usual answer in a romantic form:

> The belief that events are determinately related to the state of things immediately preceding them is now held by all competent thinkers in respect to all kinds of occurrences except human

2. These difficulties have been worked out by Sir Karl Popper, "Indeterminism in Classical Physics and in Quantum Physics," *British Journal for the Philosophy of Science* 1 (1950).

3. The numbering "PD-III'" distinguishes this corollary from Sellars' PD-III, which presents x's doing A at t as a function of the state of the universe at t, rather than immediately before t.

relations . . . Step by step in successive departments of fact conflicting modes of thought have receded and faded, until at length
they have vanished everywhere, except from this mysterious
citadel of the will. ([13]: 62-63.)

Anti-determinism is a beleaguered city, which modern science is slowly
reducing: indeed, only the citadel, "human relations", or "the will",
still withstands the besieger, and it is unlikely to resist much longer.

Sellars rightly repudiates this. *Inter alia*, he knows, as Sidgwick did
not, that the profoundest of all nineteenth-century philosophers of science, C. S. Peirce, laughed at the notion that determinism is rendered
highly probable by the progress of science:

> [T]his question ought not long to arrest a person accustomed to
> reflect upon the force of scientific reasoning. For the essence of
> the necessitarian position is that certain continuous quantities
> have certain exact values . . . . To one who is behind the scenes,
> and knows that the most refined comparisons of masses, lengths,
> and angles, far surpassing in precision all other measurements,
> yet fall behind the accuracy of bank accounts . . . the idea of
> mathematical exactitude being demonstrated in the laboratory will
> appear simply ridiculous. ([8]: 329-30.)

Determinism is not among the conclusions of scientific inquiry, except
in the sense that the "conceptual framework" within which scientific
inquiry is conducted is among them ([11]: 144). If scientific inquiry in a
particular period involves determinism, it is as one of its presuppositions
(as Collingwood would say—see [4]: 34-37), or as part of its "paradigm"
or "disciplinary matrix" (as Kuhn would say—see [5]: 10-51, 176-91).
Sellars himself prefers to say that determinism is considered by determinists to be part of the scientific "image"[4] of man ([11]: 145).

Here a distinction is useful. In speaking of the scientific image of
something, one may mean either the image in fact presupposed in
pertinent normal[5] scientific investigations, or what, in some scientific or
philosophical group, is believed to be that image. In what follows, I shall
use the phrase 'the scientific image of *x*' for the former only; and in
speaking of the latter, I shall use phrases of the form '*y*'s opinion about
the scientific image of *x*'.

Since normal science at any time has many branches, and since from
time to time it changes radically, the scientific image of man varies

4. For Sellars' use of the word "image" in this connection, see [10]: 5ff.
5. The concept of "normal science" is taken from Kuhn: see [5].

according to what branch or period of normal science is in question. Following C. S. Peirce, Sellars is interested above all in *ultimate* normal science: that is, in normal science as it will be in the scientists' heaven "when all the facts are in." Although Sellars does not dissemble his expectation that the ultimate scientific image of man will be deterministic, he is careful not to assume it, because he recognizes that, in the present state of science, contrary expectations may reasonably be held. Instead, he proposes a thought-experiment, which determinists and anti-determinists alike may attempt: namely, to investigate whether the traditional conception of man as possessing free will can be maintained, on the supposition (which confessedly may prove false) that the ultimate scientific image of man will be deterministic.

To the many, not all of them determinists, who have ceased to think in terms of the traditional doctrine of human free will and the moral notions associated with it, such a thought-experiment would be academic trifling. Sellars is not of their number. While it is plain that he would not abandon determinism even if he were to become persuaded that it could not be reconciled with his belief in free will, neither would he, like Paul Edwards and John Hospers,[6] divest himself of all or part of that belief with any sense of liberation.

The reason for this does not appear in his papers on the reconciliationist thesis, where he jocularly describes the "manifest image" of man in the world, of which the traditional doctrine of free will is a part, as

> correspond[ing] to the world as conceived by P. F. Strawson— *roughly* it is the world as we know it to be in ordinary experience, supplemented by such inductive procedures as remain within the framework [of pre-scientific thought]. ([11]: 145.)

However, in his fundamental paper, "Philosophy and the Scientific Image of Man," Sellars emphatically declares that "the concept of the manifest image of man-in-the-world is not that of an historical and bygone stage in the development of man's conception of the world and his place in it" ([10]: 7). On the contrary, the manifest image is the conceptual "framework" in terms of which man first came to be aware of himself as man-in-the-world; and it remains the framework in terms of which he defines his essence: "if man had a radically different conception of himself he would be a radically different kind of man" ([10]: 6-8). Hence Sellars rejects a Spinozist view of the relation of the manifest image to the scientific image, in which the former is dismissed as false

6. See Sidney Hook (ed.), *Determinism and Freedom* (New York: 1961).

and the latter accepted as true. Instead, he compares the two images to the two images obtained by looking through a stereoscope with one or the other eye dominating, and proposes, as the aim of philosophy, to "describe . . . how the two images blend together in a true stereoscopic view" ([10]: 9).

What is the representation of free will in the "manifest image" of man, the image in terms of which he defines his own essence? Sellars begins with a point that is not in question: when a man thinks of doing something of his own free will, he thinks of himself as being able to do something else instead. And the proposition that x, in doing A at t, could have done something else, *prima facie* contradicts Sellars' statement of determinism, namely, that x does A at t only if it is physically necessary that, given the state of the universe immediately before t, x does A at t.

The most influential recent reformulation of the classic dissolution of this difficulty in the Hobbes-Mill reconciliationist tradition is by G. E. Moore:

> What, for instance, is the sense in which I *could* have walked a mile in twenty minutes this morning, although I did not? There is one suggestion, which is very obvious: namely, that what I mean is simply after all that I could, *if* I had chosen; or (to avoid a possible complication) perhaps we had better say "that I *should, if* I had chosen." ([7]: 211.)

Moore went on to make clear that he took "if I had chosen" to be equivalent to "if I had so willed" ([7]: 212-13.)

If Moore's analysis is correct, then plainly, for all that has been shown, x could have refrained from doing A at t (i.e., would have refrained had he so willed), even though the state of the universe before t had been such that it was physically impossible for x at t to have refrained from doing A; for the state of the universe immediately before t might have made it physically impossible for x at t to have willed anything but to do A.

Moore's analysis, however, has recently been heavily attacked. In a well-known paper, J. L. Austin contended that Moore made at least two mistakes. First, since "I could have if I had chosen" does not mean the same as "I should have if I had chosen", it was a mistake to substitute the latter for the former "to avoid a possible complication." Secondly, in neither of the conditional clauses offered by Moore as analyses of "I could have walked a mile in twenty minutes this morning" is the "if"-clause a normal conditional clause, signifying a connection between cause and effect ([1]: 155-62, 165).

It is open to a defender of Moore to reply (as Chisholm has done in his article "J. L. Austin's Philosophical Papers"[7]), that, in the sixth chapter of *Ethics*, Moore left no room for doubt that, as an analysis of "I could have (although I did not)," he preferred the second of his conditional sentences ("I should have, if I had chosen") to the first. It would seem to follow that he did not think the two synonymous. However, this rebuttal does not dispose of Austin's second objection: that, since the "if" in "if I had chosen" or "if I had so willed" is not the "if" of causal condition, it has not been established that "I should have, if I had chosen" is compatible with the determinist thesis that, given the immediately prior state of the universe, it was physically necessary that I did not do what I could have done.

Austin's objection is lent support by widespread dissatisfaction with the traditional doctrine that, in voluntary action, what is done is (partly) caused by an appropriate volition. This dissatisfaction has many sources, ranging from Ryle, on one hand, denying the very existence of most traditional explanatory inner episodes, and analyzing volitions, along with desires, emotions, and thoughts, in terms of public dispositions and episodes, to Davidson, on the other hand, admitting some traditional inner episodes, namely desires, but disregarding volitions as superfluous.

It is at this point that Sellars enters the discussion. He does not follow Chisholm and others in testing the chain of Austin's argument for weak links. In the light of the work of such critics, Austin's analysis of "I should have if I had chosen" as a past-tense expression of intention, like "I should have married him, if I had chosen", now seems far from persuasive (cf. [1]: 162). Nor is it evident that Moore's analysis can be held to succeed in reconciling "I could have done *A*, although I did not" with determinism only if the "if" in "I should have done *A*, if I had chosen" is an "if" of *causal* condition. Although objections like these may be dialectically effective, Sellars is more ambitious. He aims not to refute the particular objection to Moore which Austin advanced, but to destroy the position from which Austin advanced it; and his strategy is to rehabilitate the traditional theory of volition.

Sellars' philosophy of mind is strongly Prichardian, but he is a Prichardian who avoids the pits into which Prichard himself fell. He

7. R. M. Chisholm, in *Mind* 73 (1964): 21-22.

agrees with Ryle that problems about mind are most effectively tackled by way of third-person examples: the difficulties posed by what Ryle calls "avowals" distract attention from what is crucial. However, unlike Ryle, he treats much of our mentalistic vocabulary as being explanatory as well as descriptive. When a man utters the sentence "It is snowing," his utterance expresses a proposition about the weather (in one sense of "express"), and also (in another sense of "express") an act of thought. That he performed that act of thought is normally part of the causal explanation of why he uttered that sentence. The "mentalistic" sentence "He thinks that it is snowing" does indeed describe him, and does indeed entail that he has certain dispositions, of which his utterance was one manifestation; but he has those dispositions *because* of an occurrence—*because* he thinks a certain thought. In this case, that thought consists in raising the question, "What is the weather now?" and answering, in view of some available evidence, "It is snowing." Generally, as Sellars puts it, "thoughts can be initially characterized as mental episodes having a propositional form" ([11]: 150); that is, as episodes analogous with uttering the sentence that expresses what is thought.

Not all acts of thinking satisfy this initial characterization; for not all are thinkings *that*.[8] Human beings also think about what to do, that is, they think practically as well as theoretically; and the thought-episodes that constitute the conclusions of practical thinking are what Sellars calls "intendings". Intendings are episodes which H. A. Prichard, in accordance with nineteenth-century philosophical psychology, called "volitions"; and Sellars uses that word also (see [11]: 155). Unlike thinkings that, intendings or volitions are typically expressed, not by overt speech acts, but by doing or trying to do what is intended. The mental episode of intending-to-do A is normally the cause of doing-A, although it would be a mistake to infer that x's intending-to-do-A causes x to do A ([11]: 156).

Sellars anticipates three blunders that make nonsense of this analysis. (1) Volitions must not be confounded with more specific acts of practical thinking: for example, choosings—which necessarily involve alternatives, while volitions do not; or decidings—which necessarily involve deliberation, while volitions do not ([11]: 154). (2) Even more important, volitions must not be confounded with actions; for actions are the sort of thing that can be done voluntarily, whereas volitions are mental acts

8. Sellars draws upon a familiar distinction of Ryle's: see [9].

which it makes no sense to describe as either voluntary or involuntary ([11]: 156). Sellars is always careful to distinguish the genus, mental act, from one of its species, mental action.[9] (3) Since volitions are not actions, they cannot be tryings; for trying to do A is the action of doing "one or more things which one thinks likely in the circumstances to constitute [the action of] doing A" ([11]: 156).

Enough has now been said of Sellars' theory of action to provide a foundation for his analysis of "x could have done A at t (but did not)." That analysis consists of four related definitions, which, following my earlier practice, I shall translate from Sellars' symbolic notation into English, supplemented by the symbols 'x', 'A', and 't', to which we must now add 'P' as a dummy name for a period of time, and 'G' as a dummy characterization of a set of circumstances (see [11]: 167).[10]

> (1) Throughout P, circumstances G prevent x from doing A
> =df. (Throughout P, x is in G) and (that throughout P, x is in G is physically compossible with x's willing, at any time during P, to do A) and (it is physically necessary that, if, throughout P, x is in G, then, x does not do A at any time during P).

[As we have seen, Sellars speaks of any temporal state of a deterministic system as "physically necessary" given any of the system's earlier states. Generalizing, he conceives any state of affairs S_2 within a given system to be "physically necessary" given some other state of affairs S_1, if and only if the laws of the system are such that, given those laws, the occurrence of S_2 is deducible from the occurrence of S_1. Hence S_2 is "physically compossible" given S_1, if and only if, given the laws of the system, the *non*-occurrence of S_2 is *not* deducible from the occurrence of S_1 (cf. [11]: 167).]

9. This distinction is a technical one, and does not pretend to conform to ordinary usage ([10]: 11, 41-43). The action of the heart is neither voluntary nor involuntary (in the sense in which "involuntary" implies "might have been voluntary"); and Sir David Ross did not flout ordinary usage when he used the expressions "morally good act" and "morally good action" indifferently (cf. *The Foundations of Ethics* (Oxford: Oxford University Press, 1939): 290-92). Earlier, in *The Right and the Good* (Oxford: Oxford University Press, 1930): 7, Ross had proposed a technical distinction, different from Sellars', and less traditional.

10. I have departed from Sellars in giving Sellarsian definitions of being in a position to do, having the ability to do, and being able to do, *throughout* a period, rather than *during* a period. This will simplify my position later. I have also read his abbreviation for "x does A at some time during P" as "'x does A at some time during P' (or, where appropriate, 'x does A at any time during P')," in accordance with his instruction for the abbreviation immediately following ([11]: 167).

(2) Throughout *P*, *x* is in a position to do *A* =df. There are no circumstances *G*, such that, throughout *P* or any period within *P*, *G* prevent *x* from doing *A*.

(3) Throughout *P*, *x* has the ability to do *A* =df. If, throughout *P*, *x* is in a position to do *A*, then (it is physically necessary that, if at any time during *P*, *x* wills to do *A*, then *x* does *A*).

(4) Throughout *P*, *x* is able to do *A* =df. (Throughout *P*, *x* is in a position to do *A*) and (throughout *P*, *x* has the ability to do *A*).

In definitions (2), (3), and (4), "throughout *P*" in the *analysandum* can be replaced by "at *t*", provided that, in the *analysans*, the sentence "For some period *p*, *t* falls within *p*", is added as a conjunct, and the dummy name "*P*" is replaced by the variable "*p*".

In the light of these analyses, Sellars has no difficulty in demonstrating, on Moorean lines, that the principle of determinism, as it relates to actions, namely,

PD-III'. *x* does *A* at *t* only if there is no action incompatible with *A*, such that it is physically possible, given the state of the universe immediately before *t*, that *x* does *that* action at *t*,

is perfectly compatible with the representation of man in the 'manifest image' as sometimes able to do particular actions he does not do. Any particular case of this general proposition may be rendered in Sellars' terminology, as follows:

(i) At *t*, *x* does *A*; doing *A* is incompatible with doing *A'* at the same time; and at *t*, *x* is able to do *A'*.

From it, by simplification, we obtain

(ii) At *t*, *x* is able to do *A'*.

On the other hand, taking another conjunct of (i), namely, 'at *t*, *x* does *A*', together with PD-III', we may infer by *modus ponens* that

(iii) There is no action incompatible with *A*, such that it is physically possible, given the state of the universe immediately before *t*, that *x* does *that* action at *t*.

Since A' is an action incompatible with A, we may infer from (iii) that

(iv) It is not physically possible, given the state of the universe immediately before t, that x does A' at t.

Are (ii) and (iv) incompatible? *Prima facie*, they are. It at least *sounds* like a contradiction to say both that x is able to do A' at t, and also that, given the state of the universe immediately before t, it is physically impossible that x do A' at t. Yet, according to Sellars' analysis, the contradiction is only apparent. By his definition (4), (ii) expands into:

(v) For some period p, t falls within p; and throughout p, x is in a position to do A'; and, throughout p, x has the ability to do A'.

It is the first and third conjuncts in (v) that matter; and they, by Sellars' definition (3), expand into:

(vi) For some period p, t falls within p; and if, throughout p, x is in a position to do A', then (it is physically necessary that, if at any time during x wills to do A', x does A').

This, Sellars points out, is obviously compatible with (iv); for it does not imply that it is physically possible for x to do A' at t, but only that it is physically possible for x to do A' *if he wills to do* A' (cf. [11]: 166). And determinists will maintain that any earlier state of the universe, by reference to which it is physically impossible that x does A' at t, is also such that, by reference to it, it is physically impossible that x *wills* to do A' at t. Since (vi) is no more than an expansion of (ii), if (vi) is compatible with (iv), then (ii) is also compatible with (iv). There is no inconsistency in maintaining both determinism and that sometimes a man is able to do what he does not do.

Sellars now offers an arresting explanation of why, although (ii) and (iv) are not incompatible, they nevertheless appear to be so. It is that

(iv) It is not physically possible, given the state of the universe immediately before t, that x does A' at t

is naturally interpreted as

(vii) The state of the universe immediately before t prevents x from doing A' at t.

In other words, it is tempting to construe the antecedent state of the universe, which makes x's doing A' at t physically impossible, as a set of circumstances which *prevent* x's doing A' at t. And, by Sellars' own definitions, if there are circumstances preventing x from doing A' at t, then x neither is in a position to do A' at t (by (2)), nor is able to do A' at t (by (4)).

Although it may have been sanguine of Sellars to imply that it is, intuitively, an evident mistake to construe (iv) as (vii) (cf. [11]: 170), given his definition (1), that it is a mistake is demonstrable. According to (1), circumstances G which, throughout P, prevent x from doing A' satisfy two conditions:

(*a*)   that, throughout P, x's being in G is physically compossible with x's willing to do A' during P;

and

(*b*)   that it is physically necessary that, if, throughout P, x is in G, then, during P, x does not do A'.

Condition (*a*), by requiring that a circumstance, which prevents an action's being done, must be compatible with that action's being willed, entails that no antecedent state of the universe, by reference to which that action's being willed is physically impossible, can count as a preventing circumstance. But, since it is just such states which, according to determinists, make it physically impossible that agents do what they are able to do, determinism does not imply that, when a man does not do what he is able to do, he is prevented by an antecedent state of the universe from doing so (cf. [11]: 171).

A similar result can be derived for condition (*b*), but the process of derivation is less direct. Throughout P, the circumstances G prevent x from doing A', only if it is physically necessary that if, throughout P, x is in G, then throughout P, x does not do A'. Sellars interprets this as implying that the circumstances preventing an action obtain throughout the period in which it is prevented. But the relevant corollary of determinism, namely,

(iv)   It is not physically possible, given the state of the universe immediately before t, that x does A' at t,

has to do with the state of the universe *before* the time at which x does not do A'. Sellars acknowledges that this discrepancy can be removed verbally, for example, by the definition

(D)   Throughout P, x is in G =df. t, but not the time immediately before t, falls within P, and immediately before t, x is in G'.

It remains only to construe G' as a state of the universe such that, if it obtains immediately before t, it is physically impossible that x do A' during P. Sellars rejects 'circumstances' like G, so defined, as pseudo-circumstances and considers it perverse to construe 'G' in his definition (1) as covering them. And, if they are excluded, the antecedent state of the universe is not the sort of thing that can *prevent* one from doing something, or from willing to do it ([11]: 170, 172-74).

Sellars' complex argument, if my exposition has done anything like justice to it, has combined, with great subtlety, two classical reconciliationist themes. They are that anti-determinists (1) have misunderstood what human freedom of action is, and (2) have confounded causal necessity with some form of compulsion. Sellars believes that the first mistake can be corrected, and the soundness of a Moorean analysis of "can do otherwide" as "well do otherwise, if . . ." made manifest, by a correct theory of action. His analyses of "is able to," and related concepts, which enable him sharply to distinguish inability to do what one does not do from the deterministic physical impossibility of one's doing it, are defensible if his theory of action is sound. That is why he sees the anti-determinists' second mistake as cardinal: many of them, who would not reject his theory of action, have failed to develop analyses like his only because of a deep-seated tendency to conceive the deterministic causal conditions of an action as conditions preventing any alternative (cf. [11]: 170).

While not implausible, this explanation is questionable. If my own philosophical education was at all typical, most contemporary anti-reconciliationists were thoroughly inoculated against the fallacy of confounding causal necessity with compulsion before they had ever encountered a sophisticated anti-reconciliationist argument, e.g. Thomas Reid's or C. D. Broad's. It remains possible that they are subconsciously swayed by a confusion which they consciously repudiate, but resorting to undetectable subconscious processes may be left to second-rate psychoanalysts.

The consideration that has prevailed with most anti-reconciliationists, like much else on this difficult topic, has been beautifully put by Moore.

There is, therefore, much reason to think that when we say that we *could* have done a thing which we did not do, we *often* mean merely that we *should* have done it, *if* we had chosen . . . And for my own part I must confess that I cannot feel certain that this may not be *all* that we usually mean and understand by the assertion that we have Free Will . . . But, no doubt, there are many people who will say that this is *not* sufficient to entitle us to say that we have Free Will . . . They will say . . . : Granted that we often *should* have acted differently, *if* we had chosen differently, yet it is not true that we have Free Will, unless it is *also* often true in such cases that we *could* have *chosen* differently. The question of Free Will in such cases has been thus represented as being merely the question whether we ever *could* have chosen, what we did not choose, or ever *can* choose, what, in fact, we shall not choose. ([7]: 216-18.)

Paradoxically, Sellars' work increases the force of this consideration; for it disposes of the two senses of "could have chosen otherwise" in which, according to Moore, it is often true that a man could have chosen otherwise than he did.

The first is "simply the old sense of [could have done otherwise] over again": namely, that a man could have chosen differently, if he had chosen to choose differently, understanding the expression "chosen to choose" as "made an effort to induce himself to choose" ([7]: 218-19). Sellars' analyses, however, obviate such an interpretation of "chosen to choose." In them, "choose" must be construed (as Moore himself sometimes construed it, e.g., in [7]: 212) as "will" (in the sense of "perform an act of volition"); but the expression 'willed to will' is senseless if both the first and second 'will' are so construed, and both are taken to refer to the same time.

Moore's second sense of "could have chosen otherwise" derives from "one of the commonest senses of the word 'possible'," namely, "that in which we call an event 'possible' when no man can *know for certain* that it will *not* happen" ([7]: 219). It is unquestionably true that often nobody, including the man himself, can have known what choice a man would make, until he made it. Hence, in this sense of "possible", it is often possible that a man choose otherwise than he does, that is, often he can choose otherwise than he does. However, in another connection, Sellars rightly dismissed what he called "epistemic predictability" as irrelevant to the issue of reconciliationism ([11]: 144).

Sellars, of course, amply acknowledges Moore's reason for hesitating to analyze free will as freedom to do otherwise than we do, if we so will.

Someone might grant [he confesses] that determinism is compatible with . . . being *able to do* something [other than what one does], but yet he might argue that this is a superficial truth. If one cuts deeper, one finds—so he claims—that determinism is

incompatible with the idea that one could have *willed to do* anything other than what one did. ([11]: 171.)

Furthermore, as we have seen, not only does Sellars brush aside, as
irrelevant to the free-will problem, analyses of "can will to do otherwise" in terms of epistemic predictability ([11]: 149-50), but, in addition, he embraces a theory of action more adequate than Moore's,
which precludes him from analyzing "is able to will" on the same lines
as his analysis of "is able to do" ([11]: 156-57, 171-72).

What would Moore have concluded, had he been persuaded by Sellars' arguments that his two analyses of "able to will" were either
untenable or irrelevant to the free-will problem? In *Ethics,* he recognized that there might be another sense of "able to will" besides those
which he thought he had analyzed, but added that "nobody, so far as I
know, has ever been able to tell us exactly what that sense is" ([7]: 221).

Sellars provides an analysis of such another sense, and argues that, in
this sense, ability to will otherwise than one wills is not incompatible
with determinism. As we have seen, Sellars' analysis of ability to do
cannot be mechanically adapted to analyzing ability to will, because it
would generate the expression "will to will" in an incoherent sense
([11]: 171-72). So Sellars begins again, with a definition of "prevent from
willing" which supplements his definition of "prevent from doing".[11]

> (1a) Throughout *P,* circumstances *G* prevent *x* from willing to
> do *A* =df. (Throughout *P, x* is in *G*) and (it is physically
> necessary that, if, throughout *P, x* is in *G*, then through-
> out *P, x* does not will *A*).

And this provides a foundation for a definition of "being able to will":

> (2a) Throughout *P, x* is able to will *A* =df. There are no cir-
> cumstances *G*, such that, throughout *P* or any period
> within *P, G* prevent *x* from willing *A*.

No distinctions comparable to those between being in a position to do,
having the ability to do, and being able to do, hold for willing. There is no
difference whatever between being in a position to will and being able to
will.

Given Sellars' analysis, is determinism compatible with ability to will
otherwise than one wills? If that ability exists, then some propositions
such as these are true:

11. Sellars' treatment of ability to will is very compressed, and he does not formally
enunciate the definitions which I give. However, he presupposes them. (Cf. [11]: 172-74).

(H1) Throughout P, x is able to will A.

(H2) Throughout P, x does not will A.

Let us also stipulate:

(H3) t falls within P.

(H4) The moment immediately before t does not fall within P.

(H5) "S" is a true description of the state of the universe immediately before t.

Determinism certainly implies that:

(3a) If, at t, x does not will A, then it is physically necessary that, if immediately before t the universe is in S, then, at t, x does not will A.

Now, from (H2), (H3), and (3a) it follows that:

(4a) It is physically necessary that, if immediately before t the universe is in S, then, at t, x does not will A.

And from (H1) and Sellars' analysis (that is, (1a) and (2a) together) it follows that:

(5a) There are no circumstances G, such that *both* throughout P or any period within P, x is in G, *and* it is physically necessary that, if throughout P or any period within P, x is in G, then x does not will A during P or that period within P.

It is evident that, if having participated in S immediately before t counts as being in some circumstances G throughout P, then (5a) yields:

(6a) It is not the case *both* that, throughout P, x participated in S immediately before t, *and* that it is physically necessary that if, throughout P, x participated in S immediately before t, then x does not will A during P.

Now, stipulating that x did participate in S immediately before t, and eliminating superfluous period designations, we obtain from (6a):

(7a) It is not the case that it is physically necessary that, if x participated in S immediately before t, then x does not will A during P.

Having stipulated that *x* did participate in *S* immediately before *t*, since we may substitute "immediately before *t* the universe is in *S*" for "*x* participated in *S* immediately before *t*", we may infer from (7a) that:

> (8a) It is *not* the case that it is physically necessary that, if immediately before *t* the universe is in *S*, then *x* does not will *A* during *P*,

which, since *t* falls within *P*, is the direct contradictory of (4a). Within our stipulations, this contradiction can be forestalled only by abandoning the possibility of such conjunctions as (H1) and (H2)—that is, ability to will otherwise than one wills; or by abandoning (3a)—that is, determinism.

Are any of our stipulations questionable? Not those concerning the relations between *t, P,* and *S,* or *x*'s participation in *S,* which Sellars himself endorses, and which are obviously compatible with determinism. But it may be remembered that, in discussing circumstances preventing action, Sellars flatly denied that a state of affairs obtaining before the period in which *x* is prevented from doing *A* can be a circumstance preventing his doing it. As might have been expected, he now denies that a state of the universe obtaining before the period in which *x* is prevented from willing *A* can be a circumstance preventing his willing it. And if, by some artificial definition, a situation obtaining before a given period is represented as equivalent to one obtaining during it, he insists that the equivalent so represented must be dismissed as a "pseudo-circumstance" (cf. [11]: 169-70, 172-73).

On the final page of "Fatalism and Determinism," however, Sellars appears to express misgivings about this solution,

> After all, it might be said, "*x*'s having heard an explosion at *t*," defines a physically relevant circumstance which obtains with respect to *x* during a subsequent period of time. There are various things which he may not be capable of during the period—e.g. feeling peaceful and unafraid. ([11]: 174.)

This seems a very strong counter-example indeed to the thesis that all states of affairs that obtain before the period in which *x* is able to will *A*, but does not, are pseudo-circumstances of his not willing *A*, and hence cannot be circumstances preventing him from willing *A*. Sellars appears tacitly to accept it as decisive, because he proceeds to give an altogether new argument for writing off prior states of the universe as "pseudo-circumstances":

. . . this very example brings out the essential difference between deterministic pseudo-circumstances and genuine circumstances. For the law which relates hearing explosions at *t* to not being in certain states during the subsequent period is a *specific* law of nature, an "historical law" which is paralleled at the physical level by historical laws pertaining, for example, to elastic substances. It is with reference to "real" circumstances that abilities and hindrances are explained. ([11]: 174.)

A pseudo-circumstance, as Sellars now conceives it, is not a state of affairs obtaining before the period in which *x* was prevented from willing *A*, but a state of affairs that is not related by specific laws to *x*'s not willing *A*.

This will not do as it stands. If determinism is true, then there are specific laws (although we do not know them) relating *x*'s not willing *A* at a given time during *P* with the state of the universe immediately before *P*. Hence, according to Sellars' new criterion for "real" circumstances, it would appear to follow that *x*'s participation in a certain state of the universe immediately before *P* is a real circumstance of his not willing *A* during *P*.

Sellars may possibly have used the phrase "specific laws of nature" in the sense of "specifiable—that is, *known*—laws of nature." His position would then resemble Moore's suggestion that *x* is able to will *A* at *t*, if nobody can know before *t* that *x* will not will *A* at *t*. The objection to such an interpretation is that it falls foul of Sellars' convincing argument that the sort of predictability that is in question in controversies about free will is not epistemic ([11]: 150).

Sellars has not, therefore, succeeded in providing an analysis of ability to will, according to which determinism is compatible with ability to will otherwise than one wills. Yet I doubt whether this matters much. For it seems to me highly probable that, following his general strategy of analyzing ability to will in terms of the absence of conditions preventing willing, he can find an analysis of conditions preventing willing that will do what he wants. The concept of a condition preventing the willing of *A* is restricted, I am strongly inclined to think, in a way in which the concept of a condition under which the willing of *A* is physically impossible is not. And if that is so, then ability to will otherwise than one does (understood as the absence of conditions preventing it) is compatible with determinism.

Even if the details of his theory can be put right, Sellars has not allayed all doubts about its foundation, namely, Sellars' conviction that only one who in one way or another confounded causation with compulsion would imagine free will to be incompatible with determinism. It is because of this conviction that he believes that free will can be reconciled with determinism by showing that the deterministic conditions, by reference to which our volitions are physically necessary, are not conditions that prevent us from willing otherwise.

But is it true, as a matter of historical fact, that competent philosophers have, in the last hundred years, confounded causation with compulsion? No doubt popular writers on the subject, both antideterminist and determinist, have committed this and other outrageous blunders. Yet I take it that whatever interest such blunders may have is not philosophical, just as whatever interest popular fallacies in religious apologetics may have is not theological. To mention some antireconciliationist philosophers by name: did Thomas Reid in the eighteenth century, or Henry Sidgwick in the nineteenth, imagine that if a man's acts of will are causally determined, then they must be compelled? Do C. D. Broad, or Richard Taylor, or R. M. Chisholm now imagine it?

Consider Sidgwick. He did not argue against the reconciliationist thesis on any ground at all. Instead, after surveying the "cumulative evidence for determinism," which he acknowledged to be "formidable," he recorded the following:

> . . . when I have a distinct consciousness of choosing between alternatives of conduct, one of which I conceive as right or reasonable, I find it impossible not to think that I can now choose to do what I so conceive—supposing that there is no obstacle to my doing it other than the condition of my desires and voluntary habits,—however strong may be my inclination to act unreasonably, and however uniformly I may have yielded to such inclinations in the past. ([13]: 65.)

In short, he simply found it impossible to conceive his choices as psychologically predetermined. He did not begin by expounding a conception of free will, and then, by means of some middle term (e.g., "not compelled") try to show that free will, so conceived, excludes determinism; rather, it was not until he confronted determinism that he clarified his conception of free will.

> I can suppose that my conviction of free choice *may* be illusory [he went on]; that if I knew my own nature I *might* see it to be predetermined that, being so constituted and in such circumstances, I should act on [a certain] occasion . . . contrary to my

rational judgment. But I cannot conceive myself seeing this, without at the same time conceiving my whole conception of what I now call "my" action fundamentally altered. . . . ([13]: 65-66.)

That Sidgwick's anti-reconciliationist analysis of free will also corresponded to the popular conception of it, is attested by G. E. Moore himself, in a paper published in 1898:

> Professor Clifford gives a statement of the doctrine of Free Will, as commonly understood, which seems to be so clear as to be worth quoting: "Whenever a man exercises his will, and makes a voluntary choice of one out of various possible courses, an event occurs, whose relation to contiguous events cannot be included in a general statement applicable to all similar cases. There is something wholly capricious and arbitrary, belonging to that moment only; and *we have no right to conclude that if circumstances were exactly repeated, and the man himself absolutely unaltered, he would choose the same course.*" ([6]: 181.)[12]

To repeat: those, like Clifford and Sidgwick, who understand the doctrine of free will in this way, neither argue nor need to argue that it is incompatible with determinism. That incompatibility is written into its very definition. What urgently calls for explanation is how reconciliationists have overlooked the conception of free will that Clifford and Sidgwick put forward.

In view of his praise of Clifford's statement of the common doctrine of free will as "so clear as to be worth quoting," it is surprising that Moore, fourteen years later, after acknowledging that there might be a sense of "he could have chosen" different from either "he would have chosen, if he had chosen to" or "nobody was in a position to know that he would not have chosen," should have added, "But nobody, so far as I know, has ever been able to tell us exactly what that sense is" ([7]: 221). Had he forgotten Clifford's statement? Or had he come to think that it was not exact?

To my knowledge, C. D. Broad has been alone in not only recognizing that most of "those who profess to believe in Free Will" have pretty

---

12. For the passage quoted, Moore gives the reference "Essay on 'Right and Wrong' in [W.K. Clifford] *Lectures and Essays* (1866), p. 318." Many anti-determinists would dispute Clifford's statement that a causally undetermined event must contain "something wholly capricious and arbitrary." My attention was drawn to this paper of Moore's by a very fine essay by Theodore Redpath, "Moore on Free Will," in Alice Ambrose and Morris Lazerowitz (eds.), *G.E. Moore: Essays in Retrospect* (London and New York: 1970).

much the same concept of free will as Sidgwick and Clifford, but also pointing out what he takes to be an incoherency in that concept. According to Broad, the common concept of free will is that volition satisfies two conditions, a negative and a positive. The negative condition is that it is not causally predetermined: this is the condition specified by Clifford when he wrote:

> we have no right to conclude that if circumstances were exactly repeated, and the man himself absolutely unaltered, he would choose the same course. ([6]: 181.)

Clifford did not succeed in expressing the positive condition. He referred to it when he wrote

> There is something wholly capricious and arbitrary, belonging to that moment only . . . (ibid.),

but he did not say what it was; and, as Broad points out, believers in free will would "quarrel with" the view that an act of volition is an "accident"—in Clifford's words, "capricious and arbitrary" ([2]: 214). On the contrary—this is Broad's statement of the positive condition—they would maintain that acts of volition are caused

> *by the agent or self*, considered as a substance or continuant, and not by a total cause which contains as factors *events in* and *dispositions of* the agent. ([2]: 214-15.)

Acts of volition are events, but their causes are not prior events to which they are related according to laws of nature: They "originate from causal progenitors which are continuants and not events" ([2]: 215). It is evident that an act of volition caused by a continuant which could have caused a contrary act is not causally predetermined. That an agent x caused a certain volition (say, the willing of A) at t, does not imply that there are laws of nature according to which x's willing A at t is deducible from x's existence at t. Broad's name for causation of this kind is "non-occurrent causation"; Chisholm's "agent causation" is now more common.

The concept of non-occurrent or agent causation is ancient and reputable.[13] That, like other familiar and primitive categories (e.g. Aristotle's *potentiality*), it is not usefully definable, does not show that

13. See [3]: 20-22; and Richard Taylor, "Causation" in Paul Edwards, ed., *The Encyclopedia of Philosophy* (New York: 1967), vol. II, esp. 57-59.

it is in any way illegitimate. Of course, a Humean or an early Logical Positivist would reject it as violating his theory of meaning; but Sellars, in his devastating criticism of concept empiricism ([10]: 307-16), has disposed of such objections for us. The concept of non-occurrent causation may, like the concept of phlogiston, not apply to anything that exists; but it may not be rejected as a concept unless some defect is found in it.

Broad claims to have found such a defect:

[I]t is surely quite evident [he writes] that, if the beginning of a certain process at a certain time is [caused] at all, its total cause *must* contain as an essential factor another event or process which *enters into* the moment from which the [caused] event or process *issues*. I see no *prima facie* objection to there being events that are not completely [caused]. But, in so far as an event *is* [caused], an essential factor in its total cause must be other *events*. How could an event possibly be [caused] to happen at a certain date if its total cause contained no factor to which the notion of date has any application? And how can the notion of date have any application to anything that is not an event? ([2]: 215.)[14]

What is most baffling about this passage is not that it is obscure, but that Broad is unaware that it is. What on earth did he have in mind when he implied that the notion of date has no application to anything that is not an event? It is true that a continuant, say Julius Caesar, cannot be said, like an event, to take place at a certain date; but it would be absurd to jump to the conclusion that the notion of date has no application to him. Do not his birth and death have well-known dates? And, taking a volition of which believers in free will would say that Julius Caesar was the cause, for example, his volition, at a certain moment *t* in 49 B.C., to cross the Rubicon, how is it "quite evident" that Julius Caesar, who was alive and well at *t* in 49 B.C., could not possibly have been the non-occurrent cause of that volition?

I conclude that Broad's analysis enables us to give a clear answer to Moore's question: In what sense do believers in free will assert that a free agent is able to will otherwise than, at a given time, he does will? They assert it in this sense: that (i) willing as he does at the time is not

14. In this quotation, I have substituted appropriate forms of the verb "to cause," in brackets, for corresponding forms of the verb "to determine." Unless Broad's use of "to determine" in this passage is synonymous with "to cause" (as I think it is), he would have misrepresented the position taken by advocates of non-occurrent causation.

deducible, according to laws of nature, from the state of the universe at an earlier time (Broad's negative condition); and (ii) he himself, as non-occurrent cause, at that time, of a certain volition (Broad's positive condition) could, at that time, have been non-occurrent cause of some alternative volition. The "could" in (ii) is absolute: that it is not analyzable into "would have, if . . ." is implied by (i).

This concept of free will, and the concept of non-occurrent causation that is included in it, may have as little application to the real world as the concept of phlogiston. But, like the concept of phlogiston, it appears to be a perfectly clear and coherent concept. Broad has certainly failed to show that it is not.

Unlike most reconciliationists, Sellars does not simply ignore the concept painstakingly elaborated and dismissed by Broad. But, in a discussion of Richard Taylor's *Action and Purpose* (Englewood Cliffs, N.J.: Prentice-Hall, 1966), he attacks the concept of non-occurrent causation, on the assumption that it is derived from the "interventionist" sense of causation, in which a person is said to cause something by doing something else, as in the sentence

Jones caused the match to light by striking it.

Now there are minimal, or "basic," actions which do not consist in bringing something about by doing something else; and to such actions the question, "By doing what?" does not apply. Taylor concludes that minimal or basic actions simply have agents as non-occurrent causes. To this, Sellars replies that, since the question "By doing what?" is inapplicable to such actions, "the concept of persons as causes with which we have been working is inapplicable" to them ([12]: 241).

Sellars buttresses this criticism by the further claim that

the sense in which, according to Taylor, persons cause their actions amounts to no more than that they do them: indeed, in the last analysis, to no more than that persons act. ([12]: 242).

Taylor might indeed agree that non-occurrently causing an action is no more (and no less) than doing it, or than acting. So a male sibling is no more than a brother; but, so he might claim, just as by thinking of brothers as siblings we get clearer about what brothers are, so by thinking of doing actions as causings of a certain kind, we get clearer about what acting is. Sellars adds:

Nobody would think of dancing a waltz as causing a waltz. Taylor may have been misled by the fact that we do speak, for example, of "making" a gesture, and "making" in some sense is certainly "causing." But, surely, "Jones made a gesture" stands to "Jones gesticulated" as "Jones performed a waltz" stands to "Jones waltzed," and the appearance of causation is an illusion. ([12]: 242.)

Here, Sellars is historically wrong: taking a waltz as a sub-set of the bodily actions of a dancer waltzing, Taylor and myself, at least, *do* think of dancing a waltz as causing a waltz. So thinking is not perhaps common, but that is because thinking about causation is not common. It is true that nobody would *say* that dancing a waltz is causing a waltz, unless he had been thinking philosophically about causation and action.

Taylor, I suspect, has unnecessarily alienated Sellars by attacking his doctrine (which I accept) that volitions are (occurrent) partial causes of the movements involved in bodily actions. Although it would be out of place here to develop a general theory of action, it seems to me to be defensible *both* that persons are non-occurrent causes of their basic or minimal actions, *and* that they are non-occurrent causes of the volitions that are initial stages of their actions.[15] If Sellars is right in conceiving volitions as the initial stages of actions, and if the concept of non-occurrent causation has any application to the real world, then performing an act of volition would be a palmary example of non-occurrent causation.

Taylor, and philosophers of like mind, have not introduced the concept of non-occurrent causation by illegitimately extending to cases of non-interventionist causation something true only of interventionist causation. On the contrary, from Aristotle to the present, they have done so because of reflection on such chains of causal explanation as "A staff moves a stone, and is moved by a hand, which is moved by a man" (Aristotle, *Physics* III, 256a; quoted by Chisholm as epigraph to [3]: 11). The ultimate movement in a finite series of movements is sometimes *not* the first cause in the series. We do not have: moving stone, caused by moving staff, caused by moving human hand—*finis*; but rather: moving stone, caused by moving staff, caused by moving hand—*caused by man*. And further reflection on the first cause in this series shows that it involves causation of a kind different from that involved in the earlier stages. Nor is it correct to infer that causal series terminating in human actions are what primarily gave rise to reflections of this sort: the series

---

15. My views on these matters are largely derived from R.M. Chisholm. See, *inter alia*, [3], and "Some Puzzles About Agency" in Karel Lambert, ed., *The Logical Way of Doing Things* (New Haven: 1969).

which philosophers primarily studied was that of creation, which termi-
nated in a divine *fiat*. If human agents are non-occurrent causes, then,
as Chisholm has said,

> we have a prerogative which some would attribute only to God:
> each of us, when we act, is a prime mover unmoved. In doing what
> we do, we cause certain events to happen, and nothing—or no
> one—causes us to cause those events to happen. ([3]: 23.)

That there is a sense of "free will" in which free will is incompatible
with determinism is not in itself of much interest to Sellars; nor even that
some distinguished philosophers have believed that we have free will in
that sense. It would be of interest to him only if free will in that sense
were implicit in the "manifest image" of man in the world. Now a
cardinal point in Sellars' distinction between the manifest and the
scientific images of man in the world is that the latter alone makes use of
scientific techniques of theory construction.

> There is one type of scientific reasoning which [the manifest
> image], by stipulation, does *not* include, namely that which in-
> volves the postulation of imperceptible entities, and principles
> pertaining to them, to explain the behaviour of perceptible things.
> ([10]: 7.)

With good reason, Sellars regards the principle of determinism as a
principle pertaining to postulated imperceptible entities: it was, in fact,
introduced in connection with atomism. It follows that free will, as
Sidgwick, Clifford, and Broad understand it, cannot belong to the manifest image, because it is defined in terms of the principle of determinism.

Sellars' stipulation that the manifest image excludes the postulation of
imperceptible entities and the principles pertaining to them goes some
way to explain why he writes as though there is only one manifest image,
and one "perennial philosophy" ("the 'ideal type' around which
philosophies in what might be called, in a suitably broad sense, the
Platonic tradition, cluster"—[10]: 8) which refines and endorses the
manifest image. It is true that he also writes of "the scientific image"
but, as I understand him, this is an abbreviation for "the *ultimate*
scientific image," the image of man derived from theoretical science
"when all the facts are in" (cf. [10]: 37). There are, in fact, as many
scientific images of man as there are distinctive intellectual periods in
the history of science. Sellars does not allow for a plurality of manifest
images because he conceives the manifest image as corresponding to

"the world as we know it to be in ordinary experience," supplemented by such "inductive procedures" as do not involve postulating imperceptible entities ([11]: 145), and he does not believe that ordinary experience, so supplemented, can give rise to more than one image.

This distinction between the manifest and the scientific images of man seems to me to be drawn in the wrong place. In venturing to say so, I am treating the distinction itself as a theoretical one, in terms of which the nature of certain philosophical issues can be explained. It was from Sellars that I learned to think of the fundamental problems that confront a philosopher as arising from real or apparent conflicts between two images or conceptual frameworks in terms of which he thinks about man, one of which is what he takes to be the image of man in science as it will ultimately be. The second image, Sellars' "manifest image," is the image of man implicit in the thinking according to which he conducts his life in the world—personal, social, and political. But it would be wrong to follow Sellars in describing this image as corresponding to the world as we know it to be in ordinary experience, supplemented by certain inductive procedures, as though ordinary experience were its source. On the contrary, what a man's ordinary experience is depends in some measure on what manifest image underlies his thinking.

This becomes evident when we reflect that a man's religion, if he has one, is part of the manifest image in terms of which he thinks about himself and other men. No religion is arrived at by simple observation and induction: many religions, in fact, postulate imperceptible entities, e.g. immaterial gods, immaterial souls. It follows that there may be many manifest images of man, although different manifest images may have much in common. And that is what, in my opinion, we find: the manifest image of man held by a cultivated Hindu seems to me to differ in important ways from that held by a cultivated Christian or Jew; but they have enough in common for each to be able to respect the image held by the other. The image of man held by a Dyak headhunter, say, is another matter: while a Hindu's image of man will require him to respect the Dyak, it also requires him to abhor the Dyak's image. And in this, it seems to me, the Hindu is right.

There are many manifest images of man because in his ordinary life in the world, as well as in his scientific thinking, man postulates the existence of entities which he does not see or touch, and for which he has no direct inductive evidence. If this is so, it is arbitrary to stipulate that a man's manifest image cannot refer to entities or principles which he first thought of scientifically. What could be more natural than that a man whose image of himself is orthodox Christian—an immaterial soul informing a living body—should investigate the implications of that image with respect to a deterministic conception of the physical world? Sidgwick, whose image of man was Christian, although his theology was not, was doing that when he inquired whether, in deliberately choosing between an unattractive rational action and an attractive irrational one, he could conceive his choice as causally determined.

Among the various manifest images of man that are held at the present time by cultivated persons, it seems to me perfectly certain that there is at least one according to which man has free will in a sense incompatible with determinism. That image is historically connected with the images of man in orthodox Christianity and orthodox Judaism, but it does not presuppose any particular theological position and is compatible with atheism. As far as I can tell, mine is such a manifest image, although a man may be mistaken about his manifest image of himself, just as he may about his scientific image. It seems to me almost equally certain that there is another manifest image of man, held by a growing number of cultivated persons, according to which the sense in which man has free will is compatible with determinism. Sellars' analysis of that sense, while incomplete, is the best known to me. The difference between, say, Sellars and Richard Taylor, which Sellars sees as a difference about the content of the same manifest image, I see as something less tractable: a clash between two incompatible manifest images.

In our present circumstances, the conflict between these two incompatible manifest images of man may well generate more heat than the conflict between either and any given scientific image. Still, the fundamental question will remain: is the manifest image according to which free will is incompatible with determinism in conflict with the *ultimate* scientific image of man? Despite the conviction of some philosophers that they are self-reproducing automata, the present state of the theoretical sciences seems to me to provide no grounds for an informed forecast of how human action will be treated in theoretical science "when all the facts are in." If that is so, it would be folly to abandon a reasonably grounded manifest image because of forecasts, necessarily ill-supported, about the ultimate scientific image.

REFERENCES

[1] J. L. Austin, *Philosophical Papers*, edited by Urmson and Warnock (Oxford: Oxford University Press, 1961).

[2] C. D. Broad, *Ethics and the History of Philosophy* (London: Routledge & Kegan Paul, 1952).

[3] R. M. Chisholm, "Freedom and Action," in Keith Lehrer, ed., *Freedom and Determinism* (New York: Random House, 1966).

[4] R. G. Collingwood, *An Essay on Metaphysics* (Oxford: Oxford University Press, 1940).

[5] T. S. Kuhn, *The Structure of Scientific Revolutions* (second edition; Chicago: University of Chicago Press, 1970).

[6] G. E. Moore, "Freedom," *Mind*, N. S. 7 (1898): 179-204.

[7] G. E. Moore, *Ethics* (Oxford: The Clarendon Press, 1912).

[8] C. S. Peirce, *The Philosophy of Peirce: Selected Writings*, Justus Buchler, ed. (London: Kegan Paul, Trench, Trubner, 1940).

[9] Gilbert Ryle, *The Concept of Mind* (London: Hutchinson, 1949).

[10] Wilfrid Sellars, *Science, Perception and Reality* (London: Routledge & Kegan Paul, 1963).

[11] _____, "Fatalism and Determinism," in Keith Lehrer, ed., *Freedom and Determinism* (New York: Random House, 1966).

[12] _____, "Metaphysics and the Concept of a Person," in Karel Lambert, ed., *The Logical Way of Doing Things* (New Haven: Yale University Press, 1969).

[13] Henry Sidgwick, *The Methods of Ethics* (seventh edition; London: Macmillan, 1907).

The Legend of the Given
WILLIAM S. ROBINSON
Iowa State University

To SAY of an object that it is a myth is to imply that that object does not exist. To say that it is a legend, however, implies neither its existence nor its nonexistence. Thus, if I say that I will show that the given is a legend, it must not be anticipated that I will attempt to prove that there is a given. My aim will only be to argue that it has not been shown to be a myth. More precisely, my aim will be to examine the arguments in "Empiricism and the Philosophy of Mind"[1] and to argue that they do not show the given to be a myth.

I will be interested in these arguments only in a special way. Sellars argues against several views which are based on the acceptance of a given. I am ready to agree that he has succeeded in refuting each of these views. But the consequences which are and should be drawn from the rejection of the given can be drawn only if every view which embraces a given is false. Thus, what one would like to have is an argument against the given *as such*. Fortunately, such an argument can be derived from Sellars' more particular arguments by easily justifiable generalizations. I will set out this argument and criticize it. This procedure will not only enable us to decide whether or not the given has been shown to be a myth; it will also help to provide a connected view of several portions of EPM. It will, furthermore, make clear what is required of any view of the given which hopes to survive the Sellarsian critique.

Our first task in developing an argument against the given as such is to define the notion of the given. Sellars does not state a general definition,

1. Reprinted in Wilfrid Sellars, *Science, Perception and Reality* (London: Routledge & Kegan Paul, New York: Humanities Press, 1963): 127-96. Parenthetical references in text and notes are to pages of this volume. The article under discussion will be referred to as EPM.

but there are a few particularly salient remarks which will serve as a basis for our formulation. One of these is as follows.

> . . . the point of the epistemological category of the given is, presumably, to explicate the idea that empirical knowledge rests on a 'foundation' of non-inferential knowledge of matter of fact . . . (128)

Just what kind of explication is required is not specified here. We will eventually have to discuss what kind of explication is required, but for the time being we will leave this question open. It will, however, be convenient to have an abbreviation for this characteristic of the given. I shall speak of "an explication of a foundation view," by which I shall mean exactly an explication of the kind described in the foregoing passage.

Another important characteristic of the given is that it "presupposes no learning, no forming of associations, no setting up of stimulus-response connections" (131). More explicity still,

> . . . they all [i.e., forms of the myth of the given] have in common the idea that the awareness of certain *sorts*—and by 'sorts' I have in mind, in the first instance, determinate sense repeatables—is a primordial, non-problematic feature of 'immediate experience'. (157; cf. 159)

There are three further characteristics of the given which should be mentioned. (i) Concepts applicable to the given are independent of each other (147f).-(ii) There is an association between (a) some words and (b) some given items for which the person to whom they are given has no symbols prior to the forming of the association (161f). (iii) The myth of the given holds that there are self-authenticating, non-verbal episodes (167, 169). These characteristics are, however, of subordinate interest and will not be included in our definition of the given. For, first, they are not clearly supposed by Sellars to apply to the given generally. And, second, their applicability in certain cases seems to be a consequence of the characteristics already mentioned; they are not independent specifications of the given.

Turning our attention to the first two characteristics of the given introduced above, we can ask whether both of these are necessary. I believe that a primordial awareness of sorts which was not required to explicate a foundation view might be entitled to be called a "given." But since I will not be arguing for such a given, I will follow Sellars' intention and regard both characteristics as central to the notion of the given. Accordingly, the definition which I shall use is:

Definition I. Something is given (is a single given item) if and only if
(i) it is a primordial awareness of sorts; and
(ii) it is required to explicate a foundation view.

A clarification of "primordial" is required. The basic notion here is that of independence. We must, however, be careful. Sellars points out that Locke, Berkeley, and Hume all take for granted that we can be aware of determinate sorts *"simply by virtue of having sensations and images"* (160). And I think we should leave open the possibility that having a sensation is a necessary as well as sufficient condition of awareness of determinate sorts. The following definition allows for this, and is, I think, sufficiently cautious.

Definition II. An awareness is *primordial* if and only if there are no necessary conditions for its occurrence except:
(i) conditions which follow analytically from the concept of an awareness of sorts;
(ii) having a sensation or image; and
(iii) conditions which are also necessary conditions for having sensations or images.[2]

This definition, together with Definition I, gives us the concept of the given which we are to discuss.

We will begin our examination by looking at Sellars' discussion of the sensing of sense contents, which occurs very early in EPM. A portion of his argument can be cast as a series of overlapping dilemmas. The first pair of alternatives is this.

(1) Either (a) the givenness of sense contents is defined in terms of non-inferential knowledge of sense contents; or (b) the givenness of sense contents is a *"basic* or *primitive* concept of the sense-datum framework"* (130).

(a) is not further discussed in what immediately follows, nor need it be. For on this alternative, the given is a primordial awareness which just *is*

2. Thus, for example, an awareness could be counted as primordial even if it were believed that a necessary condition of it were the existence of a self, provided that such a condition was also regarded as necessary for sensations or images.

non-inferential knowledge of matter of fact, viz., that a sense content is of a certain character. The refutation of such a possibility is a topic to which Sellars returns in later sections of EPM.

Let us for the moment follow our text and return to alternative (b). If one adopts this view, one is faced with this further pair of alternatives.

> (2) Either (c) sensing is a "unique and unanalyzable act" (130); or (d) sensing is analyzable.[3]

The view resulting from the adopting of (c) along with (b) is rejected as follows.

> What, then, of the logical connection in the direction *sensing sense contents → having non-inferential knowledge*? Clearly it is severed by those who think of sensing as a unique and unanalyzable act. (130)

The view obtained by adopting (d) along with (b) is confronted with a further choice.

> (3) Either (e) sensing is analyzable in non-epistemic terms; or (f) sensing is analyzable in epistemic terms.

Both alternatives are rejected by Sellars. The reason given against (e) is that epistemic facts cannot be analyzed without remainder into non-epistemic facts. The reason given against (f) is that it leads to the following triad, which is inconsistent, and which cannot be avoided without consequences unacceptable to the sense-datum theorist.

> A. *X senses red sense content s* entails *x non-inferentially knows that s is red.*
> B. The ability to sense sense contents is unacquired.
> C. The ability to know facts of the form *x is ϕ* is acquired. (132)

We have remarked that in this discussion what is sensed is given. We are not, of course, entitled to the converse assertion. Yet, if we regard the points we have been reviewing as applying to givenness in general and not only to sensing, it is not at all obvious that they do not continue

3. The term "given" no longer appears in these statements. However, in this discussion we may assume that what is sensed is given. The justification for this is as follows. On p. 129, Sellars sets out to explain why a certain kind of sense-datum theorist must use "the word *know* and, correspondingly, the word *given* in two senses." In the discussion that follows the word "given" does not occur. But "sensed" does occur, and is clearly the word whose use in two senses corresponds to the use of "know" in two senses.

to hold, and for the same reasons. If (c) is untenable for the reason given, then so is (c'), "Something's being given is a unique and unanalyzable occurrence." Likewise, if givenness is epistemic and epistemic facts cannot be analyzed without remainder into non-epistemic facts, then (e'), "givenness is analyzable in non-epistemic terms," is no better off than (e). Similar considerations hold for (f'), "givenness is analyzable in epistemic terms."

Let us suppose that Sellars would accept our generalized version of his argument against sense-datum theories as a correct outline of his strategy against the given in general. Then, the rejection of the given depends on the rejection of (a), (c'), (e'), and (f'). Conversely, if, as I believe, Sellars has not shown the given to be a myth, it must be because he has not succeeded in rejecting one of these four claims.

The fact that I have not discussed the argument against (a) may suggest that it is the rejection of this claim that I find problematic. However, I wish to make it quite clear that I shall at no time challenge the rejection of (a). What I find problematic is rather the rejection of (e'). Since this claim will occupy our attention for some time, let us provide ourselves with a clearer statement of it.

There are two reasons for revising (e'). First, it contains the term "analyzable", a term which might lead to quite extraneous difficulties. Second, Sellars gives a list of examples of non-epistemic analyses (pp. 130f), and I want to avoid giving the appearance of committing myself to the view that it is in one of these ways that givenness is to be analyzed. Both matters will be taken care of if we consider, instead of (e'), the assertion

(4) *Something is given to x does not entail x has non-inferential knowledge.*

If we substitute the terms of our definition of the given, (4) becomes

(5) *x has a primordial awareness of sorts of a kind which is required to explicate a foundation view does not entail x has non-inferential knowledge.*

This formulation enables us to divide our discussion into two parts. For, (5) cannot be true unless

(6) *x has a primordial awareness of sorts does not entail x has non-inferential knowledge*

is also true. Thus, we can ask first whether a rejection of (6) would be justified. If so, then (5) can also be rejected, then (4) . . . and finally the given. But if not, then we can ask, second, whether the rejection of (5) can be accomplished when we take into account the second characteristic of the given, i.e., its being required to explicate a foundation view. The two parts which follow correspond to these two questions.

I

It will be convenient to have the denial of (6) stated in positive form, namely, as

> (7) *x has a primordial awareness of sorts* entails *x has non-inferential knowledge*.

We have just given the reason why Sellars is not committed to (7) merely on account of his rejection of (5). In fact, however, Sellars takes (7) for granted in EPM. I say that he takes it for granted, because there is no explicit argument for it in EPM. This makes our task complex and difficult. It will be broken down into three parts, as follows.

First, I will construct an argument for (7) which can be drawn from Sellarsian materials. If there were not such an argument, we might turn directly to a criticism of (7). But if, as is the case, there is such an argument, it does not matter whether it is explicit or not. If (7) *can* be defended on Sellarsian principles, we must know how it can be defended. The construction of this argument will, furthermore, bring out a very fundamental premise in Sellars' view.

Second, I will give a close examination of sections IV, V, and VI of EPM. This is necessary at some point, since we must sooner or later determine whether there is in these sections an argument against the given which would proceed on lines not disturbed by the criticisms which I shall make. Part of what I shall do is to dispel the appearance that there is such an argument. But this examination is also necessary in order to show that something very close to the fundamental premise arrived at in the first part of my discussion is operative in EPM.

Third, I will show why the fundamental premise arrived at in the first part of my discussion is not one that we ought to accept.

§1. Turning to our first task, let us observe that (7) follows from

(8) *x has a primordial awareness of sorts* entails *x has primordial classificatory consciousness;*

and

(9) *x has primordial classificatory consciousness* entails *x has non-inferential knowledge.*

Regarding (8) there is no difficulty. The argument for it is that it is unimaginable what sense could be attached to calling something an awareness *of sorts* if one denied that it was in any way classificatory, or that it was a consciousness. This reason can be accepted by anyone, whether Sellars or a defender of the given.

Since I deny (7) and assert (8), I must deny (9). Now, Sellars seems just to take (9) for granted. At one point, for example, he uses the phrase "all knowledge *that something is thus-and-so*" in apposition to "all classificatory consciousness" (131). However, since the point is important, I want to raise the question whether there is not some further argument by which Sellars might support (9).

I believe that there is. In order to present it, we need the notion of a concept. Definition III and the comments which follow it will explain how I will use the term "concept" in this essay.

> Definition III. A concept is a mind dependent ability to be in a state which corresponds to a property.

To have a concept is to have a certain ability to be in a certain state. To use a concept is to use that ability, that is, to actually be in a certain state. I shall also speak of *a use* of a concept; this is simply an occurrence of being in a state, where the ability to be in that state is a concept. I have purposely left it open what the states mentioned in definition III are states *of,* since this question need not be decided for any purpose envisioned here. Abilities which are concepts are, however, mind dependent, by which I mean that, by definition, such *abilities* cannot be possessed by anything which neither is nor has a mind. Thus, the *states* mentioned in definition III are states which logically could not be had by anything unless that thing either had a mind or were itself a mind. "Mind" and "mental" I shall have to take as terms whose meaning is already understood. I will only add that "mental" is not to be understood in a limited way as including only what might be called intellectual abilities. Abilities to sense are also to be regarded as mental. Finally, our definition of "concept" will be useful only if we leave rather open what is meant by "correspond." But whatever further sense we might come to give it, the following two conditions must hold. (i) Every state can be associated with exactly one property. (ii) No two properties can be associated with the same state. In a very closely related sense we can, of course, say that concepts correspond to properties.

While there will be disagreement about how "mind" and "mental" should be explicated, I think everyone will agree that if something classifies, it either is or has a mind. Thus, having classificatory consciousness is being in a mind-dependent state, and should have been so regarded even if we had not already called it "consciousness." But classifications (i.e., individual cases of classificatory consciousness) also meet the above necessary conditions for corresponding with properties; every classification can be associated with exactly one property, and no two properties can be associated with the same classification.[4] This does not conclusively establish that classifications correspond to properties. However, since I cannot imagine a ground for denying this, I will assume that they do so correspond. It then follows that having classificatory consciousness involves using a concept.

We are now supplied with the first premise of an argument for (9). I will state this argument now and provide further explanation below.

(10) *x has primordial classificatory consciousness* entails *x makes a primordial use of a concept.*

(11) *x makes a primordial use of a concept* entails *x immediately subsumes[5] something under a concept.*

(12) *x immediately subsumes something under a concept* entails *x has non-inferential knowledge.*

Therefore, (9).

Subsumption is a difficult notion, but as with the notion of a concept, we do not have to answer all the questions that might be raised in order to proceed. The basic idea behind subsumption is surely that subsumption under a concept results in a proposition (in one sense of this term), that is, a mind dependent state which corresponds to an assertion.

4. Part of the support for this involves the stipulation that what might be called, for example, "a classification of something as red and round" is to be regarded as being really two classifications, one of something as red and one of something as round.

5. "x *immediately* subsumes" = df "x subsumes in a manner having no necessary conditions except (i) conditions which follow analytically from the concept of subsumption; (ii) having a primordial awareness; and (iii) conditions which are necessary for having a primordial awareness."

Assertions which would be relevant examples in this discussion are ones having the form "this is f."

Turning our attention to (12), we can see that a defense of it would have two parts. First, one would argue that the presence of subsumption ensures the presence of a claim, that is, of the kind of thing that could, in principle, be an object of knowledge. Second, one would argue that the immediacy of this kind of claim, its dependence on primordial awareness alone, gives it an authority which entitles it to be called "knowledge."

Does Sellars accept (12)? This is a difficult question to decide, but I believe that he does accept it. My reason is that Sellars never tries to drive a wedge between *belief* based on immediate experience and *knowledge* based on immediate experience. If Sellars thought that (12) were false, it would be quite in character for him to raise the question "What has subsumption under concepts got to do with the foundations of empirical knowledge, in view of the fact that such subsumption does not entail that there is knowledge?" I say this would be in character, since it is exactly this sort of question that Sellars raises with respect to the sensing of particulars (128f). Thus, the fact that Sellars does *not* raise such a question with respect to subsumptions is some evidence that he would not reject (12). Further support comes from reflecting on some of the arguments which he does give. He seems willing enough to admit the hypothetical, "*If* one could apply concepts on the basis of immediate experience alone, then the result of such application would be knowledge." What Sellars characteristically attacks is the antecedent of this claim.

The premise remaining to be discussed is (11). This premise is not explicitly stated in EPM, but the following passage from "Being and Being Known"[6] gives us reason to suppose that Sellars would subscribe to it. In this passage, the "predicative word ·white·" is a concept according to our definition.

> To which it can be added that the predicative word ·white· doesn't make sense apart from statement; ·white and triangular thing· presupposes ·(this) thing is triangular·. Predicates cannot be in sense unless judgment is there also.

6. Reprinted in *Science, Perception and Reality*, pp. 41-59. The quotation is from p. 49. The date given for the first presentation of this paper is 1960, four years later than that of EPM. However, there is no reason to suppose that this paper represents a change, as opposed to a clarification and expansion, of Sellars' view.

That (11) is a *basic* premise for Sellars cannot be obvious. However, does not argue for the assertions just quoted in "Being and Being Known." Nor do I know of a place in which (11) or any equivalent proposition is argued for. Finally, I cannot think of an argument for (11) which could be claimed to be constructed out of Sellarsian materials. I believe, therefore, that with (11) we have come to a "rock bottom" principle of Sellars' system.

We have also come to the nub of my criticism of Sellars. For I believe both that (11) is false and that, in spite of the fact that it is not stated in EPM, it lies behind a crucial part of its argument. Naturally, I will offer a reason for thinking that (11) is false. Before I do this, however, I want to return to the text of EPM, exhibit a portion of its structure, and show how (11) is relevant.

§2. To begin our second task, let us return to

(8) *x has a primordial awareness of sorts* entails *x has primordial classificatory consciousness.*

We have seen that Sellars can accept this. But, of course, this does not mean that he accepts the view that there are primordial awarenesses of sorts. The sections of EPM which we are about to examine may be usefully regarded as containing an argument, based on (8), and leading to the conclusion that there are no primordial awarenesses of sorts.

(8) and (10) yield

(13) *x has a primordial awareness of sorts* entails *x makes a primordial use of a concept.*

To make use of this, we need the following definition, which stipulates one sense for "independent."

Definition IV. A concept C_1 is independent of another concept C_2 if and only if having the concept C_2 is not a necessary condition of having the concept C_1.

A concept C_1 is independent of a class of concepts if and only if it is independent of each member of that class.

A concept is independent if and only if it is independent of every other concept.

Does the fact that a use of a concept is primordial entail that that concept is independent? I am not sure. For I do not know how to rule out the possibility that a necessary condition of having a sensation or image of one sort is being able to have sensations or images of other sorts. This suggestion is somewhat plausible where there are "privative" sorts. For example, it might be that anything that could be said to have a sensation of red must also be capable of having a sensation of black. If so, and if we have primordial awarenesses of sorts simply by having sensations or images, then a necessary condition of a primordial use of the concept red would be the ability to make a primordial use of the concept black; thus the concept red in such a case would not be independent.

However, it is clear that if there is a primordial use of a concept, that concept must be independent of every concept which cannot be acquired simply by virtue of having sensations or images. Among the concepts which clearly cannot be so acquired are those of various kinds of physical objects, the concept of standard conditions for observation, and the concept of a normal observer. If we agree to refer to these concepts under the heading "physical concepts," we can state our conclusion in the following form.

(14) *x makes a primordial use of the concept C_1 entails C_1 is independent of physical concepts.*

Combining (14) with a version of (13) altered only so as to include a reference to a particular sort, which we will designate by the name of its corresponding concept, we get

(15) *x has a primordial awareness of sort C_1 entails C_1 is independent of physical concepts.*

Since one could hardly deny that red is an example of a sort of which we have primordial awareness without cutting himself off from traditional empiricism, I shall take red as such an example. Applying (15) to this example yields the conclusion that there is a concept of red which is independent of physical concepts.

Since we shall have to refer to such concepts on several occasions it will be convenient to have a name for them. I will call concepts which are independent of physical concepts *ur-concepts*.[7]

7. The term is Sellars' and can be found in *Science, Perception and Reality*, pp. 334f. There is a possibility that Sellars would consider it part of the definition of an ur-concept that a use of it be subsumptive. This is not true by definition in my use of the term. Otherwise, Sellars' term is appropriate for my meaning.

It is clear that Sellars denies that there are ur-concepts. Consider the following passage.

> Now, I think it is clear what a logical atomist . . . would say. He would say that I am overlooking the fact that the logical space of physical objects in Space and Time rests on the logical space of sense contents, and he would argue that it is concepts pertaining to sense contents which have the logical independence of one another which is characteristic of traditional empiricism . . . Until you have disposed, therefore, of the idea that there is a more fundamental logical space than that of physical objects in Space and Time, or shown that it too is fraught with coherence, your incipient *Méditations Hegeliènnes* are premature. (148)

Nothing is to be drawn from the occurrence of the term "independent" in this passage, for it is used here in a sense different from the one which I have been using; its sense is given by the schema "C_1 is independent of C_2 if and only if 'C_1 applies to x' does not entail 'C_2 applies to x' and conversely." The passage has been quoted because it mentions the possibility of a logical space more fundamental than that of physical concepts. Since Sellars evidently believes he can dispose of such a possibility, and since, if there were ur-concepts, they would form a logical space more fundamental than that of physical concepts, Sellars is committed to denying that there are ur-concepts.

In order to understand Sellars' argument against ur-concepts we must introduce the notion of a descriptive content. My aim here is not to give a fully detailed exposition of this notion but only to remind the reader whence it comes.

Consider the following situations.

   (a) Seeing that x, over there, is red.
   (b) Its looking to one that x, over there, is red.
   (c) Its looking to one as though there were a red object over
        there. (151)

We can distinguish three aspects of these situations.

(i) *Propositional Content.* One who is in any of these situations is one who is having an experience to which can be ascribed a propositional content. In this case that content is "that x, over there, is red" (151). Subject to a qualification concerning the existential form required for (c), we can say that this propositional content is common to the experiences had by those who are in any of the situations (a), (b), or (c).

(ii) *Endorsement*. A propositional content can be endorsed fully, partially, or not at all. This is what is done in (a), (b), and (c), respectively, and it is this difference in endorsement which is behind the difference in what is asserted in these cases.

(iii) *Descriptive Content*. This is the notion which we have been leading up to, and for whose sake we have discussed propositional content and endorsement. For the notion of a descriptive content is introduced by Sellars as follows.

> The propositional content of these three experiences [i.e. those in (a), (b), and (c)] is, of course, but a part of that to which we are logically committed by characterizing them as situations of these three kinds. Of the remainder, as we have seen, part is a matter of the extent to which this propositional content is endorsed. It is the residue with which we are now concerned. Let us call this residue the *descriptive content*. (151)

We can clarify this notion by saying that the descriptive content of an experience is that which would make the experience a *seeing* (as opposed, say, to a believing) *provided* that the propositional content were true (cf. 152). Now, so far we have only an extrinsic characterization of descriptive content. The crucial question concerning descriptive contents—one that is under discussion for three sections of EPM—is, "What is the intrinsic character of descriptive contents?"

Before taking up the answers to this question, let us connect the need to do so with our previous discussion. Sellars is about to argue, in detail, that descriptive contents cannot be intrinsically characterized by using ur-concepts. How could such an argument have any bearing on whether or not there are ur-concepts—on whether or not we can dispose of the idea that the logical space of physical concepts rests on a more fundamental logical space of ur-concepts? Clearly, the argument can have such a bearing only if we suppose that

(16) *There are ur-concepts* entails *descriptive contents can be intrinsically characterized by using ur-concepts.*

Since I think Sellars is justified in supposing this, I will merely sketch the background for such a supposition. Strictly speaking, the consequent of (16) follows from "There is a reason to suppose there are ur-concepts" (cf. section III, last paragraph, p. 149). We will, of course, assume that no one will assert that there are ur-concepts without some reason. Now, the reasons that seem available for saying that there are ur-concepts all involve the view that ur-concepts are somehow applicable to sense experience. But such applicability cannot arise *via* the propositional content or through endorsement, for having these requires abilities beyond those required by having primordial awarenesses of sorts, and hence beyond those required by having ur-concepts. Thus, the applicability of ur-concepts to sense experience must arise through their applicability in some fashion to descriptive contents.

Sellars recognizes four answers to the question "What is the intrinsic character of a descriptive content?" I will state these using an example, viz., the descriptive content of the experiences (a), (b), and (c) above.

A_1. The descriptive content is an (ur-) red thing. (Not, of course, a (physical) red thing.)

A_2. The descriptive content is a sensation of (ur-) red.

A_3. The descriptive content is a primordial awareness of (ur-) red.

A_4. The descriptive content is an impression of red, where "impression of red" is a highly refined concept whose acquisition is an extension of, and therefore depends on the possession of a highly developed system of, physical concepts, including (physical) red.

A_4 is Sellars' own answer. Clearly, A_4 is not available to a proponent of ur-concepts. The first three answers are all of those that are available to him.

Concerning A_1, Sellars makes a general point and considers a particular case. The general point is as follows.

. . . we can scarcely say that this descriptive content is itself something red unless we can pry the term 'red' loose from its prima-facie tie with the category of physical objects. (152)

The separability of the term 'red' from its tie with physical objects is such an immediate consequence of the view that there are ur-concepts that, taken as an *argument* against that view, the foregoing would be question-begging. However, we may read this remark of Sellars' as a *challenge* to the proponent of ur-concepts to explain how anything could be entitled to be called a concept of *red* if it were applicable to something other than physical objects. This challenge remains formidable even though we have no proof that it cannot be met.[8]

The particular case that Sellars discusses represents one attempt to meet this challenge. The crux of this attempt is the claim that "seeing an object entails seeing its facing surface" (152), where this is not regarded as a *theory* about sensing, but is alleged to be a statement of what appears upon *analysis* of ordinary perception. The attempt continues by arguing that surfaces thus become intelligible upon analysis of ordinary perception, as does the coloredness of surfaces. But surfaces are not physical objects. Thus, we have arrived at the intelligibility of, for example, red items which are not physical objects.

Sellars' criticism of this attempt to make the applicability of 'red' to non-physical objects intelligible consists in pointing out that our agreement that we always perceive this side rather than that side *of a physical object* simply does not commit us to recognizing a new class of two-dimensional particulars. This I take to be a correct and sufficient reply. Thus, one *prima facie* attractive way of spelling out A_1 can be rejected. I think it is fair to say that while A_1 in general has not been decisively refuted, enough has been said to make this an unpromising alternative. Let us turn to A_2.

This alternative is taken up in section V of EPM. As Sellars points out, certain interpretations of A_2 render it a merely verbal answer which brings us no closer to an intrinsic characterization of descriptive contents. I shall henceforth be concerned with A_2 only as interpreted so as to provide a not merely verbal answer. This interpretation is that speaking about *sensations of red,* for example, helps us because " . . . sensation of . . . " contexts are to be understood as non-extensional. The way in which such a move would help is that it would allow us to use an ur-concept (e.g., red) in characterizing descriptive contents, without committing us to the existence of red items which are not physical objects.

The crucial question that A_2, so interpreted, faces is "How is the non-extensionality of ' . . . sensation of . . . ' contexts to be justified?" Sellars' discussion may be set out in the form of an argument, as follows.

---

8. Cf. Sellars' remark two pages earlier on the possibility of a non-physical object having the same redness as physical objects have: "And while this is, perhaps, not entirely out of the question, it certainly provides food for thought" (150).

(17) It can be explained how " . . . sensation of . . . " contexts can be non-extensional in just three ways, either
  (i) by assimilating sensations to thoughts; or
  (ii) by taking, e.g., "sensation of a red triangle" as having
       the sense of "episode of the kind which is the common
       descriptive component of those experiences which
       would be cases of seeing that the facing surface of a
       physical object is red and triangular if an object *were*
       presenting a red and triangular facing surface"
       (cf. 156); or
  (iii) by equating the sense of " . . . sensation of . . . "
        with that of Sellars' " . . . impression of . . . "

(18) Adopting (iii) results in a view coincident with A_4, which,
as we have seen, cannot be held by one who believes
there are ur-concepts.

(19) Adopting (ii) amounts to giving up the quest for an *intrinsic*
characterization of a descriptive content. Thus (ii) cannot
be adopted by a proponent of ur-concepts (cf. (16) above).

(20) Sensations cannot be assimilated to thoughts.

(21) Therefore, since none of the possible explanations of the
non-extensionality of ". . . sensation of . . ."contexts
is open to the proponent of ur-concepts, A_2 is not an
answer that he can give to the question about the intrinsic
character of descriptive contents.

As in the previous case, I think A_2 has been shown to be unpromising,
but without having been quite refuted. For A_2 might be rescued if one
could show that there is some alternative not covered by (17). However,
since I am not aware of such an alternative I will pass on to A_3.

This alternative is taken up in section VI of EPM. The criticism
begins as follows.

. . . they [forms of the myth of the given] all have in common
the idea that the awareness of certain *sorts* . . . is a primordial,
non-problematic feature of 'immediate experience'. In the context
of conceptualism, as we have seen, this idea took the form of
treating sensations as though they were absolutely specific, and
infinitely complicated, *thoughts*. (157)

The backward reference is to the discussion of A_2, in particular the point made above in (20). From this fact and the structure of the passage just quoted, we might gather that A_3 is a general view, with respect to which A_2 is a specific version. Viewing the matter in this way, we might expect to find Sellars outlining alternative specific versions and constructing arguments against them.

However, this is not what Sellars goes on to do. The remainder of the discussion of A_3 is devoted to showing that Locke, Berkeley, and Hume all share the assumption "that we have an unacquired ability to be aware of determinate repeatables" (159). Sellars makes it clear, furthermore, that he believes that Locke, Berkeley, and Hume treated such awarenesses as thoughts. Consider, for example, the following remarks.

> Hume, on the other hand, assuming that there are occurrent thoughts of *determinate* repeatables, *denies* that there are occurrent thoughts of *determinables*. I shall spare the reader the familiar details of Hume's attempt to give a constructive account of our consciousness of determinables, nor shall I criticize it. For my point is that however much Locke, Berkeley, and Hume differ on the problem of abstract ideas, they all take for granted that the human mind has an innate ability to be aware of certain determinate sorts—*indeed, that we are aware of them simply by virtue of having sensations and images.* (160)

The only evidence in this passage (or anywhere in this section) for Hume's agreement to the italicized assertion is the claim made at the beginning of the passage, viz., that Hume assumes that there are occurrent thoughts of determinate repeatables. In order for the latter claim to be evidence for the former without further argument, awarenesses of determinate sorts must be taken to *be* thoughts. Thus, Sellars is tacitly assuming that Hume, at least, accepts this identification.

We are now faced with a puzzling situation. The strategy which led up to section VI requires a refutation of A_3. Yet, what is done in this section does not even appear to be such a refutation. We could try to resolve the puzzle by taking Sellars to be proceeding as follows. He has just rejected the assimilation of sensations to thoughts. Now he encounters another assimilation, this time of primordial awarenesses of sorts to thoughts. Perhaps he regards these assimilations as so similar that whatever serves as a ground for rejecting the former will be sufficient for rejecting the latter. This view, however, does not resolve the puzzle.

For if this were what Sellars had in mind, there would have been no need for a new section and a new alternative. The refutation of A_3 would have been just a special case of the refutation of A_2.

The solution is rather this. While Sellars does not believe that there are primordial awarenesses of sorts (also called unacquired awarenesses of determinate sorts), he does believe (α) that if there were such things, they would have to be thoughts. He also believes (β) that there cannot be immediate subsumptions, that is, thoughts that one could have simply by virtue of having sensations and images. Neither of these refutes A_3 by itself; jointly they do. The arguments for (β) are to be found elsewhere in EPM. It is the business of section VI to establish (α).

Let us remind ourselves of the importance of (α). The proponent of ur-concepts has been challenged to give an intrinsic characterization of descriptive contents. A_3 is one of the ways in which, it seems, he can do this, so he has not been refuted until A_3 has been shown to be untenable. But A_3 has not yet been shown to be untenable, and the only argument which seems as if it might show this rests on the assumption that primordial awarenesses of sorts have to be regarded as being thoughts.

Surprising as it may seem, Sellars does not argue for this assumption. The closest that he comes to such an argument is to make the following historical claim.

> Thus, an examination of Locke's *Essay* makes it clear that he is thinking of a sensation of white as the sort of thing that can become an abstract idea (occurrent) of White—a thought of White 'in the Understanding'—merely by virtue of being separated from the context of other sensations (and images) which accompany it on a particular occasion. (157f)

There are two things to be said about this argument. The first is that the claim attributed to Locke is compatible with the claim that an occurrence of a sensation (or a primordial awareness of sorts)[9] neither is a thought nor has the occurrence of a thought as a necessary condition. For, to begin with, that something can be separated does not imply that

9. I am treating this occurrence of "sensation" as equivalent to "primordial awareness of sorts" because of the place that this discussion has in Sellars' argument. It will no doubt be suggested that it would be better to revise my analysis of the argument. I disagree. For the fundamental division remains between (a) a use of "sensation" for which it is a crucial part of the argument that sensations *cannot* be thoughts (the use in section V); and (b) a use of "sensation" (the present one) in which the argument turns on the supposition that sensations (primordial awarenesses of sorts) *must* be thoughts.

it is separated. Further, the above passage does not exclude the possibility that separating a sensation from its context requires adding something to it. In this case, a sensation would not *be* a thought, but only part of a thought. Finally, it does not follow even from the fact that a sensation can become a thought, that it *is* ever a thought, in a sense in which the existence of the former requires the existence of the latter. A man, for example, may become a parent; but no one would conclude that to be a man is to be a parent.

The second comment to be made about the discussion of Locke, and, for that matter, about the discussion of Berkeley and Hume as well, is that no historical argument is adequate to the rejection of a philosophical view. The given, or primordial awareness of sorts, may be useful notions even if several or even all past proponents of them made significant mistakes with regard to them.

Why does Sellars not give a direct defense of (α)? I believe that it is because (α) is very nearly a fundamental principle for Sellars. On this view the structure of section VII makes good sense. For if (α) is indeed a fundamental principle, there is nothing left that Sellars can do in this section, except to try to show that it is a principle which is shared by important proponents of the given.

I say that (α) is very nearly a fundamental principle for Sellars. But not quite. For it follows from

(11) *x makes a primordial use of a concept* entails *x immediately subsumes something under a concept*

together with two other assumptions, viz., that subsumptions under a concept are thoughts, and that primordial awarenesses of sorts involve uses of (ur-) concepts. The latter of these we have already encountered; the former is clearly a Sellarsian view.

Let us review our progress with respect to the second task of part I. We have examined sections IV, V, and VI with an eye to discovering whether there is an argument therein which would not be affected by a criticism of the argument set out in our §1, and in particular by a criticism of (11). We are now able to say that there is not such an argument. For if (11) were false, it would be possible that there is a primordial use of a concept that is not a subsumptive use, and hence not a thought. If there is a primordial use of a concept that is not a thought, then (α) is false. And if (α) is false, the argument of sections IV, V, and VI cannot succeed in showing that there are not primordial awarenesses of sorts.

We have also discovered another reason for regarding (11) as fundamental for Sellars. For, it stands very close to an assertion which is taken as a first principle in EPM, and is one step more basic than that assertion.

With this point, we have completed what we set out to do in this section. Let us now turn to the examination of (11).

§3. Let us begin by distinguishing (11) from

> (11a) *x makes a primordial use of a concept* materially implies *x immediately subsumes something under a concept.*

While I will argue that (11) is false, I will not argue that (11a) is false. The refutation of (11a) would be a very large undertaking indeed. It would require us to show that the admission of non-subsumptive uses of concepts is an essential part of a view which yields the most comprehensive and coherent view of our world. At this point, it should be remembered that I have not offered to show that there is a given, but only to argue that that notion is not yet ready to be consigned to mythology. What this objective requires here is only that I argue against (11). Now, (11) can be shown to be false by showing merely that the denial of (11a) makes sense. (11) is false if the falsehood of (11a) is possible. This possibility can be shown to be open if the denial of (11a) can be made intelligible, that is, if non-subsumptive uses of concepts can be made intelligible. This is what I will try to do.

Let us note, first, that in one sense of "possible" it is rather obviously possible that (11a) is false. For a use of a concept is the actualization of an ability to be in a state corresponding to a property, while a subsumptive use of a concept is the actualization of an ability to be in a state corresponding to an assertion. When a use of a concept and a subsumptive use of a concept are so described, it is obvious that the first does not logically require the second.

Mere logical possibility, however, is not enough for our purposes. What we need, in order to be quite convinced that there could be a non-subsumptive use of a concept, is to understand what it would be like to find one. This is best accomplished by providing an example, although we shall have to recognize that no example can be quite uncontroversial. The example of a non-subsumptive use of a concept which follows is not an example of a primordial awareness of sorts; it is, however, analogous to primordial awarenesses in certain respects which will be commented on below.

If I count the books on my shelf, I may say, as I point, "One, two, three, . . . ". These words reflect a state of mind corresponding to the properties 'first book counted by me on this occasion', 'second book counted by me on this occasion', etc. But I have not *subsumed* these books under concepts corresponding to these properties. Nor, indeed, *could* I have correctly done so until I had counted them. Even if I had said "This is the first book, this is the second book, . . . ," this would only look like subsumption, but would actually be counting. Of course, my counting does provide a ground for subsumption, by myself or another, of these books under such concepts as "first book counted by me on this occasion." But this is not to say that the original counting is itself a case of subsuming.

It may be that Sellars overlooks the possibility of a non-subsumptive use of a concept because of undue attention to sense-datum theories. In at least one strong tradition—one which Sellars clearly recognizes (128)—a sense-datum is an entity which can exist, and have the properties it has, whether it is given to anyone or not (and, whether anyone is aware of it or not). I do not know of any way of thinking of such an entity being given, except by thinking of it as subsumed under a concept. One must begin with an entity having a certain property. Then one has to add the awareness of it. Finally, one has to get these connected, and the only way it appears that one can do this is to make the awareness a use of a concept which subsumes the entity under that concept.

There is, however, another way of conceiving sense-data—although perhaps one should change the name with the view. On this conception, a sense-datum is not an entity that can exist and have the properties it has without anyone being aware of it. Thus, on this view, there is nothing to be brought under a concept until a use of a concept has already occurred. A red sense-datum, for example, would just be a primordial awareness of the sort red, involving a use of the (ur-) concept 'red', but not a subsumptive use. Such a use of a concept is analogous to the use of the concept "first book counted by me on this occasion" in counting. Here, it will be recalled, there is no subsumption, and there cannot be until a non-subsumptive use of the concept has occurred. A further analogy arises from the fact that my counting provides a ground for later subsumption under such a concept as "first book counted by me on this occasion." In the case of a primordial awareness of red, the initial non-subsumptive use of ur-red provides a ground for a later subsumptive use of that concept.[10]

One *could*, of course, represent every use of a concept in a sentence. Thus, a primordial awareness of red could be represented as a "This is red" awareness. This possibility, however, is not significant. We *could* also change a familiar ceremony and create knights by having the sovereign say "So-and-so is a knight." This performance would, however, remain quite different from the same utterance by anyone else, or by the sovereign at any later time.

I believe that I have said enough to make the notion of a non-subsumptive use of a concept intelligible. Let us draw some conclusions. First, (11) is false. Thus, we are not debarred from using ur-concepts in an intrinsic characterization of descriptive contents. Hence, Sellars' argument does not prevent us from holding that there are ur-concepts, primordial uses of concepts, and primordial awarenesses of sorts. We have not, of course, proved that there are such things; but our aim has been only to show that they are not yet certifiable myths, and this much we have done. Further, a review of the connections between (11) and (7) will show that in making the denial of (11) intelligible we have also made the denial of (7) intelligible. For if there can be primordial awarenesses of sorts without subsumptive uses of concepts, there can be such awarenesses without there being non-inferential knowledge. Finally, as far as we can tell from reflection on the fact that the given must be a primordial awareness of sorts, the given can be analyzed non-epistemically. For it can be analyzed as a non-subsumptive use of an ur-concept.

It may be, however, that an epistemic component has to be added to the analysis when we take into account the fact that the given also must be required to explicate a foundation view. Whether or not this is so is the central question of part II.

---

10. My main argument in this essay may appear to be weakened by the absence of an historical example at this point. For, Sellars might be defended by claiming that he had at least shown all views based on the given up to the time of writing EPM to be myths. In view of this, I feel entitled to say that I think that sense-data as I have conceived them are exactly Humean impressions; and that what Sellars has done is not to show that the given is a myth, but to show us how we must clarify the notion of the given, both in any future use of that notion and in our interpretations of historical figures. It must be obvious, however, that my interpretation of Hume differs greatly from that of Sellars. Since this disagreement cannot be gone into here, I will limit my references to Hume to the remark just made.

II

Let us remind ourselves that a foundation view is, by definition, a view to the effect that empirical knowledge rests on a foundation of non-inferential knowledge of matter of fact. To decide whether that which is required to explicate this view must be analyzed so as to contain an epistemic fact, we must first decide just what is required in order to explicate such a view. It will simplify matters if we take for granted in what follows that primordial awareness of sorts is required (this is necessary if there is to be a given) and direct our discussion to the discovery of what further conditions must be placed on this awareness, if it is to explicate a foundation view.

One suggestion as to what may be required is this.

> (22) The explication of a foundation view requires that the primordial awareness of sorts used in the explication *be* non-inferential knowledge of matters of fact.

It is clear that if (22) is true there is no hope of analyzing the given non-epistemically. It is not so clear, however, whether Sellars thinks (22) is true. At one point, he says:

> On alternative (*a*)[11] the fact that a sense content was sensed would be a *non-epistemic* fact about the sense content. Yet it would be hasty to conclude that this alternative precludes *any* logical connection between the sensing of sense contents and the possession of non-inferential knowledge. For even if the sensing of sense contents did not logically imply the existence of non-inferential knowledge, the converse might well be true. (129)

Sellars does not criticize this view, but goes on to set out alternatives. If he thought that what is required to explicate a foundation view must *be* non-inferential knowledge, we might expect that he would reject the alternative just mentioned immediately. Thus, the fact that he does not do so gives us some reason for thinking that Sellars does not believe (22).

Yet, one page later, he dismisses a view for no other reason than that it severs "the logical connection in the direction *sensing sense contents* → *having non-inferential knowledge*" (130). But the severance of the connection *in this direction* is a sufficient reason for dismissing a view only if (22), or at least an analogue of it designed to apply specifically to sensing sense contents, is presupposed.

11. This is not the same as *our* "alternative (a)" above.

I will not try to settle the question as to whether or not Sellars accepts (22). It is enough to offer a dilemma. If Sellars' case really depends on accepting (22), then it can be defeated by finding another satisfactory statement of what is required in order to explicate a foundation view.[12] We shall in fact find such an alternative statement. If, however, Sellars' case does not depend on accepting (22), it must be able to be made out on the basis of some other statement of what is required for the explication in question. Let us turn, therefore, to such other statements. Consider

(23) The explication of a foundation view requires that the primordial awareness of sorts used in the explication be a necessary condition for non-inferential knowledge.

I believe this is a step in the right direction, but it is too strong a requirement. If (23) is true, for example, revealed knowledge is impossible. But I don't think anyone would say that a philosopher had failed to explicate the idea that empirical knowledge rests on a foundation of non-inferential knowledge of matter of fact *solely* on the ground that he had not shown revealed knowledge to be *impossible*. Further, a defender of the given who rested his case on (23) would have to claim that a Sellarsian account of knowledge could not possibly be true. But surely it would be enough for him to establish merely that the Sellarsian account is not true.

What we need is roughly a statement to this effect. Something explicates a foundation view if, assuming that what we all take for granted about our world and ourselves is true, it follows that we wouldn't have non-inferential knowledge of matters of fact if we did not have the item used in the explication. To put this in a clearer and simpler form we need the following definition.

Definition V. *p* is a contingently necessary condition of *q* relative to *r* if and only if

---

12. There may be a temptation to cut off this possibility by holding that Sellars is assured of the truth of (22) because he makes it true by definition. (This is tantamount to including 'being non-inferential knowledge' in the definition of givenness.) Such a move would indeed simplify the present discussion, as also several others in this essay. Unfortunately, it would also have the effect of making Sellars' results irrelevant to some traditional views. Price, for example, is at some pains to distinguish sensing from knowing, in his introduction of sensing sense-data. *Vide* H. H. Price, *Perception* (London: Methuen, 1932): 5, 17-18, and esp. 7. Furthermore, section I, para. 3 of EPM (128-29) is barely intelligible on the assumption that Sellars is taking (22) as *definitionally* true.

(i) *r* is a contingent statement

(ii) *q* does not entail *p*

(iii) *r* and *q* together entail *p*. [13]

Let *B* represent our background knowledge, that is, an enormous conjunction of assertions about our world and ourselves, including philosophically relevant assertions, provided they are not ones which are controversial in the present discussion. Then we can give a revised statement of what is required to explicate a foundation view, as follows.

(24) The explication of a foundation view requires that the primordial awareness of sorts used in the explication be a contingently necessary condition, relative to *B*, of our having non-inferential knowledge of matter of fact.

The following two propositions present a sketch of an explication of a foundation view which meets the requirement of (24) but not the stronger requirements of (23) or (22).

(25) Empirical knowledge would not be available to beings of the kind we are, living in the kind of world we live in, unless there was some non-inferential knowledge of matter of fact; and

(26) Subject to the same general conditions, we could not have non-inferential knowledge of matter of fact unless we had primordial awareness of sorts.

I believe that (24) is true, or, at least, that nothing stronger than (24) is true. My reason is this. First, (25) and (26) together satisfy (24), but nothing stronger. Second, if the program suggested by (25) and (26) were carried out successfully, primordial awareness of sorts would have been used to explicate the idea that empirical knowledge rests on a foundation of non-inferential knowledge of matters of fact. My support for this second premise rests only on my general understanding of empiricism. If we substitute 'the given' for 'primordial awareness of sorts' in (24) and (26), we arrive at some statements which, it seems to me, give us an accurate picture of what the given is supposed to do. To put the point a little differently: one could, of course, insist that it is essential to one's notion of the given that a requirement for explicating

13. This is a version of an idea of Nagel's. *Vide* Ernest Nagel, *The Structure of Science* (New York: 1961): 559f. Where *p* is of the form "There are *N*s," one can also say that *N*s (there being *N*s) are contingently necessary conditions.

a foundation view stronger than (24) be met. But then, I think one would have to withdraw the claim to be arguing against all forms of the given as found in traditional empiricism, and settle for a critique of only some particular versions. This clearly runs counter to Sellars' intentions.

There is no argument in EPM against the adequacy of (24). This, I think, is not surprising. For if what I have said is correct, it must appear to Sellars that there is very little to choose between (24) and (22). He will naturally take primordial awareness of sorts to be knowledge. If this were so, then, while (22) would still not be strictly true, a primordial awareness of sorts which satisfied (24) could not fail to have what is required of primordial awarenesses in (22).

We have seen, however, that the view that primordial awareness of sorts is knowledge rests ultimately on (11), which is false. We are, therefore, entitled to assert the possibility of a primordial awareness of sorts that is not knowledge. Now, it is clear that (24) by itself does not require primordial awarenesses of sorts to be knowledge, or to be something whose existence entails that there is knowledge. Thus, we have found a way in which a primordial awareness of sorts could be used to explicate a foundation view, without having had to admit an epistemic component into our analysis of the given. This completes the task of part II.

The conclusion with respect to our main thesis follows directly. There is an analysis of the given which does not involve an epistemic component. What the given is, is a non-subsumptive use of an ur-concept which satisfies the further condition in (24). Once again, we have not tried to prove that there is such a thing, but only that it is a live option which has not been ruled out. It follows, even from such a limited claim, that

(4) *Something is given to x* does not entail *x has non-inferential knowledge*

is true. A review of our discussion at the beginning will show, however, that if Sellars' campaign against the given in EPM is to be successful, (4) has to be false. I conclude that while Sellars has ruled out several important versions of the given, and may have narrowed the possibly successful conceptions of the given down to one, he has not shown the given to be a myth. It is, rather, a legend, which may be false, but in which there may yet be some truth.

·~·5·~·
The Sensuous Content
of Perception

ROMANE CLARK
Indiana University

A MAN sees a small, bouncy, red, rubber ball. There is some one thing he has seen, but how much seeing has he done? How many perceptual acts have occurred? Adequate philosophical theories of perception should, no doubt, provide schematic characterizations, instances of which would be, or yield, answers to questions like these.

In this paper I consider some aspects of Professor Sellars' views on perception, particularly with reference to the sensuous character of perception. I am only marginally concerned here with Sellars' broader philosophical themes concerning the naturalistic and materialistic bases of perception. I borrow, however, from these broader considerations his assumptions that judging (that something is the case) is best understood by analogy with overt speech, and that perceiving is a species of judging.

Some jargon will be useful in developing our themes. To avoid the "success" connotations of notions like 'see', and to generalize over the range of sense modalities, I shall often speak of (psychical) agents sensuously believing that something is the case or of agents being sensuously aware of something. The ascription of sensuous beliefs to an agent does not imply that what he believes is the case; nor does saying that an agent is sensuously aware of something imply that the object of his awareness exists. These idioms will be our perceptual analogues of 'thinks that' and 'thinks of'.

It is currently fashionable to construe the logic of the ascription of mental acts to psychical agents as a modal logic.[1] If we combine current

1. The fashion was created by Hintikka. See [3], [4].

109

fashion with the assumptions borrowed above, it is plausible to think that the logic of the ascription of sensuous beliefs to agents is itself also thereby a species of modal logic. This is plausible, for, on those assumptions, perceiving is a species of judging. Moreover, if perceiving is a species of judging, and if judging is to be understood by analogy with saying, then it looks as though it should be fruitful to consider the analogy of seeing to saying.

Consider, now, the following three propositions:

(1) Perceptions are judgments.

(2) Sense impressions are constituents of perceptions.

(3) Sense impressions are not conceptual or cognitive items.

By 'judgments' we understand, not evaluations, but thoughts: those mental occurrences the verbal expressions of which are assertions. I borrow the term 'sense impression' from Sellars' writings. I do not know how closely it coincides with 'sensation' as that term has been used by other philosophers. Sense impressions must, however, at least include experiences of what Aristotle called the "proper sensibles." (How much more, if anything, the term 'sense impressions' covers remains open here.) The term covers, that is, at least, experiences of those sense qualities awareness of instances of which would not occur if some single sense modality were destroyed. (If my eyes are put out, my capacity for experiencing instances of red (although not my capacity for remembering, or imaging, them) will be removed. Putting my eyes out will not similarly remove my capacity for experiencing instances of spatial relations. Presumably, when one is sensuously aware of something red, he often—in normal circumstances at least—has a sense impression of *red*. But whether one who is sensuously aware of a small, bouncy, rubber ball *can* have *a sense impression* of the size, nature, matter, or kind of what he is sensuously aware remains undetermined now.)

The truth of any two of (1)–(3) above may appear to imply the falsity of the remaining proposition. Evidently, qualifications concerning notions like 'constituent' will be required to turn these appearances into reality. We need in particular to know how, on a given theory of perception, sense impressions are thought to be related to sensuous beliefs. But in any case, this (putatively) inconsistent triad of propositions can be exploited to sharpen certain contrasts which exist among some philosophical theories of perception.

A naive realist, for example, might accept (1) and (2) but deny (3). (I note parenthetically that such a naive realist cannot be, in Sellars' sense, "an adequately critical direct realist" ([7]: 255; see also [5], [6]. He cannot be, for the latter, according to Sellars, affirms (3)). Everett Hall was such a naive (but inadequately critical direct) realist who accepted (1) and (2) but denied (3) ([12]).

One might accept (1) and (3) but deny (2). Coupled with a suitable gloss of 'constituent of', Sellars and Professor Geach seem to be philosophers who would take this line ([5], [6], [7]; [1], esp. pp. 64ff, 122ff).

No doubt there are those who accept (2) and (3) but deny (1). (I have no one especially in mind.) Perhaps this is even the natural view, a view many or most of us shared before coming into contact with the contributions of philosophers like Brentano and Husserl, or Sellars, or Hintikka to the Philosophy of Mind.

We ignore this last view here. We assume instead that (1) is true, that perceptions are judgments. We seek now grounds for accepting or rejecting (2) and for accepting or rejecting (3).

Evidently, (2), the proposition that sense impressions are constituents of perceptions, is *in some sense* true. In what sense it is true is not clear. For it is not clear in general what the constituents of judgments may be. We speak of mentally judging that something is the case and, in doing so, of thinking of an object and of mentally attributing something of it. We abstract and distinguish the judgment which results from these occurrent acts. But where in the judgment is the mental element of reference matching the act of thinking about something, and where is the mental element of ascription matching the act of attribution? And if, (1), perceptions are judgments, then perceivings, like thinkings, presumably are composite acts, and perceptions, like thoughts, presumably are logically complex entities. Where, then, in a perception is the referential element, and where in the perception is the ascriptive element of the perceptual judging?

It is a merit of Sellars' characterization of thought as a theoretical entity whose overt, external model is speech that verbally accommodating remarks about concepts as the constitutents of thoughts can be given some substance. The model is even more helpful, and more exact, for perception in particular than it is for thought in general. For a perception, like an assertion, is a logically complex entity the occurrent, related acts of which have material conditions and properties governing their manifestations. We distinguish, of course, assertions from assertings, the acts of making assertions. And we distinguish the sentence and the words uttered in the making of an assertion from the assertion and from the act itself. Further, sentences and words, we have learned, are themselves types, occurrences of which have their own material and occurrent properties. Some of these are, by convention, crucial features in determining what sentence or word a given token instance is. A given word instance, accordingly, is at once a material entity, an occurrent word instance, a word which, as used on an appropriate occasion, is, say, an ascription of a property. It is, *qua* token of a type, a symbol which occurs in the sentence used in making some assertion. The present point is that the material conditions and features of the word which are, by convention, fixed as the determinants of the physical occurrence determine it to be an instance of a conceptual element. The word, as a physical constituent of a sentence, is used to express a conceptual element of the sentence which is used to make a statement.

Something like this is true of sense impressions as mental occurrences which naturally, and not by convention, figure in the occurrence of perceptions. Note, at least, in the first place that the occurrence of sense impressions is a necessary condition for the occurrence of perceptions. It is of some importance to distinguish the reason for this being so from the fact, if it is one, that certain physiological states of the brain, say, are necessary conditions for the occurrences of certain judgments. It would be wrong to view perceptions as merely judgments plus some sense impressions. It is not as though a judgment exhausts the content of a perception with some correlated sense impressions serving as mere causal mechanisms, the material triggers for the occurrence of the judgment. For this would fail to distinguish perceptions from other judgments which may be materially induced by sensory stimulation, but which in no sense are perceptions, and which in no sense count as seeing what is judged. It may happen that I think or judge that the ball is red, that I am concurrently subject to the appropriate sensory stimulation, and yet be quite false that I see that the ball is red. I may not be attending to what is before me.

First-person, non-inferential knowledge of what I sensuously judge, like first-person, non-inferential knowledge of what I am thinking, is one of the motives for construing perception as a form of judgment. And occurrences of sense impressions are necessary conditions for occurrences of perceptions in this further, important sense: first-person, non-inferential knowledge of what I perceive is *thereby* also first-person, non-inferential knowledge of my current sensuous impressions.

The fact is that a sensuous belief, the perception, say, that some object before me is red, requires a conscious awareness of the color of the object (although not, of course, necessarily a sense impression of *red*). Failing this, the belief is not a sensuous belief. It is not a *perception* of the object's color.

It is the occurrence of sense impressions relative to acts of sensuous belief which accounts for much of what is unique about perception as the species of judgment which it is. For sensuous beliefs differ from non-sensuous ones primarily in those elements of the perception which tie the act, the occurrent sensuous belief, to the occasion of its occurrence. We can detect, but cannot think of, something we know not what. We can think of, but cannot see, one who is absent. (We can, of course, have sensuous beliefs about one who is absent. We mistake, perhaps, something before us for him. What we cannot do, however, is have affirmative sensuous beliefs about him as being out of the range of the given sense modality.) Distance, obstructions, and perspective may prevent my seeing, but not believing, what is the case.

Sense impressions, then, are not merely necessary conditions of sensuous beliefs. They are constituents of them. Perhaps this is a truism. In any case, this fact is, in itself, of limited interest. Anyone who maintains (1) and (3) above, but denies (2), surely means to deny that sense impressions are themselves conceptual or cognitive constituents of sensuous beliefs. The considerations cited in reaching our truism suggest, I believe, that such a denial of (2) is wrong. But they do not force this conclusion. Everything depends, then, on now finding further considerations for determining the way in which sense impressions figure in sensuous judgments.

If we place this issue in the context of the general assumptions which initiated the paper, and which were borrowed from Sellars' writings, an interesting thesis rather naturally falls out. Since it is not a thesis which Sellars shares, and since it concerns the role of sense impressions in perceptions, it will be of some interest to develop it and to compare it with what Sellars actually maintains about sense impressions.

The initial assumptions, we recall, were that judging is best understood by analogy to speaking, and that perception is a species of judgment. Evidently, a certain strong, formal resemblance exists between those statements in which we, as scribes recording the occurrences of the events, ascribe certain assertions to individuals and to those statements in which we ascribe certain thoughts to them. Evidently, there is a strong, formal resemblance between assertions and judgments in their own rights. Sellars has written extensively concerning speech as the model for thought. We assume here, without review, the "Thought-Speech" analogy and Sellars' characterization of it ([5], [6], [7]).

The "Thought-Speech" analogy, plausible as it may seem, is, as described by Sellars, less persuasive when perception (which is, on present assumptions, a species of thought) is compared with speech. For one thing, there is the familiar fact that experiences, and so our sensuous beliefs, outrun our powers of description. This is not simply the "one-picture, a-thousand-words" theme. In principle, the situation is worse. I may, for example, have to show you what I cannot tell you. The fact is that colors, for instance, shade continuously from hue to hue but not so our words for colors. I can detect, discriminate, and even reidentify sounds, traces in the air, and perhaps peripheral movements, each being things the recognition of which I can only teach you by confrontation. David Kaplan somewhere put it like this, "If we cannot even say it with words, but have to paint or sing it, we cannot believe it with words." It might once have seemed plausible to insist that I think in English, say. But it is not at all plausible to insist that I perceive in English. I do not. It follows that if sensuous believing is a species of thinking, the "Thought-Speech" analogy is, in one version, misleading. The model of thought as an internal version of overt speech misses an important feature of perception. And the feature which it misses is directly related to the occurrence and nature of the sense impressions which occur in our sensuous beliefs.

It is of some importance to note that the present failure of the analogy is on the side of the model, of overt saying. The point is not that the palpable model entities have features which the alleged, theoretical, hidden entities being modeled do not. That is familiar enough and acceptable. Speech after all is linear and used for communication, features which no one requires of thought. The failure lies the other way around. This is to say that the analogy misses instead something essential to what is modeled, something essential to the nature of sensuous belief. My complaint is not that the "Thought-Speech" analogy reverses our priorities, explaining thought in terms of speech, rather than the other way around. (I think it does, in fact, do this but that is another issue.) My complaint is rather that the analogy fails to do justice to what made it seem plausible and helpful in the first place.

If one stops to think about it, it is quite amazing that Sellars offers a model of thought based upon overt speech acts and yet offers a quite distinct and unrelated model of the occurrence of sense impressions. Yet perceptions are a species of thought, and sense impressions are (however their role may be characterized) intrinsic to perceptions. Somehow, one would have thought, the model of sense impressions has got to get linked with that of thoughts. Otherwise, our theories of thought—and so, too, our theories of perceptions as well, as a special species of thinking—should be theories quite unrelated to the occurrences of sense impressions. Or, turned around, the present point runs counter to Sellars' separation of the models of thought and sense impressions in a quite direct way: since a theory of thought must include, as genus to species, that of perception, and since occurrences of sense impressions are necessary conditions for the occurrence of acts of perception which they constitute, there can be no adequate, general model of thought which does not *thereby* model the role of sense impressions in the making of sensuous judgments as well.

Sellars' model of thought we know to be overt speech. Sellars' model of sense impressions is sketched like this:

> Analysis reveals a *second* way in which the sense of "impression of a red triangle" is related to the sense of "red and triangular physical object." The first has already been characterized by relating "S has an impression of a red triangle" to "S is in that state [brought about in normal circumstances by the influence of red and triangular physical objects on the eyes] etc." The second consists in the fact that visual impressions of red triangles are conceived as items which are analogous *in certain respects* to physical objects which are red and triangular on the facing side . . .

> (a) Impressions of red, blue, yellow, etc. triangles are implied to resemble-and-differ in a way which is formally analogous to that in which physical objects which are triangular and (red or blue or yellow, etc.) on the facing side resemble-and-differ; and similarly *mutatis mutandis* in the case of other shapes.

> (b) Impressions of red triangles, circles, squares, etc. are implied to resemble-and-differ in a way which is formally analogous to that in which physical objects which are red and (triangular or circular or square, etc.) on the facing side resemble-and-differ; and similarly *mutatis mutandis* in the case of other colors. ([7]: 258-59.)

Sellars' model of sense impressions (as *states* of a psychical agent) is, thus, that of a bunch of physical objects with certain properties. The structural relations which exist among the manifestations of these physical attributes model those which, on his theory of mind, obtain among certain states of the agent.

Evidently, then, Sellars' models of thought and of sense impressions are radically unrelated; they are literally as diverse as chips of wood and guttural mouthings. Unrelated as they are, not both can be satisfactory models for the full range of thought, including as that does sensuous judgments and so also sense impressions. One of the models, at least, must then go. The question is whether either model is salvageable and throws illumination upon our original inquiry. That inquiry was concerned with the question: What is the relationship of the sensuous content of our acts of perception to the perceptual acts of which they are constituents? What can be an adequate model of thought which will reflect this relationship?

What made the "Thought-Speech" analogy plausible in the first place resided in some very general, very pervasive features common to each. Both thought and speech are intentional; each has truth-values; the ascription of the occurrence of an act of either kind to an agent exhibits formal similarities to the ascription of the other kind to him; each is the subject of immediate, reflexive awareness; and so on. None of these similarities, of course, requires, or even suggests, that thought be viewed as internalized speech. A view like that is a further consequence of some given philosophical theory of thought. The analogy supports as well (and also as little) the opposite view: the view that speech is mere externalized thought. Neither of these further philosophical stances is relevant here. What is relevant here is not the priority of thought to speech, or of speech to thought. What is important is the fact that these analogous features do exist. The fact that they do exist ensures that, so far forth, then, speaking is a plausible, overt model for the covert mental occurrences which we call thinking. The intentionality of thought, for instance, *is* analogous to the intentionality of statement. And this is a fact of great importance.

The further point is that these very general and very pervasive features are shared by perceptions as well. Sensuous beliefs, like nonsensuous judgments and like overt sayings, are intentional, have truth-values, and are the objects of reflexive self-knowledge. They exhibit similar, common, formal features as well. It is worth remarking that in these important respects, the disanalogy we noticed earlier between seeing and saying, the fact that sensuous experience outruns our capacities for verbalization, no longer counts against the model. For the model is no longer a model of thought as internalized speech, but a model of perception as sharing the intentionality and general formal properties of the ascription of assertions to speaking agents. Given this account, moreover, a perfectly natural model of sense impressions is forthcoming. It falls out as a by-product of the model of a full theory of thought, a theory which includes, of course, sensuous thinking.

The model of sense impressions, implicit in the model of thoughts, is simply this: as predicates are to declarative sentences, as ascriptions are to assertions, as concepts are to judgments, as ascribing is to stating, so, too, sense impressions are to perceptions. Predicative ascriptions of qualities to objects in ordinary assertions of fact are the overt analogues, the models, of sense impressions as constituents of sensuous judgments. The using of conventional entities to characterize objects of reference is analogous to the having of natural entities—sense impressions—in seeing how an object is. In the natural, non-conventional, "language" of perception, sense impressions are ascriptions of sensuous qualities to the objects of perception. Sense impressions are the predicate "words" of perceptual, mental "assertions." The model goes through unusually well. For conventional words reveal and highlight features necessary to our characterizations of sense impressions. As we remarked earlier, conventional words are, materially, physical entities the production of which is the conventional mechanism by which we as agents perform certain functions necessary to the act of assertion. Equally, the having of sense impressions is the natural material base for the occurrence of acts of perception. The occurrences of sense impressions in acts of perception are the vehicles for the ascription of qualities to what is before one as the use of predicate words in the making of assertions is our way of describing an object of reference. As predicate words, the use of which is essential to assertions, are conceptual elements of assertions, so too, sense impressions, the occurrence of which is essential to perceptions, are conceptual elements of perceptions. Thus, the occurrence of a sense impression is the predication of a sense quality to an object, and so it is in this way that sense impressions are cognitive or conceptual elements of sensuous beliefs. That sense impressions are constituents of sensuous judgments in just this manner amounts to accepting the truth of (1) and (2) but the denial of (3) in the original trichotomy of propositions which initiated our discussion. It is, of course, accordingly, a view which is incompatible with that familiar from Sellars' writings. Sellars, we know, affirms (3).

The analogy between conventional quality words and sense impressions is, I believe, strikingly apt. Fundamentally, there is, of course, the familiar ordering of determinates under determinables in patterns of incompatibility. The record of these relationships, fixed in the correct usage of color words, is the conventional reflection of those quasi-analytical truths of perception that, e.g., nothing can be (at once) both red and green (all over). The sense impressions, falling within a given sense modality, are the primitive base in experience of such structures. This has implications within the theory, as we shall see later, in determining the identity of a single, basic, sensuous judgment.

But other similarities between sense impressions and quality predicates go through as well. There are, for instance, in a quite direct and not altogether trivial sense, sensuous homonyms as there are verbal homonyms. For just as two words may be identical in sound but differ in meaning, the contexts of their occurrence making, perhaps, the intended ascription clear, so also two sense impressions may, in their occurrent sensuous content, be identical while the contexts of their occurrence may make it quite evident that different qualities are ascribed by these occurrences to what is before one. A sense impression of an elliptical shape, say, in a given context, is, we know, a necessary constituent of the perception that the object seen from a certain perspective is round. This is, of course, something to be learned, case by case. Children and foreigners come to distinguish not merely words of different sound, but words which have the same sound but different meanings. So, too, we all come to distinguish the import of sense impressions, qualitatively indistinguishable, by the contexts of their occurrences. This is possible because we distinguish the occurrent properties of sense impressions and their semantical functions. We do this quite as we distinguish the occurrent properties of quality words and their semantical functions. This distinction itself is further evidence of the analogy of sense impressions to predicate words and the appropriateness of the model.

Words, of course, can be attended to in their own right. They can occur in isolation; they can be given voice, perhaps, solely for their amusing or pleasant euphony. They can be abstracted from their occurrences in the contexts of assertion. We can reflect upon them as items with their own occurrent properties. But so too are sense impressions items which can occur in isolation, which can be savored for their own characters, and which can be reflected upon in abstraction from their occurrences in the contexts of perceptual judgments. Of course, the capacity to recognize words as occurrent entities which are qualitatively the same is a necessary, though not sufficient, condition to perceiving some of them as homonyms. Equally, it is the capacity to recognize sense impressions as the same in their qualitative content which is a necessary condition for the acquisition of the distinction between how things appear and how things are, and for distinguishing occurrences of sense impressions which, although they are the same in their sensuous natures, nonetheless function in the different contexts of their occurrences as different ascriptions.

Semantically, predicates are sometimes formally viewed as those linguistic elements which are assigned functions. These functions take individuals as arguments into truth-values or perhaps facts. The homonyms of a natural language, then, are words which, though identical in sound, are, in the formal sense, assigned different functions. Homonyms differ in meaning at least in the precise and limited sense that, for certain arguments, they determine opposite truth-values. Homonyms are accidentally the same in certain occurrent properties. They are however quite different words with quite different meanings. The determination of which word an homonymous occurrence expresses is largely a matter of sensitivity to context. In practice, this involves discrimination both of its syntactic function in the larger linguistic context of its occurrence and of the pragmatic circumstances of the occasion of its utterance as well.

Something quite like this is true, I believe, of sense impressions as well. Viewed formally, we can think of these, too, as functions taking individuals into truth-values or facts. A pair of different sense impressions belonging to the same sense modality will, in contexts of occurrence which are otherwise the same, yield sensuous judgments which cannot both be true. And the same sense impression in different contexts of occurrence may yield sensuous judgments of opposite truth-values. Such impressions are, then, literally different sensuous ascriptions of what is before one. The determination of what sensuous ascription a given occurrent impression embodies involves sensitivity to the natural context of its occurrence and is a function of the state and knowledge of the observer as well. (These similarities of words and sense impressions are, of course, quite distinct from the further fact that a sense impression, of *red*, say, no more itself exemplifies the color it ascribes than does an arbitrary inscription of the word 'red'. This last one is, it happens, black.)

So far I have suggested that, contrary to Sellars' view of things, we accept propositions (1) and (2) and deny (3). I have suggested that perceptions are a species of thought, that sense impressions are indeed constituents of perceptions, and that sense impressions in fact are cognitive constituents of them. I have argued that, as constituents of perceptions, sense impressions play a role in natural experience analogous to the role conventionally performed by certain predicates in acts of assertion. (We have noted that, of course, it is *predicates* which occur in *statements* (in a theoretical sense which Sellars has been concerned to explicate in a certain manner). Predicate *words*, by contrast, are English or French words, say, and occur in *sentences*.) It is in this way, analogous to predicate words, that sense impressions are properly viewed as conceptual entities rather than mere causal mechanisms. This is the view of Everett Hall's naive realism ([2]). Hall, like Brentano, thought that all psychical occurrences are intentional, and so, he believed, they are all conceptual occurrences. Hall, it is clear, would have felt quite at home adapting Sellars' "Thought-Speech" analogy to his own purposes. He did himself explicitly invoke the model of predication for the explication of sense impressions. Sellars has directly commented upon Hall's "intentional realism" ([6]). We shall turn to his criticisms and to certain hard cases for Hall's view in a moment. We pause now for a few brief, and so unfair, last comments on Sellars' own characterization of sense impressions and their material model. These comments are based upon the passages quoted from him above.

Granted that our visual sense impressions of colored triangles resemble and differ from one another in a manner formally analogous to the way in which triangles of various colors on the facing side do, what are we to make of the fact? What insight does knowing these things about physical objects convey about sense impressions? (Contrast this with viewing the occurrences of sense impressions in perceptions by analogy with that of predicates in assertions, *and all that that entails*.) The gist of Sellars' account lies in the existence of a one-to-one relation between a psychical agent's states and the manifestations of certain material qualities of physical things. Perhaps a central difficulty with the view can be most briefly put by noting the science fiction it tempts us to indulge in. For surely there are, or may be, indefinite patterns of structures on each side of this one-to-one correlation. The facing objects in their complex physical states may well exhibit all sorts of patterns of physical properties invariant with certain states of observers. And on the other side, we can imagine all sorts of brain states invariant with patterns of physical stimulatory bombardments. Indeed, if we are allowed (on pain of otherwise begging questions) to be liberal enough with the concept of an observer, the numbers of scattered or submerged or cross-linked physiological states that may exist in just the required patterns of occurrence are probably scarcely more limited than our imaginations. What this misplaced scientism shows about sense impressions is difficult to tell. But in any case the model does not illuminate what is special and interesting about sense impressions as mental phenomenon: the fact that, and the way in which, the havings of sense impressions are *awarenesses of* the sensible qualities of material things, or, more accurately, of the way in which they are impressions of sensibly qualified material things. What the model does presuppose, of course, is the causal link between environment and experience which ties the occurrent impression, in the standard case, to one's surroundings. That fact, however, was never in question. The determination of the causal mechanisms was never the philosopher's task.

I revert, instead then, to our earlier model, to the view that sense impressions function semantically like certain predicates, the quality adjectives, of natural languages. Pointed questions like the following naturally arise. If sense impressions function in perceptions, semantically, as do predicates in ordinary assertions of fact, what then are their arguments? What, literally, are the occurrent references the application of certain sense impressions to which yields on that occasion a specific perception? Moreover, the set of perceptions, after all, consists not merely of ascriptions of qualities to the objects before one. It comprises as well recognitions and classifications of what is before one, of what something is made, or what a thing may do or be doing. Each of these is something that we on occasion sensuously judge. Each is something that we can know or believe by perception. How, then, are sense impressions related to these other sensuous beliefs? Finally, we need to know and say something about the nature of perceptions as judgments. What is their logic? How many judgments does a given perception embody? How does one tell? How should direct-object constructions, the sensuous awareness of objects, be construed? In what does the distinctness and identity of a sensuous judgment consist? These and other related questions are questions of what, on a given theory, sense impressions and sensuous judgments come to. They are accordingly questions upon which the present account of sense impressions must hazard answers, if it is to be at all a plausible candidate as a theory of the sensuous element in judgment. Some of these are questions which Sellars raised in his examination of Hall's "intentional realism" ([6]). The remainder of this paper is devoted to some comments on these questions.

Earlier, we employed a misleading idiom, speaking of the sense impression of *red*. The underlining is a symptom of a theoretical embarrassment. Our sense impressions are not of qualities but of qualified objects. I see, not colors, but (in the standard case) colored objects; I hear, not sounds, but sounding objects; I feel, not pains, but portions of my anatomy that hurt. My visual sense impression is an ascription of a color, say, to that which is visually before me, not to the impression itself. But what, for example, is, in the simplest cases, before me? To what is the color ascribed? By what natural forms does singular reference manifest itself in sensuous judgments?

No doubt in common cases the object of awareness to which the sensuous ascription is applied is some instance of a natural kind. No doubt in common cases natural reference to these comes *via* a sensuous recognition or identification of the instance as a certain case of the given kind or *via* a reidentification of the same object. But these common cases, familiar as they may be, are theoretically too complex for the level of analysis to which we aspire here. We do not have sense impressions of *ball* or *rubber*, and so we do not have epistemologically primitive singular references to balls or to things of a given material nature, as being such. Sense impressions are primary occurrences in the acquisition of knowledge. But sense impressions have secondary importance in explanatory power in the corpus of our sensuous beliefs. In general, the sensuous awareness that what is before me is a car ranks higher in the intellectual scheme of things than seeing something, I know not what, to be green. Evidently, then, a theory of sense impressions requires, as a theoretical characterization of the acquisition of knowledge, the ascription of sense qualities to entities prior to the later classifications which they may help to make available of those entities. We may think of perceptions of these minimal sorts as "basic perceptions." These are basic in two senses. First, they are ascriptions of simple sensuous qualities, the proper sensibles. Second, they have no internal, logical complexity. Each is simply a (single) qualitative ascription to a (single) object of reference. What are the vehicles of singular reference in basic perceptions? Hall put the point paradoxically: ". . . I have perceptions which are descriptive or predicative throughout . . ." And Sellars replied with puzzlement: ". . . how [can] a pure perception . . . be a *sentence*, and yet be 'predicative throughout'. . . . Must not pure perceptions contain expressions referring to an object in order to be able to characterize an object?" ([6]: 110.)

Sellars is right. Perceptions, if judgments, must contain referring elements. *A fortiori*, basic perceptions must. There are two comments to be made in explaining how this requirement, which must be fulfilled, is fulfilled, although basic perceptions nonetheless consist solely of sensuous ascriptions. The first comment is a mere palliative. Basic perceptions, we note, are required by theory, not necessarily encountered in practice. It may never be that an articulate user of language has, or recalls, basic perceptions at the point at which he has mastered language in a serviceable way. These are idealizations postulated to account for the empirical basis of the acquisition of the more complex, but standard, forms of sensuous belief.

Idealizations or not, the question requires an answer. It is true in a sense that basic perceptions are ascriptive throughout. Their sensuous content resides in the sense impression of which they consist. But they have a reference. And if the reference which they have is not itself carried by some articulate conceptualization of individualized, embodied, sense qualities, then it must be carried demonstratively. And it is. The sheer occurrence of an impression of a proper sensible, any at all, is in fact a putative ascription. We may later come to learn when to withhold such predications. But in basic perceptions, the occurrence of a sense impression in the context of its occurrence provides itself the demonstrative element of the sensuous judgment. Sense impressions are, after all, impressions of sensibly qualified objects putatively before one within the range of the given sense modality. It is the sensuous content of the occurrent impression which in the context of its occurrence determines the ascriptive element of the basic perception. It is the material occurrence of the impression in the given context which provides the demonstrative reference of that experience.

We can exploit Sellars' own writings to make our present point. In "Naming and Saying," he considers a perspicuous language in which predication is carried not by the juxtaposition of referring and predicate expressions but by writing names so that they manifest the qualities or relations to be ascribed their referents. Thus, writing the name "John" in red might be the vehicle to state what we should put in words by writing "John is red." In keeping with the "Thought-Speech" analogy, Sellars' perspicuous language provides the perfect linguistic vehicle to model basic perceptions. Basic perceptions are demonstrative occurrences which ascribe the content of the occurring sense impression to what is before one. The model of the basic perception that this before me is red is, in the perspicuous language, accordingly an occurrence of the demonstrative "This" written in red. Or, vocally, an occurrence of the vocable "This" uttered shrilly would be the vehicle by which we state that this is shrill. Just as the occurrence of a demonstrative is, in appropriate contexts, a reference to something in the surroundings, so too the occurrence of a sense impression is a reference to something before one of which he is aware. And just as the vehicle of reference in the perspicuous language manifests what is ascribed to the object of reference, so too the content of the sense impression is ascribed to that to which its occurrence makes demonstrative reference.

Semantically, sense impressions are functions taking the contexts of their own occurrences as arguments into truth-values or facts. They yield (perceptual) truths if the demonstrative references of their occurrences have the sensuous characters which their contents ascribe. The occurrence of a sense impression is an ascription the verbalization of which would run schematically thus: "This, sensuously before me, is thus and so." (All psychical phenomena, Brentano thought, have objects, and the occurrences of sense impressions are, after all, mental occurrences.)

This view has further implications for a theory of perception. Basic perceptions are now to be identified *via* the sense impressions which occur in them and the contexts of their occurrences. This means, for instance, that the following perceptions—this before me is red and round; this before me is red and sticky; this before me is red and that before me is green—are not individual perceptions of conjunctions of sense attributions to things. They are rather conjunctions of perceptions of things. Common, complex perceptions of what is the case in standard acts of awareness not only are not single basic perceptions, but on the present account, involving, as they typically do, awarenesses of the kinds and natures of things, they are not basic perceptions at all. They are, on the present account, clusters and groups of what, upon analysis, presuppose individual sensuous ascriptions of simpler kinds. The psychical agent, then, who sees that the object before him is a small, bouncy, red, rubber ball, has sensuously judged that something before him is red and has judged a whole lot more besides. (How much more, and how, the difficult questions which really interest us, are not questions the themes for answers to which I can provide here.) It is each basic perception, each ascription of a sense impression, coupled with the contextual reference of its occurrence, which counts as a single, distinguishable, minimal, perceptual act.

Sellars, by contrast, commenting upon clusters of ascriptions, puts it thus:

> The point at which I am driving is, in Kantian terms, that the perception of a manifold must not be confused with a manifold of perceptions. Thus, if we leave 'and' out of the language of pure perceptions, one could not pure-perceive an object to exemplify a number of properties all together. . . . Thus it could be argued that conjunctive perception involves a "conjunction introduction move" from the component perceptions. The important thing would be that the inner language of perception proper contained the logical apparatus for making this move, so that the move could occur *in it*. ([6]: 112-13.)

But, surely, Sellars' Kantian introduction of the logician's categories into the forms of the manifold of sense cannot *in general*, at least, be right. It is not right, surely, for basic perceptions. A psychical agent, assume, sensuously believes on a given occasion that something before him is ϕ, and he sensuously believes on that same occasion that something before him is ψ. Does it indeed then follow that the agent believes on that occasion that something before him is both ϕ and ψ? Since these are basic perceptions, the primitive experiential base of awareness by assumption on the theory, these perceptions are, at least sometimes, ascriptions of proper sensibles to what is before the agent. And if this is so, then, since one does not on the same occasion simultaneously have multiple sense impressions in the same sense modality of the same object, our agent's ascriptions must in fact be cross-modal ascriptions. (One, perhaps, is visual; the other perhaps tactual. Thus, the agent may know (by sight, say) that what is (visually) before him is red. And, on the same occasion the agent may know that what is (tactually) before him is sticky.) But surely there is no contradiction, however broad our categories of rationality, in supposing that the agent does not know or believe on this occasion that what is red is what is sticky. If so, he need not believe that some one thing before him is both. Evidently, "conjunction introduction" is *not* part of the logic of "inner sense," if this is the logic of basic perceptions.

Unlike Sellars, I do not think of the logical connectives as part of perceptual judgments. Certainly not on the primitive level of basic perceptions. There are, in fact, some logical gadgetry and a philosophical stance which suggest viewing matters quite oppositely. We think instead of Gentzenian reductions, of backward reasonings; perhaps these are Peircean abductions, rather than the introduction into sense of Kantian categories. In any case, given that an agent does sensuously believe that something both ϕ's and ψ's (where perhaps these are the ascriptions of sense impressions), we may indeed posit both that the agent sensuously believes that this is ϕ and sensuously believes as well that this is ψ. As in all good theorizing, we assume in such a case the simplest sufficient conditions which will account for the fact to be explained. If the agent believes both things, then he must believe each and be in command as well of the concept of conjunction. But, note, this is not to be in command of a perceptual conjunction, whatever that may be.

It is, I believe, part of the logic of perception that the ascription of any perception to an agent entails that there exists a sense impression which the agent experiences. It is, further, part of the logic of perception, if the present account is right, that the ascription of the perception of a conjunction to a psychical agent implies a conjunction of such ascriptions to him, indexed to the same occasion. But the converse, we have argued, is not true. This is of some interest, for it suggests a seam at which the logic of sensuous judgment gets stitched to the total corpus of an agent's beliefs. Thus, while it does not follow from the fact that a psychical agent sensuously judges on an occasion that P, and also sensuously judges on that occasion that Q, that the agent therefore on the given occasion sensuously judges that both, still it does follow that he must (virtually) judge (albeit non-sensuously) on that occasion that both P and Q. For what one sensuously believes, one believes. And an agent who believes each of two things is, if rational, an agent who virtually accepts their conjunction. This is nice, for it suggests that we can keep a primitive experiential base for perception unsullied by the intrusion of Kantian categories of logic. On the other hand, the introduction of logical connections among beliefs and so, with it, the further possibility of relating certain complex and non-basic perceptions, e.g. of kinds, to basic sense impressions remains quite available.

We cannot further explore here the formal features of Hall's "intentional realism."[2] It is clear how some of the questions which remain dangling must be treated by the theory. Direct-object constructions, for instance, give way on this view to that-constructions. One hears, not sounds, but sounding objects; in being sensuously aware of an object, one sensuously judges something of how it manifestly is. But however these further matters go, the main point which remains is this: an adequate theory of perception can characterize sense impressions as cognitive elements in perception without, thereby, incorporating the full, formal powers of conventional language into our primitive experiences.[3]

2. Some brief remarks of mine concerning quantification into epistemic ascriptions have been an object of criticism by Robert C. Sleigh, [8]. I hope to respond to these in detail soon.

3. I am indebted to Ausonio Marras for helpful comments and criticisms of a draft of this paper. There has been neither space nor time to make more than minimal corrections in the wording of the text; more substantial alterations and amplifications in the light of his comments must be postponed.

REFERENCES

[1] Peter Geach, *Mental Acts* (London: Routledge & Kegan Paul, 1957).

[2] Everett Hall, *Our Knowledge of Fact and Value* (Chapel Hill: University of North Carolina Press, 1961).

[3] Jaakko Hintikka, *Knowledge and Belief* (Ithaca, N. Y.: Cornell University Press, 1962).

[4] _____, "On the Logic of Perception," in Norman S. Care and Robert H. Grimm, eds., *Perception and Personal Identity* (Cleveland: The Press of Case Western Reserve University, 1969).

[5] Wilfrid Sellars, "Empiricism and the Philosophy of Mind," in H. Feigl and M. Scriven, eds., *Minnesota Studies in the Philosophy of Science*, Vol. I (Minneapolis: University of Minnesota Press, 1956).

[6] _____, "The Intentional Realism of Everett Hall," *Southern Journal of Philosophy* 4 (1966): 103-15.

[7] _____, "Phenomenalism," in Hector-Neri Castañeda, ed., *Intentionality, Minds, and Perception* (Detroit: Wayne State University Press, 1967).

[8] Robert C. Sleigh, "Restricted Range in Epistemic Logic," *Journal of Philosophy* 69 (1972): 67-77.

·~ ·6· ~ ·

Perceptual Objects, Elementary Particles, and Emergent Properties

REINHARDT GROSSMANN

Indiana University

I F WE analyze a perceptual object far enough into its spatial parts, we arrive eventually at so-called elementary particles. Physicists tell us that, to the best of their present knowledge, these particles have certain properties and lack others. In particular, they tell us that the elementary particles of which perceptual objects consist do not share with these objects all their properties. Particles have properties which perceptual objects do not have, and conversely. For example, while perceptual objects are colored, the elementary particles of which they consist are not colored.

According to some philosophers, this discovery of the physicists poses a problem. They accept the discovery but feel that it proves that a perceptual object cannot really be one and the same thing as the structure consisting of the particles which are the spatial parts of the perceptual object. This conclusion follows, presumably, from a straightforward application of Leibniz' principle that entities with different properties must be different. It may lead to the view which is so aptly expressed in Eddington's claim that there are really two tables, with one of which, the perceptual table, he has been familiar from earliest years, and with the other of which, the physical table, he has more recently become acquainted ([5]: xi-xii). Or it may lead to a denial of the existence of one of Eddington's two tables. Some philosophers insist that physics be granted the last word when it is a question of what there is; and since physics apparently shows that elementary particles have no color, they conclude—no matter how absurd that may sound—that there are no perceptual objects. Perceptual objects, they sometimes add by way of explanation, are merely appearances to human observers of structures of imperceptible particles. Other philosophers maintain that common sense has the decisive say when it is a matter of what exists; and since there are clearly tables, and since they are equally clearly colored, they insist that there can be no such things as elementary particles. According to the spirit of this position, elementary particles are merely logical constructions, inventions of the human mind. There are, finally, some philosophers who accept the physicists' theory and who agree with Eddington that there are indeed two tables, but who also claim that the two tables are, in some sense of the term, identical. They hold that the perceptual table is, strictly speaking, not the same as the spatial structure of elementary particles. But they also hold that these two different things are in a certain way coordinated with each other. It is this particular coordination which common sense is prone to confuse with sameness or identity (see [1]: 40-58).

There are also philosophers who find all of these positions unacceptable; and since they do not see how one could possibly avoid one of these positions if one accepts the physicists' theory, they feel compelled to contradict the physicists. Since the perceptual table is quite obviously colored, so they argue, the physicists must be simply wrong when they tell us that elementary particles have no color. Other philosophers take the opposite way out. The facts of physics do not show, according to their view, that there is no perceptual table, but merely that it is not colored.

However, we do not have to choose among these, in my opinion, equally unacceptable alternatives. Here is a case where we can eat our cake and have it too. We can agree with the physicist and, at the same time, live in peace with common sense.

Common sense is right: there are perceptual objects, and they are colored. But it is also true that, say, a table consists of elementary particles and that these particles are not colored. The physicist is not mistaken either. However, it does not follow that there must, therefore, be two tables, as Eddington claims. A table consists spatially of elementary particles—that is, entities of a certain kind, which have certain properties, which stand in certain relations to each other, and which are the ultimate spatial parts of a table. Compare the table with another perceptual object, say, a chessboard consisting of sixty-four squares.

This chessboard consists of sixty-four squares in the very same spatial sense in which the table consists of elementary particles.[1] And just as it does not follow that there must be a second chessboard (a geometrical chessboard?), so it does not follow that there must be a second table in addition to a perceptual one.

Of course, the table is not identical with any one of its particles, just as the chessboard is not the same as any one of its squares. More importantly, the table is not even identical with the class of its elementary particles; and the chessboard is not the same as the class of its squares. The table and the chessboard are both spatial wholes, not classes of any kind. They belong to an entirely different ontological category, namely to the category of what I shall call *structures*. The table is a spatial structure whose ultimate spatial parts are elementary particles. The chessboard is a spatial structure whose spatial parts—but not its ultimate spatial parts—are squares.

Are we, then, implying that Leibniz' principle does not hold in this case? Are we committing ourselves to the view that one and the same perceptual object, the table, can be both colored and also not colored? Of course not. The physicist does not claim that the spatial structures which are tables are not colored. He merely maintains that certain very small spatial parts of these structures, elementary particles, are not colored. He merely claims that certain very small spatial parts of the table do not have the same properties as the table itself. But this should not come as a philosophical shock to anyone. We do not have to consider such esoteric entities as elementary particles in order to see that the spatial parts of a perceptual object may not have the same properties as the perceptual object of which they are parts. For example, some squares of the chessboard are white, but the chessboard itself is not white; only parts of it are white. Or imagine a square A whose diagonals have been drawn, so that it consists of four triangles. A is square, but none of its four spatial parts has this property. On the other hand, every one of the four parts of A is triangular, even though A itself is square. To sum up, if we acknowledge that a perceptual object may have properties which are quite different from the properties which its spatial parts have, then we are not forced to accept one of those unsatisfactory positions listed earlier. In particular, we do not have to duplicate

---

1. More precisely, the chessboard consists of "rectangular solids" with two square sides. When I speak of squares, I really mean here these bodies.

tables, nor do we have to choose between perceptual objects, on the one hand, and elementary particles, on the other.

Tables are colored, elementary particles are not. But the former consist, in a spatial sense, of the latter. There is no puzzle. No drastic revision of our beliefs—including those of the physicist—is necessary. Why, then, is there the appearance of a philosophical issue? I shall venture a guess. Perhaps, our defense of common sense clashes with a rather pervasive philosophical dogma. Let us see.

I

Sellars, who has discussed this matter more thoroughly and more astutely than most contemporary philosophers, argues that we have to choose, as I put it, between perceptual objects and elementary particles, between the manifest image, as he puts it, and the scientific image (see [11]). Does he mean to say that there are no perceptual objects, that only the elementary particles of the physicists' theory exist? I do not know for sure. There are statements which seem to speak for this interpretation. For example: "According to the view I am proposing, correspondence rules would appear in the material mode as statements to the effect that the objects of the observational framework *do not really exist—there really are no such things*" ([11]: 126). On the other hand, Sellars states repeatedly that his view is to be interpreted as a claim about the framework of perceptual objects. For example: "To say that there are no such things as the physical objects of the perceptible world is, of course, to make a point *about* the framework of physical objects, not *in* it ([11]: 97). Now, to talk about the framework of perceptual objects, one may think, is to talk, not about perceptual objects pure and simple, but rather about a linguistic and/or conceptual system. Hence, one may conclude that Sellars does not mean to deny the existence of perceptual objects in any straightforward fashion, but that he is advocating the rejection of some kind of linguistic and/or conceptual system. Of course, what comes to mind in this connection is Carnap's well-known distinction between internal and external questions of existence.[2] But it is not clear—at least to me—whether or not Sellars

---

2. Compare Carnap's statement: "And now we must distinguish two kinds of questions of existence: first, questions of the existence of certain entities of the new kind *within the framework*; we call them *internal questions*; and second, questions concerning the existence or reality *of the system of entities as a whole*, called external questions" ([2]: 206).

wants to use Carnap's distinction in this context without, at least, some modifications and, perhaps, even drastic ones.

Be that as it may, if Sellars is talking about linguistic and/or conceptual frameworks rather than perceptual objects as part of the furniture of the world, then it is not at all obvious that the framework of common sense and the framework of physics clash, as long as we keep them apart (cf. [8]). Why could we not make use of both frameworks—side by side, as it were—without praising either one as the "true" or "basic" framework? It is clear that Sellars does prefer the framework of the scientist—the scientific image—and that his preference is not just a matter of taste. He believes that the framework of the scientist is not on the same footing with that of common sense. The framework of the scientist is adequate, the framework of common sense is not: ". . . although the framework of perceptible objects, the manifest framework of everyday life, is adequate for the everyday purposes of life, it is ultimately inadequate and should not be accepted as an account of what there is *all things considered*" ([11]: 27). But just when we are ready to make up our minds that Sellars does indeed want to say that perceptual objects do not really have the properties which common sense ascribes to them, we read in the same context that "the claim that physical objects," what I call perceptual objects in this paper, "do not really have perceptible qualities is not analogous to the claim that something generally believed to be true about a certain kind of thing is actually false" ([11]: 27). One gets the impression from these and similar passages that Sellars is on the side of the physicist, that he does reject some of our common-sense beliefs about perceptual objects, but that he tries to soften the blow to these most cherished beliefs by formulating his rejection in terms of the distinction between questions within and questions about the framework of everyday life. However, irrespective of whether or not Sellars does indeed believe that the scientific framework and the framework of everyday life are irreconcilable, I shall hold him to at least this much, namely, the view that a perceptual object cannot be colored if it is a structure consisting of elementary particles. How does Sellars argue for this view?

II

Sellars maintains that a perceptual object cannot be identical with a structure of elementary particles "in that simple sense in which a forest is identical with a number of trees" ([11]: 26). However, he also concedes that "there is nothing immediately paradoxical about the view that an object can be both a perceptible object with perceptible qualities *and* a system of imperceptible objects, none of which has perceptible qualities"; for, as Sellars asks rhetorically, "Cannot systems have properties which their parts do not have?" ([11]: 26). Indeed, cannot a table have properties that the particles of which it consists do not have? According to Sellars, the answer is affirmative as long as we have only certain properties in mind, but it is negative if we think of the colors of perceptual objects. Quite clearly, he wishes to draw a distinction between two kinds of properties. What are these two kinds?

Sellars' explication is at this point not as clear as one would wish. A structure of pieces of wood, according to him, can have the property of being a ladder, even though none of its parts is a ladder. What holds here for the property of being a ladder, holds presumably for many other properties. These properties have in common, in Sellars' words, that "these properties are a matter of the parts having such-and-such qualities and being related in such and such ways" ([11]: 26). The color of a pink ice cube, on the other hand, is in his view a property of an entirely different kind. He holds that one cannot plausibly maintain that the color of this pink ice cube is a matter of its parts (elementary particles) having such–and–such imperceptible qualities and standing in such–and–such imperceptible relations to each other. Sellars puts it this way: "Pink does not seem to be made up of imperceptible qualities in the way in which being a ladder is made up of being cylindrical (the rungs), rectangular (the frame), wooden, etc." ([11]: 26). The principle of this division of all properties of perceptual objects into those that are merely a matter of the parts' having certain properties and standing in certain relations to each other, and those that are not, is as follows: "If an object is *in a strict sense* a system of objects, then every property of the object must consist in the fact that its constitutents have such-and -such qualities and stand in such-and-such relations, or, roughly, every property of a system of objects consists of properties of, and relations between, its constitutents" ([11]: 27).

What Sellars is driving at, I think, is this. The colors of objects are alleged to be *irreducible* properties of such objects. If one holds that a perceptual object is a structure of elementary particles, then no property of such a structure could be irreducible. Hence one cannot hold both that the colors of perceptual objects are irreducible properties of these objects and also that perceptual objects are structures of elementary particles. Sellars' main contention is thus that all the properties of a structure must be reducible rather than irreducible. Structures, in his view, cannot have irreducible properties. What properties they do have are reducible to the properties of their parts and the relations among these parts.[3] In one sentence, Sellars holds that there are no *emergent properties*.

Sellars gives the property of being a ladder as an example of a reducible property; presumably, this property can be "defined" in terms of the properties of and the relations among the parts of the ladder. The color pink, on the other hand, can, allegedly, not be so defined. Before we can evaluate Sellars' argument, we must try to clear up the notion of reduction which is here at work. We must attempt to explicate the relevant sense in which a property may be said to *consist* of other properties and relations.

III

Consider a perceptual object, *A*, which is both square and red. Assume that someone decides to abbreviate the sentence '*A* is square and *A* is red' first by '*A* is square and red' and then by '*A* is squed'. Do we now have a property—represented by the expression 'squed'—which consists in the relevant sense of the two properties of being square and of being red? Is there a property of being squed which can be reduced—in the sense which we wish to explicate—to the two properties of being square and of being red? The question of reduction is premature. At this point, there is absolutely no reason for assuming that the expression 'squed' represents a property, and hence there is no reason for assuming that it represents a reducible property consisting of other properties. From the fact that there exists the abbreviation '*A* is squed' and, therefore, the expression 'squed', it does not follow that there also exists a property squed. We must not read into the abbreviation anything that cannot be gotten out of the abbreviated expression. In particular, we must not treat the expression 'squed' as if it were a predicate which represents a property.[4] Otherwise, we may come to believe,

3. Sellars speaks in this connection of a *principle of reducibility* ([11]: 35).
4. Of course, this point has often been made. Compare, for example, [4]: 323. But its lesson has seldom been drawn.

mistakenly to be sure, that the abbreviation proposal does not only introduce a completely arbitrary shape 'squed', but also a property squed. If we treat 'squed', not as a completely arbitrary expression, but as a predicate, then we make covertly the entirely unjustified ontological assumption that there exists such a property as squed. It follows, therefore, that it would be a mistake to think of 'squed' as representing a property which can be *reduced* to other properties, since it *consists* of other properties. If the expression 'squed' is introduced in the manner described earlier, then there simply is no such property as squed, and the question of reducibility cannot even arise.

It would, of course, be easy to avoid hidden injections of ontological assumptions under the cover of mere abbreviation proposals by choosing only expressions without prior meaning as parts of so-called *contextual definitions*. But this elementary precaution, significantly enough, clashes in most cases with the very reason for using a contextual definition. In most cases, there is no point at all in proposing a contextual definition, unless one tries to smuggle in certain ontological assumptions through the use of misleading expressions in the abbreviation. Consider, for example, the so-called contextual definition of class terms. One usually proposes to use the expression '*e* is a member of the class determined by the property *F*' as just another expression—one can hardly call it an abbreviation—for the fact that *e* is *F*. If this alleged definition were really a mere abbreviation proposal, no intelligible purpose could possibly be served by using such expressions as 'class' and 'member'. These words should be avoided at any cost; for they cannot but give the mistaken impression that one is talking about classes and their members when all one is talking about are properties and the things that have them. On the other hand, if the intention is to introduce classes and membership—as distinguished from properties and exemplification—then no mere abbreviation proposal could possibly turn the trick. The words 'class' and 'member' must then be used with their ordinary meaning. The proponent of this contextual definition cannot eat his cake and have it too. Either the shapes 'class' and 'member' in the alleged abbreviation have no prior meaning of their own, or they mean here what they usually mean. In the first case, one merely creates unnecessary confusion by using them and, hence, should avoid them. In the second case, the contextual definition cannot really be a harmless abbreviation proposal. On closer inspection, it turns out to be a disguised equivalence statement, namely, the statement that for all *e* and for all F, e is a member of the class determined by F if and only if e is F. This equivalence statement should never be called a definition; for, as Frege remarks: "One must never present as a definition that which requires proof or an intuition to establish its truth" ([6]: 5). It is in reality a law that connects the theory of classes (set theory) with the theory of properties (monadic predicate logic). As such, it presupposes the existence of classes and of the membership relation just as much as the existence of properties and of exemplification. Almost all so-called contextual definitions turn out to be disguised equivalence statements void of any reductive ontological power.

From the fact that 'A is squed' is an abbreviation of 'A is square and red' it does not follow, as I have argued, that there exists a property, whether reducible or not, represented by the expression 'squed'. Yet, it is a dogma among philosophers and, especially, among logicians that an expression like 'squed' represents a property. They rely in all such cases on what I shall call the *principle of property abstraction*. According to this principle, there always exists a property F such that an entity e has this property if and only if . . . e . . . is the case, where the dots indicate any well-formed propositional context.[5] If this principle were true, then there would be such a property as squed. Furthermore, if the principle of property abstraction holds, there seems to flow from it an explication of the notion of a reducible property. A reducible property, one might be tempted to say, is simply a property which exists by the principle of property abstraction. For example, if the well-formed propositional context involved mentions the properties U, V, W, etc., then the abstracted property, F, would be said to consist of the properties U, V, W, etc. But things, as it turns out, are not that simple. The so-called principle of property abstraction consists really of two principles. Depending on which one of these two principles we have in mind, there are two quite different explications of the notion of a reducible property.

Consider the allegedly abstracted property squed. What property could that possibly be? What further property is common to all square and red things and only to such things? There is no plausible candidate. But this seems to show that we have no reason for accepting the principle of property abstraction in its full generality. Granted that some things have additional properties if and only if they have some other properties, there seems to be quite a number of exceptions to this rule. But is it not true that even though there does not exist a third property,

5. I talk here only about properties, but what I say applies automatically to relations.

on a par with square and red, there exists, at least, the property of *being both square and red*? And if there exists this property, then there is after all no exception to the principle of property abstraction; for there always exists the property which is represented by the relevant propositional form. It is this additional idea, it seems clear, that convinces many of the soundness of the principle of property abstraction. But we must be quite clear that we have discovered a new principle—hidden behind the principle of property abstraction, so to speak—to the effect that every well-formed propositional form represents a property. I shall call this the *dogma of complex properties*. This dogma must be quite carefully distinguished from what I shall call from now on the principle of property abstraction proper. Without the dogma of complex properties, as we have seen, the principle of property abstraction proper has very little to recommend itself.

The dogma of complex properties, if true, would yield the following explication of a reducible property. To say of a property that it is reducible is to say that it is represented by a well-formed (complex) propositional form. Such a property reduces to the properties mentioned in the propositional form. But this explication is not forthcoming, alas, because the dogma of complex properties is false.

If we assume that it is a fact that the individual thing A is both square and red, then A most certainly exists, and so do the two properties square and red. But there is no third property, there is no other entity belonging to the category of property, that could be called the property of being both square and red.[6] I know of no argument that establishes the existence of such a third property. Quite to the contrary, the briefest of reflections seems to show that no complex propositional form whatsoever represents a property. If it is a fact that A is identical with A, then there exists the entity A and also—at least in my view—the relation of identity. But there is no such thing as the property of being identical with A. If it is a fact that A is to the left of B, then the relation of being to the left of exists as well as A and B, but there is no such thing as the property of being to the left of B. To believe that there exist such entities as the property of being both square and red, the property of being identical with A, and the property of being to the left of B is sheer ontological superstition.

6. Of course, we may go on talking about such properties as the property of being both square and red. But we must always remember—when it matters to ontology—that to say of something that it has the property of being both square and red is really to say that it is square and red.

To see this clearly, consider the fact that A is to the left of B. If we accept the dogma of complex properties, then we are committed to the view that in this case there exist, not only the relation of being to the left of, but also the two additional properties of being to the left of B and of A's being to the left of something. Since these are three different entities, there must also be three different facts of which these entities are constituents, namely, the fact that A stands to B in the relation of being to the left of, the fact that A has the (relational) property of being to the left of B, and the fact that B has the (relational) property that A is to the left of it. Yet it is quite obvious that there is only one such fact, namely, that A is to the left of B. As Ramsey once put it: ". . . the theory of complex universals is responsible for an incomprehensible trinity, as senseless as that of theology" ([9]: 118).

It may be objected to our rejection of the dogma of complex properties that complex properties must exist, because there is something common to A and B if A as well as B is both square and red. If A and B have something in common, so the argument goes, what they have in common must be a property which both of them share, namely, the property of being both square and red. Now it is true that—in a manner of speaking—there is something common to A and B in this case. But what they have in common is not a property. Rather, A and B are constituents of similar facts. The similiarity between the fact that A is square and red and the fact that B is square and red does not consist in that these two facts contain, in addition to different individual things, one and the same complex property, but, rather, in that both of them contain the same constituents in the same order: both facts contain as further constituents *exemplification* (each fact contains this constituent twice), *square, red,* and *and.*[7] We may express this similarity by saying that the structure of (the rest of) the two facts is the same. It is this identity of structure of two facts which is the common element in all those cases where one is tempted to speak of a common complex property. In short, it is not A and B which have something in common, a shared property, but the two facts.

There is another objection against our view. If there are several things which are both square and red, then there exists the class of all those things which are square and red. But how could this class exist, it may be said, unless the complex property of being square and red existed, for,

---

7. There is a criterion for the identity of facts (states of affairs): two facts are the same if and only if they have the same constituents in the same order the same number of times.

surely, this property must determine the class? According to this argument, every class must be determined by a property. But this assumption is false. There are many classes for which no determining property exists. For example, the intersection of any two (existing) classes exists, even if there is no property which determines the intersection; the power set of every (existing) class exists, whether or not there is a corresponding property; there also exists for every (existing) class the union class, irrespective of whether or not there exists the relevant property; and so on. Starting with a collection of entities which are not classes, there exists the class of all subsets of this collection. There exists, furthermore, the class of all subsets of this second class. And so on. Moreover, there also exists the union of all the classes of this hierarchy, and this union, in turn, has a power set. And so on. All these classes exist quite independently of whether or not there are any corresponding properties.[8] This reply to the objection, I submit, agrees well with the spirit in which Zermelo approached the axiomatization of set theory.

I conclude, then, that we cannot explicate the notion of a reducible property in terms of the dogma of complex properties. But what about the principle of property abstraction proper? Granted that complex propositional forms do not represent complex properties, granted, therefore, that the principle of property abstraction proper does not always hold, could we not use it to explicate the notion of a reducible property at least whenever it does hold? Assume that there exists, as a matter of brute fact, a certain property, *squed*, such that a thing is squed if and only if it is both square and red. Does it make any sense to claim in this case that squed is a reducible property, and that it reduces to the two properties square and red? I do not think so. There are three properties involved here, ontologically speaking, and to speak of reduction would be utterly misleading. The situation is precisely as I have described it: there are three properties involved, but these properties are "connected" with each other; an entity has one of these properties if and only if it has the other two. It would be as misleading to speak of reduction in this case as it would be if we were to say that coextensive properties are reducible to each other.

Of course, when we turn to perceptual objects and their spatial parts, the situation is slightly different. But this difference makes no difference

8. That not every class is determined by a property is only one side of a coin. The other side consists in the fact that not every property determines a class, as the set-theoretical paradoxes show.

for our point. The properties which are "connected" are not properties of the same thing. Rather, one of these properties is a property of a perceptual object, while the rest are properties (and relations) of parts of the perceptual object. The relevant equivalence statement, therefore, reads like this: A perceptual object has the property F if and only if its elementary particles have the properties U, V, W, etc., and stand in the relations R, S, T, etc. to each other. It is clear that we cannot explicate Sellars' notion of a reducible property in terms of such equivalences; for, then, we would have to say that the color pink is a reducible rather than an irreducible property of perceptual objects.[9]

Since this last attempt at explicating Sellars' notion of a reducible property fails, it may seem that there simply is no acceptable explication and, hence, no clear notion. I am convinced that this conclusion is basically sound. But I also believe that Sellars' point can be made in a different way. The sentence 'A is a ladder', we may say, is merely short for the longer sentence 'A consists spatially of such-and-such pieces of wood of such-and-such shapes which stand in such-and-such relations to each other'. The idea is, of course, that the longer sentence mentions only properties of and relations among spatial parts of A. When we say that A is pink, on the other hand, we are not abbreviating in this fashion a longer statement about the properties of and relations among the parts of A. Let us grant, for the sake of the argument, that these two assertions about the expressions 'ladder' and 'pink' are true. Then we can reformulate Sellars' principle of reducibility as follows: All statements which purport to attribute properties to a system of entities are in reality mere abbreviations of longer statements about the properties of and relations among the parts of the system. Notice that according to this reformulation, structures simply have no properties and, in particular, no properties that *consist* of other properties (and relations). That this is the only viable version of Sellars' principle is the lesson of our previous considerations. Sellars' argument now comes down to this. If a perceptual object were a structure consisting of elementary particles, then all statements which purport to attribute properties to the perceptual object would have to be, in reality, abbreviations for statements about proper-

---

9. This, however, is the notion of reduction which plays an important role in the traditional discussion of emergent properties. Compare, for example, the following definition of emergence by Hempel and Oppenheim: "The occurrence of a characteristic W in an object w is emergent relatively to a theory T, a part relation Pt, and a class G of attributes if that occurrence cannot be deduced by means of T from a characterization of the Pt-parts of w with respect to all the attributes in G" ([7]: 336).

ties of and relations among the parts of the perceptual object. But a statement to the effect that a certain perceptual object has a certain color is not an abbreviation of this sort. Therefore, a perceptual object cannot be identical with a structure of elementary particles.

Since I agree with Sellars that statements about the colors of perceptual objects are not abbreviations, but since I also claim—in opposition to Sellars—that perceptual objects are structures of elementary particles, I must reject this principle of reduction. Structures, I maintain, have properties of their own. They have properties which are not reducible—in the sense explicated above—to properties of and relations among their parts. Once pointed out, it seems rather obvious that the principle of reduction is actually false. Nor do we have to compare colors of perceptual objects with the rather esoteric properties of elementary particles to see that it is false. Recall the square A with its diagonals drawn. It consists of four triangles which stand in certain spatial relations to each other. A has the property of being square, even though none of its four spatial parts has this property. It cannot be an abbreviation to say that A is square; for there are squares which do not consist of triangles but consist, for example, of smaller squares. There are even squares which have no perceptible spatial parts. In general, shape—just like color—is an emergent property. It is not reducible—in the sense explicated above—to the properties of and relations among the spatial parts of the shaped object.

On the other hand, I do not claim that structures have all the properties commonly attributed to them. I granted earlier, for the sake of comparison, that the property of being a ladder is a reducible property, that is, that there really is no such thing. Perhaps, there isn't; although I must confess that I am inclined to think that there is. But I am quite sure about some other alleged properties of structures. Take, for example, the "property" of the series of natural numbers of having a first but no last element. To attribute this "property" to the series, I am certain, is to say that there is an element such that all other elements of the series are larger than this one, while there is no element which is the largest. Therefore, our thesis is not that all the alleged properties of structures exist, but merely that there are properties of structures. More specifically, we hold that colors and shapes are emergent properties of spatial structures. We are not committed to accept such suspect properties as "the will of the people," "the mood of the crowd," and the like. It is not to be decided by an a priori argument whether there are properties of structures. This is entirely a factual matter. There are properties that belong quite clearly to certain structures; there are also alleged properties of structures which rather obviously do not exist; and in some cases there may be justified doubt. I am here defending only two essential assertions. First, there are structures. Second, there are properties of structures.

We are now in a position to appreciate the full force of Sellars' argument against the identity of perceptual objects with structures of particles. Nothing less is at stake than the existence of emergent properties. It must be admitted that the recent tradition is on Sellars' side. The commonly accepted view is that the properties of structures can be "defined" in terms of and, hence, "reduced" to properties of and relations among the parts of such structures. It is this widely accepted view, I submit, which is, at least in part, responsible for the notion that the scientist's discovery of colorless particles clashes with the common-sense belief in colored perceptual objects.

IV

In a different context, Sellars raises another objection against the view that perceptual objects are structures of elementary particles.[10] His argument is interesting not only for its own sake, but also because it throws some light on the important notion of structure. Sellars argues, if I understand him correctly, that one cannot show that, say, pink can be attributed to a structure, unless one shows that some statement of the form 'pink (. . .)' is true, where the expression filling the blank belongs "to the conceptual space of a set of elements, and [has] the appropriate logical form for referring to an aggregate of [the] elements" ([3]: 300). It will not do, according to Sellars, to fill the blank with an expression for a perceptual object, say, the description expression 'the table in front of me'; for the "problem of in what sense tables are 'in fact' aggregates is left completely unilluminated" ([3]: 300). What Sellars has in mind may be that one assumes what one is supposed to prove if one (a) points out

10. See Sellars' rejoinder to B. Aune's comments in [3]: 299-300. There exists also still another argument by Sellars, the so-called grain argument. (See, especially, [10].) I do not discuss this argument in my paper, because it reduces—if I understand it correctly—to the same kind of argument as the one which we have been talking about in terms of the color pink.

that one can say that the table is pink—that this is a proper statement—and (b) concludes that pink is a property of structures; for then one simply takes for granted that the table is a structure, without explaining in what sense and how it is a structure. If this is Sellars' point, let us substitute for the statement 'The table in front of me is pink' the more detailed sentence 'The structure which consists of such-and-such particles standing in such-and-such relations to each other is pink', where the blanks have to be filled in by the physicist, so that we have a very detailed description of the structure under consideration in terms of its physical constituents. It is my impression, though, that this elaboration would still not satisfy Sellars; for what he is driving at is that, if we fill the blank in 'pink (. . .)' with a genuine expression for an aggregrate (structure), we will get "a number of subjects" for the property pink, so that this property will have to be relational. We will then get something of the form 'pink $(x_1, x_2, x_3, \ldots)$,' and pink will be a relation holding among x_1, x_2, x_3, etc. But since pink is quite clearly not a relation, as is agreed by all parties to the dispute, pink cannot be a property of structures. According to this interpretation, Sellars is saying that, if we try to give a detailed analysis of the perceptual object and do not just assume that it is a structure of elementary particles, then we will inevitably arrive at a statement in which pink is attributed, not just to one subject, but to several such subjects. Hence we shall have to give up the view that pink is a property rather than a relation.

However, the statement which was mentioned above, containing the detailed description of the table, shows clearly that this undesirable consequence does not appear. The phrase 'the structure which consists of such-and-such particles which stand in such-and-such relations to each other' describes a single entity, not a multitude of entities. Therefore, to say that this structure is pink is to attribute pink to a single entity, not a multitude of entities. Pink does not turn into a relation among particles, but remains a monadic property of perceptual objects. The description of a perceptual object, it is true, is *in terms of* a number of its parts, but it is not a description *of* these many parts. What can fill the blank in 'pink (. . .)' and, at the same time, inform us about the detailed structure of the perceptual object is a description of this object in terms of the properties of and relations among its parts. Analogously, the property of being square does not have to be conceived of as a relation if we say that the object before us, A, which consists of the four triangles a, b, c, and d in such-and-such spatial relations to each other, is square.

The property of being square is attributed to a single thing A, not to the four triangles of which A consists. This reply to Sellars' argument presupposes, of course, that an "expression belonging to the conceptual space of a set of elements, and having the appropriate logical form for referring to an aggregate of these elements" can be a *description* of a *single entity* in terms of its parts, their properties and relations. But I cannot think of any reason why such a description should not qualify.

It may be the case that Sellars took his cue from the common practice of referring to a class (set) by an expression of the form '$(A, B, C, . . .)$.' If we put a predicate in front of such an expression, we get something that seems to represent some kind of relational predication; a relation seems to be predicated as holding among the entities A, B, C, etc. But we must not be misled by this superficial similarity. In reality, the expression '$(A, B, C, . . .)$' means something quite different when it is used to represent a class from when it is used to represent the various entities among which a certain relation is thought to hold. In the former case, '$(A, B, C, . . .)$' is just another way of writing the definite description 'the class which consists of the elements A, B, C, . . .'; and this is a description of a single entity. This description of a single entity, to be sure, is not in terms of its parts—as it is in the case of a structure—but in terms of its elements or members.

Structures, at any rate, must not be confused with classes. There are at least two reasons, though, why an identification of structures with classes appears to be natural. Firstly, some structures belong to the subject matter of classical set theory. Ordered classes, for example, are nothing but structures in our sense. Secondly, certain structures are often viewed as classes, namely, as classes which contain in addition to the usual elements also certain relations among these elements. For example, the series of natural numbers is sometimes identified with the class whose members are the natural numbers together with the relation of being greater than (or equal) between natural numbers. But, of course, the series of natural numbers is not the same entity as this class.

Nor must structures be confused with entities of any other basic category. They are neither properties, nor individual things, nor states of affairs, and so on. They form a basic category of their own. And spatio-temporal structures—perceptual objects and their parts, that is —form a subcategory of that most important kind of furniture of the world.

REFERENCES

[1] M. Brodbeck, "Mental and Physical: Identity vs. Sameness," in P. K. Feyerabend and G. Maxwell, eds., *Mind, Matter, and Method* (Minneapolis: University of Minnesota Press, 1966).

[2] Rudolf Carnap, *Meaning and Necessity,* enlarged ed. (Chicago: University of Chicago Press, 1956).

[3] Hector-Neri Castañeda, ed., *Intentionality, Minds, and Perception* (Detroit: Wayne State University Press, 1967).

[4] A. Church, *Introduction to Mathematical Logic* (Princeton: Princeton University Press, 1956).

[5] A. Eddington, *The Nature of the Physical World* (Cambridge: Cambridge University Press, 1928).

[6] G. Frege, review of Hilbert's *Die Grundlagen der Geometrie*, translated as "On the Foundations of Geometry," *Philosophical Review* 69 (1960): 2-17.

[7] C. G. Hempel and P. Oppenheim, "The Logic of Explanation," in H. Feigl and M. Brodbeck, eds., *Readings in the Philosophy of Science* (New York: Appleton-Century-Crofts, 1953): 319-52.

[8] D. B. Marquis, *Scientific Realism and the Antinomy of External Objects* (Ph. D. thesis, Indiana University, 1970).

[9] F. P. Ramsey, *The Foundations of Mathematics* (London: Routledge & Kegan Paul, 1931).

[10] Wilfrid Sellars, "Philosophy and the Scientific Image of Man," in R. G. Colodny, ed., *Frontiers of Science and Philosophy* (Pittsburgh: University of Pittsburgh Press, 1963): 37-78.

[11] _____, *Science, Perception and Reality* (London: Routledge & Kegan Paul, 1963).

·~·7·~·

The Elusiveness of Categories, the Archimedean Dilemma, and the Nature of Man: A Study in Sellarsian Metaphysics

JAY F. ROSENBERG

The University of North Carolina at Chapel Hill

I

THE ontological enterprise is the attempt to delineate the most general complete answer to the question "What is there?". The enterprise has two dimensions. Positively, it rests upon epistemology. Viewing "What is there?" as a question among questions, the philosopher produces an account of the epistemological grounds of an adequate answer. We *discover* what there is. How we discover it, what we have discovered, and, perhaps, what we are likely to discover, form the subject matter of positive ontology. Negatively, the enterprise rests upon analysis. Philosophers discourse about entities or putative entities more or less problematic in nature—numbers, qualities, classes, propositions, facts, and the like. Whether the entities be putative merely and, if so, what such discourse amounts to is the subject matter of negative ontology. In his positive ontology, Sellars is a scientific realist, in his negative ontology, what I shall call a linguistic nominalist. The two stances are, of course, not unrelated. Thereby hangs a long tale, much of which will emerge as we proceed. Let me begin, then, by picking up some of the threads of Sellars' negative ontology. Since he is a synoptic and systematic thinker, following them will take us a considerable distance—and in some unexpected directions.

II

2. The thesis of linguistic nominalism may be succinctly stated in first approximation thus:

> . . . that the abstract entities which are the subject matter of the contemporary debate between platonistic and anti-platonistic philosophers—qualities, relations, classes, propositions, and the like—are linguistic entities. They are linguistic expressions. ([10]; [16]: 229.)

3. Like Carnap, Sellars sees discourse putatively about abstract entities as discourse in the material mode of speech. Thus,

  (1) Redness is a quality

is viewed, roughly, as a transposed version of something like

  (2) 'red' is a monadic predicate.

As anyone who has worked with the basic Carnapian move will recognize, *caveats* are essential. The fundamental difficulty (first raised by Church) can be sketched in connection with translation. (1) is transcribed, for example, in German by

  (1g) Die Röte ist eine Qualität,

while (2) translates as

  (2g) 'red' ist ein monadisches Prädikat.

The invariance of the quoted item in (2) and (2g) highlights the fact that (2) is a claim about a specific word of the *English* language. Like (2) and (2g), (1) and (1g) are true or false together. (1g), however, could be used to make a true statement even if there were no English language. The truth of (1g) does not turn on the existence of any English word. Hence, since (1g) and (1) say the same thing, neither does the truth of (1). Since (1) would, but (2) would not, be true in the absence of an English language, (1) and (2) evidently have different subject matters. Discourse putatively about universals, therefore, apparently cannot be discourse about linguistic expressions. The traditional conclusion has been that (1) concerns itself with a totally non-linguistic subject matter, e.g., the entities of a platonic realm of subsistents.

4. Sellars, however, does not accept the traditional conclusion. He sees

(1) as independent of *specific* linguistic forms not by virtue of its relation to a totally non-linguistic subject matter, but rather by virtue of the fact that its mode of reference to language abstracts from what is idiosyncratic to the specific expressions of determinate historical languages. It is directed, rather, to the role or functions served in common by the different concrete linguistic materials of historical languages regarded as "materially different varieties of one and the same 'language game' " ([10]; [16]: 239). Thus, according to Sellars, (1) is insulated from the idiosyncrasies of translation not by being *non*-linguistic, but rather by being *inter*-linguistic to begin with. (1) adverts to a function shared by 'red's in English, 'rot's in German, and 'rouge's in French. Sellars uses dot-quotation to form common nouns subsuming linguistic materials thus functionally individuated. Thus ·red·s are items in *any* language which have the function (play the role, do the job) which the token exhibited between the dot-quotes has in *our* language, i.e., in the language of *use*. As translation represents a move from one language of use to another, the material between *dot*-quotes—being relativized to the *used* language—is thus translated as well. Asterisk-quotes, by contrast, form common nouns subsuming linguistic materials · as *structurally* individuated. *rot*s, thus, are items having the *shape* of the token exhibited between the asterisks. In English, *rot*s are ·rot·s, while, in German, *rot*s are ·red·s. Thus Sellars sees ordinary quotation, relatively innocuous in *intra*-linguistic contexts where structure and function run parallel, as systematically ambiguous between structure and function in *inter*-linguistic contexts, where a single structure may answer to diverse functions (as *rot*s may be ·rot·s or ·red·s) and a single function may be served by items of various structures (as *red*s, *rot*s, and *rouge*s may all be ·red·s). And he sees the ontological idiom as our ordinary language resource for coping with this ambiguity. But, being framed in terms appropriate to discourse about objects, it, too, misleads, though in a wholly different way.

5. In second approximation, then,

> (1) Redness is a quality

is to be analyzed as

> (3) ·red·s are monadic predicates.

Bits of language considered simply as belonging to the natural order—inscriptions and utterances viewed solely in terms of "empirical properties and matter-of-factual relations''—Sellars calls 'natural-linguistic objects' ([21]; [18]: 212). Viewed externally, then, the proximate subject matter of philosophers' ontological discourse is such natural-linguistic objects. But the discourse is discourse about them not *qua* natural-linguistic objects but rather as *functionally* individuated items and fit subjects for *normative* claims. Philosophers' ontological discourse is the classificatory discourse of a functional metalanguage transposed into the material mode of speech, but the proximate subject matter of that discourse is the *tokens*—inscriptions and utterances—over which, for example, the universal quantifier implicit in (3) ranges:

(4) $(x)(x$ is a $\cdot$red$\cdot \supset x$ is a monadic predicate).

Thus the rubric ''linguistic nominalism''. 'Linguistic', since, *à la* Carnap, Sellars analyzes ontological discourse as a transposed form of metalinguistic discourse. 'Nominalism', since, according to Sellars, the proximate subjects of that discourse properly analyzed are, considered externally, particulars only—utterance tokens and inscriptions.

III

6. But what is it for some natural-linguistic object to have a role or function? If to be a $\cdot$red$\cdot$ is to be an item in any language which has the function which the exhibited token has in our language, are we not then committed to an ontology embracing, at least, functions or roles? The answer, of course, is that we are not, and to see it, we need only pursue a favorite Sellarsian analogy a bit. What is it to be a pawn in chess? It is surely *only* to be subject to chess-normatives in the appropriate way. A pawn is any item which may advance along a file one square at a time, capture diagonally, queen at the eighth rank, and so on. *Which* items of the natural order (pieces of wood or ivory, configurations of electrons in a computer) are pawns will vary from time to time, and what natural order goings-on *count* as moving, capturing, queening—indeed, what counts as a square, rank, or file—from occasion to occasion will also vary. What is invariant is the set of rules or normatives espoused by the players and the *regularities* in the natural order which are generated in response to these espoused normatives. The *esse* of a game, as Sellars

puts it, is *ludi*, to be played. To play a game is to do what one does subject to the constraints of various normatives espoused as action-guiding policies and with a specifiable end-in-view. Externally, what is manifested is regularities *in re*. 'Square' becomes colored cardboard; 'pawn' becomes piece of wood of such-and-such a shape; 'moving' becomes transportation of wood from point to point; and 'capturing' becomes physical displacement and replacement. Thus a game of chess is played out.

7. With language there are both tensions and affinities.

> . . . If all rules of language were ought-to-do's, we would be precluded from explaining what it is to have concepts in terms of rules of language. Now many rules of language *are* ought-to-do's thus,
>
>> (Other things being equal) one ought to say such and such, if in C
>
> and as such they can be efficacious in linguistic activity only to the extent that people have the relevant concepts. It is therefore of the utmost importance to note that many of the rules of language which are of special interest to the epistemologist are ought-to-be's rather than ought-to-do's. ([14]: 510.)

8. Linguistic normatives, in the primary sense, are ought-to-be's, what Sellars calls "rules of criticism". Conceptual activity (covert or overt) is through-and-through rule-governed, not in the sense of being guided by explicitly espoused rules of *action* (ought-to-do's) which require of the agents a rich prior conceptualization of the rules *qua* rules and of the evoking situations as falling under the rule-descriptions and *thus* as reasons for the actions which the rules enjoin, but rather, in the first instance, by being relevantly *assessable* according to rules of criticism the subjects of which need *not* have the concept of a rule as a rule, nor, indeed, any concepts at all. (Sellars' example: Clock chimes ought to strike on the quarter hour ([14]: 508).)

9. But, further,

> . . . the members of a linguistic community are *first* language *learners* and only potentially 'people', but *subsequently* language *teachers* possessed of the rich conceptual framework this implies. They start out being the *subject matter* of the ought-to-be's and graduate to the status of agent subjects of the ought-to-do's [the

rules of action enjoining, among other things, the *bringing about* of what the rules of criticism posit ought to be]. Linguistic ought-to-be's are translated into *uniformities* by training. ([14]: 512.)

In the second instance, then, conceptual activity—and most notably and to the point, linguistic activity—is rule-governed by being the product of agents who are trained to conform to ought-to-be's which are posited by the rules of criticism by their predecessors and teachers who espoused as action-guiding policies the correlative ought-to-do's relating to the bringing about of behavior conforming to those ought-to-be's. It is as rule-governed in this second sense that language makes contact with the chess analogy. As the espoused rules of chess constrain an agent's chess activity and precipitate from time to time uniformities of relational structure among the current physical embodiments of the chess roles constituted by those normatives, so the rules of language are reflected in the natural order by the uniform practices of the trained language users and the uniformities of relational structure among the natural-linguistic objects which are the manifestations *in re* of their conceptual activity and collectively constitute the evolving world-story. "Espousal of principles is reflected in uniformities of performance" ([21]; [18]: 216).[1]

10. The relevant uniformities, Sellars tells us, are of three types:

> I.   Language-entry transitions (world → language), e.g., the responses with ·red·s to red objects in daylight;
> II. Intra-linguistic moves (language → language), e.g., the correlations of ·a is north of b·s with ·b is south of a·s or ·thunder at t·s with · lighting at $t - \Delta t$ ·s;
> and III. Language-exit transitions (language → world), e.g., the doings of A consequent upon ·I shall now do A·s.

(See [17]: 114; [20]; [18]: 329 ff; [21]; [18]: 216.)

11. Notice that, since ·red·s, ·a is north of b·s, ·I shall now do A·s, and the like are all, considered in themselves, natural-linguistic objects—inscriptions, i.e., piles of ink or chalk, or utterance tokens, i.e., disturbances in the air—the uniformities canvassed here are all world-world uniformities, correlations between relational structures of objects *all of which* are members of the natural order. The picture

---

1. For a more leisurely and detailed development of this theme, see my [9].

Sellars gives us, then, is one of agent-persons producing and structuring systems of natural-linguistic objects in a manner which is characterizable as *rule-governed* in at least three dimensions:

first, as performances *assessable* by reference to linguistic ought-to-be's (rules of criticism);

second, by mature language users, as performances responsive to *autonomous* linguistic ought-to-do's (rules of action) espoused as explicit behavior-guiding policies (i.e., rules conceived *as* rules); and

third, again by mature language users, as performances responsive to *derivative* linguistic ought-to-do's pertaining to the bringing about of linguistic ought-to-be's conceived as explicit behavioral constraints (again, rules conceived *as* rules).

12. Sameness of function, role, or office, then, amounts to sameness of place in the "logical space" or relational structure generated by this system of linguistic normatives which finds its total *ontological* reflection in the world-world uniformities which are the linguistic actions of persons and their natural-order consequences. Synonymy, to put it crudely, is substitutability *salve* uniformities. Terms which make the same contribution to the system of language-entry, language-exit, and intra-language uniformities are terms having the same function. For that function is individuated by the relational structure induced by the total set of linguistic normatives, and the world-world uniformities resulting from the linguistic actions of persons is the total reflection *in re* of the structure.

IV

13. So much, for now, for the ontology of language. What of its epistemology? We have been taking the semantical rules of criticism, the normatives formulating linguistic ought-to-be's, as given. But, of course, they are not. In a deep sense, the correlation of relational structures, the world-world uniformities, which we have been discussing will prove to be their Sellarsian *raison d'être*. But that is a point which we must approach gradually. More immediately, we must begin to make contact with positive ontology. Sellars, recall, is in his positive ontology a scientific realist. It is to science that he turns also for the epistemological underpinnings of linguistic ought-to-be's. Briefly and

roughly put, for Sellars, *laws of nature* and *semantical rules of criticism* are one and the same. In more detail:

> . . . law-like propositions tell us how we ought to think about the world. They formulate rules of criticism, and if, as such, they tell us what ought or ought not to be the case, the fact that it is what ought or ought not to be the case with respect to *our beliefs about* the world suffices to distinguish them from those rules of criticism which tell us what ought or ought not to be the case in the world. ([17]: 117.)

> . . . law-like statements are, in our sense of the phrase, 'semantical rules', and are, *ceteris paribus*, reflected in uniformities pertaining to the verbal behaviour (and conceptual acts) of those who espouse them. ([17]: 118.)

14. Thus, for Sellars, evolution of theories and evolution of concepts go hand in hand. Theory change *is* concept change, either in the *limited* sense of introducing new intra-language moves governing old "pieces" —new language →language inferential connections—as when a new law is formulated in an old theoretical vocabulary, or in the more *radical* sense of introducing wholly new "pieces" into the game—a new theoretical vocabulary including ·molecule·s or·gene·s, for example—in postulational theory formation. Even in the latter case, however, Sellars sees the change as, in an important sense, gradual and evolutionary, for the new theoretical predicates are introduced in the first instance as *analogical* predicates, where the relevant analogies occur at the level of second-order attributes, analogies which it is the function of the *model* to control.

> As I see it, . . . models provide a basis for a more or less vague and open-textured reference to a framework of propositional functions which the predicates of a theory are to satisfy. They are specified as *the functions which* hold, with certain qualifications, of the predicates which apply to the entities of the model. I say "with certain qualifications" because the reference to a model is accompanied by what I have called a "commentary" which eliminates specific functions from the analogy and modifies others. ([19]; [16]: 348.)

15. Like Feyerabend, Sellars sees observationality as a *de facto* property of a system of predicates at a time. But, unlike Feyerabend,

Sellars sees also that the essential role of the concepts of the framework of common sense (e.g., colored physical objects, extended in space and enduring through time), in controlling the analogies in terms of which theoretical predicates are in the first instance introduced, gives those concepts a *methodological* bindingness which precludes the *piecemeal* abandonment of common sense for theoretical concepts and, thus, precludes acceptance of the full-fledged Feyerabendian "pragmatic theory of observation".

16. Hence, while Sellars assents to the contention that

> The framework of common sense is radically false (i.e., there *really* are no such things as the physical objects and processes of the common sense framework), ([19]; [16]: 354.)

he insists that this idea be clarified

> . . . in terms of the concept of its being reasonable *at some stage* to abandon the framework of common sense and use only the framework of theoretical science, suitably enriched by the dimension of practical discourse. ([19]; [16]: 354.)

It is only when the conceptual space of the theory has acquired a status which is *fully* non-analogical and, thus, not parasitic on the framework of common sense, however, that such an abandonment would not result in conceptual loss.

> It is the rock bottom concepts and principles of common sense which are binding until a total structure which can do the job better is actually at hand—rather than a "regulative ideal". ([19]; [16]: 355.)

17. Nevertheless, it is clear that such methodological bindingness is compatible with the *eventual* abandonment and replacement of any set of concepts, however observational (i.e., governed by language-entry semantical rules) they may currently be. Hence, for Sellars, the observational concepts of the common sense framework are *epistemologically* on a par with the concepts of developed postulational theories and, thus, *consonance* with such common sense observations cannot be the fundamentum of the acceptability of new laws and theories. Rather, for Sellars, the ends controlling the scientific enterprise are basically and centrally the ends of *explanation*.

V

18. On Sellars' view, accepting a new law-like statement is espousing a new principle of inference (semantical rule) as a behavior-guiding policy resulting in modification of the world-world regularities consequent upon conceptual—paradigmatically, linguistic—activities. This view places the epistemology of science squarely in the realm of human conduct, and so it is not surprising to find Sellars arguing that the fundamental forms of reasoning governing the acceptance of new laws and theories are one and all forms of *practical* reasoning. An inductive argument emerges as a schematized practical argument.

The major premiss of the first level probability argument, i.e., briefly,

a proposition is probable$_M$ if it satisfies condition C

has the sense of

there is a good argument of kind M for accepting a proposition if it satisfies condition C

and, hence, since the conclusion of this argument is a practical one, the sense of

there is a good argument of kind M which has as its conclusion 'I shall accept a proposition, if it satisfies condition C'.

In short, the major premise of the first order probability$_M$ argument tells us that the *complete* practical reasoning which culminates in

I shall accept h

(where this acceptance is bound up with probability$_M$), has the form

I shall bring about E
(but bringing about E implies accepting a proposition, if it satisfies condition C)
so, I shall accept a proposition, if it satisfies condition C
h satisfies condition C
so, I shall accept h.

Thus,

h is probable$_M$

where the subscript indicates a specific mode of probability, asserts the availability of a good argument for 'I shall accept *h'*, the ultimate major of which is the intention to achieve a certain end, and the proximate major is the appropriate intention to follow a certain policy with respect to accepting propositions. ([12]: 207-8.)

19. What are these epistemic ends which govern the various modes of probability and, hence, the scientific enterprise as a whole? Two cases are of central concern here—the probability of *theories* and the *nomological* probability, or probability of lawlike propositions, upon which it is grounded. To fix the relevant ends, Sellars first examines the policies of action which they are to justify. Let us consider the probability of theories first. The appropriate practical reasoning for the probability of theories, according to Sellars, concludes thus:

> T is the simplest available framework which generates new testable lawlike statements, generates acceptable approximations of nomologically probable lawlike statements and generates no falsified lawlike statements (from now on, the statement that T has this complex property will be represented by '$\phi(T)$').
> Therefore, I shall accept T. ([12]: 209.)

The policy, then, is accepting frameworks which are ϕ. What is the end, E, which justifies the policy?

> But why should one accept the policy? By what end is it analytically implied? Surely the state of being in possession of such frameworks logically implies accepting such frameworks *if one does not already have them*. And that this state is the end in question is supported by the fact that it simply unpacks the concept of *being able to give non-trivial explanatory accounts of established laws*. ([12]: 210; second italics mine.)

20. For the nomological probability which is presupposed by the probability of theories, the results are similar. The policy to be justified in this case is the adoption of rules of inference which project the observed frequency of a property in a class to unobserved finite samples from the class (with "universal" laws being that special case in which the observed frequency = 1). And the epistemic end, E, which justifies the policy,

> . . . is the state of being able to draw inferences concerning the composition with respect to a given property Y of unexamined finite samples (ΔK) of a kind, X, *in a way which also provides an*

explanatory account of the composition with respect to Y of the total examined sample, K, of X. ([12]: 215; italics mine.)

In more detail, the practical reasoning underlying nomological probability runs:

> I shall be able to draw inferences concerning the composition with respect to a given property Y of unexamined finite samples (ΔK) of a kind, X, in a way which also provides an explanatory account of the composition with respect to Y of the total examined sample, K, of X.
>
> Being able to do this involves coming to have (where I do not already have) principles of inference which accord with the evidence in the sense that they project the composition of the evidence in a way which generates an explanatory account of this composition.
>
> n/m of all examined As is B.
>
> The implication 'that ΔK is a finite unexamined class of As implies that approximately n/m ΔK is B' accords in the above sense with the evidence.
>
> Therefore I shall accept this principle of inference. ([12]: 216-17.)

21. The epistemic ends controlling the acceptance of new laws and theories, then, are ends concerned with "the realizing of a logically necessary condition of being in the very framework of explanation and prediction, i.e. being able to draw inferences concerning the unknown and give explanatory accounts of the known" ([12]: 219). Roughly, we accept the law or theory which permits inferences to new cases or laws while providing the *best explanatory account* of the cases or laws which we already know.[2]

22. Now this conclusion may seem peculiar. Surely, it will be objected, the epistemic end controlling the scientific enterprise can be nothing less than the possession of *empirical truth*. The relevant epistemic states must surely be, not merely the ability to give explanatory accounts, but rather the ability to give *explanations,* i.e., *true* explanatory accounts; not merely the ability to infer predictions, but rather the ability to infer *true* predictions. To cut the scientific enterprise off from the quest for empirical truth as Sellars does is not only to falsify radically the essential character of that enterprise, but surely also to undermine the very

---

2. For a similar conclusion, see [3] and [2]. I have applied this point to the philosophy of linguistics in [6] and [7].

possibility that science can be the fundamentum of the claims of positive ontology, the prime thesis of Sellars' scientific realism.

23. To this objection, Sellars offers both a negative and a positive reply. Negatively, his reply is to insist that the epistemic ends controlling the scientific enterprise must be the sort of things that can be known to be realized, be known to obtain. While this condition is met by the ends in terms of which Sellars analyzes the acceptability of theories and laws, in light of the standing possibility that any theory may be superseded by a better theory, however, it is *not* similarly met by the proposed end-in-view of the possession of empirical truth.

24. Positively, however, Sellars replies that the assertions licensed by an acceptable semantical rule *are* true, and, indeed, it is a mere tautology to say so. For the generic concept of truth—the *meaning* of 'true', on Sellars' account—precisely *is* correct assertibility, that is, assertibility "in accordance with the relevant semantical rules, and on the basis of such additional, though unspecified, information as these rules may require. . . 'True', then, means *semantically* assertible ('S-assertible') and the varieties of truth correspond to the general varieties of semantical rule" ([17]: 101). Thus, for Sellars, while the epistemic end-in-view *controlling* the scientific enterprise cannot be the possession of empirical truth (for a state which cannot be known to be realized cannot ground a valid practical reasoning), that the scientific enterprise *issue in* empirical truth is itself a necessary truth, for the products of that enterprise are precisely semantical rules, assertibility in accordance with which *is* truth.

25. But, to cast a finer net, while the *generic* concept of truth is S-assertibility, its specification for the primary concept of *empirical* or *matter-of-factual* truth leads to a deeper set of considerations grounded in an analysis of the distinctive *function* of first-level factual discourse. Like Wittgenstein in the *Tractatus,* Sellars sees this function as one of *picturing*. The primary concept of *factual* truth, for Sellars, is truth as correct picture. Atomic statements are pictures which are

> . . . correct or incorrect in terms of the semantical rules of the framework within which they are statements. They are true (S-assertible) if correct, false if incorrect. ([17]: 119.)

> The *criterion* of the correctness of the performance of asserting a basic matter-of-factual proposition is the correctness of the propo-

sition *qua* picture, i.e. the fact that it coincides with the picture the world-cum-language would generate in accordance with the uniformities controlled by the semantical rules of the language. Thus the *correctness* of the picture is not defined in terms of the *correctness* of a performance but vice versa. ([17]: 136.)

VI

26. Picturing, for Sellars, is not a semantic relation, but a relation *in re,* a relation between two relational structures. It is, in fact, precisely that correlation of natural-linguistic objects and non-linguistic objects, that set of world-world uniformities, to which we have already adverted. To say that first-level factual discourse pictures the world is, roughly, to say that the system of linguistic productions *qua natural-linguistic objects* forms a relational structure isomorphic to the system of items in the natural order which *qua semantical objects* those linguistic productions are about. Thus,

> A statement to the effect that a linguistic item pictures a non-linguistic item . . . is, in an important sense, an object language statement, for even though it mentions linguistic objects, it treats them as items in the order of causes and effects, i.e. *in rerum natura,* and speaks of their functioning in this order in a way which is to be sharply contrasted with the metalinguistic statements of logical semantics, in which the key role is played by abstract singular terms. Thus it is essential to note that whereas in
>
> > '*a*' (in L) denotes O
>
> the 'O' of the right-hand side is a metalinguistic expression, in
>
> > '*a*'s (in L) represent O
>
> it is not. ([17]: 137.)

The former is roughly equivalent to

> For some INSENSE, *$*a*$*s (in *L*) are INSENSE's and INSENSE's are (equivalent to) ·*O*·s

(where 'INSENSE' is a metalinguistic variable taking dot-quoted individual constants as substituends—see [17]: 137-38), while the latter corresponds rather to something like

> The regularities involving *$*a*$*s (produced by *L*-speakers) are isomorphic to the regularities involving *O* (in the world).

27. I have been speaking of *isomorphism,* but the 'fit' between systems of natural-linguistic objects and systems of non-linguistic objects, like any correlation of relational structures, is one which admits of degrees.

> [P]ictures, like maps, can be more or less adequate. The adequacy concerns the 'method of projection'. A picture (candidate) subject to the rules of a given method of projection (conceptual framework), which is a correct picture (successful candidate), is S-assertible with respect to that method of projection. ([17]: 135.)

28. A conceptual framework (system of semantical normatives) controls the production of natural-linguistic objects, the regularities of relation among which then correspond more or less to the regularities among the non-linguistic objects which they variously represent. Since the picturing relation thus generated admits of degrees, it follows that

> . . . one conceptual framework can be more 'adequate' than another, and this fact can be used to define a sense in which one proposition can be said to be 'more true' than another. ([17]: 134.)

Less metaphorically, responsive to the earlier identification of theoretical evolution and conceptual evolution, we can distinguish

> . . . between the conceptual structure to which a proposition *belongs* and the conceptual structure *with respect to which its truth is defined.* ([17]: 134.)

In other words, while the so-called 'absolute' sense of 'true'—and the *ultimate* cash value of 'S-assertibility'—remains assertibility in *our* conceptual structure, here and now, it makes sense to view our conceptual structure as merely one stage in the evolution of a series of conceptual frameworks which are, in the picturing sense adumbrated above, increasingly adequate. Consequently, we may consider the assertibility—in accordance with the semantical rules of conceptual structures which are more or less evolved *counterparts* of our own—either of propositions belonging to our current conceptual structure or of propositions which are themselves more or less evolved counterparts of those which we can formulate with our current conceptual resources.

29. And now we are in the position to take the last step and

> . . . conceive of a language which enables its users to form *ideally* adequate pictures of objects . . . ([17]: 140.)

This language (which Sellars naturally enough calls "Peirceish") forms the fundamentum of a notion of *ideal* truth. What is true, then, *in the last analysis* is what would be correctly S-assertible according to the semantical rules of the *Peirceish* conceptual framework, and 'what really exists', in the sense of Sellars' scientific realism, is what the Peirceish conceptual structure would posit as the ultimate furniture of the world, what is correctly pictured by first-level factual statements of Peirceish.

30. Peirceish, of course, is but a regulative ideal.

> Although the concepts of 'ideal truth' and 'what really exists' are defined in terms of a Peircean conceptual structure they do not require that there ever be a Peirceish community. ([17]: 142).

Nevertheless, Sellars insists that it is an *intelligible* regulative ideal, given literal content by the notion of the adequacy of a conceptual framework *qua method of projecting more or less adequate pictures*.

> Peirce himself fell into difficulty because, by not taking into account the dimension of 'picturing', he had no Archimedean point outside the series of actual and possible beliefs in terms of which to define the ideal or limit to which members of this series might approximate. ([17]: 142.)

VII

31. This, then, is a sketch—and, let me emphasize, *only* a sketch—of one strand of Sellars' deep and intricate philosophy. It leads from ascent to the formal mode through linguistic rules of criticism, natural laws as semantical rules, practical reasoning and the epistemic ends of scientific inquiry, and the conception of factual discourse as picturing the world to a renovated Peircean conception of ideal truth. While fascinating sideroads—many of which Sellars himself has fruitfully explored—lead off from each juncture of this path, the path itself provides more than enough discussible topography. In what follows, I should like to pick up three themes for further exploration. I will first raise a problem from the beginning, from negative ontology. Call it "The Elusiveness of Categories". Wittgenstein has a 'solution' of sorts for it, and while I'm not at all happy with his solution, I don't myself have a better one, so I shall leave this issue as an open question. Second, I will discuss a theme

from the end, theory convergence and Peircean limit concepts. There is a problem here too. Call it "The Archimedean Dilemma". For this one, I have a solution which I shall do my best to lay out. These two discussions bring pressure to bear from two different directions on Sellars' account of the picturing relation, exploring its limitations, first from the standpoint of negative ontology and, then, from the standpoint of positive. Finally, I shall return to the middle and say a bit about epistemic ends. Here I intend to indulge my propensity for speculative metaphysics. Call it a study of "The Nature of Man". But first things first.

VIII

32. Consider the following ontological thesis:

(T) Facts are not objects.[3]

Sellars, as I understand him, would assent to two claims about (T)—first, that it is misleadingly put, being the material mode transposition of a thesis perspicuously formulated in a functional metalanguage, but, second, that it is *true*. Or, more precisely, the metalinguistic thesis for which it is a material mode surrogate is true. What metalinguistic thesis? Well, 'fact', in this truth-neutral sense, is the material mode counterpart of 'sentence', and 'object' of 'name' ('referring expression', 'individual constant'), so (T) puts unperspicuously roughly the metalinguistic thesis that

(T*) Sentences are not names.

And that Sellars accepts (T*) is clear enough.

---

3. Two comments: First, the choice of thesis is not crucial. Any of several others would have done as well. Second, as always in ontological discourse, a few cautionary terminological remarks are in order. Here I am using 'fact' in the *truth-neutral* sense of the Tractarian *'Sachlage'*. In this sense of 'fact', both true and false sentences may be used to state facts. Thus, 'situation' or 'state of affairs' would do as well as 'fact'. On the other hand, I do *not* intend that objects be conceived as "ontologically simple", Tractarian *'Gegenstände'*. Thus, 'things' or 'particulars' would do as well as 'objects'. (But *not* 'individuals'. There is *a* reading of (T) on which "Facts are not individuals" comes out false—cf. [10]; [16]: 253—and I need a thesis which is unambiguously Sellarsianly *true*.)

33. What is important to us here, however, is that (T*) *is* contentious. Not all philosophers would accept it. Frege, for example, held that sentences *are* names—specifically, names of truth-values. According to Frege, every well-formed sentence has, in addition to a sense, a referent. It denotes either the True or the False. (T*), then, is not only disputable; it has been disputed. And so arguments are called for. Are there relevant arguments concerning the putative distinction between sentences and names claimed by (T*)?

34. Of course there are such arguments, deep and cogent arguments deriving from Wittgenstein's *Tractatus*. But, and this is the heart of the matter, the arguments turn upon drawing a categorial *ontological* distinction between sentences and names. Indeed, they turn upon the very ontological distinction with which we began. Briefly, sentences are not names because names are natural-linguistic *objects* and sentences are natural-linguistic *facts*. And facts are not objects. This, in broad outline, is the structure of the problem which I call the Elusiveness of Categories. Let us look at the details.

35. How is it possible to use language to make claims about the world? A classical, though unacceptable, answer appeals to *reference*. Language is about the world by virtue of the fact that bits of language (names) *stand for* bits of the world (objects). If that were the *whole* story, however, there would be no essential difference between a sentence and a mere list of names. Yet a mere list makes no claim. So a sentence cannot be a mere list of names. Here the road forks. Frege hews to the referential model. But recognizing the need to differentiate a sentence from a list, Frege insists, too, that a sentence contains at least one *non-name*. Yet his semantics undermines his good intentions. Frege multiplies relations of *standing for*—an expression *denotes* its referent and *expresses* its sense—but he applies all of them across the whole range of linguistic forms. Subjects, predicates, and sentences alike—all of them have *both* senses *and* referents. True, the referents of predicate expressions are concepts—*'ungesättigt'* entities categorially different from the objects which are the referents of subject terms—but that is a difference in the world where we need a difference in the words. Functionally, however, subject and predicate expressions are alike—both relate to the world by the twin ties of sense and reference. A Fregean *non-name,* thus, turns out to be a name after all, but the name of a *non-object*. On the side of ontology, Frege gives us only the metaphor of "unsaturatedness", and on the side of language, no func-

tional difference at all. However ingeniously modified, the referential model remains a dead end.

36. Wittgenstein's answer is one which we have already met. Language (and here let us limit ourselves to first-level matter-of-factual language) represents the world by *picturing* it. The picturing theme is a vast one, of course, but its primary impact for our current discussion can be spelled out quickly.[4] Let me quote Sellars' exposition:

> What Wittgenstein tells us is that while superficially regarded the statement [aRb] is a concatenation of the three parts 'a', 'R', and 'b', viewed more profoundly it is a *two-termed fact*, with 'R' coming in to the statement . . . as bringing it about that the expressions 'a' and 'b' are related as having an 'R' between them. And he is making the point that what is essential to any statement which will say that aRb is not the names 'a' and 'b' have a relation word between them . . . but that these names be related (dyadically) *in some way or other* whether or not this involves the use of a third sign design. ([15]; [18]: 226; first italics mine.)

37. Now Sellars rejects the *full* Tractarian view that the only *essential* feature of the picturing relation is that n-adic atomic facts be pictured by n-adic configurations of names (i.e., by n-adic *linguistic* facts).

> It was, indeed, a significant achievement to show that it is n-adic configurations of referring expressions that represent n-adic states of affairs. But of itself this thesis throws no light on the crucial question: What is there about *this specific* n-adic configuration of referring expressions that makes the configuration say that the items referred to are related in *that specific* n-adic way? ([21]; [18]: 213-14.)

38. For the Tractarian schema

> Linguistic fact pictures nonlinguistic fact,

Sellars substitutes the richer scheme

> (natural-linguistic objects) O_1', O_2', . . . , O_n' make up a picture of [objects] O_1, O_2, . . . , O_n by virtue of such and such facts about O_1', O_2', . . . , O_n'. ([21]; [18]: 215.)

Yet this account "preserves in a modified way the Wittgensteinian theme that it is configurations of names that picture configurations of objects" for "the occurrence of an elementary statement is to be con-

4. For a more extended discussion, see my [5], [9], and [8].

strued as the occurrence *in a certain manner* of the names of the objects referred to" ([21]; [18]: 215). Pursued directly, this Sellarsian modification of the Tractarian account would bring us, again, to the correlations of relational structures, the world-world uniformities, consequent upon the linguistic activities of persons controlled by a "method of projection" which is a system of semantical normatives constituting a conceptual framework.[5] But enough has been said for our purposes here to see that the features of the picturing account which generated our initial puzzle are still with us. For Sellars accepts the view that a *necessary* condition of picturing is a categorial *ontological* distinction between names and sentences. And whether that distinction be described as one between linguistic objects and linguistic facts, between natural-linguistic objects and configurations of such objects, or between names and names occurring in a certain manner, it does not alter the essential point—that the distinction is precisely the categorial ontological distinction between objects and facts with which we began, though now restricted to the domain of language as it is manifested in the natural order.

39. This, then, is the Elusiveness of Categories. The rock-bottom categorial distinctions of ontology cannot be elucidated by metalinguistic ascent because the *truth* of the very metalinguistic claims proposed as analyses of the material mode ontological theses ultimately *presupposes* the very distinction putatively drawn by those theses. And here, I think, we reach the deepest understanding of Wittgenstein's thesis that "What *can* be shown, *cannot* be said". This, of course, is the Wittgensteinian 'solution' which I alluded to earlier. According to it, ultimate categorial distinctions belong to the realm of what is showable only. They "make themselves manifest", but any attempt to render them explicit is futile. In Sellarsian-Carnapian terms, if we attempt to *state* a categorial distinction, we find ourselves talking in the material mode. And this is misleading. So we ascend to a functional metalanguage—the formal mode—transposing our putative ontological thesis into a putatively metalinguistic one. But the resulting metalinguistic thesis is contentious. *And the correct defense of that thesis turns upon our ability to draw the very categorial distinction with which we began.* Our attempt to give explicit statement to a categorial thesis of ontology has met with futility.

5. For the corresponding earlier Sellarsian version of this story, see [21]; [18]: 215-22.

40. The only alternative, then, seems to be Wittgenstein's—relegate categorial ontological distinctions to a special realm which we *call* the realm of the merely showable, recognizing thereby that any attempt to state such a distinction will meet with *just this sort* of futility. Now this seems to me an alternative which is as defeatist as it is unenlightening. As I said earlier, I am not at all happy with it. But at this point I see no other, better, alternative, and so I must be content simply to commend this difficult question of categorial distinctions to your attention.

IX

41. We have not yet finished putting pressure on Sellars' version of *picturing,* however, and a second look at the proposed role of the picturing relation as a fundamentum for first-level matter-of-factual truth provides a convenient place to begin the development of our second problem. Recall that Sellars insists that the correctness of an elementary proposition as a picture is *criterial* for the correctness of the assertion-performance which, *qua* justified by semantical rules, constitutes the truth of that proposition. "Thus the *correctness* of the picture is not defined in terms of the *correctness* of a performance but vice versa" ([17]: 136).

42. The point is a delicate one and it has its consequences. For while the correctness of an assertion-performance *with respect to a system of semantical rules* is something which can be judged from *within* the conceptual structure constituted by those semantical rules, Sellars' requirement, that the adequacy of the semantical rules themselves ultimately be measured by the adequacy *as pictures* of the first-level assertions which they license, suggests that we need a standpoint which is *neutral* as among diverse conceptual structures from which we can judge the degree of fit between a system of natural-linguistic objects and a system of non-linguistic objects in a way which does not *presuppose* that one conceptual framework is more adequate than another.

43. And, indeed, this is a consequence to which Sellars appears to assent, for, recall, he characterizes the notion of correctness of picture as an Archimedean standpoint *outside* the Peircean series of actual and possible beliefs, intending thereby to provide some non-metaphorical

content for Peirce's notion of a limit point for scientific inquiry. Thus Sellars hopes to answer the challenge of such philosophers as Quine, who find the Peircean model intrinsically unintelligible:

> Peirce was tempted to define truth outright in terms of scientific method, as the ideal theory which is approached as a limit when the (supposed) canons of scientific method are used unceasingly on continuing experience. But there is a lot wrong with Peirce's notion besides its assumption of a final organon of scientific method and its appeal to an infinite process. There is a faulty use of numerical analogy in speaking of a limit of theories, since the notion of limit depends on that of ''nearer than,'' which is defined for numbers and not for theories. ([4]: 23.)

44. But can Sellars' conception of the picturing role of first-level matter-of-factual discourse thus provide content for the Peircean limit notion? That the matter is doubtful may be brought into sharper relief by reemphasizing another Sellarsian point, that statements to the effect that a natural-linguistic object, X, represents a non-linguistic object, Y, (briefly, that X pictures Y) are wholly in the object language ([17]: 137). Here, however, we must surely ask *which* object language, and it seems inevitable that any answer will again tie us down to one specific conceptual framework or another. A conception of *what* is pictured, in other words, seems to be available only from *within* a *single* conceptual scheme, and that will not do for an Archimedean standpoint.

45. Now Sellars recognizes this difficulty, and in a single passage of *Science and Metaphysics* he attempts to meet it:

> Are the individual variables we use tied exclusively to the individual senses of our current conceptual structure? Are the predicate variables we use tied exclusively to our conceptual resources? It is obvious that the only *cash* we have for these variables is to be found in our current conceptual structure, but it is a mistake to think that the substituends for a variable are limited to the constants which are here-now possessions of an instantaneous cross-section of language users. The identity of a language through time must be taken seriously, and a distinction drawn between the *logical* or 'formal' criteria of individuality which apply to any descriptive conceptual framework, and the more specific (material) criteria in terms of which individuals are identified in specific conceptual frameworks; and, similarly, between the logical criteria which differentiate, say, *n*-adic from *m*-adic predicates generally, from the conceptual criteria (material rules) which give distinctive

conceptual content to predicates which have the same purely logical status.

Thus the purely formal aspects of logical syntax, when they have been correctly disentangled, give us a way of speaking which abstracts from those features which differentiate specific conceptual structures, and enables us to form the concept of a domain of objects which are pictured in one way (less adequately) by one linguistic system, and in another way (more adequately) by another. And we can conceive of the former (or less adequate) linguistic system as our current linguistic system. ([17]: 139-40.)[6]

46. But, as suggestive as this passage is, it seems evident that "the purely formal aspects of logical syntax" are just not rich enough to do the requisite job. The easiest way to highlight the limitations of Sellars' proposal is to recognize that the *counterpart* in a more-highly-evolved conceptual framework of a predicate in our, or some other, "less adequate" conceptual framework may well turn out to be a relation of *different polyadicity*. There is every indication, for example, that the counterpart concepts of our common-sense color concepts will be, minimally, dyadic, rather than the strictly monadic predications of the physical-object framework. "Logical criteria which differentiate, say, n-adic from m-adic predicates generally" give us no hold on the problem of *identifying* counterpart predicates of *different* polyadicities in different conceptual frameworks. Again, as Sellars himself recognizes, it is entirely possible for the counterpart concept of some *individual* sense in our conceptual scheme to belong to a logical category which is distinct from that which is occupied by the less-well-developed concept. Indeed, Sellars deems it likely that objects in our conceptual framework will have as counterparts in successor frameworks not objects but, rather, *virtual classes* of objects ([17]: 149-50). If a particular conceptual framework is an explanatory dead-end, we shall even find within it concepts which have *no* counterparts in highly developed conceptual schemes which are "on the right track". Thus no predicate in current science is a more highly evolved counterpart of 'phlogiston'. If such fundamental matters as the *number* of objects available *in re* to be pictured and the polyadicities of the relations into which they enter are open to reconceptualization in successive conceptual frameworks, we must surely conclude that logical syntax alone, however thoroughly

6. For a heroic early attempt to actually *carry out* parts of such a program, see Sellars' [11].

disentangled, is inadequate to the task of guiding the formation of "the concept of a domain of objects which are pictured in one way . . . by one linguistic system and in another way . . . by another" ([17]: 140). The only alternative is to grant that there can be *no* system of concepts which is *both* framework-neutral *and* descriptive. The myth of the *gettable,* in that sense, must be recognized as being as pernicious as the myth of the *given.*

47. But if this is so, Quine's criticisms of the Peircean notion of ideal truth would seem to carry the field. For we have lost the "Archimedean standpoint" from which we could view Peirce's limit concepts as more than mere metaphors. This is the problem which I call the Archimedean Dilemma. How, if there is no framework-neutral standpoint from which to assess the relative adequacy as pictures of the systems of propositions generated in accordance with the semantical rules of different conceptual schemes, are we to give content to the Peircean notion of a limit toward which successive conceptual systems evolve?[7]

X

48. To begin to approach this problem, let us return to the primary and natural home of limits and convergence and examine the nature of convergence to a limit for number series. What does it mean to say that the infinite series of rationals

$$1/2, \ 2/3, \ 3/4, \ 4/5, \ . \ . \ .$$

converges to the number 1? It means that, as you go out in the series, the individual members of the series get arbitrarily close to 1. More precisely, if we represent the members of our series by 'A_1', 'A_2', . . ., etc., to say that the limit of the A_i-series is 1 ($\lim_{n \to \infty} A_n = 1$) is to say that

$$(\epsilon) \ (\exists N) \ (n) \ (n > N \ \supset \ \left| A_n - 1 \right| \ \leq \ \epsilon).$$

In general, a series $S_1, S_2, \ . \ . \ .$ converges to the limit L, ($\lim_{n \to \infty} S_n = L$), if and only if

$$(\epsilon) \ (\exists N) \ (n) \ (n > N \ \supset \ \left| S_n - L \right| \ \leq \ \epsilon).$$

---

7. The Archimedean Dilemma has a strict counterpart as an *internal* problem of philosophical methodology. Hall has called it 'the categorio-centric predicament'. See [1] for an extended discussion.

(For every increment, ϵ, there is a point in the series, N, beyond which every member, S_n, of the series is within ϵ of the limit L.) This is the *Weierstrass condition* for convergence. Notice that, even though the limit of the series of A_i is not a *member* of the series of A_i, in order to make use of the Weierstrass definition of convergence *we must know, and be able to say, what that limit is.* The model of convergence which Sellars utilizes is a model based upon Weierstrass' definition. Consequently, in order to give content to the notion that conceptual frameworks converge to a limit, Sellars finds it necessary to attempt to specify, from without, the character of the limit to which the series of frameworks is to converge. This is the demand for a framework-neutral standpoint which gives rise to the Archimedean Dilemma.

49. But we have argued that there is no way of characterizing a limit point for conceptual evolution in framework-neutral terms. Is there any analogue to this difficulty in mathematics? Consider the series of rationals

2/1, 4/3, 10/7, 24/17, 58/41, 140/99, . . .

which converges to the square root of 2. Again, the limit of the series is not a member of the series. But, more significantly, the limit of the series is not even a member of the *system of numbers to which the members of the series belong.* For the square root of 2 is demonstrably irrational, provably incapable of being represented as any ratio of integers. Is there any way in which, while remaining entirely within the system of *rational* numbers, we can demonstrate that this series (call it the B_i-series) converges? That is, can we demonstrate that *there is* a limit to which the B_i-series converges without being able to demonstrate, or even to *state,* that the series converges to the limit L, for any specifiable L? The answer, interestingly enough, is that we can. Rather than using the Weierstrass notion of convergence, where members of the series get arbitrarily close to a *known limit,* we can demonstrate simply that the series of B_i converges to *some* limit by establishing, instead, that, as we go out in the series, individual members of the series get arbitrarily close *to each other.* More precisely, the series of B_i converges if and only if

$$(\epsilon) \, (\exists N) \, (m) \, (n) \, (m > N \ \& \ n > N \ \cdot \supset \cdot \left| B_m - B_n \right| \leqslant \epsilon).$$

(For every increment, ϵ, there is a point in the series, N, beyond which any pair of members, B_m and B_n, are written ϵ of each other.) This is the *Cauchy condition* for convergence. Unlike a case in which use is made of the Weierstrass condition, convergence can be demonstrated by appeal to the Cauchy condition *even if the limit to which a series converges is not capable of being explicated in terms of the concepts governing the members of that series*. The requisite analogue for conceptual frameworks is clear. A temporal series of conceptual systems can be shown to be evolving towards *some* limit if it can be established that pairs of systems grow successively and arbitrarily closer to each other. This is the requirement, but it is still phrased metaphorically. Is there a way of breaking the metaphor and providing a *literal* content for the notion of conceptual systems approaching, not an ideal limit specified in framework-neutral terms, but rather *each other* ? To do so requires that we take a closer look at the epistemology of theory succession and, more particularly, at the requirement of explanatory adequacy which is the *sine qua non* of acceptability for a theory. In virtue of what relation between a successor theory and its predecessor(s) is it the case that the new theory can be said to provide an explanatory account of the laws of the old?

50. On the now-classical Hempelian account of explanation, a successor theory provides an explanatory account of a set of predecessor laws if and only if the new theory *entails* the old laws. It is clear, however, that, while deducibility relations will be of crucial importance, this straightforward *identification* of explanation and deducibility cannot hold up under scrutiny. Most significantly, the Hempelian identification fails because it presupposes meaning-invariance of terms between old and new theories, a possibility analytically precluded by our earlier identification of natural laws with a subset of the semantical rules which are constitutive of meanings *qua* linguistic roles or functions. Theory change *is* concept change, and so there can be no question of strict entailment relations between new laws and old. But each old law *will* have a *strict counterpart* in the new theory. Why not require, then, that these strict counterpart laws be deducible from the basic principles of the new theoretical framework? This brings us to the heart of the matter, for it will rather be a consequence of the principles of the new theory that the *strict* counterparts of the old laws are *literally false*.

51. Let me provide a handful of illustrations. Kepler's Laws of Planetary Motion specify that the path of a planet about the sun is an *ellipse*. Yet it is a consequence of Newton's Laws of Motion and Universal Gravitation that the orbit of a planet will *not* be an ellipse, since no

planet is subject *solely* to the central gravitational force of the sun as the *total* determinant of its motion. The Law of Universal Gravitation asserts that *every* two bodies attract one another with a determinate gravitational force, and the Second Law of Motion posits that *any* force produces a consequent acceleration in the bodies upon which it acts. It follows that, while roughly elliptical in the large, planetary paths will necessarily be highly irregular in the small, for each planet is subject not only to the central solar gravitational force, but equally to the perturbational gravitational forces resulting from the presence in the solar system of other planets, satellites, asteroids, and interplanetary gas and dust. Again, Galileo's Law of Falling Bodies specifies that the acceleration in free fall of a body near the surface of the earth is constant. But, according to Newton's theories, acceleration in free fall results from the action of gravitational forces which vary continuously with the changing distance of the falling body from the center of the earth. It follows that the absolute magnitude of the acceleration will *not* be constant, but will rather be a continuously varying function of the distance of fall. Finally, to take an example from another area of science, the Boyle-Charles Gas Law specifies that the volume of a sample of gas of fixed mass varies directly as the temperature of the sample and inversely as the pressure. But the counterpart concepts of temperature and pressure in the kinetic theory (mean kinetic energy of the molecules composing the sample and relative frequency of collisions between those molecules and the walls of the container) are not thus regularly related to volume. Rather, a correction factor must be introduced into the equation, depending, among other things, upon the absolute diameter of the molecules in the sample and the degree to which the collisions between those molecules are not perfectly elastic.

52. The upshot is that the new theories do not provide explanatory accounts of the old laws by entailing their strict counterparts in the successor framework. Rather, it is an analytic consequence of the basic principles of the new framework that the strict counterparts of the predecessor laws are literally false, for the new principles entail laws which are *inconsistent* with the strict counterparts of the old laws. And this basic fact about theory succession is something Sellars himself not only recognized but, indeed, in certain contexts, stressed. As he has put it, theories

> . . . *explain empirical laws by explaining why observable things obey to the extent that they do, these empirical laws*; that is, they

explain why individual objects of various kinds and in various circumstances in the observation framework behave in those ways in which it is inductively established that they do behave. Roughly, it is because a gas is —in some sense of 'is'—a cloud of molecules which are behaving in certain theoretically defined ways, that it obeys the *empirical* Boyle-Charles law. ([13]; [18]: 121.)

53. Strictly speaking, then, theories do not provide a direct explanatory account of their predecessor laws. Rather they provide an *indirect* explanatory account of predecessor laws by providing a *direct* account of the *success* of those laws. And this point is not, as Sellars seems to suggest, limited to the relationship between postulational microtheories and inductively established macro-regularities. It applies to the relationship between *any* pair of theories related as predecessor and successor. Just as it is because a gas is a cloud of molecules that the empirical Boyle-Charles Law is as good an account of the behavior of gases as it is, so it is because a *molecule* is a system of protons, neutrons, and electrons, with determinate masses and charges, interacting in ways specified by the theory of subatomic particles, that the *kinetic* theory is as good an account of the behavior of gases as *it* is.

54. In general, then, the *prime* explanatory function of a new theory, and, thus, as we have seen, the fundamental constraint on its acceptability, is to account for the *success* of its predecessor(s). And this accounting essentially involves idealizations and limit concepts. Its structure is this: The basic framework principles of the new theory must have three analytic consequences. First, they must have the consequence that the strict counterparts of predecessor laws are literally false. But, second, they must *also* have the consequence that those strict counterparts are *true in the limit*. The orbit of a planet *would* be an ellipse were there no perturbational forces; the acceleration of a freely falling body *would* be constant were its distance from the center of the earth constant; the strict counterpart of the Boyle-Charles Law *would* be literally correct were molecules of zero diameter and collisions between them perfectly elastic. And, finally, the new theory must have the consequence that the relevant limit is one which is *closely approximated* by the world as it is posited in the successor framework to be. The perturbational forces acting upon a planet are *near zero;* the relative change in distance between a falling body and the center of the earth is *near zero;* and molecules have *near zero* diameters, collisions between them being *almost* perfectly elastic. Thus, it follows that the strict counterparts

within the successor framework of the old laws are *good approxima-tions* to what the successor theory now asserts to be the actual state of affairs.

55. A successor theory, in other words, allows us to calculate the *magnitude* of the deviation of the accounts provided by its predecessor(s) from what the new theory now tells us is actually the case. And here we have precisely the raw materials which we need to construct a version of Cauchy convergence for scientific theories. The degree to which two theories approach one another can be measured by the absolute numerical magnitude of the correction factors which must be introduced into applications of the strict counterparts of predecessor laws to arrive at the values determined by their successors. Inasmuch as the absolute numerical values of the requisite correction factors become increasingly smaller as we move from successor theory to successor theory, we may say, non-metaphorically, that the theories are approaching each other.

56. This solution to the convergence problem incorporates *both* the insights of Sellars *and* the insights of Quine. For we may now say, with Sellars, that it is the "purely formal aspects of logical syntax"—in this case, the framework-neutral but *descriptively empty* (content-free) concepts of pure mathematics—which enable us to give a non-metaphorical sense to the Peircean limit concept, while *also* agreeing to the Quinean contention that the notion of limit is "defined for numbers and not for theories". For theories generate numbers. And as the absolute numerical magnitudes of the correction factors introduced by theory succession converge, *in the well-defined sense of pure mathematics*, to zero, so we may say that the theories themselves are growing successively closer to each other.

57. And this shows, too, that it is no mere accident that the notion of scientific progress has been historically tied to the extent to which a discipline projects *quantitative measures* of its theoretical parameters. For, if the argument to this point has not been misguided, it is only after a discipline has introduced quantitative measures over its subject matter that there *can* be any literal sense given to the notion that successive theories within that discipline have a *direction* and represent progress, more or less rapid, in that direction. Since the acceptability of a successor theory turns fundamentally upon its ability to account for the successes of its predecessor(s), since it is essential to such an account that

the strict counterparts of old laws in the new framework be *closely approximated* limit cases or idealizations of laws of the new theory, and since the notion of a close approximation makes *literal* sense (is well-defined) only for *numerical measures,* it follows that theories in a non-quantitative discipline cannot be related as predecessor and successor but, at best, merely as *alternatives* to one another.

58. If my colleagues in the social sciences find this "transcendental deduction of 'quantitativism' " objectionable, I can only plead, as Sellars does in connection with his own "transcendental deduction of 'finitism' ", that "I am not alone in thinking that the issue is not an empirical one" ([17]: 148). If we must abandon the myth of the gettable and recognize that no conceptual system can be both framework-neutral and descriptive, as I have argued that we must, then I can see no alternative solution to the Archimedean Dilemma.

XI

59. Before proceeding to my final theme, let me pause to collect a few morals concerning the picturing relation and its role in Sellars' philosophy. Sellars gives picturing two major jobs to do. First, as the sole genuine relation between linguistic and non-linguistic entities (natural-linguistic objects and non-linguistic objects), picturing is to provide the ultimate basis *in re* for the normative claims of a functional metalinguistic discourse. The cash value for the pseudo-relations of functional semantics is to be provided by the regularities of picturing consequent upon the linguistic activities of persons. Indeed, the very possibility that language make claims about the world at all depends, in the last analysis, precisely upon the possibility that first-level statements be related to states of affairs in the world as pictures of them. Further, since the *content* of philosophers' ontological discourse is to be explicated by semantical claims in a functional metalanguage, the picturing relation is to be the ultimate basis for the analysis of such discourse as well.

60. Second, since the picturing relation is posited to admit of continuous refinement toward a characterizable limit, it is to serve also to supply non-metaphorical content for the Peircean notions of 'completed science' and 'ideal truth', an Archimedean standpoint outside the

series of actual and possible conceptual frameworks against which the adequacy of those frameworks may be neutrally measured.

61. That we must appeal to picturing to resolve the first cluster of problems seems to me an unavoidable conclusion. The relation of language to the world cannot be elucidated—indeed, as I see it, cannot even be *understood*—in any other terms. But the problem of the Elusiveness of Categories shows us how little, in the last analysis, such an appeal accomplishes in coping with prime *ontological* concerns. In particular, the need to ground the picturing function of factual discourse by categorial ontological distinctions prevents the metalinguistic ascent of linguistic nominalism from providing a fully formal analysis of philosophers' ontological discourse. Categorial ontological distinctions, while *in one sense* purely formal, emerge as, in another important sense, *real* distinctions, primitive realities so fundamental that they are presupposed by the very functioning of *any* mode of representation, formal or contentive, and, thus, incapable of any representational elucidation in terms still more basic. In the first case, then, Sellars' appeal to picturing, while fundamentally *correct*, is, in a deep sense, *impotent* to provide a path leading totally out of the jungle of classical ontological puzzlements.

62. In the second case, the conclusion is much the reverse. The picturing relation *would* provide the Archimedean standpoint which Sellars sees as a requirement of a non-metaphorical understanding of theory convergence, were it possible to have knowledge of the degree of adequacy of a system of linguistic pictures in a manner *neutral* as among conceptual frameworks. But adequacy of picture *cannot* be thus neutrally assessed and so, I have argued, Sellars' appeal to the picturing relation in the second case is basically *incorrect*. In this case, however, we have an alternative. By attending to the epistemological details of theory succession, we were able to locate a determinate measure of the distance between a *pair* of theories and, thus, to make non-metaphorical sense from within of the tending of the scientific enterprise toward *a* limit, although a limit which there is now no need to formulate, *per impossibile,* in framework-neutral terms.

63. Thus, incorrect in one instance and significantly impotent in another, the conception of picturing central to Sellars' philosophy turns out to be a more limited tool for the unravelling of philosophical perplexities than he believes. Yet, for all that, picturing *is* the ultimate—indeed,

the only genuine—relation between language and the world. That Sellars could see this, and see it as clearly as he has, remains a philosophical accomplishment of the first magnitude, an accomplishment that cannot be diminished.

XII

64. And now let me, finally, bring this already unwieldy study to a close by developing a few speculative remarks concerning the epistemic ends-in-view controlling the scientific enterprise and, more broadly, inquiry into the world in general and the representations (pictures) which result from it. The epistemic ends, you will recall, are essentially the ends of explanation. The prime requirement of acceptability for lawlike statements turned out to be the realization of a necessary condition for being in the framework of explanation and prediction, the controlling end-in-view being the possession of principles which license inferences to unknown cases while optimally explaining what is known. Similarly, the epistemic end controlling the acceptance of new theoretical frameworks emerged as the state of "being able to give non-trivial explanatory accounts of established laws" ([12]: 210). Now the question which I wish to pose here is itself the request for an explanatory account. People seek explanations. Their doing so is the ultimate "motive force" of the scientific enterprise and, more broadly, of all representings of the world. But *why* do people seek explanations? Why do people have the epistemic ends which they in fact do have and thus come to produce representations of the world? It is this question which will be exercising us for the balance of the essay.

65. Now a first reaction might well be that the question itself is misguided. It asks for what can't be given. In the case of any *individual* person, perhaps, a psychoanalytic account might be given of why *he* has and pursues the ends with which we find him, but there is no *more general* account to be given of why *people* have and pursue the ends with which we find them. From the philosophical point of view, the most we can say is that people just *do,* generally, have these ends and pursue these activities, and that that must be an end to the matter.

66. While there is doubtless *some* merit to this reaction, I think that we must finally respond to it by dismissing it. First, we must dismiss it

because, insofar as it contains merely a polemic against raising questions of a certain sort, it counts as "blocking the road to inquiry", and Peirce's injunction against such epistemological obstructionism is as valid today as when first issued. But, second, we must dismiss it because, insofar as it contains a diagnosis of the putative illegitimacy of our question, the presumptive evidence seems contrary to the grounds of that diagnosis. For the "will to explain" is not, as the reaction seems to suggest, an idiosyncratic feature of isolated persons or groups of persons. Rather the search for explanations seems to be characteristic of man *as a species*. While the nature and sophistication of the particular explanatory accounts offered varies widely from culture to culture and, within a single culture, from epoch to epoch, the *presence* of explanatory accounts seems itself to be a cultural invariant. From the elemental mythologies of primitive man to contemporary postulational microphysics is a great distance measured in terms of sophistication. But *epistemologically* myth and microtheory are brothers. Each is a system of beliefs and principles accepted because it provides, at the time of its acceptance, the *best available explanatory account* of a range of phenomena. That people's systems of beliefs and representations of the world grow out of and are controlled by the end of explanation is too pervasive a feature of human life to be dismissed as a brute and unexplainable fact.

67. On the other hand, the contrasting immediate reaction that men seek explanations simply because they wish to *understand* their world must also be dismissed. Here, however, the basis of dismissal is not that the proposed reply is incorrect. Rather it is all *too* true. For the connection between explanation and understanding is analytic. What we understand and what we can explain are not just contingently coextensive. Rather, it is a *necessary* truth that we understand *only* what we can explain. The process of explaining a range of phenomena *is* the process of coming to understand those phenomena. And since it is a necessary truth that we understand only what we can explain, to say that men seek explanations *in order* to achieve understanding is itself to offer no explanation but merely a *rephrasal* of our original question. *Why* do people seek to understand the world?

68. An appropriately sophisticated answer sees scientific inquiry as activity in the service of higher ends. What we do not understand, the reply runs, we cannot predict and we cannot control. Only when we understand the world, therefore, can we act most effectively in optimiz-

ing all those factors which conduce to the good life for man. The ends of understanding (explanation) are, indeed, the ultimate ends controlling the *scientific* enterprise. But, viewed more broadly, that enterprise itself is but a *means* to a more fundamental end—the achieving of the good life for man. And, thus, in this broader context, the epistemic ends-in-view of understanding are to be seen as merely *proximate* ends, and the belief-systems and representations which they generate are to be seen as means or instruments for the attaining of the *genuinely* ultimate ends of *all* human activity.

69. As attractive as this "epistemological instrumentalism" may seem, I believe that we must finally reject it also. For it does not fairly reflect the essential *autonomy* of the epistemic ends of explanation. And this is so because epistemological instrumentalism mislocates the relation between understanding and the good life. To be sure, there *is* a necessary connection, but it is *not* the relation of necessary means to an autonomous end. It is, in fact, even *closer* than that. What we must recognize is that understanding is an *essential part* of the good life for man. The relation of human understanding to human happiness is not like the relation between buying a car and owning it; it is, rather, much more like the relation between eating an apple and enjoying it. Here the activity is a constituent of the enjoyment. *What* we enjoy is *eating the apple.* If I may be permitted a somewhat archaic mode of expression, the enjoyment is *supervenient* upon the eating, not *consequent* upon it as effect upon cause nor separable from it as end from means. Human understanding and the good life for man are related in *that* way. The latter is not consequent upon nor separable from the former but, rather, supervenient upon it. Understanding is itself a wholly autonomous human good and, thus, not *merely* a precondition of human happiness but rather a prime constituent of that happiness. Epistemological instrumentalism, therefore, will not do.

70. What alternative, then, is left us? As I see it, our only choice is to begin to take Aristotle seriously: Every man *by nature* desires to know. What I propose is that we must properly regard our explanatory question concerning the epistemic ends controlling the scientific enterprise as an *empirical* question and, thus, one which *falls within the legitimate scope of that enterprise itself.* Thereby we turn the methodology upon itself as subject. And when we do so, we may find that our *problem* undergoes a radical Copernican inversion. Let me briefly explain what I have in mind.

71. We have been asking for an explanation of why, with respect to epistemic ends and, more broadly, with respect to the representations of the world consequent upon the human epistemic activity controlled by those ends, man is as he is. Taken seriously, the Aristotelian proposal suggests that humans seek to understand and thus to represent the world as a matter of *natural* necessity. It is a law of nature that man, as a species, searches for explanations of phenomena and thereby comes to project representations of his world. Since it is the job of *science* to develop theoretical frameworks which provide explanatory accounts of natural laws, it now becomes a part of that enterprise to develop a comprehensive theoretical account of man-in-the-universe from which it will follow that men seek to understand and represent the universe of which they are a part. And the way to do *this* may well be by means of a *total* conception of the *universe* as a physical system which of natural necessity *evolves* subsystems that in turn necessarily project increasingly adequate representations of the whole. Crudely, our universe necessarily "grows knowers" and thereby comes to reflect *itself* (*picture* itself) within itself.

72. Such a theory would treat man and the universe as explanatorily *correlative*. The fundamental nature of man would, of course, be explained by an appeal to the general character of the physical universe of and within which man is an evolutionary product. But, equally, the fundamental nature of the physical *universe* would be explained by showing that in a universe of that sort, and *only* in a universe of that sort, *could* there evolve a species of entities which generate representations of the total physical system of which they are but a part and thereby *come to inquire* into the fundamental nature of that system. "If the universe weren't the way it *is,* there couldn't be anything in it *capable* of asking what it *was* like."

73. Nor is this Copernican explanatory inversion totally alien to the thinking of contemporary physical theorizers. The physicist John Wheeler and his students have recently begun to speculate about just such an account of the "very large numbers" of physics—the ratio of electrical to gravitational forces, for example. It now begins to appear that, if such fundamental constants were very much different from what they are, the most fundamental physical preconditions of life could not be instantiated within the universe at all. Thus the proposal has been made that we explain the *universe* by reference to *us*. The universe *did* evolve us, after all, and it would not be a trivial result if it could be shown

that *only* a universe of this sort (where "this sort" is now to be specified in precise and quantitative theoretical terms) *could* evolve us.

74. Here, indeed, is a synoptic view of man-in-the-world. We cannot understand the universe until we understand it precisely *as* a universe which is such that, within it, a species of entities evolves which seeks to understand and represent it. And we cannot understand *ourselves* and our epistemology until we understand them both as *products* of this total evolutionary system and as *parts* of the very process of its evolution. And is there anything like this in Sellars' philosophy? Well, at one time there *was*. In 1948, Sellars sketched a distinction

> . . . between a broader and a narrower sense of "empirical system." The narrower sense would cover only such relational systems as include "minds" which "know" the system in which they are embedded. The broader sense would cover any systems which could be said to be a system of exemplifications of universals. With this distinction in mind, one might introduce the phrase "concrete system" to stand for this broader sense, and use the phrase "empirical system" for those systems which are "self-knowing", to which alone the term "empirical" is appropriate. An exploration of the concept of self-knowing concrete systems would take us into the heart of epistemology, for, indeed, in the material mode of speech, epistemology is nothing other than the pure theory of such systems. ([11]: 305.)

A universe which evolves a subsystem of entities who necessarily generate, within the whole of which they are a part, a representation of that whole is surely nothing other than a "self-knowing concrete system" in this early Sellarsian sense.

75. But we need not turn to Sellars for an anticipation of these speculations. The reader has doubtless been hearing echoes for some time; let me now say that they are intentional. For, although newly clothed in respectability by our appeals to empirical science, our universe thus conceived as understandable only as a total system evolving *within* itself a representation *of* itself is a philosophical old friend: the Hegelian Absolute evolving to self-consciousness. Nor is the turning of the methodology of science in upon itself as subject any different from Hegel's identification of subject matter and method in *Die Phänomenologie des Geistes*. Sellars proposes that we now understand Kantian *noumena* in terms of the posits of postulational microtheory.

What I am suggesting here is that we can now understand the self-actualization of the Hegelian Absolute as well, in terms of a synoptic empirical theory of man-in-the-universe which views the epistemic activities of persons and the fundamental nature of the physical arena in which those activities occur as explanatorily correlative, neither being understandable without recourse to a conception of the other.

76. To pursue this topic further would, I fear, generate quite another study, no shorter surely than the present one. So this is not the place to pursue it. But I firmly believe that it is a topic well worth pursuing. And if my readers do not find such an attempt to resuscitate the central themes of Nineteenth Century Idealism particularly congenial to their contemporary idioms, I can cheerfully reply that it is a habit which, like almost everything else philosophical, I learned from Wilfrid Sellars. [8]

8. This essay was completed in 1970. The ensuing four years have provided ample opportunity for second, and even third, thoughts. In consequence, much of what I said in this essay I would now say differently, and some of it (Section VIII, for example) I would now not say at all. My current views are comprehensively represented in two forthcoming works: an essay, "The 'Given' and How to Take It—Some Reflections on Phenomenal Ontology" and a book, *Linguistic Representation* (Philosophical Studies Series in Philosophy, D. Reidel Publishing Company., Dordrecht, Holland).

REFERENCES

[1] Hall Everett, *Philosophical Systems* (Chicago: The University of Chicago Press, 1960).
[2] Harman, Gilbert, "Enumerative Induction as Inference to the Best Explanation," *The Journal of Philosophy* 65 (1968): 529-33.
[3] _____, "Inference to the Best Explanation," *The Philosophical Review* 74 (1965): 88-95.
[4] Quine, W. V., *Word and Object* (Cambridge, Mass.: The M.I.T. Press, 1960).
[5] Rosenberg, Jay F., "New Perspectives on the *Tractatus*," *Dialogue* 4 (1966): 506-17.
[6] _____, "Synonymy and the Epistemology of Linguistics," *Inquiry* 10 (1967): 405-20.
[7] _____, "What's Happening in Philosophy of Language Today," *American Philosophical Quarterly*, 9 (1972): 101-6.
[8] _____, "Wittgenstein's Self-Criticisms, or 'Whatever Happened to the Picture Theory?'," *Noûs* 4 (1970): 209-23.
[9] _____, "Wittgenstein's Theory of Language as Picture," *American Philosophical Quarterly* 5 (1968): 18-30.

[10] Sellars, Wilfrid, "Abstract Entities," *Review of Metaphysics* 16 (1963); reprinted as Ch. IX, pp. 229-69, of [16].

[11] _____, "Concepts as Involving Laws and Inconceivable Without Them," *Philosophy of Science* 15 (1948): 287-315.

[12] _____, "Induction as Vindication," *Philosophy of Science* 31 (1964): 197-231.

[13] _____, "The Language of Theories," in *Current Issues in the Philosophy of Science*, Herbert Feigl and Grover Maxwell, eds., (New York: Holt, Rinehart, & Winston, 1961); reprinted as Ch. 4, pp. 106-26, of [18].

[14] _____, "Language as Thought and Communication," *Philosophy and Phenomenological Research* 29 (1969): 506-27.

[15] _____, "Naming and Saying," *Philosophy of Science* 29 (1962): reprinted as Ch. 7, pp. 225-45, of [18].

[16] _____, *Philosophical Perspectives*   (Springfield, Ill.: Charles C Thomas, Publisher, 1967).

[17] _____, *Science and Metaphysics* (London: Routledge & Kegan Paul; New York: Humanities Press, 1968).

[18] _____, *Science, Perception and Reality* (London: Routledge & Kegan Paul; New York: Humanities Press, 1963).

[19] _____, "Scientific Realism or Irenic Instrumentalism: A Critique of Nagel and Feyerabend on Theoretical Explanation," *Proceedings of the Boston Colloquium on Philosophy of Science* (1965); reprinted as Ch. XIV, pp. 337-69, of [16].

[20] _____, "Some Reflections on Language Games," *Philosophy of Science* 21 (1954): 204-28; reprinted as Ch. 11, pp. 321-58, of [18].

[21] _____, "Truth and 'Correspondence'," *Journal of Philosophy* 59 (1962); reprinted as Ch. 6, pp. 197-224, of [18].

· ~ ·8· ~ ·
Things, Natures, and Properties
ROBERT G. TURNBULL
The Ohio State University

O UR LANGUAGE (by which term I mean to include those languages belonging to the Indo-European family) contains rich predicational resources. Of particular and vexing philosophical moment are those which can be, in English, placed under the rubrics '*is a(n)* predication' and '*is* predication'. Examples of the former are: 'Fido *is a* dog', 'Jones *is an* artist', 'Oxygen *is a* gas', 'The chord just played *is a* minor'. Examples of the latter are: 'Fido *is* white', 'The building *is* tall', 'Peter *is* angry', 'Her smile *is* sweet'. Aristotle made the distinction between *is a* predication and *is* predication a cornerstone of his philosophy, thus giving form and background to a complex philosophical debate whose duration is measured in millenia.

Many philosophers in this century, influenced by developments in logic (notably *Principia Mathematica* of Russell and Whitehead), have, in effect, attempted *reduction* of *is a(n)* predication to *is* predication. Predications of both kinds have been alleged to find, at some remove or other, clarified expression in the (canonical) form, '*F(x)*'. Since standard forms of the (lower) functional calculus take substitution instances of the form, '*F(x) · G(x)*', as admissible, the clarificational model is "thing-property" (*is*) and not "thing-nature or kind" (*is a*). Empiricists of one kind or another, attracted by *PM* style clarifications, have generated several awkward problems which I can hint at by a few questions: Isn't it *necessary* that, if Fido is a dog, he not be a cat?; *Must* not whatever is colored have a shape?; If a particular has several properties, and one of them is replaced by another, why must the particular itself be replaced? How is the notion of the *bare* particular any more intelligible than that of a material substrate or Aristotelian prime matter?

185

In recent years this sort of reduction of *is a(n)* to *is* predication has gone off center stage in Anglo-American philosophy, having been replaced by (for the most part) varieties of Aristotelianism. (Strawson's distinction between sortal and characterizing universals is only one case in point.) In addition to the "awkward problems" hinted at in the last paragraph, the replacement was motivated by discomfort with the psychologizing epistemology of "acquaintance" which commonly accompanied the *PM* style reduction. Names of particulars (and, sometimes, properties) introduced by acquaintance, language learned or anchored by acquaintance with atomic facts, the cleansing of language of "meaningless" (because unverifiable) sentences—all commonly belonged to the reduction of *is a(n)* to *is*. I am in sympathy with the attack on the reduction and on the psychologizing epistemology, but I am distinctly uncomfortable in the Procrustean bed of the Aristotelian replacement. The possibility that reduction of *is* predication to *is a(n)* predication might be accomplished without generating the "awkward problems" and without accompanying psychologizing epistemology is attractive to me.

Wilfrid Sellars published two articles more than twenty years ago which attempt serious exploitation of this possibility, viz., "Concepts as Involving Laws and Inconceivable Without Them" [2] and "The Logic of Complex Particulars" [3]. These were followed by a third, "Particulars" [4] (reprinted in [5]; page references in what follows refer to the reprinting), which developed further, amplified, and corrected some of the ideas of the first two papers. These papers are remarkably detailed and exhibit the usual Sellarsian dialectical acumen. In what follows, I shall first attempt to state the main themes and arguments in them which are germane to the reduction of *is* to *is a(n)* predication and then turn to a sympathetic critique. Needless to say, I think Sellars in these papers accomplishes a great deal.

Though I shall rather freely move among the three papers, I shall use [3] as the primary source, for in it what I have called the "reduction of *is* to *is a(n)* predication" is developed most carefully and completely. I shall begin by summarizing the main development of [3] so as to provide an Ariadne's thread to guide the reader through the complex of argument, digression, and critical comment which follows.

Suppose that behind the logic of terms and sentences of "our" language—sentences with the surface logical grammar of both *is* and *is a(n)* predication—there is a "simple", but unused, level whose basic non-relational sentences are about particulars which have one and only one non-relational property. One might even say of such particulars that their non-relational properties *are* their natures. Complex particulars, the "things" of the surface grammar, are constructs from basic particulars; better, the sentences of surface grammar express facts which are "logical constructions" out of facts of the basic level. *Is* predications of the surface level assert the "ingredience" of a basic particular in a complex. *Is,* in the Sellarsian scheme, is therefore defined, and crucial—or should I say *material?*—in the definition of the *is a(n)* of the basic particulars level. *Ingredience* is, however, defined in terms of *co-ingredience-in-a-thing*. If one attends to certain patterns of co-ingredience-in-a-thing, the definition of *is a(n)* at the surface grammatical level comes into view: *Is a(n)*, at the 'thing"-level, is a matter of exemplifying or exhibiting a given pattern of co-ingredience. Thus 'Fido is white' asserts the ingredience of at least one basic particular whose "nature" is white in the complex particular, Fido. And 'Fido is a dog' asserts that the complex particular, Fido, exemplifies or exhibits a certain pattern of co-ingredience-in-a-thing.

In [3], the assumption of a level of particulars which is "basic" and which can have one and only one non-relational "simple" property—what Sellars calls a 'quale'—is argued for only in the sense that the assumption, together with the "construction" machinery, enables us to make sense of important parts of what I have called "surface grammar discourse". I have no quarrel with that sort of argument and will, in due time, have something to say about its success in [3]. In "Particulars", however, where he is attacking the notion of the "bare particular", Sellars attempts to show that "it is only possible to think of a basic particular as exemplifying two or more simple non-relational universals" ([5]: 287) if one is guilty of confusing particulars and facts. The strongest argument he gives fails, as, in 1963, he recognized ([5]: 289, fn.). I shall, nevertheless, reproduce it, for reflection upon it will enable me to make an important point.

Suppose 'Greem' designates a quale and that α is greem. α is, so far forth, incomplex, for Greemness is not part of it—otherwise we should be confusing α with the fact that α is greem. Call the class of basic particulars which exemplify Greemness 'Grom'; call a member of that class a 'Grum'. Make appropriate assumptions, *mutatis mutandis*, for kleemness, klom, and klum. Sellars writes,

> . . . once the confusion between particulars and facts is completely avoided, the notion that a basic particular can be an instance of two *qualia* not only loses all plausibility, but is seen to be absurd.

A basic particular which is an instance of Greemness is not a bare particular standing in a relation to Greemness, it is a grum. A basic particular which is an instance of Kleemness is not a bare particular standing in a relation to Kleemness, it is a klum. Surely, however intimately related a grum and a klum may be, they cannot be identical! ([5]: 288-89.)

The argument, as Sellars notes, fails if

Grum $=_{df}$ greem-item

and

Klum $=_{df}$ kleem-item.

And there is no reason to think that these identities do not obtain.

On the preceding page, Sellars makes much of the notion that α, "without internal complexity", could hardly be both a grum and a klum. And he is at pains to deny that α is a bare particular "standing in a relation" to whatever quale it exemplifies. I think that the matter of "internal complexity" can be put more perspicuously and that there is a tough argument which can be put to the defender of "polyqualified" basic particulars.

In accordance with the standard lower functional calculus, there is no logical impossibility in a certain particular's exemplifying only F and G at t_1 and exemplifying only F and H at t_2. (Indeed, it might exemplify only H and I at t_3.) A good many philosophers have, nevertheless, been uncomfortable about this possibility and have insisted that, if a particular (*not*, of course, a "natured" substance) were to cease having *any* one of its (simple) non-relational properties, it would cease to exist. Part of the motivation for the insistence is, of course, some version of a sense-data or sensa theory in accordance with which sense particulars have no persisting natures other than the properties they exemplify and also have no "hidden" properties. Indeed, the only argument I know which has been used to support the principle, "Change of any property, change of particular", is a dubious psychologizing epistemology of sense-data (or their equivalent). And this, for reasons we need not pursue here, will not do. It *might* be argued that, since the calculus permits polyqualified particulars and since the calculus really does work for ontological purposes, it is simply arbitrary to insist on monoqualification. But the arbitrariness works the other way. In virtue of what principle is there one particular rather than several when several properties are "clustered"? The appeal at this point is, doubtless, to some alleged principle(s) of space and/or time. However sophisticated the principles and their defense, the appeal—for the most obvious example—comes to: The color and the shape are both "in the same place at the same time", so there cannot be two particulars; for it is impossible for two particulars to be "in the same place at the same time". Though I am prepared to quarrel with the principle where it concerns bottom-level particulars, I wish merely to point out that the appeal here is really to a *nature* which allows some property-clusters in a particular and disallows others. But, if there are such natures (which are not themselves non-relational properties), then we are, in principle, back with Aristotle, and talk of "simple" particulars must be abandoned. (What I am incidentally underlining is, of course, the embarrassment of the usual list of synthetic a priori candidates: Whatever is colored must be extended; Whatever has pitch must have timbre; etc.) Such natures would, of course, provide the "internal complexity" which Sellars deplores, though he does not explicitly consider the above argument.

Also in "Particulars", Sellars treats colored basic particulars as having "the logical properties of points" in "continua" ([5]: 290). He writes:

> It is these points which are the basic particulars, and the *quale* which they exemplify has no designation in ordinary usage. We might well introduce the word 'greem' for this purpose. It is a *synthetic* necessary truth that the instances of *greem* are points in a *continuum*. On the other hand, 'x is *green*' = 'x is a *continuum* of which the elements are *greem*'; so that 'x is *green*' analytically entails 'x is extended'. ([5]: 290.)

I can see no reason for identifying basic particulars—as discussed so far at least—with points, even *greem* points. I agree that '*x* is green' analytically entails '*x* is extended' and agree as well that this analytical entailment depends upon the construction of complex particulars. But surely the multiplication of synthetic necessary truths and the puzzles of continua are, if possible, to be avoided. What is more disturbing, however, is the implication that instances of greem either singly or collectively have extension and, if extension, some shape or other. This, of course, threatens the doctrine that each basic particular has one and only one non-relational property. I should think that doctrine is better served by adumbration with "colored" particulars being *simply red*, *green*, etc., "shaped" particulars being *simply square*, *round*, etc., and so on, it being clearly understood that complex particulars, "made up of" instances of colors and shapes, are necessarily (analytically) colored if shaped and shaped if colored. I shall, however, leave this matter until the last section of the paper—the "sympathetic critique".

In what follows, I shall use the initial lower-case letters of the Greek alphabet as variable terms for basic particulars and subscript those letters to form constants. I shall use initial upper-case Greek letters in an exactly similar way for qualia. Thus, on the Sellars scheme, sentences of the form,

$$A(\alpha) \cdot B(\alpha),$$

are "illegitimate" ([3]: 307 and elsewhere). This requires Sellars to say,

> . . . while there are atomic functions, and while every set of atomic functions must have an axiomatics, there is nothing which could be called a "calculus" of atomic one-place functions. ([3]: 331.)

To this comment may be added his comment in "Particulars" concerning basic particulars' instancing one and only one simple non-relational property:

> Furthermore, it is not to be as a mere matter of fact that this is so, as though these particulars *could* exemplify more than one, but do not happen to do so. It is to be a defining characteristic of the conceptual frame we are elaborating that no particular belonging to it *can* exemplify more than one simple non-relational universal. ([5]: 286.)

Finally, I should note Sellars' insistence, both in [2] and "Particulars", that no sentence of the form, '$A(\alpha)$' is either a contradiction or an analytic truth. Thus α_1, though it *is* A_1, *could* be or have been A_2; what it *could not* be or have been is *both* A_1 and A_2. These last modal comments require adversion to [2].

The scheme of [2] is comparatively simple to state, though its development is intricate, and it is easy to misconstrue it. In it Sellars is concerned to state a doctrine of "real connections" which is not open to objections which he raises against C. I. Lewis. To do so, he distinguishes between the laws of logic (truths wherein the descriptive terms occur vacuously), which determine the logical modalities; laws of nature or "*P*-laws" (with predicate terms occurring essentially), which determine causal modalities; accidental generalities (again with predicate terms occurring essentially); and, finally, individual matters of fact (with basic particulars and qualia as bedrock elements). These, in turn, lead to distinctions between (a) possible worlds *per se,* (b) families of possible worlds each having a distinctive set of laws of nature, (c) individual worlds in a given family, determined by differing sets of basic particulars and concerning which an accidental generalization may hold. Thus in no possible world and, *a fortiori,* in no family of possible worlds *could (logically* could) a substitution instance of a contradiction obtain. In no possible world of a given family *could (physically* could) a violation of the laws of nature which determine that family obtain.

Sellars' argument for the synthetic necessity of laws of nature is, in effect, an application of the principle of the identity of indiscernibles to universals or properties, with non-identity of "most determinate" universals anchored in difference of exemplifications, thus:

> . . . *diversification of the most-determinate qualitative universals is to be understood in terms of relations which obtain between all particulars, actual and merely possible, which exemplify these universals. This thesis will lead us to the conclusion that universals and laws are correlative, that a family of possible histories* [worlds] *exemplifying the same universals is ipso facto a family of possible histories conforming to the same laws, differing only in their "initial conditions".* ([2]: 299-300; italics in original.)

Sellars' idea is that, if most determinate non-relational properties were not "tied" together in plena of exemplificational patterns (i.e., of different basic particulars in possible worlds of a given "family"), they would be indiscernible and hence not different. Each possible world of a "family" is therefore a gapless arrangement of particulars, arranged by their exemplification of one or another of the non-contradictory and structured set of laws determining the "family". The extension of a term in one of the laws is therefore a class of particulars drawn from the many worlds in the "family"; much more narrowly considered, its extension ("real" extension, if you will) is the class of particulars exemplifying it in a single world (of the "family"). The modality of a law statement is thus to be thought of as a matter of its holding for all (joint) exemplifications in all the worlds of a "family". A mere regularity holding for a single world justifies no 'could' which would require its holding for all possible worlds of a "family". The logical modalities, therefore, on the Sellars account, differ from the causal modalities in having extension to *all* possible worlds whereas the causal modalities have extension to all worlds of a given "family". Thus they support different subjunctives in ". . . were, . . . would . . ." conditionals.

Sellars defends the above account in [2] with the terms of the physical laws designating properties which characterize *complex* particulars. In a footnote (to p. 300), he briefly summarizes the important definitions of [3], definitions implementing the "construction" of complex particulars to which we shall turn shortly. He does not, however, work out his argument in the (as we shall see) rather staggering detail which those definitions would require. And this is unfortunate.

In the first place, it is impossible to formulate laws which have the form, '$(x)(F(x) c\text{-implies } G(x))$' (whatever the connective may be), if the values of x are basic particulars; for, in that case, as will be remembered, co-exemplification is not permitted. *Prima facie,* therefore, "universals and laws are correlative", as Sellars develops the case, only if the universals characterize complex particulars and the laws relate complex particulars. And this holds, *secunda facie*, for Sellars uses the standard form given above in later phases of his account of [2]. In the second place, difference of extension of qualia is guaranteed, for no basic particular exemplifies more than one quale. And, in the spirit of Sellars' [2], we must suppose possible basic particulars for all qualia—and thus guaranteed differentiation of extension.

Given these considerations, we are justified in taking at least some of the universals which qualify complex particulars as collecting sequential uniformities among basic particulars, others as collecting static uniformities among basic particulars, and the remainder (perhaps) merely as qualifying a complex particular by virtue of qualifying some basic particular(s) collected in the complex particular by one or other of the first two kinds of universals. The first two kinds (call them 'causal' and 'co-exemplificational') of universals would, trivially, be subject to the identity of indiscernibles. If they collect the same, they *are* the same. That a complex particular had one of the third kind (call it an 'ingredient universal') of universals in it by virtue of having either a causal or co-exemplificational universal might well be taken as an *analytic* necessity.

One may then think of laws which relate causal and/or co-exemplificational universals and ingredient universals as built into the concepts we have of causal and co-exemplificational universals and reflected in what I earlier called the "surface grammar" of a large number of terms in our language. (Indeed, the idea that "thing" or "kind" terms build in laws and function as such in explanations has a venerable history and remains attractive to many.) On this view scientific progress would be largely a matter of "adopting" different concepts and thus introducing different universals for collecting sequential and static uniformities among basic particulars. And on this view species-genera hierarchies of causal and co-exemplificational universals "materially" capture the analytic (i.e., not synthetic) interconnections between such universals, interconnections which "materially" parallel linguistic or conceptual analytic necessities. What I am suggesting will be recognized as akin to the 17th and 18th Century rationalists' idea of "analysis". By such "analysis" the investigator was supposed to discover, perhaps even by experiment, which "definitional" ingredients in a concept must be eliminated, kept, or added. Such concepts do, indeed, "involve laws" and are "inconceivable without them".

What I am questioning in the Sellars account, in [2], is therefore threefold:

(1) whether diversification of universals (even apparently "most determinate" ones at the level of causal or co-exemplificational universals) requires laws in the sense of *synthetic* necessities;

(2) whether an argument made in terms of the "surface grammar" of terms for causal and co-exemplificational universals can legitimately be transferred to basic particulars and qualia without suffering a change; [*Must* there be synthetic necessities holding between basic particulars—by virtue of the qualia they exemplify—if there are (analytic or synthetic) necessities holding between complex particulars and between complex particulars and their "parts"?]

and

(3) whether, given that the thesis of basic particulars with one and only one quale each can be argued for on other grounds, the diversification of universals at the level of qualia in any sense requires either synthetic or analytic necessities.

If we suppose that the demon of the "given" has been exorcised, there is no objection in principle to recognizing "particulars", whether "actual" or merely "possible", with which no one is acquainted. Indeed, one may properly insist that, in the straightforward senses of 'acquaintance' provided by the perception verbs of our language, we are acquainted only with complex particulars—though not, of course, *as such*. Basic particulars need be countenanced only for convenience in exposing the rationale of our language or, for what comes to the same thing, ontological purposes. I am prepared therefore to accept the apparatus of [2], i.e., possible worlds as divided into families of possible worlds, with individual possible worlds as members of some family or other, families being specified by non-contradictory structures of laws (laws being, as I argued above, modes of collecting uniformities among basic particulars). I am prepared as well to accept the idea that each world "exists", in the sense that it is a gapless construct which ideally exploits a logical-cum-nomological modal feature (or set of features) of our language. In the same vein, I should go even farther and suggest that the systematic attempt to answer the question, 'Which world is the *real* world?', involving as it does an answer to the question, 'Which family of worlds is the *real* family?', is not a philosophical attempt at all. The question about the real family is one to which science asymptotically seeks an answer, producing successively non-final language or conceptual changes, the non-finality reflecting what, in another genre, is described as the always probabilistic character of inductive generalization. The observation of "things" as of a kind or nature (or, if you please, as basic particulars collected into putative sequential and/or static uniformities) is, on this accounting, conceptually informed and thus "involves laws". All this is, I think, in fundamental agreement with the main claims of [2]. And it is compatible with the fact that a living language, at any given time, operates at several levels of generality and embodies conceptual tangles and gropings.

In "Particulars", in the process of summarizing some features of [2], Sellars argues that no sentence of the form, '$A(\alpha)$', is either an analytic or contradictory proposition. On the other hand, if, for example, α_1 is A_1 in possible world W_1, then there is no possible world in which α_1 is A_2—though the latter would be (to use a phrase which Sellars calls "clumsy and confusing") a possible state of a possible world. Sellars' defense of the claim that, if a basic particular has a certain quale, then there is no possible world in which that same particular has a different quale, is the argument that, otherwise, there would be bare particulars:

> If the challenge were pressed, 'Why isn't what you are calling "a possible but not actual state of W_1", just another world, say W_2, so that whereas in W_1 x_1 is a grum, in W_2 x_1 is a klum?' the answer would lie in pointing out that this objection involves the mistake of

bare particulars. To see this, we need only remind ourselves that x_1, a particular belonging to W_1 is *ex hypothesi* a grum. Now, to say that it is logically possible for x_1 (which is a grum) to be a klum, in short, to point out that 'x_1 is kleem' is not a contradiction, does not in the slightest entail that x_1 is somehow neutral as between Greemness and Kleemness, i.e. is a bare particular. Thus, while it is a possibility with respect to W_1 that x_1 be kleem, there can be nothing identical with x_1 which *is* a klum, and hence no world which includes x_1 as an instance of Kleemness. Each world, then, has its own set of particulars, there being no overlap between the particulars of one world and those of another. ([5]: 295.)

As we have noted earlier (and as Sellars himself noted), the argument based on the non-identity of a grum and a klum is flawed (above, p.187). It will be remembered that the flaw consisted of the straightforward possibility that a klum might be construed as a kleem-item and a grum as a greem-item, there being nothing logically awkward in one and the same item's being both a kleem-item and a greem-item.

I wish now to press a point which will bring us back to the matter of *is a(n)* and *is* predication. Sellars, in distinguishing between the quale Greenness, the class Grom, and Grums as members of the class, takes predications of the form, '$A(\alpha)$', as of the *is* variety. (Otherwise there would be no temptation to talk of greem-items.) This allows talk of greem-items, even as we may, at the surface level, talk of green-items, red-items, square-items, etc. Still at the surface level, it is important to note that it is just nonsense to talk of man-items, dog-items, bear-items, etc. Where *is a(n)* predication is involved, the distinction between *being F* and *being an F-item* cannot exist. If, then, predications of the form, '$A(\alpha)$', are of the *is a(n)* variety, Sellars' strong argument against bare particulars works, and his argument concerning possible states of possible worlds (granted its other features) also works.

It is worth noting, as well, that construing basic particulars as having one and only one quale becomes much more intuitive if one thinks of the predications as *is a(n)* predications. Surface grammar allows a "thing" to have any number of properties (expressed in *is* predications) but only one nature (expressed in *is a(n)* predications) except for acquired "natures", for example, x's being both a man and a carpenter. One must therefore say that, at the level of basic particulars and qualia, *all* predications are nature or thing-kind predications (*is a(n)*) and *none* are property predications (*is*). Sellars' failure to recognize this, even as late as

1963 ([5]: 289, fn.), is astonishing, especially so when he explicitly recognizes that his strong argument against bare particulars fails. I suspect that a partial explanation is to be found in his preoccupation with administering the *coup de grace* to bare particulars in terms set by their proponents.

The case for construing basic particulars as subject only to *is a(n)* predications (except when combined in complexes) is strengthened when one considers that, in "Particulars", Sellars attempts to show how qualia and "classes of their instances" can be identified. The obstacle to asserting their identity is, as he correctly sees, the fact that "it makes sense to say that the world might have contained no instances of two *qualia* F and G, even though in point of fact it does do so. F and G, then, would both determine the null class of basic particulars" ([5]: 296-97). His own machinery of possible worlds, allowing for the members of a class to be distributed through several worlds, though totally lacking in some, assures the non-identity of classes determined by any two qualia. The troublesome fact that there *might* be no instances of two qualia is removed by ostensible reification of possibilities—a reification whose sting is removed by the recognition that the existence of possible worlds is all one with idealized exploitation of the depth grammar of our language. The identity of qualia and classes is, nevertheless, made even more intuitive by the recognition that qualia predication must be taken as *is a(n)* predication and that, consequently, locutions of the form '*A*-item' lack sense. Indeed, if the latter did make sense and an *A*-item could be a *B*-item, the identity of qualia and classes might fail with the possibility that all and only *A*-items are *B*-items. The mono-predication is crucial.

At long last we can turn to the "construction" of complex particulars as adumbrated in [3]. In explication of *is* predication (though he does not explicitly recognize it as such), Sellars starts with the notion of *ingredient in* (symbolized by '*I*'), and his first approximation has the following form:

$$(\exists \alpha)(\exists A)(I(\alpha, x_1) \text{ and } A(\alpha)).$$

This *approximates* the correct form of *is* predications, as in such sentences as 'Peter is angry', and is to be read 'There is a basic particular and there is a quale such that at least one such particular is ingredient in a certain complex particular (Peter), and that particular is an anger'. Sellars' actual formulation (the above is mine) does not take account of the *is a(n)* predication following the 'and', and he does not explicitly separate the variables, x, y, etc., and their subscripts (i.e., constants) from the undefined signs for basic particulars. But he writes as follows:

> I, or Ingredience, is a relation between an ingredient particular and a complex particular of which it is an ingredient. *But prior to I are the relations between a set of items by virtue of which they are ingredients.* ([3]: 320, italics in original.)

So I have used 'α' instead of Sellars' 'x' and reserved 'x' and its subscripts for complex particulars. Sellars proceeds to a "definition in use" (his term) for 'I' in order to recognize the "prior" character of certain "relations" between complex particulars, thus

$$I(\alpha,x) \text{ if and only if } x = \Phi (. . ., \alpha, . . .). ([3]: 320.)$$

I think that what Sellars actually intends is stronger than the 'if and only if' suggests, i.e., something sufficiently strong for the treatment of 'I' as a genuinely *defined* sign. Genuine definition of 'I', however, requires a finer-grained treatment of '$\Phi(. . .)$' than Sellars ever provides. The "relations" packed into the latter's designation have to be those I mentioned earlier in portmanteau fashion by talking about sequential and static uniformities in basic particulars. Thus complex particulars (values of x) could be mentioned by some such phrase as 'the α's, the β's, etc., such that . . .' where the gap following 'that' is to be filled by argument variables, and also terms for qualia, descriptive relations between basic particulars, logical connectives, and operators. Even for relatively "simple" complex particulars the complexities would be staggering, but what is sought is conceptual and "in principle" clarification. It is clear that Ingredience cannot usefully be taken as any sort of relatively simple whole-part relationship. (One is reminded of Aristotle's comment at *Categories* 1a24-5, that by " 'present in a subject' I do not mean present as parts are present in a whole.") What is needed is some account of what might be called a "thing-making" relation or relations and then an additional account of the kind or kinds of basic particulars a thing *must* have to be the sort of thing it is and which it *may* have. I shall try my hand at a sketch of this account in the last section of this paper.

Staying with the surface grammatical example, 'Peter is angry', we might represent it by

Anger/Peter/

and, assuming for schematic purposes that Peter = $\Phi(. . ., \alpha, . . .)$, we get

Anger/Peter/ =def. $(\exists \alpha)(I(\alpha, \Phi(. . ., \alpha, . . .)))$ and Anger(α).

Anger, in the above, is taken, of course, to be a quale, and qualia are said in good Aristotelian fashion to be present in complex particulars by virtue of their being exemplified by basic particulars which are constituents of complex particulars. Clearly, on this accounting, a complex particular may have many simple properties or qualia, i.e., many *is* predications of qualia may be made of it. *Strictu sensu*, the *is* predication in our example is of *is angry*, the *is a(n)* predication being of *is an anger* and made of a basic particular ingredient in the complex particular. So understood, *is* predication, occurring as adjectival (and, I should argue as well, adverbial) predication in the surface grammar, is definable in terms of both *is a(n)* predication (for basic particulars) and ingredience. I should note that Sellars, in [2] as in "Particulars", does not recognize qualia predication as *is a(n)* predication.

Sellars next notes that some "properties" of complex particulars are complex. His schema for their predication has the following form:

(1) $(\exists \alpha)(\exists \beta) . . . I(\alpha, \Phi(. . ., \alpha, . . .))$ & $I(\beta, \Phi(. . ., \beta, . . .))$ & $. . .$
   & $A(\alpha)$ & $B(\beta)$ & $. . . .$

As Sellars actually writes, that schema has the form:

(2) $(\exists y)(\exists z) . . . I(y,x)$ & $I(z,x) . . .$ & $g(y)$ & $h(z) . . . .$ ([3]: 321.)

For an adequate parallel of Sellars' actual formulation, we should have to write (1) as

(1a) $(\exists \alpha)(\exists \beta) . . . I(\alpha, \Phi(. . ., \alpha, \beta, . . .))$ & $I(\beta, \Phi(. . ., \alpha, \beta, . . .))$
   & $. . .$ & $A(\alpha)$ & $B(\beta)$ & $. . . .$

Given the (possibly) complex character of '$\Phi(. . .)$', such complex "properties" may be very complex indeed, may be "causal", etc., even though they do not as such limit the "nature" of a thing or complex particular. Consider such "properties", for example, as being migratory, being musical, etc.

Sellars then adds to (2) the following:

(3) $\sim(\exists w)I(w,x)$ & $(w \neq y)$ & $(w \neq z)$ & $. . .$ ([3]: 321.)

If we suppose that a surface grammatical sentence having the form '$f(x)$' is "unpacked" by the conjunction of (2) and (3), then, assuming the full fleshing out, x will be completely specified. Sellars calls the 'f' where it has this sort of unpacking a "θ-predicate", the choice of 'θ' being dictated "because of its relation to the initial sound of 'things' " ([3]: 322). Thus, if we define expressions having the form '$\theta(t)$', we get something like

(4a) $\theta_i(t)$ =def. $(\exists\alpha)(\exists\beta)[\ldots \& I(\alpha,\Phi(\ldots,\alpha,\beta,\ldots)) \& I(\beta,$
$\Phi(\ldots,\alpha,\beta,\ldots)) \& \ldots \& A(\alpha) \& B(\beta) \& \ldots] \& \sim[(\exists\gamma)I(\gamma,$
$\Phi(\ldots,\alpha,\beta,\ldots)) \& (\gamma\neq\alpha) \& (\gamma\neq\beta) \& \ldots] \& [t =$
$\Phi(\ldots,\alpha,\beta,\ldots)]$.

θ-properties (or, as Sellars says, concepts) are *complete* specifications of the qualia which the constituent basic particulars of a complex particular exemplify. As Sellars remarks

> To put the matter somewhat differently, if t exemplifies θ_i, then nothing can be truly predicated of t concerning its *intrinsic* character (as opposed to its relation to particulars not ingredient in it) which is not contained in the sense of '$\theta_i(t)$'. *It follows that expressions of the form '$\theta_i(t)$ & $\theta_j(t)$' are no more legitimate at the molecular level, than are expressions of the form* 'f(x) & g(x)' *at the atomic. A θ-concept specifies the complete and determinate nature of any complex particular which exemplifies it.* ([3]: 322-23; italics in original.)

With this notion of θ-characteristics or properties, Sellars is ready to state his final important notion in terms of which he distinguishes *is* and *is a(n)* predication at the surface grammatical level, viz. *Constituency*. He understands this in such a way that Constituency relates a quale (or several qualia) with a θ-characteristic, thus providing a parallel for Ingredience which relates a basic particular with a complex particular. If, then, one thinks of a complex particular's being, say, an *A*-thing as its exemplifying a θ-characteristic which has *A* as a constituent, the following equivalence holds:

(5a) $C[A,(\imath\theta)\theta(\Phi(\ldots))]$ if and only if $(\exists\alpha)I(\alpha,\Phi(\ldots,\alpha,\ldots))$ & $A(\alpha)$.

Sellars' actual formulation is

(5) $C[f, (\imath\theta)\theta(t)]$ if and only if $(\exists y)I(y,t) \& f(y)$.   ([3]: 326.)

(5a) supplies some crucial detail which (5) lacks, viz., that values of 't' must always be complex particulars, specifiable by expressions of the form, '$\Phi(\ldots)$'. Were a given value of t fully specified, the fact that a given quale is constituent in the θ-characteristic which that value of t

exemplifies would show itself. Thus sentences having the form of the left side of (5) would seem to be either analytic or contradictory, and so also those having the form of the right side of (5). For *both* Constituency and Ingredience are unpackings of Co-ingredience-in-a-thing. So when Sellars goes on to represent "Fido is an angry-thing" by

(6) $C[\text{Anger}, (\imath\theta)\theta(\text{Fido})]$, ([3]: 327)

and reads this as "Anger is a constituent of the θ-concept exemplified by Fido" ([3]: 327), he misleads. For the reading suggests that information is conveyed by the sentence which does not already show itself in the proper representation of Fido by some fully specified value of '$\phi(. . .)$'.

At long last, we get to Sellars' treatment of *is a(n)* predication at what I have been calling the "surface grammatical level". He first notes that, working with ideas like (6) in mind, there is a means of construing, say, 'Fido is angry' and 'Fido is hungry' so that both may be true. And this is surely what we wish for *is* predication. But *is a(n)* is obviously a different matter; we don't want 'Fido is a dog' and 'Fido is a cat' to be both true. Sellars thinks that "thing-kind" concepts can be handled in the following manner.

First he isolates concepts or properties referred to in the first position of Constituency statements, as anger is referred to in (6). These he calls "notes" and suggests that we may think of various classes of θ-characteristics as having typical notes. Thus angry things all exemplify some member of the class of θ-concepts which have *anger* as a constituent, and so on. Using subscripts of 'N' to form different variables ranging over notes, 'Fido is angry and Fido is hungry' is taken as having the following form:

$C[N_1, (\imath\theta)\theta(t)]$ & $C[N_2, (\imath\theta)\theta(t)]$. ([3]: 329.)

Then Sellars says,

Words for "kinds of things" are so introduced that every overlap of the classes of θ-concepts specified by the notes named by these words, contains only θ-concepts which are unexemplified either as a contingent matter of fact, or because they are physically impossible. They are so chosen, in other words, that

$\sim(\exists t)\, C[N_1, (\imath\theta)\theta(t)]$ & $C[N_2, (\imath\theta)\theta(t)]$.

We now understand how "Fido is a dog" differs from "Fido is angry". ([3]: 329.)

This is the denouement of [3]. For several reasons—all connected with Sellars' handling of Co-ingredience-in-a-thing—I don't think it will do.

I have no quarrel with the notion of Co-ingredience as such; something like it is needed for any attempt to "construct" *things* from basic particulars and qualia. What is also needed is further adumbration of "the relations between a set of items [i.e., basic particulars] by virtue of which they are ingredients" ([3]: 320) in things *simpliciter* and in things as belonging to certain thing-kinds. Quite aside from the formalization difficulties in (6) and other sentences like it, Sellars' treatment of the difference between 'Fido is angry' and 'Fido is a dog' won't do. It is no "contingent matter of fact" or "physical impossibility" which guarantees that Fido is not a cat, if he is a dog. It is a *conceptual* impossibility, and the symbolism should exhibit that perspicuously.

Leaving aside worries about the construction of things *simpliciter*, consider that many complex particulars, all of them co-ingredient collections, have what I shall call "structural features" in common (roughly, what I earlier called "causal and co-exemplificational universals"). Indeed, the specification of what Sellars calls "relations between a set of items" *is the same thing as* specifying structural features. Sellars' move from Ingredience to Constituence, i.e., going from "relations" between basic particulars to "relations" between qualia, is a move in the right direction, but, as he develops it, it leaves us with $is\ a(n)$ predication as a species of *is* predication. What is needed is a treatment of Constituence and Ingredience which allows for complex particulars (co-ingredient collections) to stand to patterns of structural features (constituence patterns) as values stand to the bound variables which they are values of or as sets of particulars instance a law.

If we suppose, as I think we must, that every complex particular has ingredient basic particulars which are arrayed in spatially and temporally contiguous sets and that those particulars instance static and sequential uniformities which can be referred to in varying degrees of generality, we can see how one and the same co-ingredient collection can be at once *a* thing, *an* animal, *a* dog, and even *a* hunting dog. If dog, for example, is thought of as a class of complex particulars which meet the "thing-requirement" (i.e., are spatially and temporally contiguous sets or groupings) and are, additionally, patterned in "dog" ways, we may think of Fido's *being a* dog as his being a complex particular which is a member of that class. Thing-concepts so thought of would, of course, be freighted with laws and indeed be inconceivable without them. Since the "dog" patterning, as it were, would run through the whole thing-set, it would be logically impossible for the thing-set to be a cat—unless, *per impossibile,* dogs really were cats.

As Aristotle correctly noted, if it is possible to make an *is* predication of a thing, it must be possible to make an *is a(n)* predication of that very same thing. Thus, if 'is angry' is true of something, 'is a dog', 'is a man', or some such must be true of that same thing. Indeed, it seems otiose to point out that every *is* predication presupposes at the very least the predication, 'is a thing'. Using a bit of Sellars' notation, this would amount to requiring that nothing could be ingredient in a specification of $\Phi(\ .\ .\ .\ )$ unless that specification were a member of what I shall call a "Φ-class". After all, one could not even say what ingredience is without the notion of co-ingredience-in-a-thing.

Sellars' move from Ingredience to Constituence is, I think, partial recognition of the need for specific and generic characterization of Φ-classes without values for basic particular variables and with non-vacuous occurrence of qualia-terms (and ranges of qualia-terms). In this connection, two matters should be noted. First, the specific and generic characterization, as it were, mandates some basic particulars or sets of basic particulars, permits others, and excludes yet others. No dog, e.g., can fail to be quadrupedal, vertebrate, and mammalian. It *might*, however, have any of a number of colors or shapes. It *couldn't* be herbivorous or oviparous. Though the characterization may vary through time and may be more explicit and distinctive for a mammalian biologist, the logical point that thing-kind concepts involve characterization of Φ-classes via lawlike patternings remains. The issue involved is not one of what or how we know but rather of the infra-structure of thing-kind terms of "our" language. Second, I see no reason to quarrel with the Sellarsian characterization of Ingredience as a means of explicating *is* predication. That a complex particular *is F* or *G* or whatever is plausibly taken to be a matter of its having ingredient in it basic particulars which exemplify qualia, whether these be thought of singly or as groups of basic particulars exhibiting structures. It is worth commenting, though the point is not new, that *is* predication at the surface grammatical level generally tells the way a thing is or how it is with that thing. Thus Fido is angry, not anger; Jones is running, not a run; and so on.

As noted much earlier, Sellars makes much of the identity of properties and classes in "Particulars". I argued then that there was a connection between the *is a(n)* predication of qualia and the identity of classes of basic particulars and qualia. I should like now to underline my own argument that *is a(n)* predication at the level of complex particulars is to be understood in terms of class membership. In this same connection and with the fundamental features of [2] in mind, one may make his peace with the idea of there being all manner of families of possible worlds with different sets of laws, including the laws packed into thing-kinds, sufficient to secure "extensions" for every non-contradictory set of laws-cum-thing-kinds, to say nothing of the possible worlds of a given family. And once again I might well note that these "exist" as gapless constructs which ideally exploit logical-cum-nomological features of our language.

The matter of the identity of properties and classes is rather different if one focuses on *is* predication. Though Socrates smiles, he doesn't belong to the class of smiles. Though Fido is angry, he doesn't belong to the class of angers. And so on. Generally, on the present account, complex particulars may be said to belong to classes determined by *is* predications which may be made of them by virtue of having ingredient in them basic particulars or patterns of basic particulars which are members of those same classes by virtue of *is a(n)* predications. The same fact can be expressed by noting that, in the case of *is* predications, one must add the phrase suffix '-thing' to form the class name (as 'angry-thing', 'smiling-thing', etc.), which is not necessary in the case of *is a(n)* predications. That a man can smile without *being* a smile or be angry without *being* an anger, but cannot be a man without *being* a man, suggests, from a different angle, that, though *is a(n)* predication is to be understood in terms of class membership, *is* predication need not. Aside from the issue of unexemplified properties (which was dealt with earlier), I think that much of the philosophical (as opposed to purely logical) worry about the identity of properties and classes can be dispelled by drawing out the implications of the differences between *is a(n)* and *is* predication. What has been laid out here is, of course, only a small start of that task or, to use a Sellarsism, a promissory note.

Several times I have taken exception to Sellars' claim that, for various reasons, we must countenance "synthetic necessities". Though I grant, of course, that modal terms like 'can', 'must', etc., as well as subjunctive counter-factuals, require explication somehow in terms of "necessities", I find those "necessities" to be either overtly or covertly logical or analytic. Sellars would grant, I believe, that, though the fundamental lawful interrelations are at the infra-level of basic particulars and qualia, our reasonings take place at the level of *is* and *is a(n)* predications concerning complex particulars, that is, at what I have called the surface grammatical level. At *that* level, both *is* and *is a(n)* predications *presuppose* uniformities. Thing-kind terms, in particular, build in laws, so that, if appropriate sequential and static uniformities among *is* predications do not obtain, then the *thing*, whatever it may be, simply isn't a member of the relevant Φ-class or, what comes to the same, does not fall under the thing-kind term in question. *A fortiori,* the thing-term cannot be used to explain the necessity of a given *is* predication's obtaining for that thing. (*That* necessity, should it obtain, is, of course, covertly analytic, since, if it failed to obtain, the thing in question would not exhibit the uniformity required by the applicability of the thing-kind term.) The failure of thing-kind terms or concepts to support (observationally) justified *is* predications, on this reckoning, is not an invitation fo find synthetic necessities or to adopt language for expressing such necessities. It is rather an invitation to shift concepts (whether the same term in the sense of token or token-class is used or not) to one which presupposes (a) different (uniformity or) uniformities—or, what comes to the same, is the concept of a different Φ-class. As I noted earlier, what I have in mind is similar to the rationalist idea of "analysis"— without the rationalist blur between ontology and science which reified the ideal exploitation of the modal features of our language into the proper objects of science. (Cf. Leibniz' insistence that metaphysics goes beyond and completes physics.)

A final comment concerning basic particulars. It will be remembered that Sellars, in "Particulars", treats basic particulars (at least the colored ones) as "points in a continuum". In commenting on that, I suggested taking the notion that basic particulars have one and only one non-relational property very strictly. A given basic particular, α_i, is, say, a red *and nothing else* (saving its relations to other basic particulars). Another, α_2, is, say, a square *and nothing else*. Such particulars do not "exist" in the sense in which every "existing" particular must have a shape, if colored, and a color, if shaped. This suggests an analysis of the simplest "existing" particulars. Consider:

$$\text{red}(x) \cdot \text{square}(x) =_{\text{def.}} \text{red}[\alpha] \cdot \text{square}[\beta] \cdot \phi^{\ulcorner}\alpha,\beta^{\urcorner} = x.$$

I have used square brackets, '[ ]', for the *is a(n)* predication of qualia and '$\Phi^{\ulcorner} \ldots ^{\urcorner}$' for what, with apologies to Nelson Goodman ([1], Ch. VII), could be called "concretizing". This would be a first move towards Sellars' 'Φ(. . .)'. Without laying out the necessary detail for a proper account, I should like, obviously, to suggest the lines I would take to account for the necessity of 'Whatever is colored is extended' and other such necessities (e.g., 'Whatever has pitch has a timbre'). The general argument which the accounting would supply is, of course, support for the claim that all such necessities are (covertly) analytic.

We may, as well, think of basic particulars as temporally related and having, as it were, temporal extension, some "lasting longer" than others. Indeed, in a fleshed-out account, I should argue for the possibility of a given basic particular's being both prior to and later than another. Part of the reason for that argument is that, with that possibility, we could make sense of a given *non*-basic particular's changing its shape but not its color without having to be exchanged for another particular and without the assumption of "natures". Suppose that x is first round and red, then oblong and red, and then square and red. Using something like the concretizing device of the above paragraph, we may think of x as four basic particulars (one each for red, round, oval, and square) whose concretizing includes the temporal overlap of the red basic particular with all of the other three. Again, I can here offer the merest sketch. I may hope, however, that the idea of the construction of "existent" from "non-existent" particulars is tolerably clear and also the point of the idea.

I set out to show that three early papers of Wilfrid Sellars pointed out a way for plausible reduction of *is* predication to *is a(n)* predication, though Sellars did not explicitly so define his task. I have long regarded those papers as brilliantly suggestive and am grateful for the opportunity to pull together my thoughts concerning them. Their themes and doctrines cover a great deal of philosophical ground, however, and I fear that an article-length critique hardly does them justice.

REFERENCES

[1] Nelson Goodman, *Structure of Appearance* (Indianapolis: Bobbs-Merrill, 1951).
[2] Wilfrid Sellars, "Concepts as Involving Laws and Inconceivable Without Them," *Philosophy of Science* 15 (1948).
[3] _____, "The Logic of Complex Particulars," *Mind* 58 (1949).
[4] _____, "Particulars," *Philosophy and Phenomenological Research* 13 (1952); reprinted in [5].
[5] _____, *Science, Perception and Reality* (London: Routledge & Kegan Paul; New York: The Humanities Press, 1963).

· ~ · 9 · ~ ·
The Indispensable Word 'Now'

RULON WELLS
Yale University

§1. *Twofold aim of paper.* Better than any other philosopher, Wilfrid Sellars has grasped and pointed up a certain elusive insight about time. My first and lengthier project in this paper is to state, develop, and examine this insight, an insight that is succinctly formulated with the help of the word 'now'.

Sellars incorporates this insight into a metaphysic which is in one respect monistic—there is only matter, or body; mind and body are identical; the Manifest Image is to be dropped in favor of the Scientific Image—and in another respect dualistic—besides the real order there is the logical order. Not finding in Sellars himself any regular or even any preferred label for this metaphysic, I venture to coin the term 'biordinalism', picking on the notion of the two orders as signaling its monism-with-dualism.

I shall not here undertake to do for Sellars' biordinalism the same job of statement, development, and examination as for his insight into the Now, but shall only undertake to show that the metaphysic is independent of the insight. My second project, then, is to show that one can without any sort of inconsistency accept the insight without accepting the remainder (the monism-with-dualism) of the metaphysic into which Sellars incorporates it.

The articulation between the two projects is logically simple. The first project culminates in a syllogism: (1) Every language adequate to the description of experience contains the word 'now' (or equivalent); (2) the language of science does not contain the word 'now'; therefore (3) the language of science is not adequate to the description of experience. The second project considers two other syllogisms, logically equivalent to each other, which build on the conclusion of the first. One of these syllogisms argues: (3) The language of science is not adequate to the description of experience; (4) the language of science is adequate to the description of reality; therefore (5) some language adequate to the description of reality is not adequate to the description of experience. The other syllogism argues: (6) Every language adequate to the description of reality is adequate to the description of experience; therefore (7) the language of science is not adequate to the description of reality.

The minor premise of the first of these equivalent syllogisms denies the conclusion of the second, so that it conclusion must deny the major premise of the second. Propositions (4)—the minor premise of the first—and (6)—the major premise of the second—cannot both be accepted (though they can both be rejected; they are contraries, not contradictories). In the background of the present paper, though only in the background, is the fact that some people, Sellars for one, accept (4), and others, for example myself, accept (6). Sellars' metaphysic, as an argued position, depends upon (4) conjointly with (3); the acceptance of (3) leaves the question whether to accept (4) or (6) quite open.

The first project of the present paper is to establish (3) as itself the conclusion of a previous argument.

§2. *From McTaggart to Sellars.* From Sellars' point of view, all that is useful in McTaggart's account of time is his distinction of two aspects. He largely disagrees not only with the conclusion of McTaggart's account, but also with the details of the account itself. To venture in criticism just a tiny step beyond Sellars, I must also on my own initiative urge against McTaggart two further objections. The minor one is that his labels for the two aspects are poor; there is nothing obvious or particularly helpful to the memory in calling Past, Present, and Future the A-series, and the series of times related by earlier and later (before and after) the B-series. The more important criticism is that while it is quite proper to speak of *the* B-series (singular), to speak correspondingly of *the* A-series presupposes the false Hegelian account which I shall take up in §10. Every distinct now determines a distinct A-series, so that we ought to speak of A-series (plural), in contrast with the B-series (singular).

In spite of Sellars' rejection of most of McTaggart's account, there is in the end a partial agreement. Sellars does hold that A-series are unreal (more precisely: do not belong to the real order), though not for McTaggart's reason. His reason is, as sketched in §1, that natural science on the one hand excludes A-series and on the other hand exhausts the real order.

It may go beyond what Sellars has actually said, but I daresay would not be unacceptable to him, if we perform a conceptual operation on A-series and on the B-series so as to distinguish the two aspects in a different way. In any A-series, the two extreme terms are related by B-relations to the central term: The Past (relative to a Present) is all those instants that are earlier than the Present instant, and the Future is all those instants that are later than it. We may be said to have conflated every A-series with the B-series. It is an immediate and important consequence of this conflation that the other two terms of any A-series are uniquely determined by their B-relation to the central term. The Present is the central term in importance as well as in order. As will be developed in §8, every Present, or Now, is able through conflation with the B-series to represent and to reconstitute its entire A-series. Conflation—the fact that every instant is both (a) a term in the B-series and (b) involved either as a term—the Present—or as a part of the Past term or of the Future term—of every A-series—has a linguistic reflection that will be considered in §16.

I propose to construe ordinary English sentences like 'Now it is 12 o'clock' as identities, 'Now = 12 o'clock'; 'now', construed as a noun, will be abbreviated 'n', and 'c' will be a dummy symbol for any expression which refers to an instant qua term of the B-series. An instant, considered in this aspect, I call a c-date; the letter 'c', unlike McTaggart's 'A' and 'B', is intended to be mnemonic, and to recall the words 'clock' and 'calendar'.

So the canonical way of expressing the conflation of the B-series with an A-series is an identity $n = c$, where n is the central term of that A-series and c is a c-date, i.e., is a date qua belonging to the B-series. To utter such an identity, or whatever the surface structure of one's language transforms it into, is called in English 'telling the time', and the standard forms of question calling for such an identity are 'What time is it?' and 'Can you tell me what time it is?'

§3. *The physicist's limitations.* Now what I take to be Sellars' insight, readily expressed in the New Way of Words, is this: The physicist can't tell us what time it is.

This proposition may seem surprising, because one might think that the physicist is par excellence the one who can tell us what time it is. But it is because the proposition is paradoxical that it is well suited to expressing an important insight. A humdrum expression of the same insight is that the physicist's concern with time, and his expertise, lies exclusively in the B-series.

It may be helpful to make three points in support of this proposition, points which if I can't quote them from Sellars I take to be implicit in his discussions. These three points explain the paradox away. (1) The physicist cannot *qua physicist* tell us what time it is. (2) Identities of the sort $n = c$ may figure in the physicist's data, and yet be excluded from his conclusions. (3) The physicist can tell us what is the best clock—in other words, he is expert in making inferences which yield corrections of various actual clock-readings, but these inferences have apparent c-dates as their inputs and real or true c-dates as their outputs. In inferences of this class, inputs as well as outputs are purely within the B-series.

§4. *In what way the physicist is expert.* Point (3) illuminates point (1). To see into the physicist's expertise, let us consider error and its correction. One of the defining characters of the expert is that in case of disagreement between an expert and a non-expert, the expert is (as a rule, perhaps not always) right and the non-expert wrong. How might a non-physicist be wrong about what time it is, and subject to correction by the physicist? We may confine attention to the case where the mistaken judgment is not a mere guess, but has some basis, and we may consider the mistake as consisting of a mistake in inference from this basis. The physicist's expertise lies (a) in not making mistakes in inference from this basis, and (b) in being aware of other bases from which to make inferences of this sort. The mistake in inference is a physical mistake, not a logical one, because the inference is a material, not a formal (deductive) inference. We are not here concerned with point (b). The effect of the physicist's expert correction is to replace one c-date by another, and it can be given this fundamental canonical form: The time which seems to be c_1 is really c_2. This correction makes no reference, explicit or implicit, to any A-series. Besides this fundamental form of expert correction, there will be various derived forms; for instance, the expert physicist may for a given appearance (apparent time) give the correct time without giving it as a correc*tion* of some *incorrect* time. In the fundamental form of judgment wherein the physicist displays his expertise, the identity will have singular descriptions on both sides; one will describe a phenomenon, or appearance, and the other will specify a real time.

Concerning point (2), I need only briefly comment that if identities of the form $n = c$ figure in the physicist's data, they don't figure essentially, i.e. indispensably; a physicist who records data using A-terms did not need to do so, since he could have used B-terms exclusively.

As a last clarification of the physicist's expertise, I should like to emphasize that when I speak of the physicist as correcting a mistake in inference, I am not committing myself to a doctrine of the datum in any obnoxious version. It is not peculiar to defenders of the epistemological datum to hold that mistakes fall into categories, in other words that if so-and-so be alleged to have made a mistake, it is fair to ask 'What *kind* of a mistake?'. To put the same thought into yet other words, if someone 'goes wrong', it is fair to try to pinpoint it, to inquire *where* he went wrong. And if the non-physicist is shown by the physicist to have made a mistake about (to have gone wrong about) the time, I don't see what heading his mistake could fall under except that of, e.g., 'thinking that his watch was right', or the like. To think that his watch is right is to think that since his watch says 12 o'clock, it is 12 o'clock; or, to describe it in our canonical terms, it is, on the basis that his watch says 12 o'clock, to infer that it is 12 o'clock. It is in the word 'since' that his mistake is concentrated, and that is where the physicist corrects him.

§5. *A misapprehension about corrigibility.* If it comes to the public as paradoxical news that the physicist cannot tell us what time it is, the reason is that very few people have gotten straight the elementary distinction between A-series and the B-series. Perhaps McTaggart's distinction should not be called elementary. Perhaps it should be built into the definition of 'elementary' that an elementary point is easily and widely grasped. Call it elementary or not, in any case the distinction involves some subtle and delicate insights into meaning (and identity of meaning, or synonymy), and the promulgation of the point suffers from the fact that the physicist need not be meticulous about it, precisely because it does *not* concern him. It is by a comedy of errors that the physicist neglects a point that seems to concern him because it doesn't really concern him, and then the non-physicist, thinking that the physicist is careful about everything that seems to concern him, thinks that the physicist must have given a correct account of the point.

In general, people are careless and un-knowledgeable about identity. They are inept in distinguishing varieties of identity, and think that any identity $X = Y$ warrants saying 'X, i.e. Y, . . . '. This casual negligence, in the case at hand, freely says 'n, i.e., c, . . . '. Even great philosophers have lapsed from their own profounder insights into this negligence. (Russell, at those times when he suffered this lapse, thought that these identities made '*now*' superfluous in an ideal language.) I take it as part of Sellars' signal merit, in dealing with the Now, to view this negligence as mistaken and indefensible.

§6. *No scientist can tell us what time it is.* We should not simply identify the scientist with the physicist. In view of Sellars' elaborate critique of reductionism—a topic to which he has given more attention than to any other in the philosophy of science—we should consider the possibility that some science other than physics could tell us what time it is.

Actually, this possibility need not detain us very long. The only plausible candidate is psychology, and psychology turns out to be in no better position than physics. It is not because of what distinguishes physics from psychology that physics is unequal to the task; it is because of what they have in common. It is the general features of natural empirical science, not any special features—whatever they may be—of physics that exclude A-serial terms. It is because science, even when describing (as psychology does) the experience of time, employs constants that refer to instants qua terms in the B-series, and variables ranging over these, but excludes A-constants. Even those who distinguish between *Natur-* and *Geisteswissenschaften* will not distinguish between them in this respect; the distinction will be drawn, rather, on the basis that the former explain and the latter understand (*verstehen*); and this distinction will entail that the final output of the latter will contain constants where the former would not consider an output final until it had universally quantified variables. But even the *Geisteswissenschaften,* when they employ constants of time (date-constants), can confine their attention exclusively to the B-series, and if they were to bring in A-terms, would forfeit their claim to being sciences.

The conclusion so far is that science cannot tell us what time it is. To rephrase the point more technically, science cannot verify or falsify—cannot establish the truth or the falsity of—any canonical identity $n = c$. (These terms 'verify, 'falsify', 'establish' are not restricted to conclusive or definitive verification, etc.; they are meant to apply also to even probable, partial, or otherwise less than conclusive verification, etc.)

But it follows from this that 'now' is excluded from the language of science. For the principle of parsimony would preclude its lying there unused; there could be a place for it only if there were a use for it. To be used means to occur, non-vacuously, in sentences expressing propositions that are amenable to verification and falsification. But identities $n = c$ are not amenable to verification or falsification by science. It may seem that there is one possibility still left open: that 'now' might occur (and non-vacuously) in some other linguistic environment than that of identity. This possibility will be closed out in §8, where it is shown that every occurrence of 'now' in an environment other than identity is tantamount to an occurrence in the identity-environment.

§7. *Verbal Tenses and A-expressions.* It seems that in ordinary English the choice of one verbal Tense rather than another accomplishes the same determination of meaning as the choice of one A-expression such as 'now', 'formerly', 'in the future' rather than another.

Expressions that are used to signify one or another determination of an A-series will be called A-expressions. A partial list of the A-expressions of ordinary English is the following: (1) the nouns 'now', 'past' (as in 'the past'), 'yesterday', 'today', 'tomorrow'; (2) the adjectives 'former', 'current', 'contemporary', 'prospective', 'present', 'future' (in some but not all of their occurrences); (3) the adverbs 'then', 'formerly' ('now' in some occurrences might seem to be an adverb, but I shall argue that it can always fairly be construed as a noun); (4) the two-word sequences whose first word is 'last' or 'next' and whose second word is 'time', 'week', 'month', or 'year'.

Some of these expressions can be grouped into pairs or larger groups whose members have the same meaning, in other words into groups of synonyms; e.g., 'now' (functioning as a noun) and 'the present time'; 'in the past' and 'at some former time or times'. There may be differences in rhetorical effect and in use between expressions that have the same meaning. Occasion will arise in §§17-19 to make the distinction between meaning on the one hand and effect and use on the other hand somewhat more definite.

When a language contains groups of synonymous expressions, one speaks of redundancy. It is possible to drop all members but one of such a group without any loss in the language's power to signify meanings. (There may be loss of rhetorical effect or the like.)

Besides the A-expressions listed above in (1)-(4), English has another group. If the single word 'walks' be analyzed into the two morphemes 'walk' (which here functions as a verbal stem) and 's' (the ending), we see that the ending signifies three things at once: the Third person, the Singular number, and the Present tense. In 'walked', the morpheme 'ed' signifies Past Tense only, without distinction of Person or of Number. In the terminology of Roman Jakobson, the meaning of 's' is a bundle of semantical 'distinctive features', of which we are here only interested in the third. It is the defining characteristic of the so-called inflecting languages that their nouns, adjectives, and verbs include morphemes that signify bundles, i.e., that signify more than one meaning at a time. English inflection is rudimentary compared with that of German or of Greek; if all its endings were like 'ed' rather than like 's', it would not be called an inflecting language at all.

In languages whose verbs inflect for Tense, the expression of Tense (for example English 's') will also, simultaneously, be the expression of at least one other meaning. The project of rationally reconstructing such languages in the way of dropping the expression of Tense from the verb is more complicated than the project for languages all of whose Tense-expressions are like 'ed' in that they express Tense and nothing more. And the details would vary considerably from one language to another. But it is important for the main purpose of the present paper to make the point that it could be done, and done in a way that employs 'now' as the sole A-expression of the resulting language, without loss in the power of signifying meanings. The principal change is that occurrences of 'now' would have to be made obligatory rather than optional as they are in ordinary English.

We owe the contrast between optional and obligatory features to Franz Boas. Languages differ, Boas observed, more in what they must say than in what they can say. Applying Boas' distinction to English, we might think that for English verbs to signify the distinction between Past, Present, and Future time is obligatory, not optional.

Actually, this is not so, for two reasons. I shall undertake to show, first, that it is not so, and second, that even if it were so, a suitably reconstructed English with 'now' as its sole A-expression could signify the same distinction.

The first reason why it is not true that an English verb is obliged to signify the distinction between Past, Present, and Future time is that each grammatical Tense has other uses besides the expression of seman-tical Tense. No more than the merest sketch of these uses is appropriate here, just enough to illustrate the point. It is customary to distinguish at least three senses or uses (they used to be called 'forces') of the Present tense: (a) a literal, strict sense; (b) a narrative, or historical Present (perhaps this should be called, not a distinct *sense* from (a), but only a certain *use* to which (a) is put); and (c) a Gnomic Present, neutral as regards time, which occurs in the necessary truths of mathematics, in the antecedents of if-then propositions when the event referred to is in the future, in statements about the physical world that are not mathematically true but that are true at all times, and elsewhere. Now English grammar divides verb-forms into those that do and those that do not contain an expression of grammatical Tense; the former (e.g., 'walks', 'walked', 'will walk', 'is walking', 'is', 'was', 'were', 'will be') are called finite, the latter (e.g., 'to walk', 'walking', 'to be') infinite; English grammar further requires that every complete sentence contain at least one finite verb. Every complete sentence, then, will contain something which either expresses grammatical Past tense, like 'ed' in 'walked', or grammatical Present tense, like 's' in 'walks', or grammatical Future tense, like 'will' in 'will walk'. Grammatical Tense is truly obligatory in English. But there is nothing in English to force the grammatical Present tense to be taken in sense (a), rather than in (b) or (c). And the grammatical Past tense and the grammatical Future tense likewise have other uses than their literal ones. And this is why we are constrained to distinguish semantical from grammatical Tense, and to conclude that semantical Tense is not obligatory in English.

The second reason is that the distinction between Past, Present, and Future time can be evaded. English uses Gender to distinguish sex, as for example in the pronouns 'he' versus 'she'. But one can evade the distinction by saying 'he or she'. Similarly the distinction between Singular and Plural number can be evaded—'he or she walks or they walk'. In just the same way, disjunction makes it possible to evade the distinction of Tenses. And so, even if in English each of the grammatical Tenses had only its literal sense, it would still be possible by disjunction to evade commitment as to whether the event referred to was earlier than, simultaneous with, or later than the time of the speech-act. If Boas's distinction between obligatory and optional features is to be valid, it must be understood in some limited way such that the possibility of evasion by disjunction does not invalidate it.

So much for the first point. It is not absolutely obligatory that every complete English sentence that refers to a datable event shall specify whether, relative to the time of uttering the sentence, the event referred to is Past, Present, or Future.

The next point is that whatever is accomplished by verbal Tense can be accomplished by other means. I take it that the phrase 'verbal Tense' is redundant, i.e. that by Tense we understand not just a distinction of meaning, but that distinction effected by certain formal means, namely by one or another ending that is bound with a verb stem to form a single word. It is not essential that the ending be inflectional, i.e. that it simultaneously express at least one other meaning as well as Past, Present, or Future; but it is essential that the expression be part of a single word; 'periphrastic tenses', like English 'will walk', are called tenses only by courtesy. Now in whatever sense the expression of the difference between Past, Present, and Future is obligatory in ordinary English, this obligatory character cannot depend on the fact that the expression of the difference is part of the same word as the stem of the verb that expresses the meaning which the difference modifies. We could, then, preserve this obligatory character if we modified ordinary English in two steps, the second of which compensates for the first. In the first step, distinctions of grammatical Tense are done away with; the only finite verb-form will be the former grammatical Present tense, and its sole meaning will be, Gnomic Present. In the second step, it is stipulated that every occurrence of a finite verb-form be accompanied by one of the three A-expressions, 'formerly', 'now', and 'in the future'.

This two-step reconstruction is crudely sketched, but I dare say the sketch is sufficient to make the point that so far as English grammatical Tenses have the effect of expressing the difference between Past, Present, and Future, the same effect can be gotten with 'now', etc., provided that we change certain rules governing them from 'may occur' to 'must occur'. And this justifies us in saying that the verbal Tense-expressions, taken literally, are themselves A-expressions. We may advantageously employ Sellars' concept of linguistic role here and say that there is a certain role played both by 'now' and by 's' in ordinary English, and a certain other role, specifically different, generically the same, played by 'formerly' and by 'ed'; and that what distinguishes 'now' from 's' in ordinary English is that occurrence of the one is optional, of the other obligatory.

§8. *'Now' the sole A-expression*. We may achieve a further narrowing or pinpointing of focus if we impose on English the 'rational reconstruction' (logical positivism) or 'regimentation' (Quine) that 'now' will be the sole A-expression; and that it will occur solely in identities. The two steps that achieve this result, and the purpose of achieving it, will now be explained. The sense in which 'now' is one expression in all its occurrences, though infinitely homonymous, will be explained in §§10-11.

Because of conflatability (§2), A-expressions other than 'now' can be dropped in favor of some paraphrase which contains the word 'now'; for instance, 'the past' can be paraphrased as 'some time earlier than now'. But these paraphrases do not conform to the proposed restriction that 'now' shall occur only when collocated with the identity-symbol. In the instance just given, 'now' is collocated with the expression 'earlier than'. But the solution could not be more simple. Instead of saying 'some time earlier than now', or, more explicitly, 'some time, x, which is earlier than now', we will say 'some time, x, which is earlier than some time, y, which = now'. In a formalized language with quantifiers, ordinary English 'He walked' would be rendered as '$(\exists x, y)$(He walks at time x and x is earlier than y and y = now)'. These versions not only sound odd but are a good deal more inconvenient than their originals; but these objections have no bearing on whether they adequately render the meaning.

This maneuver of confining 'now' to identities is possible because of the theorem (PM*13.195; Quine, *Mathematical Logic* *234b; etc.), $\phi x \equiv (\exists y)(y=x \& \phi y)$. We are merely giving this familiar theorem an unusual application. English (even suitably regimented English) not being a formalized language, the distinction between primitive and defined expressions does not obtain within it; an expression either occurs or does not occur, and no distinction is drawn between those necessary equivalences which are tautologies disguised by definitions and other necessary equivalences. But in the process of suitably reconstructing English, one may sometimes take advantage of necessary equivalences by dropping one member in favor of the other; this is the nearest counterpart in an unformalized language to the formalized technique of taking one member as definiendum and the other as definiens. Because of such equivalences, the language which ordinary English would become if we modified it by (a) dropping tense-distinctions, (b) dropping all A-expressions except 'now', and (c) confining the occurrence of 'now' to identities would be no poorer in expressing meanings than is ordinary English.

The rationale of these modifications is that they make it seem as though 'now' could be gotten down to an exceedingly meager employment. And this semblance lets us bring out, in order to reject, a certain false expectation. Suppose someone had the project of showing that A-expressions are, in principle, superfluous. Our result might seem to help his project, for we might be thought to have *all but succeeded* in eliminating them. Total victory is in sight! But the proper reading of our result is precisely the opposite. It was possible to confine all

A-expressions (including Tense-expressions) to 'now', and 'now' to occurrence in identities, precisely because these identities furnish a spark, or seed, from which to reconstitute the entire range of A-expressions. The confinement was a victory only in the lexicon and the syntax, not in the semantics. It is handy (for our present purpose), but not significant.

§9. *Tokens of 'now'*. Sellars' discussion of the Now, in later as well as in earlier papers, is mostly carried on in terms of tokens and types. In particular, he makes much of the thesis that three statements differing from one another only in tense may all belong to the same type, although differing appreciably as tokens.

We can simplify the discussion, without falsifying it, by considering only tokens of 'now' tokened by some one person. Any two such tokens, I assume, are tokened at different times; each of these times may be treated, in our present discussion, as an instant, and each is describable as a c-date in the B-series. If one reaches the conclusion—as I shall—that no two such tokens of 'now' belong to the same type, this does not exclude the possibility that two tokens of 'now', uttered simultaneously by different people, belong to the same type. But, while we need not deny this possibility, we may leave it out of present account as a mere complication. Let us confine attention, then, to the class of all the tokens 'now' actually uttered (tokened) by some one speaker. Regarding the principle of assigning different tokens to the same type, there are just two possibilities that are at all plausible, namely the two extreme views; intermediate views are possible, but not plausible. One extreme view is that no two of his tokens belong to the same type; the opposite extreme is that all of them belong to the same type.

The latter view is the more common; the former I take to be Sellars', and it is also the one which I defend. For the latter view, the locus classicus is Chapter One of Hegel's Phenomenology.

§10. *Hegel's mistake*. Hegel has an uncommon way of putting the common view, a way that has the merit it is intended to have, of belonging to a 'shape of consciousness' that must be left behind in the dialectical advance. This way speaks not of types but of universals; the 'now' is some sort of universal.

The easiest way of seeing the mistake is to consider the Now functionally. Let us help ourselves by a fiction. Consider replacing the one word 'now' by an infinity of words (a denumerable infinity, as of the natural numbers). The fiction may be described by a metaphor drawn from present-day technology: It amounts to replacing one re-usable container by an endless supply of discardable containers, each bearing the label 'Use once and throw away'. If it be objected that the fiction can teach us nothing because it feigns something impossible, the objection can be met by a distinction. If the objection is that the fiction assumes an infinite vocabulary of *simple* signs, whereas the only admissible infinity is that of complex sequences of simple signs, the answer exploits a point made by Tarski in connection with quotation-names; the same point can be made in connection with subscripts. An expression such as ' 'p' ' or 'x_1' is complex in one way and simple in another; somewhat as the word 'as' is made up of two letters, but functions semantically as a single unit, so the quotation-name ' 'p' ' and the variable-name 'x_1' function as single units. Thus they function as simple signs, and yet (taken in the other way) comply with the requirement that only by complex sequences can there be an infinity of signs. They are structurally complex, but functionally simple.

If the objection is that the words used to take the place of 'now' would get longer and longer and soon unmanageably long, we may bring in another consideration. The only purpose of the subscripts is to insure that the same type is never used twice. Given that, because each user has a finite life, there is a finite number of types that he can actually use, it will suffice to preclude re-use if we furnish him with more types than he can use. It might still be claimed that the number of types is 'unmanageably' large, and the length of the longest ones 'unmanageably' long; I shall not attempt here to reply to *that* claim. At least there is a limit to the length. This principle is used in certain stores where, instead of people queuing up, each person upon entering takes a numbered ticket and waits until his number is called. Ambiguity is avoided if the number of tickets is finite but larger than the number of customers waiting at any one time.

And, at last, let us consider the effect of the following convention: that the number of simple signs is infinite (the signs, if they be arranged in alphabetical order, will contain longer and longer subscripts), but by convention one simply omits all subscripts. This convention, applied to the infinite register of signs, yields just the rules that we have with 'now'. If we had infinitely many signs, each consisting of 'now' plus its own unique subscript, and then applied to each of these the convention of omitting (deleting) the subscript, then the result would be an infinitely homonymous sign, whose homonymy (ambiguity) would be resolved, if at all, only by the extralinguistic context. So we may conclude that 'now' as actually used is virtually the result of such a convention, applied to such a register; meaning by 'virtually' that the result is the same as if there actually were such a register and such a convention. I see this conclusion as warranting the further conclusion that, for any one person, no two tokens of 'now' belong to the same type.

§11. *'Now' as a pseudo-universal.* The infinite homonymy (or ambiguity—it is not necessary for present purposes to distinguish between the two) of 'now' is not troublesome in those cases when it is resolved by the extralinguistic context. Those cases are the cases when the hearer knows an identity of the form 'The time when 'now' is uttered $= c$'. Of course the expression 'the time when 'now' is uttered' is itself infected with infinite homonymy since it doesn't unhomonymously specify which 'now' is meant. This infinite homonymy must be what Reichenbach was trying to get at when he described 'now' as token-reflexive. The seriously homonymous cases are those where the hearer lacks knowledge of any suitable identity. A delightful instance is the one recounted by Spengler, and meant to prove the Greeks' lack of a modern time-sense, involving some agreement that is to last for 'a hundred years from today', but without any suitable identity to pin down for others when 'today' was.

There is a rule involved in the use of the term 'now', and being subject to a rule is what it has in common with universals; but it is not a rule that lets a single instance of the term apply to, or denote, two or more instances of its referent, and that is why it is not a universal. We may commemorate these two facts together by calling it a pseudo-universal. The further fact that we can in ordinary English speak of 'Any now', 'a succession of nows', 'the constantly changing now', etc., does not establish it as a true universal, because these usages are adequately explained by supposing that in them 'now' is used in some metalinguistic way (in particular, the one that Carnap calls 'autonymous' and Bloomfield 'hypostatic'), and moreover a way such that what is involved is not a *word* 'now', where for two tokens to belong to the same word they must not merely have the same sound but also bear the same meaning, but just the *sound* 'now'. And likewise, when we speak of 'the Now', it is not one word of which we speak, but one sound (or one string of letters), which is used to produce a potential infinity of words. Each of these words has in turn a potential infinity of tokens, but (according to Sellars' suggestion) no more than one token that looks or sounds like 'now'.

§12. *A rationale for assigning tokens to types.* The view that no two now-tokens belong to the same type is susceptible of various further determinations, and Sellars has given us one such determination. By way of preparing for an exposition of his theory, I will say something about sense and reference, then I will consider identity-criteria for assigning tokens to types (and, in particular, criteria which peg identity of type to identity of sense), and third I will consider Sellars' particular theory, which involves a conception of subtypes.

§13. *Russell's approach and Frege's.* One of Russell's theories of egocentric terms is that they are proper names, according to the definition (taken from Mill but given a strict reading) that they denote without connoting. On this theory, in an identity '$n = c$', the left member is a proper name and the right member is (or abbreviates) a singular description. The description, when expanded, would give way to a variable whose values are instants. Russell's presentations of his theory of descriptions leave it open whether a one-to-one correlation of substituends and values of his variables is presupposed; if it is not, then there may be 'more' instants, in a technical sense, than there are possible expressions denoting or describing instants.

Frege's theory is in the end not so very different from Russell's formally, but is developed semantically by Frege along very different lines. His theory of identity, if we adapt our statement of it so as to refer exclusively to identities containing a 'now' and another constant, is that both members of the identity have sense, as well as reference, and that when the identity is true they have the same reference even if they have different senses.

Although Russell's formal theory of singular descriptions neither entails nor presupposes his epistemology of knowledge by acquaintance and knowledge by description, there is no special nonformal motive for using his formal theory unless one means to assume his epistemology. Since Sellars doesn't mean to assume it, and since it is primarily Sellars' treatment of the Now to which I am addressing myself, I can confine myself to considering Frege-like theories.

§14. *Identity-criteria for types.* Sellars' theory of time includes an assignment of Tense-expressions to types. This is easily adapted to certain rational reconstructions which eliminate Tense-expressions in favor of other A-expressions, but it is not easily adapted to the particular rational reconstruction which retains 'now' as sole A-expression. I therefore propose for temporary consideration another reconstruction, which differs from ordinary English (a) in dropping verbal tenses in favor of other A-expressions, (b) in splitting 'then'—which means 'not-now, whether before or after now'—into the two expressions '*P*-then', which refers exclusively to the past, and '*F*-then', which refers exclusively to the future, and (c) in retaining as A-expressions only these three: '*P*-then', 'now', and '*F*-then'. In this reconstructed English, a verb in the Gnomic Present accompanied by '*P*-then' is necessarily equivalent in meaning to an ordinary-English Past-tense verb with Past tense in its literal sense, accompanied by 'now', to a literal Present, and accompanied by '*F*-then', in a literal Future.

This reconstructed Tenseless English perfectly duplicates the meanings of ordinary Tensed English. Sellars' assignment of occurrences of Tense-expressions to types is adapted to this reconstructed English as an assignment of occurrences of '*P*-then', of 'now', and of '*F*-then' to types. (Details are given in §§16-20.) I do not, by the way, regard ordinary-English 'then' as ambiguous. It unambiguously means not-now, but not-now is a genus that can be divided into the two species (a) not-now and earlier than now and (b) not-now and later than now; the genus is, or is necessarily equivalent to, the disjunction of these two species. The logic is the same as with parent, which is (or is necessarily equivalent to) the disjunction of the two species father and mother.

§15. *Ambiguity versus breadth of A-expressions.* The composition of time is often conceived of in this way: the Present is a single instant, the Past is an infinite series of instants ending just before the Present, and the Future is an infinite series of instants starting just after the Present. This is a picture of the composition of time. We may combine it with that picture of the A-series (pretended to be single and unique) which thinks of the Now (imagined as some sort of thing with continued identity) as singling out, or focusing attention on, the instants of the B-series one after another. Our modern technological world could offer as visual models such things as the 108 positions on a typewriter successively coinciding with the indicator, or with the infinitely many positions on a Turing-machine tape successively occupying the focus. Each of the two pictures which we have just combined is crude and even untenable; what if, for instance, the series of instants is not discrete but dense, so that we cannot speak of 'successively' or 'next' or 'one after the other'; so that, in other words, the series is not truly a succession? But nevertheless the combination of these two untenable pictures will serve to get us started in developing certain conceptions. The salient feature is that each instant has an individuality and a permanence, no matter whether it is past, present, or future.

According to this combined picture, in which the discreteness of the series is essential, one may think of the past and of the future as a succession of instants. If we turn our attention from time expressed to the expression of time, we find that there are two ways in which we can understand the expressions 'the Past' and 'the Future'; both ways are compatible with the combined picture just described. Namely, these two expressions may be thought of as ambiguous or as broad.

To bring out the difference between ambiguity and breadth, it will be sufficient to consider, as in effect we have been doing all along, only events that are instantaneous, so that 'times' may be identified with instants; no non-zero duration, that is, no interval bounded by two distinct instants, will be considered. It doesn't matter here that it is in the last analysis unrealistic to assume that fundamental events are instantaneous; because what is under consideration here is that the same event which at one time is truly described with the help of the literal Present tense or of 'now' is at some other times truly described with the help of the literal Past tense or of 'P-then', and at all the remaining times truly described with the help of the literal Future tense or of 'F-then'. In describing this tripartite truth we have no need to subdivide the time in question, and thus we virtually treat it as instantaneous. It is in connection with *other* questions that the need for subdivision may arise.

If all events in our universe of discourse are instantaneous, it is possible to take the view that the expression 'P-then', on each occasion of its use, is used to refer not to the entire series, the Past, but to some single term of that series, some single instant. On this view, 'P-then' may refer on more than one occasion of its use to the same instant, but in its range of possible referents there are infinitely many instants that it may refer to. If on one occasion of use this expression refers to one instant, and on another occasion to another instant, we may say that the expression is ambiguous—if not in the ordinary sense, then at least in one ordinary philosophical sense. And if we call it ambiguous at all, we must call it infinitely ambiguous, or, since the infinity is only a potential infinity, indefinitely ambiguous. Exactly the same with 'F-then'. Ordinary-English 'then', and reconstructed-English 'F-then' and 'P-then', may each of them be one word, or at least one sound or one

string of letters, but each of them is infinitely many types, judging by
what I understand to be Sellars' indentity-criterion for types. In §§ 16-19,
especially §16, I complete the statement of this identity-criterion.

Alongside of this view of 'P-then' and 'F-then' (and so of ordinary-
English 'then') there is another view which it is equally possible to take.
This other view is based on the logical principle which is known as
Existential Quantifier Introduction in systems that use introduction-
and elimination-rules. According to this other view, restricted to the
universe of discourse specified above, the expressions 'P-then' and
'F-then' never occur except as the virtual result of EQ-introduction. If,
for the moment, days be treated as indivisible instants, then ordinary-
English 'He walked' must be the virtual result of applying EQ-
introduction either to reconstructed-English 'He walks the day before
now', or to 'He walks two days before now', or 'He walks three days
before now', etc., without end. As is true of existentially quantified
propositions in general, there is a certain heuristic value in thinking of
the proposition introduced by EQ-introduction as logically equivalent to
a (denumerably) infinite disjunction. The reason for speaking of 'virtual'
results is to disclaim the claim that anyone who asserts an existentially
quantified proposition is prepared to assert at least one of the propositions from which it results by EQ-introduction; Russell may well be
right that the principal human use of existentially quantified propositions is to express incomplete knowledge.

Now, to finish the statement of the other equally possible view,
although a proposition containing 'P-then' or 'F-then' is the result of a
potential infinity of premiss-propositions, it is not ambiguous as
between them; rather, it is broad. To resume the heuristic fiction
mentioned above, the single broad sense of the expression 'P-then' is
necessarily equivalent to the infinite disjunction of the senses of 'the day
before now', 'two days before now', and so on, each one of which senses
is narrow in comparison.

If there is an issue as to which view to choose, it is a perfectly familiar
issue, and only the example is unusual. If we change the example from
'P-then' to 'man', the sense of familiarity is restored. One perennially
popular view says that 'man' *means* something different when it applies
to Plato than when it applies to Socrates, and so on without end.
Another perennially popular view says that though 'man' applies to
(medieval: supposits for) different individual men on different occasions
of its use, it has a constant meaning; in Frege's version of this view, it
has a constant reference and a constant sense.

§16. *Sense and type*. The difference between A- and B-expressions can be stated in terms of Fregean senses. Every true identity '$n = c$' furnishes two expressions that have the same reference, namely a certain instant. One of these, a 'now', refers to that instant *qua* central term of an A-series; the other refers to it *qua c*-date, i.e. *qua* one of the infinitely many terms of the B-series. Because the two expressions refer to the same instant qua A-term and qua B-term respectively, they have different senses.

Now it is possible to combine the view that each A-expression has the same reference as various B-expressions but has a different sense, with the first of the two perennially popular views of meaning described above, with the following result. This first popular view, applied to 'P-then' (similarly to 'F-then'), holds that 'P-then' is infinitely ambiguous; more precisely, that there is a potential infinity of distinct instants to which it may refer. Of course, if it has infinitely many referents, it has infinitely many senses, since difference of reference entails difference of sense, but not vice versa. It is possible that one and the same instant is referred to, by some one speaker but on three different occasions, first by 'F-then', next by 'now', and last by 'P-then'. The present suggestion is that these three different tokens be stipulated to have the same sense as well as the same reference.

The suggestion I have just formulated is not Sellars', but it offers a basis for his suggestion. Sellars suggests that these three different tokens should be assigned to the same type, and the suggestion I have formulated gives as a reason for doing so that they have the same sense. Now sameness of sense is perhaps not the only ground for assignment to the same type, but it is one acceptable ground, and if we do not invoke it we shall want some other.

§17. *Subtypes*. As an aid to articulating Sellars' suggestion, I will introduce the concept of subtype.

Although the distinction of token and type is widely accepted, there is no generally accepted identity-criterion for assigning different tokens to the same type. Not that there are alternative criteria between which there is rivalry; the matter simply has not been worked out. In such approximations to a criterion as there are, the leading idea seems to be functionalistic: tokens count as the same type if their function is the same. And the functions in question being linguistic, convention (as contrasted with nature) will play a large part. Sameness of type will be pegged to sameness of function: If the function performed by two tokens is conventionally reckoned to be the same, their type will be reckoned to be the same also.

A good example of perceptible differences that are conventionally disregarded is found in handwriting. Two people may write manifestly different 'hands', and yet write what counts as the same message. One way of describing this sameness would be to say that, letter by letter, their tokens belong to the same type. If, then, in addition, we want to take note of the difference, we could do it by introducing the concept of subtype and saying that their respective tokens belonged to different subtypes. Even if they wrote with the same color of ink, and wrote letters of about the same size, one hand might be neat and the other scrawly, or one bold and one weak, or one with the slant of the letters from lower left to upper right and the other 'backhand'.

The difference between two people's 'hands' might be of interest even if it had no conventional meaning: of practical interest, in some court-room question of evidence, or of theoretical interest as a clue to person-ality and character. This interest would be our reason for distinguishing subtypes even though the distinction had no basis in convention.

It might seem that there are cases where the basis for distinguishing subtypes *is* conventional. In written English ('written' in a broad sense, including not only handwritten English but also typewritten, letterpress-printed, chiseled in stone, and any other process whose result is perceived by the eyes rather than by the ears and yields elements like letterpress-printed letters), we distinguish between capital and lower-case letters. Now it might be proposed to regard capital 'A' and lower-case 'a', for example, as different subtypes of the same type. We might extend the same treatment to a Roman and the corresponding Italic letter; to a boldface and the corresponding ordinary letter; to a letter in the Bodoni typeface and the corresponding letter in Basker-ville; to an ordinary Bodoni eight-point letter and the corre-sponding ten-point.

There is no question that we want to take note of these various distinctions somehow, but the question is whether to do it by speaking of different subtypes of the same type. We might propose to take, as our criterion for sameness of type, not sameness of function but sameness of meaning. The difference between capital and lower-case letters is not used to distinguish meanings, subject to minor exceptions (such as proper names, 'Mill' versus 'mill'), and it is unconventional to mix the two varieties in the same word, except that the first letter of a proper name and of the first word of a sentence must be a capital; a sequence of letters like 'miLl' would be simply a blunder, or a stunt, or the like, without effect on the meaning. With the difference between Roman and Italic the situation is more complicated. Italic against a background of Roman has the function of indicating extra or unusually placed stress in the corresponding spoken English phrase ('*e*volution, not *re*volution'; 'it *is* true'); one might or might not consider this function a kind of meaning. Italic in longer stretches is sometimes used antiphonally, as when questions are printed in Italic and answers in Roman, or when, as in Faulkner's *The Sound and the Fury,* Quentin's reminiscences are printed in Italic. Here again, whether this is a difference in meaning depends on one's definition. At the very least, we can say that present practices don't make any and every difference of meaning expressible in this way; the sort of difference in meaning that there is between 'pit' and 'tip' could not be expressed by 'pit' versus '*pit*'.

I have gone at such length into a matter that may seem to be of specialized interest in order to prepare for another suggestion of Sellars'. One who said that 'pit' and '*pit*' (i) have the same meaning, and so are assigned to the same type, but (ii) have different functions, and so are assigned to different subtypes, might use the same approach in a much grander way to describe the differences between languages. He might propose to assign 'ink', 'encre', and 'Tinte' to the same type, while duly taking note of their conventionalized difference in function by assigning them to different subtypes. In fact, he could even characterize the difference between languages by the difference in selecting subtypes. There is a convention or rule that an utterance that selects 'ink' rather than 'encre' or 'Tinte' must also select 'pen' rather than 'plume' or 'Feder' and must also select 'black' rather than 'noir' or 'schwarz'. Scrambling 'ink', 'plume', and 'schwarz' in one utterance (so-called macaronic speech) is like scrambling Italic and Roman letters in the spelling of one word.

The suggestion is ingenious, and it may well be that many of the actual differences between languages that seem to refute it are if carefully analyzed only unsystematic exceptions or other complications that do not spoil its basic truth. Sellars's main interest in the suggestion is not an interest in the difference between English, French, and German but the intent of treating the difference between mental and physical vocabulary as the same kind of difference. It might be suggested, in the same spirit, that the difference between A-expressions and B-expressions be subsumed under the same conception of different subtypes of a single type.

It does not concern us in the present paper to examine this suggestion as applied to the mind-body problem, but as applied to A- and B-expressions it does concern us.

§18. *The rationale for having subtypes.* In its simplest version, the contrast of type and token is nothing but the contrast of universal and particular, limited to the case where the universal is a sign. In this simplest version, any two tokens of one type would be perceptibly indistinguishable from one another. Reflection (a) on the thought that our concern is limited to signs, so that to be the same thing means to be the same sign, and (b) on the thought that to be the same sign is to signify the same thing, leads us to the conclusion that two tokens may as well be treated as the same sign (the same type) if they mean the same thing, even if they are perceptibly distinguishable from each other and even if their perceptible difference has some function (other than meaning). But then we need the concept of subtype; for we need to provide for cases where perceptible distinctions are regulated by convention (Italic vs. Roman; English vs. French) or are correlated with laws of nature (e.g., different handwritings as reflecting different personalities).

It proves terminologically convenient to speak of x and y as the same subtype or different subtypes even when they are not included in the same type. Using this convenient terminology and applying it to A- and to B-expressions, we may pose our questions: Granted that every occurrence of 'now' belongs to a different subtype from every occurrence of 'then' and also from every occurrence of a B-expression, shall we ever assign (a) an occurrence of 'now' and an occurrence of 'then', (b) an occurrence of 'now' and an occurrence of a B-expression to the same type? Our answer will depend, according to the proposal made above, on whether the two occurrences have the same meaning, and so function as the same sign. It is important to be clear about the order of priority. We cannot first become clear as to whether x and y belong to the same type, and then if we wish go on to the question of whether they have the same meaning; there is no settled determinate concept of type, and one of the most obvious proposals for making it determinate determines it by pegging it to the concept of meaning. Unfortunately, the concept of meaning is itself somewhat indeterminate.

§19. *Subtypes dispensable.* If the subtypes of one type do not differ in meaning, then in that respect the plurality of subtypes is superfluous. We can use superfluity (dispensability) as a test in helping ourselves to become clear as to which functions we wish to classify as meaning-functions.

Let us return to the example of languages. In some way the plurality of languages is superfluous. This means not that it serves no purpose, but that the purposes it serves are not only incidental but minor. To be sure, *given* the plurality of languages, one may put it to use. Leibniz used Latin in corresponding with scholars, of any country; he used French in corresponding with Frenchmen, scholars or not, and with German royalty and people of the court; he used German in corresponding with other Germans. There must be some variety of meaning or some sense of 'meaning' in which his choice of language was meaningful. But presumably Latin, French, and German don't essentially differ as regards the power of signifying references and senses. If any two of the three were done away with, there would be loss of some sort of meaning, but not loss of reference-and-sense-signifying power.

So also with the plurality of typefaces and of writing hands. It is good to know of the a priori possibility of this plurality, but its actuality gives no gain in signifying power. Given the plurality, we may use it for various purposes, but there are no purposes which it and only it would fulfill.

It is not so with the difference between A- and B-expressions. This point has been stressed before and will be stressed again. On the other hand, it may well be so with the difference between the now-tokens and the then-tokens of the type 'now'. It is one thing to say that every occurrence of 'now' has the same sense as some occurrence of some B-expression, quite another to say that it has the same sense as various occurrences of 'then'. I see no strong objection to the second suggestion, whereas the first is wholly gratuitous.

§20. *To the second suggestion there is no strong objection, but there is a mild one.* Consider three different instants, an earliest I, a middle J, and a latest K. Let a certain speaker utter a token 'now' at I, 'P-then' at J, and 'P-then' at K. Let him intend all three tokens, one of 'now', two of 'P-then', to refer to the instant I. Then the second suggestion of §19 (Sellars' suggestion, as restated in terms of 'P-then', 'now', and 'F-then' instead of verbal Tenses, and with the help of the concept of subtype) is this: All three tokens belong to the same type, though the one 'now' belongs to one subtype and the two 'P-then's belong to another subtype.

The mild objection is that the three tokens should not be assigned to the same type unless they have the same sense, but there is good reason to say that the first 'P-then' and the second 'P-then' have different senses. And this creates two obstacles for the suggestion. First, since not all three tokens have the same sense, they cannot all three be assigned to the same type. At least two types must be recognized, such that the 'now' and one of the '*P*-then's belong to one type and the other '*P*-then' to the other type. Second, there is no reason to identify the 'now' with one of the '*P*-then's in sense and in type rather than with the other; so the principle of sufficient reason bids us to identify it with neither of them, and thus in the end to recognize three distinct senses and three distinct types for our three tokens. And in general, by the same argument, *n* tokens will call for *n* types.

Before I give the good reason for saying that the two '*P*-then's have different senses, let me explain why I call the objection to the second suggestion mild, not strong. (i) The reason given will be good, but not compelling and universally agreed upon. There is much uncertainty about a reasonable identity-criterion for senses. (ii) One might reject the principle of sufficient reason, or subordinate it to the demand for economy, concluding that two types are better than three, and in general $n - 1$ better than n. (iii) One might assign different tokens to the same type even while agreeing that they have different senses; in other words, one might refuse to peg type-identity to sense-identity. (a) One might do this on the ground of some as yet unthought-of, reasonable identity criterion; or (b) one might propose some relaxation of the sense-identity criterion, as for example that two senses may be correlated with the same type if they are such that there cannot ever be uncertainty as to which one is intended. (iv) Even if, arbitrarily and in violation of various principles, one unites with each 'now' some '*P*-then's (and similarly some '*F*-then's), this does not commit one to identifying any 'now' in sense or in type with any B-expression.

The good reason for saying that '*P*-then' said at *J* and '*P*-then' said at *K*, both intended to refer to the instant *I*, have different senses is this: the former may be considered to refer to *I* qua earlier than *J*, and the latter to *I* qua earlier than *K*. I take it as agreed that 'now', '*P*-then', and '*F*-then' are token-reflexive; in which case it is not inappropriate if each token of them reflects its time of tokening in its sense.

§21. *'Now' as perspectival.* From this point on, I will adopt without further question Sellars' suggestion of three subtypes, as modified by me. My remaining task is to examine proposals to consider the Now (i) perspectival, (ii) pragmatic, (iii) metalinguistic, and (iv) subjective.

As a criterion for type-identity, I have pressed sense-identity. Sellars has not taken a stand on this one way or the other. He has, instead, proposed, not as a general criterion but with exclusive reference to his three-subtype suggestion, that the three subtypes of each A-expression indicate not a difference in the world but a difference in the utterer's perspective on the world. It seems to me that this amounts to proposing reference-identity as the criterion for type-identity: all three subtypes have the same reference, namely the world. Difference in perspective could be, but doesn't have to be, subsumed under difference in sense. The point I am now concerned to make is this: the metaphor of perspective gives no support to the view that our need for three subtypes has no basis in reality.

To say that a shift from one subtype to another subtype of an A-expression reflects a shift in perspective is to use a metaphor drawn from space. But it is not the spatialization that is objectionable. It is obvious that the metaphor does spatialize, but nevertheless it escapes Bergson's objections because it temporalizes as well. It speaks not just of perspective but of shifting, i.e. changing perspective, and sheer spatialization cannot speak of change.

What Sellars wants to make use of is that it is *the same* object which is perceived under different perspectives. And no doubt this is a fair enough statement, given an ordinary, commonsensical understanding of sameness. It may even be so in all philosophical profundity, though there are philosophies (like Berkeley's) that deny it. But to suppose that it is philosophically the very same object throughout all the changes in perspective on it is to have already taken a stand on a certain philosophical issue. To advance the metaphor in support of the view that the perspectival relation is wholly external to that upon which there is perspective is to abuse it. In spatial perspective, that upon which there is perspective is in space. In B-temporal perspective, that upon which there is perspective is in B-time. If the analogy holds, then that upon which there is A-temporal perspective is in A-time. And if the analogy doesn't hold, then of course there is no validity to the metaphor, because the only philosophical use of metaphor is to assert a similarity, and a similarity of the kind called analogy. So that *if* the metaphor is valid—the metaphor which suggests that the difference between an instant now and that same instant P-then (likewise F-then) is a difference in A-temporal perspective—then that instant *is* in A-time, and the metaphor cannot be used to support the view that A-time is external to the instant. It is the same instant which is a term in the B-series and which is involved in infinitely many A-series.

I will elaborate the thought that what is an object of perspective is an object in space (or, by metaphor, in time) by a thought about external and internal relations. By external relations we mean more or less the accidental ones, i.e., those relations in which a thing might or might not stand. A certain statue on the village green stands to me in the external, accidental relation that I am six feet away from it, or a hundred feet away. But though my being six feet away is external to the statue, my being in some spatial relation or other to it is internal; it is essential, not accidental, to the statue that as long as I exist, in spatial relation to something or other, I am also, in particular, in spatial relation to the statue. My proposed terminology for expressing these two facts is to contrast detailed with general relations, saying that detailed spatial relations are external but the general spatial relation is internal to spatial things. (Afficionados of W. E. Johnson would see some resemblance—more, probably, than there really is—between my general-detailed contrast and his determinable-determinate contrast.) My distinction has an important bearing on the perspectival metaphor. Are A-temporal perspectives external to instants? It depends. Detailed A-temporal perspectives are external to them, as is beyond dispute, but it does not follow, which would be needed for excluding A-time from the real order, that the general A-temporal perspective is external.

§22. *'Now' as pragmatic.* I take it that the three-subtype theory has an ulterior motive. The eventual conclusion that Sellars means to be aiming at, I gather, is that the linguistic fact (namely, that we need three subtypes) does not reflect an extralinguistic fact about the world, but does reflect a fact, extralinguistic in some sense, about our minds. More precisely, the need to distinguish three subtypes bears on the logical order, but has no bearing on the real order. I aim to show that this eventual conclusion is possible, but not necessary.

Perhaps the proposal in early papers to treat 'now' under pragmatics rather than under semantics had the same ulterior motive, and only differed in the means chosen. The suggestion is interesting enough to deserve further discussion.

In Charles Morris' formulation, the three parts of semiotics are related not by coordination but by nesting, or subordination. Pragmatics is that part of semiotics which deals with signs in their fullness, i.e. deals with every aspect of them—not only their vehicles, and their meanings, but also their relations to their users. Here a digression is necessary, to mention another sense of 'pragmatics' that has grown up. When Reichenbach addressed himself to pragmatics, he concerned himself with token-reflexives, and simply didn't raise the question whether pragmatics had any other concerns. This had the (regrettable) effect that various subsequent writers, such as Bar-Hillel and Uriel Weinreich, adopted the adjective 'pragmatic' as *meaning* 'dealing with token-reflexives'. I mention this sense only to put it aside. Plainly whatever would be called pragmatic by Reichenbach would be called pragmatic by Morris, though perhaps not conversely; but in the usage of, e.g., Weinreich there is no trichotomous framework in the background as there is in Morris' usage, to which I now return.

The fact that in Morris' framework there is a nested structure immediately and necessarily generates a double sense of 'pragmatics' (and similarly of 'semantics', which does not concern us). Pragmatics as originally defined deals with every aspect of signs; but we cannot prevent there arising a narrower sense in which it deals with those aspects that have *not* been dealt with by syntactics nor by semantics. By comparison with this inevitably generated narrower sense, the original sense is seen as wider. My reason for distinguishing these two senses so carefully is to suggest the possibility of equivocation.

Morris' trichotomy sounds like a division of labor; and if we forget that the relation between the three parts is subordination, and think of it instead as coordination, then we could think that just as semantics (in its original and wider sense) deals with meanings but not with users, so pragmatics (in its narrower sense) deals with users *and not with meanings*. To think this would be a mistake, but a natural one. Because of the nesting relation, there is no sense, either wider or narrower, in which pragmatics does not deal with meanings.

Now what I have to intimate, as delicately as I can, is that only if we think of the pragmatic in this coordinate way can we pass from the premiss that 'now' is pragmatic to the conclusion that 'now' does not have or involve a meaning. But if this conclusion is unwarranted, then to treat the now as pragmatic does not serve the ulterior purpose of removing A-time from the real world.

§23. *'Now' as metalinguistic*. In "Realism and the New Way of Words," Sellars assigned 'now' to the pragmatic metalanguage of Omniscient Jones; i.e., he proposed to treat 'now' as (i) pragmatic, (ii) metalinguistic. The ulterior philosophical motive of both treatments may have been the same. Putting 'now' into the metalanguage might seem to remove it from direct reference to the world, by interposing the object-language as a screen. But this seeming would be an illusion unless the metalanguage was about the object-language only, *and not* about the world; in truth, a sufficiently rich metalanguage will be about its object-language *and also* about the world that the object-language is about.

Russell, at the end of *Inquiry into Meaning and Truth,* raises the question of whether it is ever valid to infer a feature of the world *W* that an object-language *O* is about from necessary features of *O* itself, and answers Yes. Our present question is whether it is ever valid to infer features of *W* from features of *M*, a metalanguage of *O*. I urge that the answer is again Yes; i.e., it is sometimes ('ever') valid. To put the same point with a double negative, we cannot claim that features of *M* never make a commitment or presupposition about *W*, and if there is an *M* with a feature that is necessary not just by definition of *M* but as indispensable in a sufficiently rich metalanguage of a language that describes *W*, then that feature reflects a feature of *W*. Now 'now' may be just such a feature. It is true that Sellars had a different, special, reason for putting 'now' in the metalanguage, namely that Omniscient Jones's *O* was subject to the limitation that it did not express non-identities of time at all; but was that the only reason?

§24. *'Now' as subjective.* In Frege's semantics, sense is not the only thing opposed to reference. Besides sense, there is representation, or idea (*Vorstellung*; cf. Geach and Black, *Translations from the Philosophical Writings of Gottlob Frege* (Oxford: Basil Blackwell, 1966): x, 59). The ground of distinction is that senses are objective, representations are subjective.

Frege didn't have or didn't find occasion to note that 'subjective' (and correspondingly 'objective') has *two* main ordinary meanings. (1) Those predicates are subjective about the predication of which people disagree, objective about which they agree. (2) The objective is the real; the subjective is that apparent which has no basis in reality. Many thinkers link the two senses by the stipulation that whatever is subjective in the first sense is subjective in the second; as a notable example, part of the argument concluding that secondary qualities are not real is that they vary from person to person. This linking, asymmetrical, leaves open the question of whether there are predicates that are objective in the first sense and subjective in the second.

A-predicates might be an instance. For every token 'now', there is an expression 'is identical with now' (abbreviated: ' = n'); each such expression signifies an A-predicate, and according to my argument, such A-predicates may be regarded without valid objection as the fundamental A-predicates, i.e., as the ones from which all other A-predicates may be conceptually derived. Applying here the distinction of §21 between detailed and general predicates, we may contrast the detailed fundamental A-predicates (plural) with the general fundamental A-predicate (singular). The purpose of doing so is to go on and say that about the general fundamental A-predicate there is no disagreement; it is objective in the first sense, and according to Frege's criterion expressions signifying it may have senses ascribed to them. If it is subjective in the second sense, then according to Frege's criterion such expressions may not have senses ascribed to them. I am not only making the obvious point that if objectivity is split in two, then a criterion depending on objectivity is split in two; I am also pointing out that A-predicates may force the split. If we peg objectivity to reality, and (as in premiss (4) of §1) reality to science, then this pegged sense of objectivity becomes discrepant from the other sense, because the general fundamental A-predicate definitely is objective in the other sense, and definitely is objective in the pegged sense.

To have pointed up this subjectivity is one of the many signal merits of Wilfrid Sellars. I have endeavored to put a finishing touch on his accomplishment by disengaging it from other parts of his total oeuvre.[1]

---

[1] A general resemblance will be noted between my position and that of Richard M. Gale in *The Language of Time* (1968). My discussion is strictly adapted to an examination of Sellars. Thus I have no occasion, for example, to take up the question of whether A-series are objective in the sense that there would be A-series, in addition to the B-series, even if there were no minds.

· ~ ·10· ~ ·

Theories and Counterfactuals

BAS C. VAN FRAASSEN
University of Toronto

W ILFRID SELLARS' analysis of the philosophical problems surrounding counterfactual assertions was, in my opinion, a major contribution to the subject.[1] But since his writing the situation has changed in this way: at that time there was no general formal logic of counterfactuals, and today there are several. (See [11], [12], [14], [7], [8].) While the logical developments have introduced a host of technical problems, they have also illuminated with startling clarity some major philosophical conflicts.

In the first part of this paper I shall attempt a critical exposition of Sellars' "Counterfactuals, Dispositions, and the Causal Modalities". Exegesis of Sellars is not easy: in his papers themes are developed to the point of perplexity, dropped, new themes taken up; finally the themes are linked, the perplexities disappear, and the union is not sterile: it engenders new perplexities. Sellars is our first master of dialectical writing since Bradley; I hope I may be forgiven a student's oversimplifications. After pointing out what seems to me to be a crucial gap in Sellars' argument, I shall address myself to the issues which are consequently left untouched in his analysis. In the Appendix I shall discuss the logic correlate to the kind of position which Sellars held.

---

1. The use of "counterfactual" covers "subjunctive" in our (and current) terminology.

1. Sellars' Analysis of Counterfactuals and Causal Modalities

Two distinct kinds of problems concerning counterfactuals occupied philosophers after the war. The first kind comprised the logical puzzles: how could there be a kind of implication for which, for example, contraposition might not hold? The second kind were more philosophical or perhaps semantic: under what conditions are such conditionals true? With respect to both kinds of problems, Sellars seemed to reach the conclusion that they are mistaken in intent, that they arise only upon a misunderstanding of the subject. The analysis that supports this conclusion seems to me extraordinarily successful. Yet, as I shall argue below, it rides roughshod over the problem which today divides the two main approaches to the subject.

1.1 *The logical puzzles*.[2] The main logical puzzles that appeared prior to 1960 are three (as we can now say with hindsight).

Contraposition is problematic. For we assert that if the match be struck it will burn because, after all, the match is dry, in oxygen, etc. But then why do we not assert that if the match be struck it will not be dry because, after all, the match does not burn, is in oxygen, etc.? Does this betoken a rejection of the inference that if A and C imply B, then A and (*not B*) imply (*not C*)?

Transitivity is problematic. Suppose that light C burns if and only if switches A and B are closed. I know that B is closed, so I am willing to assert that if A be closed, C will burn. Also, I know that if C burns, B is closed. But am I willing to assert that if A be closed, B is closed? Surely there is no *connection* between what is done to A and the state of B; and, surely, these conditionals are meant to assert connections?

Yes, in both cases, crucial features of the example concern the reliance on tacit assumptions. But as Goodman's analysis had shown right at the beginning, there is little hope of eliminating the problem by reference to ideally explicit auxiliary assumptions: there seems to be no systematic way of singling out the 'right' auxiliaries. Reliance on tacit assumptions is a crucial feature; *weakening the antecedent is problematic*. As Sellars points out, the assertion that if the match be struck it will burn does not commit us to the assertion that if it be struck and made wet, it will burn.

2. For a thorough discussion, see [12].

There is really a fourth logical problem, but it is hardly peculiar to these conditionals. What rules govern the nesting of conditionals? No subject-specific puzzles concerning the nesting of counterfactual conditionals seem to have appeared.

1.2 *The thing-kind framework*. In Parts I and II of "Counterfactuals, Dispositions, and the Causal Modalities", Sellars removed most of the interest from these puzzles vis-à-vis philosophy of science (as opposed to logic or philosophy of language generally). He points out that the disturbing examples belong to a certain class of conditionals, which naturally occur in scientific contexts, but that the puzzles disappear when attention is focused upon just that class. The apparent relevance of the puzzles is due to a "misunderstanding of the conceptual framework in terms of which we speak of what *things do* when *acted upon* in certain ways in certain kinds of *circumstance*" ([9]: 225).

The basic pattern of discourse in which these conditionals occur is described as follows:

Suppose we have reason to believe that

Ψ-ing Ks (in circumstances C) causes them to ψ

(where K is a kind of thing—*e.g.*, *match*). Then we have reason to believe of a particular thing of kind K, call it x_1, which is in C, that

x_1 would ψ, if it were Φ-ed.

And if it were Φ-ed and did ψ, and we were asked "Why did it ψ?" we would answer, "Because it was Φ-ed"; and if we were then asked, "Why did it ψ when Φ-ed?" we would answer "Because it is a K." If it were then pointed out that Ks don't always ψ when Φ-ed, we should counter with "They do if they are in C, as this one was." ([9]: 248.)

The point is that the antecedent is an *input* statement, the consequent an *output* statement, and neither input nor output statements describe *circumstances* (standing conditions). Now negations of output statements are, if anything, output statements again, so the contraposition of a conditional in this class is not in this class (nor is any nested conditional). Neither can the question of transitivity arise, since no statement can be consequent of one and antecedent of another such conditional. Finally, the application of two inputs cannot be expected to have the same effect as the application of one, so weakening the antecedent cannot be a valid rule. Scratching dry matches does not cause them to become wet; this is the simple insight that needed to be mobilized through a detailed analysis of the language of science.

Sellars does not deny that there are, and may even occur in scientific contexts, counterfactual conditionals not in the described class. But what he has described is the basic use of these conditionals in such contexts, and what he has disarmed is the suspicion that the puzzles revealed fundamental paradoxes in indispensable features of the scientific language game.

1.3 *Induction and the pragmatic turn.* Under what conditions is it true to say that Φ-ing Ks (in circumstances C) causes them to ψ? This question ties the subject of counterfactual conditionals to the traditional disputes about causation. For the warrant for the counterfactual "Were x Φ-ed, it would ψ" is exactly the assertion that Φ-ing Ks causes them to ψ, if x is a K. And the very fact that assertions of causation warrant counterfactuals has been offered as evidence against the 'constant conjunction' view of causation, and for the 'entailment view' thereof. In Part III of his paper, Sellars displays a debate by two relatively naive proponents of this view, Mr. C and Mr. E, who are forced to become less naive by the dialectical pressures built up in that debate.

Mr. C's representative statement is this:

> It would . . . be a mistake simply to *equate* lawlike statements with statements affirming constant conjunctions. . . . [A] basic lawlike statement carries with it the further implication that *it is accepted on inductive grounds* . . . . The statement, in short, *sticks its neck out*. It is this neck-sticking-out-ness . . . which finds its expression in the subjunctive mood. ([9]: 268-69.)

So Mr. C distinguishes the factual information directly conveyed by an assertion from certain information about the assertor conveyed indirectly, or contextually implied. In his interpretation of the subjunctive or counterfactual constructions, he introduces an ineliminable pragmatic element.

Mr. E starts off audaciously with claims about physical possibility and physical necessity, appearing to claim that counterfactuals convey directly factual information that cannot be conveyed directly by any statement in the indicative. But he is forced away from this audacity; it seems to me a fair summary to say that the dialogue leads to an improved, sophisticated empiricist position, and that an older Mr. E, looking back, will look back with equanimity. The crucial turn for Mr. E is depicted here:

Mr. E and his colleagues are typically prepared to grant . . . that to say that *being A* physically entails *being B* is equivalent to saying that

It is physically necessary that *A* be constantly conjoined with *B*

or, in current logistical symbolism,

$\boxed{c}\{(x)Ax \supset Bx\}$. ([9]: 272.)

This sets the stage for a resolution of the conflict in which "the core truth of Hume's philosophy of causation" is combined with the *"ungrudging* recognition of those features of causal discourse as a mode of rational discourse on which the 'metaphysical rationalists' laid such stress but also mis-assimilated to describing" ([9]: 285).

The pragmatic turn as eventually taken by Mr. E is this: induction establishes principles *in accordance with which* we reason, not just premises *from which* to reason. So the subjunctive mood, or the presence of modal qualifiers, indicates that the statement in question is one which has the role of warranting certain inferential moves.

This is accompanied by the sketch of a theory of modalities in general and causal modalities in particular, for which the deontic (as opposed to the alethic) modalities form the paradigm. I shall address myself critically to this theory below, but I am in fundamental agreement with some of its central ideas.[3] To display my agreement with this philosophical approach to science, I interject the next subsection.

1.4 *Excursion: Kantian reflections on science.* There may be some instruction in speculating on how Kant or a Kantian might react to contemporary puzzles in philosophy of science.[4] In his *Preface to the Metaphysical Foundations of Natural Science,* Kant begins almost like a rationalist:

> That only can be called science proper whose certainty is apodictic: cognition that can merely contain empirical certainty is only improperly called science. . . . ([6]: 18.)

But the qualification that removes Kant from the rationalist camp follows at once: there is *pure* and *applied* rational cognition. In any science, "only so much science is to be met with as mathematics", but this does not mean that physical theory is no more than a part of

3. For this I must blame or thank Fogelin as much as Sellars; see references.

4. I have benefited much from the mimeographed notes of, and conversations and correspondence with, Professor Gordon Brittan (University of Montana) about Kant's philosophy of science; and from [10].

mathematics. There is rational physics, a mathematical framework for the description of physical phenomena, developed *more geometrico* by spinning out the implications of our concepts of matter and motion. But the phenomena are not determined uniquely by the framework; they fit the framework; the framework is adequate to their discussion. The actual phenomena are contingent, may be thus or so, and it is their general form alone that is described in the pure, mathematical part of physical theory.

The main, perhaps the only, quarrel we have here with Kant is that he did not envisage the possibility of future scientific revolutions. By 1800, our concepts of matter and motion were highly sophisticated, and could in principle be formulated and expounded in deductive, axiomatic form (of moderate precision). Foundational studies in physics along the lines of Kant's *Metaphysical Principles* might even have enjoyed some success if they had caught the fancy of his era. But we see no reason to believe in the absolute value of a framework so expounded. The certainty of the mathematical inferences does not guarantee that the phenomena shall fit; what we *refer* to as matter may not be an instance of our concept of matter.

The pure part of our theory cannot become wrong; in principle it can be propounded in the form of a definition. But although it is apodictic, it can certainly become irrelevant. The pure part of a physical theory is mathematical. It describes a general pattern, which, in the full-fledged theory, the phenomena are asserted to fit. To say it in a later, more pictorial patois, it provides a mathematical model. The "fit" and "model" terminology is meant to yield a perspicuous description of the relation of theory to empirical fact, and the use of this terminology conveys a certain view of that relation; a view which, today as much as ever, could do with a good deal more precision.

The fit is not a unique relation; empirical structures may fit our model thus or so. In his *Inaugural Dissertation* Kant attempted a prolegomenon to any future rational cosmology, and as prime factors in "the notion of a world in general" listed matter, form, and wholeness. The form of a world, presumably described mathematically in a cosmology, "consists in the co-ordination . . . of substances" and

> the bond constituting the *essential* form of a world is regarded as the principle of *possible interactions* of the substances constituting the world. For actual interactions do not belong to essence but to state.[5]

5. N. K. Smith, ed., *Kant's Inaugural Dissertation*, p. 40.

There are many possible empirical structures that would fit the model; the non-mathematical part of the theory comprises the assertion that *whatever the actual structure be*, it fits the model. To hold a theory is to be committed to the view that whatever the empirical structures be that we shall encounter, they shall fit the model provided.

To hold a theory is to take an inductive stance toward empirical structures viewed *sub specie possibilitatis*. The proper evaluation term to apply to theories held or advanced is therefore "vindication"; commitments are vindicated, not verified. (This does not rule out that the theory might be true or false; I am only charting terminology properly applied to what Popper calls the game of science.) And the commitment to a certain view concerning the general form of the phenomena, whatever they shall be, places one in a position in which questions are received and answered *ex cathedra*. (I do not have a general account of commitment, but this feature of commitments seems to me to be as central as the adherence to a program of action, for political and moral as well as theoretical commitments.)

Accounts of scientific explanation have generally focused on the relation between explanatory premises and explained conclusion. But it is not true that the theory is corroborated or the theory holder vindicated only if a request for explanation is met with a deduction. First, requests for explanation may be justified or not justified, and the theory itself determines which requests are just. Thus Kant noted that faced with a question,

> we are well advised to leave aside the supposed grounds of the answer, and first consider what we should gain according as the answer is in the affirmative or in the negative. Should we then find that in both cases the outcome is mere nonsense, there will be good reason for instituting a critical examination of our question, to determine whether the question does not itself rest on a groundless presupposition. . . . ([5], A485.)

Thus request for explanation may be countered by a *corrective* rather than a *direct* answer. (Cf. [1].) That this distinction is not an idle one in the game of science is attested by many examples: when a theory is replaced, and the replacement is revolutionary, the new theory generally leads us to give corrective answers where the old theory attempted direct answers. (To cite one example, Aristotelian critics asked Galileo for the cause that makes a body maintain uniform rectilinear motion as described by the law of inertia. (Cf. [4]: 406.)

When the question is a just one, the theory holder vindicates his theoretical commitment if he can give an account showing how the phenomena can be as he says (*ex cathedra*, i.e., as his theory says) they are. Only in ideal cases can he deduce the observation results, via his theory, from known conditions. The Newtonian postulated universal gravitation; to vindicate his system of the heavens, the actual motion of a given planetary body need not follow from any particular given premises concerning the nearby distribution of matter. It need only be possible for him to show that it follows from various distributions of matter, at least some of which are not contradicted by observation. If the actually observed distribution is not identical with any of these, then his view implies that there is more matter waiting to be observed. His explanation is not empty, since the nature of the auxiliary hypotheses open to him is delimited by his theory, but his vindication does not require him to demonstrate the truth of a particular auxiliary hypothesis. As with ideological commitments, however, the rationale needed for vindication may eventually cripple itself by complexity.

To sum up, then, to hold a theory is to commit oneself to a view concerning the general form of any possible empirical structure, of all actual empirical structures *whatever they turn out to be*. And to make this commitment is, in part, to assume an office, to which it is appropriate to direct requests for explanation. The assumption of office is vindicated when these requests are met appropriately, and with success. But the appropriate reaction may be to refuse to attempt an explanation, to declare the explanation-request groundless. (And not general criteria of rationality, but the specific theory *itself*, determines when a direct answer is called for.) Now we may observe, from the side of pragmatics, the following function of the subjunctive mood: the use of counterfactuals in the class attended to by Sellars signals that the explainer-office has been assumed by the user.

1.5 *Sellars on modalities.* To take modalities at face value, as statements 'in the object language', is "to court serious philosophical perplexity" according to Sellars ([9]: 302). For to do so is inevitably to create a need for a metaphysical commitment: if modal statements describe, then there must be something that they describe and the description is not equivalent to that given by any indicative statement. Hence the introduction of possible worlds (alethic modality), possible states of the world and non-Humean connections (physical modality), and values (deontic modality). On the other hand, we have seen the failure of the 'nothing but' positions on these issues, and should have learned from them.

Suppose an empiricist says: "*A* physically entails *B*" (1) directly implies only that *A* materially entails *B* (always) and (2) contextually implies that the speaker has inductive grounds for his assertion. Then he will be immediately in a quandary with respect to such statements as "There is a property which physically implies *B*" or, worse, "There are causal connections which have not yet been discovered" (cf. [9]: 302). For if the empiricist is correct, the job of physical entailment assertions can be done by the conjunction of an object language (universal) material implication plus a metalanguage assertion about correct inference in our language. And then what is *actually* in our language would seem to set definite limits to what can be truly asserted in this way.

Sellars draws a number of parallels. The view that " 'Rot' (in German) means *red*" means " 'Rot' (in German) translates into 'red' (in English)" founders on the fact that *the former only* has

'Rot' (en allemand) veut dire *rouge*

as correct French translation. The view that discourse about properties is the straightforward 'material mode' correlate of discourse about predicates founders on the non-absurdity of "There are qualities which no one has yet experienced" and "There are numbers for which no designation exists in our language". Finally, the paradigm example is found in ethics:

> It is as though someone . . . had been carefully talked into the idea that 'ought' is a perfectly good concept, though not a descriptive one, and that 'Everybody ought to keep promises' contextually implies a wish, on the speaker's part, that promise keeping were a universal practice, and was then confronted with such statements as
> *There are* obligations which have not yet been recognized. ([9]: 302.)

Each of these parallels has been discussed independently by Sellars. One very attractive feature of his views is that he has offered essentially the same diagnosis and the same solution for problems in these diverse areas. His departure from a strict or naive nominalism is exactly that he recognizes that our thought and reasoning outstrip the resources that have been actualized in our language so far (or even in the fulness of time, since it is contingent when Armageddon shall occur). His emendation of the simple nominalist dicta concerning modalities and abstracta is this:

> [T]he logic of variables and quantification involves not only the *momentary* crystallized content of the language at a *cross section* of its history, but also its character as admitting . . . modification, revision, in short,development, in accordance with rational procedures. ([9]: 304.)

> [T]he presence in the object language of the causal modalities . . . serves not only to express *existing* commitments, but also to provide the *framework* for the thinking by which we reason our way . . . into the making of *new* commitments and the abandoning of old. ([9]: 302-3.)

This view of modalities is not perspicuously reflected in the usual semantic analysis of modal logic, but can be given a formal image also (see, e.g., [16], Ch. V, 2b., and references therein.)

My main criticism is not that this account of modalities, and its corollary account of counterfactuals, is inadequate with respect to the problems faced. But there is a crucial point where possible philosophical disputes are shouldered aside, exactly where the problem of counterfactuals is proclaimed a corollary to the problem of the causal modalities. That is why I said in subsection 1.3 that the crucial turn came for Mr. E in the passage I cited from page 272 of Sellars' paper. For if that is correct, then causation has always something universal in it, does not link particular events except by virtue of linking kinds of events—and if that is so, the door is opened to the empiricist, nominalist account of causation.

The debate on counterfactuals prior to 1960 did not clearly reveal that there is a fundamental parting of the ways at just that point. (Though both ways were followed by different disputants and sometimes by the same.) I take Sellars' theory to be the natural outcome of following one of these ways (and probably that followed by the majority of philosophers at that time) and in the Appendix I shall show its great degree of internal coherence. But in the remainder of the body of this paper I shall address myself to exactly the question that was evaded in the earlier debate.

2. *The Use of Counterfactuals*

There can be no sharp distinction between our background theories and the theories which we advance and advocate. Certainly it is true that we hold any theory inviolate only with the rider that conceptual revolutions are possible; that is, we accept the possibility of theoretical developments with outcomes presently inconceivable to us. History teaches us that such revisions occur and that *experientia docet*, or if it doesn't, it should. But as a distinction relative to context of inquiry, and subject to at least the vagueness of "context of inquiry", it is a useful distinction.

One who advances and advocates a theory is naturally wont to issue counterfactuals. The use of counterfactuals signals that the office of explainer has been assumed. By this I do not mean that one who issues a counterfactual thereby claims that he can explain why the counterfactual itself is true. I mean that he thereby claims to have an account of how things are in the relevant subject area, and that the phenomena will vindicate his theoretical commitments there. And it is not warranted to assert a counterfactual unless it is warranted to accept some corresponding theory.[6]

We make a general distinction, however, between warrantedness and truth. I wish to inquire into this distinction in relation to counterfactuals and I shall try to provide the inquiry with impetus in two ways: by examining (stylized) examples, and by listing some candidates for general principles governing inference involving such conditions. As a first example, suppose we are examining a car engine and I say "If that screw were (be) tightened, the engine would (will) run faster". Useful knowledge, if correct, on cold mornings. You will be right in holding my theoretical stance to be discredited if *either* you find that I am talking through my hat (i.e. without the warrant of relevant study or experience), *or* you tighten the screw and the engine does not run any faster. But that does not mean that I shall be discredited if in tightening the screw you break the gas line, no matter what the engine does. For my theoretical warrant, such as I have, was not all that led me to the assertion: I was making certain reasonable assumptions about the fixity of standing conditions.

This example illustrates the conclusion of the preceding paragraph, and also highlights the *ceteris paribus* clause that tacitly accompanies the conditional. Thus, if we use the symbol $>$ for the relevant connector, we cannot infer $(A \ \& \ C) > B$ from $A > B$. This is a generally accepted feature of the logic of counterfactual (or subjunctive) conditionals. I shall not spend much time on the generally accepted features,

6. The theoretical commitment might be quite minimal, to the effect that any adequate and correct account must have certain consequences, and that an adequate and correct account is possible.

however; I intend to focus on more controversial features, and to this end I shall now relate a fable.

Since time began, the Sailor has played Show and Kill with the Blind Man, and the world lasts as long as they play. Each shows thumb, forefinger, or little finger of the left hand, signifying elephant, man, or ant. The elephant kills the man by stepping on him, the man kills the ant, but the ant climbs into the clumsy elephant's ear and eats his brain. The Sailor agonizes over his choice, studies the hollow eyes before him, seeks to divine patterns in the other's play. They are paid off by the Dwarf, an impartial judge; his coin is love, wealth, sickness, old age, and death. What the Sailor does, does not affect the Blind Man's choice, their interaction is limited to the Dwarf. At various stages, the Sailor gains confidence in the predictability of the other's play, to the point of saying "If I were to show thumb, the outcome would be A; if I were to show forefinger, the outcome would be B".

Which of the Sailor's utterances is true? I am now not concerned with warrant, or at least not primarily with warrant, but with truth. And indeed, one central question here is whether the truth of counterfactuals depends on their being warranted.

Suppose we wish to give a thoroughly nominalist account of counterfactuals.[7] Then we can say: the use of the subjunctive, as opposed to the indicative, form has as its only function to signal the theoretical commitment. Hence the subjunctive conditional is "true" exactly if the indicative conditional follows from a theory which the utterer accepts or advocates, plus certain true assumptions made in the context, and if the theory in question is a *stable* one. ("Stable" must mean at least that the theory is never discredited by the phenomena; a thorough-going nominalist would probably resist the scientific realist's use of "true" in opposition to "vindicated".)

One simple objection we can counter immediately. We would normally say that the counterfactual assertion had been right even if subsequently the utterer's theory was discredited, but by phenomena having nothing to do with those described in the assertion in question. Well, we can take the utterer to subscribe to all sub-theories of any theory to which he subscribes; hence some of his counterfactual assertions may be true even if not all are.

There is, however, an opposing point of view. What we have called the nominalist position conflates warrant and truth, but semantics pre-

---

7. Historically, the dispute between nominalists, realists, and conceptualists seems to have concerned mainly causal properties, rather than abstract entities *überhaupt*. This classification is noticeable today mainly in the use of "scientific realism."

cedes pragmatics. Each statement is true or false, warrant apart. Coun-terfactual statements, like modal statements, describe possibilities; and these descriptions are true or false. The ontological locus of possibility is not consciousness nor language; whether or not a given statement about possibilities is true is in itself a question of fact.

The Sailor says "If I were to show elephant now, I would gain" and also "If I were to show ant now, I would lose". These statements must be true or false. How could this depend on the theory he has framed? In principle, there are several theories, none ever discredited by the facts, which nevertheless do not warrant the same counterfactuals on this occasion. Do the truth-values depend on which theory he framed? Do they depend on which theories are simpler, more elegant, more aestheti-cally pleasing, easier to formulate, easier to remember, easier to use in calculation; or on which theories give a more comfortable world-picture, or tie in with religious beliefs? And if you have an answer ready to these questions, does your answer reflect your value judgments about, say, aesthetic elegance or religious significance?

Let us call the sketched opposing account the realist account. What consequences does this account have for inference involving condition-als? The input statements are those describing what the Sailor shows, the output statements those describing whether the Sailor wins, draws, or loses, and what the Dwarf pays out (presumably depending on the history of who won over the past n plays, for some number n). The standing conditions are who won m plays ago, for each m; whether the Blind Man has died or become senile over the past interval delta of time, whether it rains or the sterile thunder brings no rain, and so on. A typical conditional of the kind we are examining is therefore

If the Sailor were now to show man, he would gain.

(I am willing to count truth-functional compounds of output statements as output statements, but not so far input statements. For I mean to limit the grammatical and logical context as severely as I can; the technical problems and possibilities have been adequately canvassed by Stal-naker, Thomason, and Lewis.)

Suppose the Blind Man shows elephant, and previous plays are not considered by the Dwarf. Regardless of what the Sailor shows, the above conditional is false. If the Sailor had shown man, he would not have won. That is, the contrary conditional, formed by negating the consequent, was true. This is the case for all the conditionals of that form: their truth-value is made perfectly determinate by the facts, but is independent of the truth-value of the antecedent. Thus we have as general principle

(I) $(A > B) \lor (A >\sim B)$.

The reason is that relevant aspects of the state of the system (what the Blind Man shows) plus the *contemplated* input determine the output, since the Dwarf reacts in a uniquely given manner to what the players show.

In addition, suppose that the Sailor shows man and does not gain. Then the Blind Man must have shown something other than what, under the circumstances, would have resulted in gain for the Sailor if the Sailor showed man. Thus what would make the assertion true (a certain act by the Blind Man) did not occur. We conclude that the following is also a general principle, although (and this may sound paradoxical) the truth-value of such a conditional depends in no way on the truth-value of its antecedent:

(II) $(A > B) \supset (A \supset B)$.

The converse is easily refuted: suppose that the Blind Man shows elephant, and the Sailor shows ant, and consider the same conditional as above.

Now (II) is again a generally accepted principle but (I) is not; and indeed, the nominalist will most certainly contest its generality. His response will certainly be that the structure of the fable is misleading us, and that the adherence to (I) would, at best, betoken drastic limitations in scope. First, we do not normally take the truth of a counterfactual to be established so easily. Suppose you know that I am advocating a theory which you doubt, and I say: if you were to adjust parameter X to value x, you would find that Y had value y. And suppose you carry out the suggested manipulation and find the described result. Then you cannot deny that I *predicted* correctly, but you will nevertheless not grant yet that my conditional assertion was true. You will say: let us try that again. And if the second time it does not work, you will say that the first outcome was accidental, and did not really show the correctness of my assertion after all. And this shows that we should reject (I) as well as such similar principles as

(III) $(A \,\&\, B) \supset (A > B)$,

which would also hold if the facts always show clearly whether a given counterfactual is true or false.[8]

8. Here the nominalist parts company with all of Stalnaker, Thomason, and Lewis.

This the realist can counter with the view that the other's conditionals are universally generalized conditionals. In certain contexts, for example in laboratory situations, it may be inappropriate to assert any but universally generalized conditionals. And of course, neither $(x)(A > B) \vee (x)(A > {\sim}B)$ nor $(A \mathbin{\&} B) \supset (x)(A > B)$ are logically true, which is all that the example shows.

The nominalist can counter secondly that two factors make the logical morals of the fable incapable of generalization. The first is that what the Sailor does has no effect on what the Blind Man does; the second is that the Dwarf is a deterministic system.

Suppose that, contrary to the story so far, the Sailor becomes convinced that what the Blind Man shows is in part determined by what he himself decides to show. I do not see how this affects the example except by transforming it into another example perfectly similar in relevant respects. The input is still what the Sailor does, but the independent system is now some ideally or physically isolable part of the Blind Man, the state of which, together with the Sailor's acts, determines the Blind Man's acts. The "underlying state" is now no longer uniquely correlated with an observable phenomenon (the Blind Man's showing) but that does not affect the logic of the situation. And the Sailor's theoretical situation need not become more precarious, although the subject of his theorizing is no longer so eminently observable; this is the kind of situation in which the Sailor may naturally be expected to turn to either microtheories or astrology.

The problem of indeterminism, however, is much more formidable. The Sailor will become very frustrated in his practical reasoning if, ever so often and quite unpredictably, the Dwarf doles out payment not in accordance with the rules of play and gain. The Sailor may then begin to talk probabilistically, and say, for example, "If I show man, then the outcome will probably be gain". And he will cease to endorse conditionals unqualified by probabilistic terms—not would they be warranted if he were to endorse them.

But the realist surely is not at the end of his tether here. Should a probabilistically qualified counterfactual be construed as denying all unqualified counterfactuals? Surely we do not so construe probabilistically qualified indicative statements. (If I say that the switch is probably, but only probably, off, I do not imply that really it is neither on nor off.) Instead, a theory of conditionals with the above logical principles can be elegantly incorporated in a theory of conditional probability. (See [11].)

As a rough indication of what that means, we can take the conditional probability that *B* is true given that *A* is true to be equal to *r*, exactly if the probability that *A* > *B* is true is equal to *r*. Thus suppose that a system is in state *X* and that the probability of output *O* given input *I* equals *r* because the system is in state *X*. Then we can say that a system of this kind is subject to a number of alternative propensities, "iffy" properties, and that in this system, at this time, the probability that it currently has the propensity to put out *O* if *I* is put in, equals *r*. These propensities are clearly such that if they were taken into account in characterizing the state, the system would not be indeterministic. But they are not being used to characterize the state, say, because they are not 'directly observable'.

However this introduction of properties of a new sort may be devoid of physical motivation. It is analogous to the attempt to provide 'hidden parameter' underpinnings for quantum theory. In a certain abstract sense, or rather in several such, it is certainly possible to do so. But unless the attempt gives rise to a new theory successfully rivaling the old, the new parameters introduced are useless metaphysics. Of course, what we are here debating is a metaphysical point, and the question whether metaphysics is useless is properly raised only about the debate as a whole as opposed to a specific move in the debate. To amend the criticism, therefore: the introduction of a special kind of property in order to ensure that the truth-value of all conditionals be made determinate by the facts is justified only if we can thereby serve better the aim of saving the phenomena elegantly.

3. *Counterfactuals and Non-deterministic Systems*

The historical point, if it is correct, that the way we talk about and conceive of physical behavior and interaction derives from a tacit assumption of determinism, does by itself nothing to discredit our conceptions. It need only be shown that our inference patterns can be valid even if applied in discourse concerning non-deterministic systems, to make our language game capable of preservation.

As a correlate example, we may consider Aristotle's discussion of the sea-battle. The facts so far entail neither that there will be a sea-battle tomorrow, nor that there will not be one (suppose). Now I can use the term "what will actually happen", and this term clearly purports to refer to a unique future state. But I have no independent way of identifying the referent of that term. I can say "One of the two possibilities must become actual; I am referring to the one that does". But that is no help; it is tautological to say that what will actually happen is the actual outcome, the possibility that will later have become actual. If the present facts did determine the future, we would have an independent way of identifying the actual outcome (it is then that possible outcome which is necessary given present facts). So indeterminism, but not determinism, undermines the use of "the actual outcome" by making it impossible for us to give some independent, uniquely identifying description of its referent.

Yet, as has often been pointed out, those who think in terms of a uniquely actual future, and have no hesitation in referring to it, do not thereby commit themselves to the view that all physical systems are deterministic (with respect to the parameters considered relevant). There is a perfectly usable, convenient world-picture in which one of the possible futures is designated as the actual one. Once we have shown that the language game governed by this picture does not preclude indeterminism, the picture cannot be ruled out by reference to indeterminism alone. (But adherence to the picture is one metaphysical stance, and a metaphysical stance too is a theoretical commitment open to discredit or vindication.)

With respect to counterfactual conditionals, we face, I think, a similar situation. The nominalist attempt to characterize the use of such conditionals has not been very successful. Within pragmatics, we are perfectly willing to agree that counterfactuals can only be warranted by theories. But some counterfactuals are surely true though not warranted (at this time)? A less nominalistically inclined philosopher attempting to carry through the interpretation of conditionals in terms of physical theory, might refer to the possible theory (or theories) maximal with respect to certain standards.[9] But on the one hand there are problems, possibly unsolvable or not uniquely solvable, involved in ranking theories with respect to completeness and simplicity. On the other hand, there seem to be standards generally accepted among scientists, attested by the use of such phrases as "good physical reasons" and "physical understanding", which have seen only the most rudimentary attempts at philosophical explication, which may or may not be 'purely psychological' or 'purely historical' or quasi-religious, but which surely would be

9. I am indebted to David Lewis for this point.

needed to explain uses of counterfactuals if this general line of approach is correct at all. I fear that the approach will only lead us into a quagmire.

But the way in which counterfactuals tend to enter our reasoning seems very remote from these deliberations. I wonder with some detachment whether the girl would leave or stay if I smiled at her, with agony whether the bomb would explode or not were I to move it. Perhaps this is because I have not reflected adequately about the problems of free will and indeterminism; the fact remains that this is how I think.

Now we have seen how the realist can save the phenomena with respect to this way of thinking. He can do this by postulating counterfacts in addition to facts, propensities, or potentialities. But that is quite a price to pay for salvation. In the case of other modalities, physical as well as logical, Sellars' writings have helped to maintain the thesis that the ontological locus of possibility is in language and consciousness. Shall we here either accept the independent reality, in some sense, of possibilities and potentialities, or foreswear the explication of the counterfactual language game?

Thomason has elsewhere proposed a general emendation of the logic of conditionals to solve related problems.[10] We can adapt his solution to the present context, and shall begin by relating it to the account of theory-acceptance sketched above.

Consider such a question as "If the Sailor won (now) would the Dwarf pay fairly?" or in general, "If X were the input, would Y result?" There are three major relevant responses that might be made:

(1) If X were the input, Y would result.
(2) If X were the input, some alternative to Y would result (Y would not result).
(3) If X were the input, the result might be or not be Y (there is no telling).

The question has (1) (Yes) and (2) (No) as direct answers. Response (3) should be sharply distinguished from such non-responsive retorts as "I don't know". For (3) is a correction of the question. It asserts that there is no such thing as the unique outcome given X. The questioner is mistaken in some way: he supposes that his question has a true direct answer, and that to vindicate our theoretical alignments in this area we must supply that answer. But that means that he supposes that input X

10. In [14]: 18, with reference to Quine's "Bizet and Verdi" problem. See also the next-to-last section of my [15].

applied to the present state (of the system in question) will be followed by a uniquely determined next state. And the system may not be deterministic in that respect.

Following Strawson, we may argue that the functioning of statements in discourse can often be illuminated by regarding them as answers to questions. Let us suppose that question Q has possible rival direct answers $A_1, \ldots, A_n$, and that we know already under which conditions these answers are *true*. Then we can add that A_i is *false* exactly if A_j is true for some $j \neq i$, and that the question *arises* exactly if one of its direct answers is true. Then clearly, if a question does not arise, its answers are neither true nor false, and this will presumably happen if the question is based on an assumption B which is true only if at least one of those direct answers is true.[11]

The kind of question discussed above I regard as having as direct answers the pair $A > B$, $A > {\sim}B$. Thus of these two, each is true if and only if the other is false. But it is possible that the question does not arise or that it is mistaken; then neither direct answer is true. That this is so is stated by response (3), which, accordingly, I formulate as

$$(3') \quad {\sim}\text{True} \ (A > B) \ \& \ {\sim}\text{True} \ (A > {\sim}B).$$

But questions purport not to be mistaken, in the sense that "the king of Baluchistan" purports to refer to an individual, and political pronouncements purport to express majority opinion. In many cases we do not know whether the purport is correct. But at one level of reasoning at least, this possibility of radical failure in our background assumptions does not affect the trustworthiness of logical principles.

I shall not enter the technicalities of the logic that accompanies this dual view. (See [14] and my [16], Chap. V, sections 3-4.) But on a semantic level we can give the view some added content by discussing abstract machines with input. Let us begin with a deterministic machine: it has as possible states the elements of a set H (the state-space), as possible inputs the elements of a set I. Its mechanics are summed up by a next-state function δ: if the state is now x and the input now applied is i, then the next state is $\delta(x, i)$. Clearly, the conditional

(4) If input j were now applied, the next state would have character C

---

11. Belnap has argued that there is no necessary connection between the possibility of questions not arising and the view that statements may be neither true nor false. I hold only that viewing statements in the way indicated *may* illuminate their role in discourse.

is true if the present state x is such that $\delta(x,j)$ has character C; if not, then

> (5) If input j were now applied, the next state would not have character C

is true. Any question of the form "If input j were now applied, would the resultant state have character C?" is well-taken; it never fails to arise. If we consider truth-functional compounds of statements, $(A > B) \vee (A >\sim B)$ is logically true here.

Consider next an indeterministic system. Its analogue to the next-state function is a relation δ^* such that: if the state is now x, and the input now applied is i, then the next state will be a state bearing δ^* to $\langle x, i \rangle$. How will the logic of the above kinds of statements go here? Well, to reduce this problem to the previous one, note that δ^* is the union of a set Δ of alternative possible next-state functions: Δ is the set of mappings δ such that $\delta(x,i)$ bears δ^* to $\langle x,i \rangle$ for x in H, i in I. If the present state is x (and the input is j), we can regard A as true (false) if and only if A is true (false) in each of the similar deterministic machines with the next-state function in Δ, when their state is x (and the input is j). Then simple conditionals like (4) or (5) may well come out neither true nor false. But the disjunction of (4) and (5) will come out true; the set of logically true statements will be as before.

The view which I have now sketched is meant as an alternative to the positions which I have called nominalist and realist. This third view is meant to do justice to the apparent fact that intuitive counterfactual discourse is guided by the realist's picture, in which in some sense every question of outcome is well-taken. But it eschews the realist's reification of counterfacts, causal properties, propensities, potentialities, or alternative possible worlds. It accepts the nominalist's conviction that a conditional could not be true unless it could be warranted, but accepts as logically true the sentences so characterized under an uncritical use of the realist's picture. If a name be allowed for the view, I would like to call it conceptualist.

Appendix: The Logic of Counterfactuals

The position which I have called nominalist is probably closest to what philosophers were inclined to adopt, especially in the earliest stages of the discussion. Attempts to give that position a precise, defensible form ended in despair, partly becaause the position did not seem to lead to an adequate semantic analysis of conditionals that satisfied the intuitive criteria. But then, the criteria were themselves not made precise until the methods of formal semantics reached the stage that made the work of Stalnaker, Thomason, and Lewis possible.

In this Appendix, I wish to show that the nominalist position does have a specific logical system associated with it, a system that can be strengthened in various ways to yield other extant conditional logics. Some of these strengthenings might be acceptable to the nominalist, perhaps with respect to certain purposes; but that reflects the usual (and desirable) flexibility of a philosophical position vis-à-vis logical principles.

The conditional logic to which I refer was mentioned in passing by Thomason, and described by him as "a *minimal* basis" for a logic of conditionals ([14]: 12 and n. 4). I shall use Thomason's designation **CMS** for the system, but shall formulate it axiomatically in such a way that no nesting of conditional connectors appears explicitly in the rules. **CMS** is a proper part of Lewis system **CO**, described by him as absolutely minimal, and I shall compare the two systems below ([7]).

The main criteria for a logic of counterfactual conditionals that emerge from the work of Stalnaker, Thomason, and Lewis, as well as the earlier philosophical discussions, seem to be these:

(1) The natural deduction rules of implication, introduction, and elimination hold.

(2) If $A > B$ is given, and A is introduced as a supposition (in a 'subordinate proof' or 'subderivation'), then B may be introduced under that supposition.

(3) Contraposition does not hold.

(4) Transitivity does not hold.

(5) Weakening of the antecedent does not hold.

Taking our cue from (1) and (2), we can formulate the logical system **CMS** as follows:

R0. If $(A_1 \& \ldots \& A_n) \supset B$ is a tautology, then $A_1, \ldots, A_n \vdash B$.

R1. $A > B, A \vdash B$.

R2. If $A, B_1, \ldots, B_n \vdash C$, then $A > B_1, \ldots, A > B_n \vdash A > C$.

Here $n = 0$ is allowed, so that $\vdash B \supset B$ by R0, and $\vdash A > A$ by R2. Also, some theorems have nested conditional connectors in them, but these we allow only for technical convenience. We note *à propos* (3)-(5), that the following do not hold in this system:

(3*) $A > B \vdash \sim B > \sim A$.

(4*) $A > B, B > C \vdash A > C$.

(5*) $A > B \vdash (A \& C) > B$.

That these indeed do not hold is perhaps not so easy to see at this point, but it will become clear upon the nominalist interpretation which we are about to give.

Let us consider a nominalist who has a theory T; he talks the language of modal logic, but hastens to explain that he considers $\Box A$ true exactly if A follows from T. He may or may not be a nominalist in the sense of denying the existence of sets, and if he does deny the existence of sets, he may or may not consider himself justified (in some other way) in using set theory. In any case, I shall use set-theoretical language to describe him. He considers $A > B$ true in a given context if there is some true assumption p that may reasonably be made in that context, such that $\Box (A \& p. \supset B)$. He agrees that the assumption may not be expressible in his language, but has some way, acceptable to him as a nominalist, of explaining what it means to say that some assumptions are not expressible in his language. Finally, he agrees that he has no general account of what assumptions are both reasonable and true in which contexts.

If this philosopher wishes to test for logical truth a statement of the form

(6) $\ldots (A_1 > B_1) \ldots (A_i > B_i) \ldots$

(in which there are no nestings of conditional connectors, which we consider irrelevant), how does he go about it? Well, according to him, (6) is true exactly if

(7) $\ldots \Box (A_1 \& p_1. \supset B_1) \ldots \Box (A_i \& p_i. \supset B_i) \ldots$

is true, provided the assumptions $p_1, \ldots, p_i, \ldots$ are all right. Now all he can say when an assumption is all right, is that it must at least be true. Hence, to rule out any unwarranted assumptions on his part, he will choose a distinct atomic sentence p_i, not occurring in (6), for each distinct sentence A_i, and see if

(8) $p_1, \ldots, p_i, \ldots \vdash (7)$

holds in modal logic.

That (3*)-(5*) are unsound principles for him is easy to see. But R0-R2 are sound principles for him. For example, $(A > B) \lor \sim(A > B)$ is logically true because $p \vdash \Box(A \& p \cdot \supset B) \lor \sim\Box(A \& p \cdot \supset B)$ is. And $p \vdash \Box(A \& p \cdot \supset B) \& A \cdot \supset B$ holds, so $(A > B) \& A \cdot \supset B$ is logically true. Finally, if $(A \& B_1 \& \ldots \& B_n) \supset C$ is logically true, so is $p \supset [\Box(A \& p \cdot \supset B_1) \& \ldots \& \Box(A \& p \cdot \supset B_n) \cdot \supset \Box (A \& p \cdot \supset C)]$; indeed, so its consequent. Thus this philosopher accepts **CMS** as correct. If it is also the strongest such system that he can accept, given that his modal logic is such or such, then we have a 'reduction' of the fragment of this conditional logic in which no nesting of conditionals occurs to alethic modal logic along the lines of Anderson's reduction of deontic logic to alethic modal logic.

Before looking at possible ways to strengthen the system, we should address this technical question. I shall do this sketchily, since ways to make it precise are straightforward given others' work. A *model structure* (ms) is a couple $\mathbf{M} = \langle K,p \rangle$ where K is a non-empty set (the possible worlds) and p a function from worlds and sentences to sets of worlds. For brevity we write $p_\alpha(A)$ for $p(\alpha,A)$; the conditions on p are

$$p_\alpha(A) \subseteq K, \qquad \alpha \in p_\alpha(A),$$

because the contextual assumptions must be true ones, although A need not be true. We define a *valuation v over* $\mathbf{M}$ to be a function from worlds and sentences into $\{T, F\}$, subject to the conditions (writing $v_\alpha(A)$ for $v(\alpha,A)$:

(i) $v_\alpha(\sim A) = F$ iff $v_\alpha(A) = T$;
$v_\alpha(A \& B) = F$ iff $v_\alpha(A) = F$ or $v_\alpha(B) = F$;

(ii) $v_\alpha(A \supset B) = F$ iff $v_\alpha(A) = T$ and $v_\alpha(B) = F$;

(iii) $v_\alpha(A > B) = F$ iff for some β in $p_\alpha(A)$, $v_\beta(A \supset B) = F$.

To show the completeness of **CMS** under this interpretation, let K be the set of all maximal consistent theories of **CMS**. If α is a member of K, and A is a sentence, define $p(\alpha,A)$ by:

$$p(\alpha,A) = \{\beta \in K: \text{for any sentence } B, \text{ if } A > B \in \alpha \text{ then } A \supset B \in \beta\}.$$

Note that $\alpha \in p(\alpha, A)$ by R1. The model $\mathbf{M} = \langle K,p \rangle$ so defined provides a counterexample to each non-theorem. For, define the function v for member α of K and sentence A by

$$v(\alpha, A) = \begin{cases} T, \text{ if } A \in \alpha \\ F, \text{ otherwise} \end{cases}$$

Then v is a valuation over **M**:

(ad i) $v_\alpha(A) = F$ iff $A \notin \alpha$ iff $\sim A \in \alpha$ iff $v_\alpha(A) \neq T$;

(ad ii) $v_\alpha(A \supset B) = F$ iff $A \supset B \notin \alpha$ iff $A, \sim B \in \alpha$ iff $v_\alpha(A) = T$ and $v_\alpha(B) = F$;

(ad iii) $v_\alpha(A > B) = F$ iff $v_\beta(A \supset B) = F$ for some β in $p_\alpha(A)$, as we shall now show.

Suppose first that $A > B$ is in α. Then $A \supset B$ is in every β in $p_\alpha(A)$, by definition of p. Suppose on the other hand that $A > B$ is not in α. Then $\sim(A \supset B)$ is consistent with the set of all conditionals $A \supset C$ such that $A > C$ is in α. For suppose it is not. Then, because the rules are finitary, there are sentences $C_1, \ldots, C_n$ such that $A, A \supset C_1, \ldots, A \supset C_n \vdash B$, and $A > C_1, \ldots, A > C_n$ are all in α. But then $A, C_1, \ldots, C_n \vdash B$, hence $A > C_1, \ldots, A > C_n \vdash A > B$ by R2, so $A > B \in \alpha$.

To substantiate the relation to modal logic, which was used above to relate the logic of conditionals to the nominalist point of view, we must yet show that any consistent theory Γ of **CMS** can be embedded in a consistent modal theory Δ in a certain way. Since we ignore nesting of conditionals (as technically convenient but philosophically irrelevant) in this context, we add to Γ all the material biconditionals

$$(A_i > B) \equiv \Box(A_i \,\&\, p_i \cdot \supset B),$$

where the syntax is now enlarged by adding denumerably many new atomic sentences $p_1, \ldots, p_i, \ldots$, and the unary connector $\Box$, and where A_i is the ith sentence of the old syntax. The resultant set Δ we shall show to be a consistent theory of any normal modal logic.[12]

We return to the model **M** $= \langle K, p \rangle$ defined for the completeness proof above. Since Γ is consistent, it is part of some member α of K. For the purpose of interpreting modal notions, we shall regard all members of K as possible relative to one another. I shall now make up a new syntax which will not contain the old syntax but into which the old syntax can be mapped in a natural way. The sentences of the new syntax are the subsets of K. For such subsets X, Y, we define:

12. For relevant information about normal modal logics, see [13] or [16], Chapter V, section 2.

$\sim X = K - X,$

$X \ \& \ Y = X \ \cap \ Y,$

$X \supset Y = \sim(X \ \& \ \sim Y),$

$\Box X = \{\alpha: \beta \epsilon X \text{ for all } \beta \text{ in } K\}.$

The natural mapping is of course $\left| A \right| = \{\alpha: A \epsilon \alpha\} = \{\alpha: v_\alpha(A) = T\}$, where v is the valuation that was defined for the completeness proof. We may take for granted, from modal logic, that if a given member α of K belongs to each member of a set of the new sentences, then that set is consistent. And we may call a new sentence X true at α exactly if α is a member of X.

Now we clearly have that

(i) $v_\alpha(\sim A) = T$ iff $\alpha \epsilon \sim \left| A \right|$,

(ii) $v_\alpha(A \ \& \ B) = T$ iff $\alpha \epsilon \left| A \right| \ \& \ \left| B \right|$,

(iii) $v_\alpha(A \supset B) = T$ iff $\alpha \epsilon \left| A \right| \supset \left| B \right|$,

and similarly for other truth-functional connectors defined in the usual way. In addition, we have as new sentences the sets $p_\alpha(A)$, which must be true at α, for each world α and old sentence A. What we should like to demonstrate now is that

(iv) $v_\alpha(A > B) = T$ iff $\alpha \epsilon \Box(\left| A \right| \ \& \ p_\alpha(A) \ . \supset \left| B \right|)$,

for from this it would then follow that for each α in K, $\alpha \epsilon \big[\left| A \right| > \left| B \right| \equiv \Box(\left| A \right| \& p_\alpha(A) \ . \supset \left| B \right|)\big]$. Then we could complete the total proof by enlarging the old syntax by adding atomic sentences $p_1, \ldots, p_i, \ldots$, and connector $\Box$; set $\left| p_i \right| = \left| p_\alpha(A_i) \right|$, $\left| \Box A \right| = \Box \left| A \right|$; and define $\alpha^* = \{B : B \text{ is a sentence of the enlarged syntax and } \alpha \epsilon \left| B \right|\}$. Clearly, Δ will then be part of α^* if Γ is part of α.

But (iv) must hold. For let β be any member of K. If $\beta \notin p_\alpha(A)$, then $\beta \epsilon (\left| A \right| \& p_\alpha(A) \ . \supset \left| B \right|)$. If $\beta \epsilon p_\alpha(A)$, then, by the definition of p, $A \supset B$ will be in β, so $\beta \epsilon \left| A \supset B \right|$. But then $\beta \epsilon \left| A \right| \supset \left| B \right|$, hence $\beta \epsilon (\left| A \right| \& p_\alpha(A) \ . \supset \left| B \right|)$. So the relation of modal logic is as we said it was.

I think that someone taking the above position and concerned with the counterfactuals in some specific language game, might well wish to add some things to the rudimentary logic sketched above. But I do not find any of the additions suggested so far in the literature of overwhelming force. To begin, if A and B are equivalent in some strong sense, then $A > C$ and $B > C$ should be materially equivalent. If we are developing the theory within a modal logic, we shall therefore be inclined to lay down the principle

$$\Box (A \equiv B) \vdash (A > C) \equiv (B > C),$$

and if we use the language of **CMS**, we shall be inclined (as I am not) to the principle

R3. $(A > B), (B > A) \vdash (A > C) \equiv (B > C).$

The second may, however, be a stronger principle than the first; in both cases, the inclination resulted from a natural (in a purely psychological sense of "natural") tendency to equate "equivalence in a strong sense" with "strictest equivalence expressible in the language".

Another conviction, more general than and encompassing the preceding, is that logical connections between A and B should engender logical connections between $A > C$ and $B > C$. This conviction may lead one to accept either of the above, or David Lewis' further

$$(A \lor B > A) \lor (A \lor B > B) \lor (A \lor B > C . \equiv . (A > C) \& (B > C)).$$

Lewis considers this to be one of the minimal principles for a logic of conditionals. Certainly from the point of view which we have explored in this section, there seems to be no obvious reason to accept it. But Lewis interprets counterfactual conditionals generally in terms of similarity relations among possible worlds, a notion that has not entered our discussion at all.[13*]

13. I would like to record my debt, no doubt already obvious, to conversations about counterfactuals with Fogelin, Lewis, Stalnaker, and Thomason and to thank the John Simon Guggenheim Memorial Foundation and the Canada Council for their generous support.

*NOTE ADDED IN PROOF: Since this paper was written in 1970, much has happened in this problem area. My own further papers on the subject are: "Probabilities of Conditionals" forthcoming in the proceedings of the University of Western Ontario Conference on the Foundations of Probability and Statistics, and "Hidden Variables in Conditional Logic" forthcoming in Theoria.

REFERENCES

[1] Nuel D. Belnap, Jr., "Questions: Their Presuppositions, and How They Can Fail to Arise," in K. Lambert, ed., *The Logical Way of Doing Things* (New Haven: Yale University Press, 1969): 23-37.

[2] R. J. Fogelin, "Inferential Constructions," *American Philosophical Quarterly* 4 (1967): 1-13.

[3] _____, "Simultaneity of Cause and Effect," presented at a Colloquium at the University of North Carolina, October 1969.

[4] A. Grünbaum, *Philosophical Problems of Space and Time* (New York: Knopf, 1963).

[5] Immanuel Kant, *Critique of Pure Reason,* N.K. Smith, tr. (New York: St. Martin's Press, 1956).

[6] _____, *Prolegomena and Metaphysical Foundations of Natural Science,* trans. by E.B. Bax (London: G. Bell and Sons), as quoted in *Philosophy of Science: The Historical Background,* ed. by J. Kockelmans (New York: Free Press, 1968).

[7] David Lewis, "Completeness of Three Logics of Counterfactual Conditionals, *Theoria* 37 (1971): 74-85.

[8] _____, *Counterfactuals* (Oxford: Blackwell's 1973).

[9] Wilfrid Sellars, "Counterfactuals, Dispositions, and the Causal Modalities," *Minnesota Studies in the Philosophy of Science* 2 (1958): 225-308.

[10] _____, "Is There a Synthetic *A Priori?*," in his *Science, Perception and Reality* (London: Routledge & Kegan Paul, 1963): 298-320.

[11] R. Stalnaker, "Probability and Conditionality," *Philosophy of Science* 37 (1970): 64-80.

[12] _____, "A Theory of Conditionals," in N. Rescher, ed., *Studies in Logical Theory* (Oxford: Blackwell's, 1968): 98-112.

[13] _____ and R.H. Thomason, "A Semantic Analysis of Conditional Logic," *Theoria* 36 (1970): 23-42.

[14] R.H. Thomason, "A Fitch-Style Formulation of Conditional Logic," *Logique et Analyse* 13 (1970): 397-412.

[15] Bas C. van Fraassen, "A Formal Approach to the Philosophy of Science," in *Paradigms and Paradoxes* (Pittsburgh: University of Pittsburgh Press, 1972).

[16] _____, *Formal Semantics and Logic* (New York: Macmillan, 1971).

·~· 11 ·~·
Wilfrid Sellars' Theory
of Induction

GILBERT H. HARMAN
Princeton University

A CCORDING to Wilfrid Sellars, there is 'no such thing as a non-deductive probability argument' ([5]:44).[1] He holds that 'the concept of such probability arguments is an illusion; the division of argument into "deductive" and "probability" arguments a mistake' ([5]: 32; *cf.* [3]: 11, 17). He suggests that what appear to be nondeductive arguments for a conclusion p may be deductive arguments for something else. For example, a deductive argument for *it is probable that p*, which asserts something about the proposition that p, may appear at first to be a nondeductive argument for (*probably*) p, which asserts that p and only 'signifies' or 'implies' what the former claim asserts about the proposition that p ([5]: 7). Sellars also suggests that a deductive argument for *it is reasonable to accept that p* may appear to be a nondeductive argument for p, since it can make it reasonable to accept that p ([5]: 33-44; *cf.* [3]: 14-20). These two points are, for Sellars, closely related, since he analyzes *it is probable that p* as *it is reasonable to accept that p* ([5]: 32; [3]: 15).

Furthermore, according to Sellars, to claim that it is reasonable to accept that p is to claim that there is a good argument for accepting that p ([5]: 45; [3]: 15, 18). 'This argument will be of the kind traditionally called practical' ([5]: 45). It 'has as its conclusion *I shall accept that-p*' ([3]: 15). '[T]he skeleton of the argument is deductive' ([5]: 46); it may be a 'deductive practical syllogism' ([3]: 26). 'This practical argument has

1. References in the text are to numbered sections, rather than to pages, of [5] and [3]. Preparation of the present article was supported in part by the National Science Foundation.

as its major premise an intention, expressed by *I shall bring about E*, which intention implies a general condition intention or policy, expressed by *I shall accept a proposition which satisfies such and such condition'* ([3]: 34). For Sellars, a study of induction must show how inductive methods forward ends which provide the major premises for the relevant practical arguments. These ends are 'constitutive of the scientific enterprise' ([3]: 60; *cf*. [5]: 57-59).

What are these ends? Sellars mentions three. First, there is the end of 'knowing where we stand with respect to the proportion of answers to certain classes of questions which are true' ([3]: 82, *cf*. 73). More exactly, this first end is that of knowing that we have answered a set of 'yes'–'no' questions in such a way that a majority of our answers are correct and, furthermore, that we know what proportion of the answers are correct ([3]: 71-74; *cf*. [5]: 43, 55). Second, there is the end of accepting the simplest law-like statements that would explain the observed composition of a sample ([3]: 42, 47, 52-56). Given Sellars' account of law-like statements, this is the end of 'being able to draw inferences concerning the composition with respect to a given property Y of unexamined finite samples (ΔK) of a kind, X, in a way which also provides an explanatory account of the composition with respect to Y of the total examined sample, K, of X' ([3]: 52). Third, there is the end of 'being able to give non-trivial explanatory accounts of established laws' ([3]: 38), which Sellars equates with being in possession of 'the simplest available framework which generates new testable law-like statements, generates acceptable approximations of nomologically probable law-like statements and generates no falsified law-like statements' ([3]: 35).

Each end is associated with a different sort of inductive argument and with a different 'mode' of probability. The first is relevant to 'the so-called "statistical" or "proportional" syllogism, [*e.g.*] *7 of these 8 objects are ϕ, therefore it is probable$_s$ that a randomly selected one is ϕ . . .'* ([3]: 70) and related arguments. The subscripted *s* here indicates the mode of probability appropriate to this sort of argument. The second of the above ends is relevant to "nomological induction' ([3]: 42) as in the argument '*n/m observed As are B, therefore it is probable$_n$ that n/m of all As are B*' ([3]: 40). The subscripted *n* indicates that it is 'nomological probability (inductive probability in the narrower sense)' ([3]: 40) that is the mode of probability appropriate to this sort of argument. Finally, the third of the above ends is relevant to theoretical inference as when one accepts the simplest theory that permits one to give non-trivial explanations of established laws ([3]: 35-39). The relevant mode of probability in this last case is 'the probability of theories', which is indicated by saying of some theory that it is 'probable,' ([3]: 35).

In this paper I shall argue: (1) that distinguishing three kinds of inductive argument or probability in the way that Sellars does serves no useful purpose, (2) that induction is a matter of inference and therefore has nothing to do with deduction, arguments, and logic, and (3) that there is no such thing as a deductive practical argument.

I

Induction is inference to the best explanation, inference to the best total explanatory account. More precisely, one attempts to modify one's antecedent views as little as possible while increasing the explanatory coherence of the result. Sometimes this is a matter of accepting a conclusion that explains what one already believes; sometimes it is a matter of accepting a conclusion explained by things which one already believes; sometimes it is a matter of rejecting a previous belief which is promoting too much explanatory complication in one's total view. Often it involves all of this and more.

It is easy to see that the second and third types of induction mentioned by Sellars are special cases of inference to the best explanation. One accepts a statistical or universal law because it best explains what one believes about the composition of a sample; one accepts a theory because it best explains accepted laws. There is no reason to suppose that a different principle is operative in the two cases; nor is there any reason to suppose that these two cases differ in principle from one in which a detective concludes that the butler must have done it because that best explains the evidence.

It is true that for Sellars accepting a law is not the same as acquiring a belief, since for Sellars laws are principles of inference. But he does not say why the difference between laws and other beliefs should make a difference in the reasons which lead to their acceptance. In any event, as I shall argue in the following section, it is a mistake to treat laws as principles of inference.

I mentioned above that inference to the best total explanatory account includes cases in which one comes to accept something that is explained by things previously accepted. For example, one infers that a person will be at a certain place at a certain time, given that he now intends to be there then. One infers that his present intention will explain his being there. Competing alternatives are that something will prevent his appearance or that he will change his mind or forget. One's inference is warranted to the extent that its conclusion is sufficiently more plausible than these competing alternatives.

Again, one infers on a particular occasion that sugar will dissolve when stirred into one's tea. That is, one infers that the solubility of sugar in hot tea will explain the dissolving of this sugar in this tea. The conclusion is acceptable to the extent that it is sufficiently more plausible than competing alternatives such as that some factor or other will prevent the dissolving this time.

The other type of inference Sellars discusses, the proportional syllogism, would seem to be an inference to the best explanation of this sort. The proportional syllogism is supposed to warrant belief that something is a B given that it is an A and that most As are Bs. This looks like a case in which one infers a conclusion that is explained by something already accepted. One infers that most As being Bs will explain this As being a B.

But it is by no means obvious that it is reasonable to believe that a particular A is a B if one knows only that most As are Bs. For one thing, there is Kyburg's lottery paradox. For each ticket in a fair lottery, Sellars' principle has one accept the proposition that it loses. By hypothesis one is also justified in believing that one of the tickets wins. One is led to accept a set of propositions one knows to be inconsistent.

Sellars quite rightly points out that accepting each member of a set of propositions is not the same as accepting their conjunction ([3]: 74). That is true; but it does not dispel one's feeling that there is something wrong with a principle that allows one to conclude, for each ticket in the lottery, that it will lose.

Sellars might appeal here to his analysis of probability. Recall that he claims that to say a proposition is probable is to say that it is reasonable to accept the proposition. Since for each ticket, it is probable that the ticket will lose, it follows that for each ticket it is reasonable to accept the proposition that the ticket loses. But one can just as easily turn the argument around. Since it is not reasonable to believe of each ticket that it will lose, and since it is probable for each ticket that it will lose, Sellars' analysis of probability must be mistaken.

We have seen that for Sellars the reasonableness of believing of each ticket that it will lose derives from a supposed end of ours that Sellars takes to be partially constitutive of the scientific enterprise. The end in question is that of knowing that one has answered a set of 'yes'–'no' questions so that a majority of one's answers are correct and, furthermore, one knows what proportion of the answers are correct. Now it is quite clear, I think, that this is not one of our ends. It is not something we immediately recognize as one of our ends (in the way that we immediately recognize our interest in explanation); and Sellars offers no argument for thinking that it is one of our ends. Moreover, it is certainly not even partially constitutive of the scientific enterprise. Science is not a matter of accepting vast sets of competing propositions in such a way that most of what one accepts is true. It is a matter of attempting to fit what one accepts into an explanatorily complete whole.

If induction is taken to be inference to the best of competing total explanatory accounts, it becomes clear that one cannot infer of a given lottery ticket that the ticket will lose. Competing total accounts will have to say for every ticket whether it wins or loses. By hypothesis, there is no reason to rule out one account in favor of another. Since no total account can be inferred, no conclusion can be drawn about a particular ticket's winning or losing.

This agrees well with the results of a knowability test of rules of acceptance. A rule of acceptance passes the test only if it is possible to come to know the conclusion by reasoning in accordance with the suggested rule. Sellars' rule fails the test, since one cannot come to know that one will lose a lottery simply by arguing from the high probability that one will lose.

II

Induction is inference or reasoning which adds to and subtracts from antecedent beliefs in the interests of explanatory coherence. Deductive logic has nothing to do with that. So called deductive 'rules of inference', such as *modus ponens,* have nothing to do with inference. They are concerned only with deductive *relations,* such as entailment. *Modus ponens* says that a proposition of the form P and a proposition of the form Q, if P jointly entail a proposition of the form Q. *Modus ponens* does not say that if one believes P and also believes Q, if P, then one can infer Q, since that is not always so. Sometimes one should stop believing P or Q, *if P* rather than start believing Q.[2] It is a familiar point that, although a logical contradiction entails everything, one should not respond to the discovery of contradiction in one's views by attempting to infer everything. Instead one should, here as elsewhere, attempt to modify one's views so as to maximize coherence and minimize change.

It is a mistake to suppose that a principle like *modus ponens* is a principle of inference. The error is compounded if one goes on, as Sellars does, to analyze nonlogical principles, such as laws of nature, as 'material' or 'physical' principles of inference. Talk about deductive principles of inference can be treated as misleading talk about entailment relations. But what sense can be made of talk about material or physical principles of inference?

For Sellars, a principle of inference can be either 'a logical principle in the narrower sense or a physical principle of inference' ([3]: 62). To accept a principle of inference includes, according to Sellars, being disposed to 'draw specific inferences' of a specified form ([3]: 48); and, according to Sellars, that involves having 'an associative disposition to think that-q on having the thought that-p' ([3]: 53). We have seen that this theory misrepresents deductive principles like *modus ponens*. One accepts *modus ponens* without being disposed to infer 'q' whenever one thinks 'p' and 'if p, then q'. Similarly, one can accept as a law of nature *all As are Bs* without being disposed to infer that something is a B whenever one happens to think it is an A. For one will sometimes decide that one was wrong in thinking that it was an A.

This should be a crucial objection to Sellars' theory. He says, 'I have long defended the view that the law-like statements which it is the object of nomological induction to establish are principles of inference and that the problem of induction cannot be solved without this insight' ([3]: 42). I have argued that the supposed insight is false. However, I am unable to discover how Sellars' solution to the problem of induction rests on that mistaken insight. Looking through his argument I find nothing that depends essentially on the claim that laws of nature are rules of inference rather than the statements in the object language they appear to be. For, if I understand his vindication of nomological induction, it rests entirely on the claim that one of our ends is to find simple laws that explain the evidence; and I see nothing in the argument that requires such laws to be principles of inference.

2. Sellars admits as much in [4]: 183 fn. But he fails to see how devastating this is for his account of induction and practical reasoning.

Be that as it may, more needs to be said about Sellars' views about deduction. On the one hand, as we have just seen, he supposes that so called deductive 'rules of inference' are literally rules of inference. On the other hand, as noted in the previous section, he denies that it is always reasonable to accept a conjunction simply because one accepts the conjuncts. For Sellars, 'conjunction introduction' is not generally acceptable as a principle of inference ([3]: 74). Conjunction introduction is the principle that 'p' and 'q' together entail '$p\&q$'. It would ordinarily be considered (misleadingly) a deductive 'principle of inference'. How are we to square Sellars' idea that deductive principles of inference are literally principles of inference with his claim that conjunction introduction is not a generally acceptable principle of inference?

A possible clue emerges in the following passage in which Sellars is explaining the connection between deductive argument and what it is reasonable to believe. He says,

> Notice that correlated with every good deductively valid argument, for example
>
> (If p, then q)$\&p$.
> So (necessarily) q.
>
> is a certain kind of second order argument, thus (roughly)
>
> '([If] p, then q)$\&p$' implies 'q'.
> '(If p, then q) & p' is true.
> So it is (epistemically) reasonable to accept 'q'. ([5]: 33.)

There are many interesting aspects to Sellars' discussion of this second argument ([5]: 34-38); but I cannot go into them here. I do want to comment on the fact that the deductive argument which Sellars first mentions in this passage has a single premise. This is interesting because it is the only complete (nonenthymematic) argument which he mentions in either of these papers ([5] or [3]) with a single premise. The argument is similar to one that makes use of a single application of *modus ponens*:

> If p, then q.
> p.
> So (necessarily) q.

However, that argument has two premises, whereas the argument which Sellars mentions has only one: the conjunction of those two premises.

Sellars' reason for rejecting conjunction introduction is that it can lead from probable premises to an improbable conclusion. A similar consideration can be urged against *modus ponens*, since both 'If *p*, then *q*' and '*p*' can be probable when '*q*' is not. In the passage from Sellars cited above, he seems to accept a version of *modus ponens* and, indeed, even says that correlated with *every* good, deductively valid argument is an argument showing that it is epistemically reasonable to accept the conclusion of the first argument. 'Every argument' should include simple instances of *modus ponens* and conjunction introduction.

This indicates that Sellars accepts deductive 'principles of inference' as principles to be used only when one accepts the conjunction of the relevant premises. For example, on this interpretation of Sellars' view, *modus ponens* authorizes the acceptance of '*q*' only if one already accepts the conjunction '(If *p*, then *q*) & *p*'. Of course, when Sellars rejects conjunction introduction, he is not to be interpreted as rejecting the principle that if one accepts '*p*&*q*' one may accept '*p*&*q*'. He is to be understood to be rejecting the principle that one may accept '*p*&*q*' if one accepts both '*p*' and '*q*'. Similarly he must be taken to reject the principle that one may accept '*q*' if one accepts '*p*' and 'if *p*, then *q*'. To the extent that on this interpretation he rejects conjunction introduction, he also rejects *modus ponens*. To the extent that he accepts *modus ponens*, he accepts conjunction introduction.

This way of taking deductive 'principles of inference' as principles of inference does not avoid the problems mentioned above. It is not always true that one may infer '*q*' if one believes '(If *p*, then *q*) & *p*', since sometimes one should instead stop believing '(If *p*, then *q*) & *p*'. And one should not respond to the discovery that a belief is logically inconsistent by inferring everything.[3]

III

It is a mistake to suppose that wherever there is inference or reasoning there is an associated logic. For example, it is a mistake to suppose that because there is such a thing as inductive inference or reasoning, there is such a thing as inductive logic. Similarly it is a mistake to suppose that because there is such a thing as practical inference or reasoning, there is such a thing as practical logic, a logic of imperatives, a logic of commands, or a logic of intention.

3. Many of the points in this and the previous section are elaborated and defended at greater length in [1].

The mistake in question derives from a mistake about deduction. One assumes that deduction has something to do with a particular type of inference or reasoning that people engage in. One assumes that in the first instance the principles of (deductive) logic are principles implicitly followed or accepted in the practice of deductive inference or reasoning. Then one notes that there are kinds of inference or reasoning that cannot be treated as deductive. For example, there is inductive inference or reasoning and there is practical inference or reasoning. Since one thinks that the principles of deductive logic are in the first instance abstracted from the supposed practice of deductive inference or reasoning, one feels that it should be possible to develop an inductive logic by abstracting the principles of the practice of inductive inference or reasoning and, similarly, that it should be possible to develop a practical logic by abstracting the principles of the practice of practical inference or reasoning.

This line of thought simply misconstrues what logic is all about. Since there is no such thing as our practice of engaging in deductive inference or reasoning, the principles of deductive logic cannot be abstracted from any such practice. The point of these principles is quite different. They are concerned, not with inference and reasoning, but with logical truth and entailment.

Inference and reasoning involve modifying beliefs and expectations as well as plans and goals. When beliefs and expectations are modified, one's reasoning counts as inductive. When plans and goals change, one's reasoning counts as practical. Usually both aspects are involved. In either case, the principle of inference is the same: maximize coherence and minimize change. In neither case does one follow deductive 'principles of inference'. Discovery of contradiction in one's belief or in one's plans is not to be met by the decision to believe or to do everything. In either case one tries to make the least change that will restore and maximize coherence.

It is true that one can speak of deductive *argument*, in a technical sense of 'argument'. In this sense, an argument consists in a set of 'premises' together with a 'conclusion'. The argument is 'valid' if the premises logically entail the conclusion, *e.g.*, if a conditional, whose antecedent is the conjunction of the premises and whose consequent is the conclusion, is a logical truth.[4] But what could it mean to speak of an inductive or practical argument? If the premises entail the conclusion,

4. The best discussion of logical truth with which I am familiar appears in [2].

the argument is deductive. If the premises do not entail the conclusion, in what sense is there any argument?

The idea that there can be such a thing as an inductive or practical argument is the result of confusing an argument in the technical sense of 'argument' with an inference in the ordinary sense of 'inference'. There are inductive and practical inferences. It does not follow that there are inductive or practical arguments. Indeed, it does not even *make sense* to suppose that there are inductive or practical arguments until further meaning is given to the notion of *argument*.

We have seen that Sellars agrees that, strictly speaking, there is no such thing as an inductive argument ([5]: 32; [3]: 11, 17). But he does hold that there are practical arguments. In particular, to claim that it is reasonable to accept that-*p* is, he says, to claim that there is a good practical argument which has as its conclusion *I shall accept that-p* ([5]: 45; [3]: 15, 18), a conclusion which, on its intended interpretation, is neither true nor false, having something like the meaning of *let me accept that-p* ([5]: 48). Since it is neither true nor false, the usual account of validity is inappropriate.

I believe that Sellars' account of validity for practical arguments can be summarized as follows. An argument is practically valid if and only if (1) the conclusion is a statement of intention that is neither true nor false; (2) at least one premise is a statement of intention that is neither true nor false; and (3) if the statements of intention mentioned in (1) and (2) are rephrased as the corresponding true or false remarks about the future, the resulting argument is deductively valid ([3]: 24-25).

For Sellars, a practical argument is a *good argument* if it is valid, its factual premises are true, and its practical premises (statements of intention) have a character of 'practical objectivity' or 'practical truth' ([5]: 48-49). Now, if the practical objectivity or practical truth of an intention to do something is the same as its being reasonable to do that thing, then to claim that it is reasonable to accept that-*p* is indeed to claim that there is a good practical argument which has as its conclusion *I shall accept that-p*, namely the argument

> I shall accept that-*p*.
> So (necessarily) I shall accept that-*p*.

However, this trivializes Sellars' reason for introducing the notion of a practical argument in the first place.

What is more, Sellars' theory can now be used to show that it is reasonable for one to accept anything which he will in fact accept. For consider the following argument, where R is any practical premise that has practical objectivity or truth:

> R.
> I will accept that-p.
> So (necessarily) I shall accept that-p.

This is a good practical argument (as Sellars defines this notion) for accepting that-p. Therefore, it is reasonable to accept that-p, since, according to Sellars, that is simply to say that there is a good argument for accepting that-p.

It is clear what has gone wrong. Sellars has identified the technical notion of argument with the ordinary notion of inference or reasoning. It may be that it is reasonable to accept something if and only if there is a good line of reasoning, in the ordinary sense, that would lead one to accept it. That does not mean that it is reasonable to accept something if and only if there is a good argument, in some technical sense, for accepting it.

To sum up. Although I have accepted Sellars' claim that induction is to be understood in terms of our ends, I have argued, against Sellars, that this gives us no reason to distinguish nomological induction from theoretical inference; and I have also argued against his claim that one of our goals is to answer a set of questions in such a way that we know that most of our answers are right and also know what proportion are right. Furthermore, although I have agreed with Sellars that it is an error to speak in the same breath of deductive and inductive inference or argument, I have disagreed with his account of deduction, and I have argued against his introduction of a notion of practical argument.

REFERENCES

[1] Gilbert H. Harman, "Induction, A Discussion of the Relevance of the Theory of Knowledge to the Theory of Induction (with a Digression to the Effect that neither Deductive Logic nor the Probability Calculus has Anything to Do with Inference)," in Marshall Swain, ed., *Induction, Acceptance, and Rational Belief* (Dordrecht, Holland: D. Reidel, 1970): 83-89.

[2] W.V.O. Quine, *Philosophy of Logic* (Englewood Cliffs, N.J.: Prentice-Hall, 1970).

[3] Wilfrid Sellars, "Induction as Vindication," *Philosophy of Science* 31 (1964).

[4] Gilbert H. Harman, *Thought* (Princeton University Press: 1973).

[5] _____, "Are There Non-Deductive Logics?," in Nicholas Rescher *et al.*, eds., *Essays in Honor of Carl G. Hempel* (Dordrecht, Holland: D. Reidel, 1969).

PART TWO
SELLARSIANA

Autobiographical Reflections

WILFRID SELLARS

ONE day in the late 1940s, Robert Turnbull and I drove to the Minneapolis airport to meet Rudolf Carnap, who was coming to speak to the graduate philosophy club and to visit his good friend Herbert Feigl. At the time, I was discussing his *Logische Aufbau* in my seminar in Philosophical Analysis, and we had scarcely settled in the car for the return journey when I began to bombard my captive audience with questions. I have long since forgotten the detail of what I was after, but I vividly remember that his first reaction was to expostulate, "But that book was written by my grandfather!" The aptness of this remark strikes me anew as I attempt to reconstruct, in outline, the philosopher-stages which preceded me-here-now. I am struck by major continuities which, like shared traits of character, run throughout the series. Other themes, like fibers in a rope, provide a counterpoint of family resemblance. Autobiography, like history, is the attempt to rethink the thoughts of others.

I was born in Ann Arbor, Michigan, on May 20, 1912. My father had for several years been instructor in philosophy at the University of Michigan. My mother, a strikingly beautiful young woman, was, like my father, a Canadian by birth and, indeed, a first cousin. In another world she would have been an artist in words and on canvas. In the actual world, she began her adult life with two small children of whom I was the elder, and her sensitivity and creativity, aside from two major works of translation and countless notebooks, remained a private dimension, yet one which, together with her good sense and strength of character, pervaded our lives.

I remember little from my early years that seems relevant. I know by hearsay that my father taught me to read at the age of three, and I can remember snatches of the experience. Reading was soon an essential part of my life and has remained so ever since. I also remember that I kept largely to myself and did not make friends easily.

Psychologists tell us that a change of environment frees us from stimuli conditioned to anxiety. It cannot, of course, remove us from ourselves but, at least in our more malleable years, can make possible quantum jumps in personal development. I have been exceptionally fortunate in this respect. At an early age, I was not only removed from old environments but placed in exciting new ones. When I was nine years old, I spent some two years away from Ann Arbor, first at school in Providence and Boston. There followed a year in Paris, where my mother, sister, and I lived on the Rue de Tournon, and I was thrown like a beginning swimmer with a rope around his waist into the strange new world of the *Lycée Montaigne*. The experience of living in Paris and struggling with classes in which I had to learn both the language and the subject matter (with my mother's constant help and encouragement) was, in contemporary idiom, mind stretching. Its effect was to snowball in subsequent years in accordance with the true, if disturbing, principle that to him who hath shall be given.

As a ten-year-old in Paris, I was overwhelmed by history. I became an ardent Jacobite, with an assist from Alexandre Dumas, Jr. We had already spent some months in England, mostly in Oxford, where the International Congress of Philosophy was to take place. My most vivid memory from this first stay in Oxford is climbing the ladder to the top of Magdalen Tower, with my mother grimly following.

On my return to Ann Arbor, I not surprisingly lived mostly in my imagination. My school work was at best undistinguished, and I remember the dismay, touched with anger, with which on one occasion my father learned my grade in spelling.

Once again, some two years later, I was saved, or so it seemed, by a change of scene. This time it was the simple move from the public schools to the high school (including junior high) run by the University's School of Education. It does not take much hindsight to realize that my status as a faculty child—which had previously been somewhat of a burden—had something to do with my sense of new horizons. Suddenly

I had rapport with my teachers, and once again learning was both possible and exciting. I even acquired the smugness of one who knows that he can get by with a minimum of effort.

I graduated from high school in 1929, upon which I went to the University summer school, taking a course in algebra. I had come to enjoy mathematics, and, while I had in no way begun to think of a career, I probably would have replied "mathematics" if asked what would by my "major." But the question had never really come up. I had no sense whatever of pressure from my parents, and before the fall semester had to be faced, it was decided, almost at the last minute, that I would go to Paris again with my mother and sister, and study at the *Lycée Louis le Grand*. My father would join us when he went on sabbatical leave the following semester. We arrived in Paris at the end of August, and I was not to return from Europe till January 1931.

At the *Lycée,* I was enrolled in the *Classe de Mathématiques* and began a program with a strong scientific orientation. Nevertheless, it was here that I had my first encounter with philosophy. I say "my first encounter" in all seriousness, for I scarcely knew that there was a subject *called* philosophy, let alone that there was such a subject. It had never come up as such in any conversation with my father, at least that I can remember; although I can, on careful reflection, see that some specific topics in philosophy must have caught my ear, particularly while accompanying my father (as caddie) when he played golf, as he frequently did, with DeWitt Parker. I clearly remember one occasion on which I heatedly (and to his scarcely concealed amusement) defended against Parker the thesis of the maturation of chances.

So I was in Paris when the stock market crashed. By this time, I had made the acquaintance of a Jewish boy, also a student at the *Lycée,* who had been educated in England. We gravitated together and were soon boon companions. He had friends who were Marxist in ideology but, to the extent that they were politically involved, strongly anti-Stalinist. Boris Souvarine was the immediate source of ideological influence; though on the horizon was Trotsky, who had just been sent into exile. I, of course, was a complete novice in these matters. But I was soon reading Marxist classics, and adding *l'Humanité* and *Le Populaire* to my daily surfeit of newspapers. My first serious reading of philosophy, then, such as it was, was in Marx, Engels, Lenin, and, in general, the philosophical and quasi-philosophical polemical literature which is the life blood of French intellectuals.

Nevertheless, my first academic contact with philosophy was, as indicated above, in a course at the *Lycée*. Even as surveys go, it was thin stuff. But it did give me a sense of how philosophical issues were classified and an acquaintance with some of the major philosophers (in French perspective). It suddenly hit me that my father was a philosopher and that I knew nothing about this dimension of his existence. What my mother was able to tell me whetted my curiosity, and, by the time he joined us in February, I was eager to explore this unexpected goldmine.

My father and I had always gotten along well together, but we had found little to talk about besides topics that arose *per accidens* from the events of the day. Indeed, he had been a distant figure who almost daily disappeared either into the University or into his study in the attic, where he turned out book after book. (The muffled sound of his typewriter in almost continuous operation—or so it seemed—was later to haunt me, when I began my own attempts at publication). Thus, there is a sense in which father and son first met that spring in Paris through the good offices of philosophy. Needless to say, I found his views congenial from the start and quickly sloughed off the pseudo-Hegelian jargon of Marxist *Naturphilosophie*. More resistant (as they should have been) were the Hegelian overtones of Marxism as a schema of historical explanation. In any event, a dialogue was initiated which has continued for some forty-two years.

That summer, my father returned to this country to earn the money to support the grand tour, the next highlight of which was six months in Germany, where I learned the language and audited courses at the University of Munich. The economic depression had continued to spread and intensify, and it was clear that in Germany, at least, if things continued to deteriorate, a social and political crisis would be at hand. I soon became convinced that Hitler would in one way or another gain power, unless the opposition could be meaningfully united, which, unfortunately, seemed increasingly unlikely. And the idea that Hitler in power could be overthrown by revolution from within struck me as utopian in the extreme.

I returned to this country in January of 1931 and saw the depression I had been reading about from afar. It is difficult to picture the horror of the period. Ann Arbor was, of course, a sheltered oasis, but the real world and, in particular, the demoralized city of Detroit, was always on the horizon of consciousness. I resumed my studies at the University and divided my time between mathematics, economics, and philosophy.

I had not attempted the French baccalaureate examination but was able to earn enough credits by examination to keep me abreast of my classmates. I was active during this period in the socialist movement on the campus and in the 1932 election campaigned on a soapbox at factory gates for Norman Thomas.

This essay, though biographical, is not intended to be a biography, and I have gone into the above variety of detail to give some indication of the context in which I began to think of philosophy as a career. Which reminds me that somewhere along the line I should have mentioned a factor which it is easy for me to forget. I had never experienced those theological anxieties which have pushed so many in the direction of philosophy and which tend to distort it into a secular substitute for religion. Indeed, as a second generation atheist, I was completely at ease about the subject and over the years I have taken great intellectual pleasure in exploring abstruse issues in theology in the classroom and in private discussion.

My first serious work in philosophy was in C. H. Langford's course on Locke, Berkeley, and Hume. Actually, it was at least as much on G. E. Moore and Cambridge Analysis as it was on the Empiricists. I was soon taking advanced courses and seminars across the whole spectrum of the subject, with the exception of ethics. In DeWitt Parker's excellent seminar in metaphysics, I was introduced to McTaggart's classic paper on the unreality of Time and chose to write my term paper on the topic. I was soon deep in the literature and found myself genuinely involved. Philosophy was no longer a storehouse of alternatives to be explored and evaluated but, from that moment on, an unfinished dialogue in which I might have something to say. I soon became convinced that the problem of time was so intimately connected with other classical problems that it, like the mind-body problem, is one of the major proving grounds for philosophical systems.

One of my vivid memories of the period is a running controversy with A. P. Uschenko in which I defended a substantialist ontology of change against the argument that when S changes from being ϕ to being ψ, S must *really* consist of an event which is ϕ and an event which is ψ to be the terms for the relation *earlier than*. My reply was a clumsy anticipation of the subsequent treatment of the topic in "Time and the World Order"[1] and, most recently, "Metaphysics and the Concept of a

---

1. In *Minnesota Studies in the Philosophy of Science*, Vol. III, edited by Herbert Feigl and Grover Maxwell (Minneapolis: University of Minnesota Press, 1963): 527-616.

Person''[2] in the latter of which Gustav Bergmann inherits the role of Uschenko. I was to remain convinced (to put it in more contemporary terms) that the basic objects of the common-sense framework are continuants rather than 'gen-identical' strings of events. I tended to think, in Aristotelian terms, of events in Time (or Space-Time) as metrical abstractions grounded in the reality of changing substances. Things couldn't *consist* of events, because events were the changes of things.

I was already in the grips of an empiricist 'abstractionism' and believed categories to be the deliverances of 'abstraction' from the 'given'. Thus, the self was given to us as substance, though it did not follow, I argued *contra* Parker, that it was conceptually necessary that all substances be 'selves'. Since I also held, in good Sellarsian fashion, that the mind as that which thinks is identical with the brain, I should have been more worried than I was about the givenness of the self. I am afraid I would have said that the givenness is somehow incomplete and generic and let it go at that. In retrospect, I seem to have thought that the self could be a substance which was a whole of material substances and yet be given as a substance without being *given as* a whole of material substances. When, in subsequent years, I attempted to think through the consequences of abstractionism as a theory of categorial concepts, the chief result was to make me receptive to Kant.

During this period, my philosophical thinking was primarily focused on Cambridge Analysis. Yet, while I was duly impressed with its high standards of rigor and clarity, particularly as exemplified by Moore, I rejected, on the whole, its results. I was also impressed, as were my younger contemporaries, with the power of the new logic. Yet I was (and remain) convinced that most transcriptions of philosophically interesting concepts into its logical forms were wildly implausible. Nevertheless, I regarded the strategy as a sound one and believed that the crucial question concerned the manner in which the technical apparatus of *Principia* would have to be fleshed out in order to do justice to the conceptual forms of human knowledge.

During this period I was being exposed to the philosophical aspects of Lewis' and Langford's *Symbolic Logic,* and it is therefore not surprising that I regarded the introduction of logical modalities as a paradigm case of this enrichment. It seemed obvious, even at the time, that this strategy should be extended to the causal modalities. The result was an

---

2. In *The Logical Way of Doing Things,* edited by Karel Lambert (New Haven: Yale University Press, 1969): 219-52.

immediate sympathy with the causal realism of C.D. Broad and, later, W.C. Kneale. Yet I was puzzled by what it could mean to say that necessity (logical or causal) was in the world, which, it seemed, must surely be the case, if modal concepts are genuine concepts and any modal propositions true. Was negation in the world? I was tempted by the approach to negation which grounds it in a 'real relation of incompatibility', and it was years before I sorted out the confusions (and insights) involved. Was generality in the world? I saw this as one aspect of the problem of universals, which was never far from my mind. It can be seen that my early reading of the *Tractatus* had had but little effect. I regarded it as almost a *reductio* of Cambridge Analysis.

After graduating in 1933, I went to Buffalo as a teaching assistant. From the beginning, I was at home in the classroom. I had already discovered, as a debater in high school, that I could present ideas persuasively to large audiences and, which is more important, think on my feet. I early developed the technique of combining lecturing with extended 'Socratic' exchanges with 'volunteers' who happened to ask the right question and could be guided (or goaded) into representing the *volonté générale* of the class. Marvin Farber led me through my first careful reading of the *Critique of Pure Reason* and introduced me to Husserl. His combination of utter respect for the structure of Husserl's thought with the equally firm conviction that this structure could be given a naturalistic interpretation was undoubtedly a key influence on my own subsequent philosophical strategy.

Although I enjoyed teaching and could contemplate this aspect of an academic career with enthusiasm, writing was quite another story. Like most American students, I had almost no experience in writing term papers until the last two years of college. Examinations I took in my stride; the constraints assimilated writing them to the debater's task of thinking on one's feet. With papers, there was always (until the last minute!) the opportunity for second and third thoughts about every step, and, as so often happens, the will-o'-the-wisp of the best made every choice look bad. It wasn't until years later that I learned that no matter how clumsy, gappy, and incoherent a first draft is, it contains the essence of what one has to say; and the comfort of finding raw material on paper to be licked into shape makes writing the next draft an entirely different experience. I have known philosophers whose first draft is the final product, and an excellent one at that. But I contemplate them with the same awe as I do Mozart, who could hear completed symphonies in his head.

I struggled, nevertheless, through an M.A. thesis on Time and, having been awarded a Rhodes Scholarship that Christmas, prepared to continue my studies at Oxford. In those days, graduate studies played a very minor role in the life of the University. I was advised to read for an undergraduate degree and have never regretted the choice. In the fall of 1934, then, I entered Oriel College and began a course of studies which would lead to a B.A. degree in philosophy, politics, and economics, with a concentration in philosophy.

Once again, I had the opportunity for a new beginning. I did an enormous amount of reading on topics with which I was already generally familiar, but in a far more critical spirit. I learned to argue with books as I learned, in tutorials, to be pushed to the limit in discussion. My tutor in philosophy at Oriel was W. G. Maclagan, now at Glasgow, who did an admirable job of questioning my dogmatisms and gently forcing me to clarify my ideas and arguments. I had already come to think of myself as having a system, and in a sense I did. But I became increasingly aware of how programmatic it was and of how little it contained that was clear and distinct.

My experience with Moore, however, had convinced me that clarity and distinctness can be achieved at the expense, to borrow a Spinozistic term, of adequacy, and that one should give one's muddiest intuitions the fullest benefit of the doubt. I had long felt that, although C. D. Broad might not be clearer than Moore, nevertheless he had a more adequate grasp of the problems they shared. I now think that this can be traced to Broad's awareness of, and technical competence in, the scientific background of these problems.

I soon came under the influence of H.A. Prichard and, through him, of Cook Wilson. I found here, or at least seemed to find, a clearly articulated approach to philosophical issues which undercut the dialectic, rooted in Descartes, which led to both Hume and 19th Century Idealism. At the same time, I discovered Thomas Reid and found him appealing for much the same reasons.

Of a piece with this development was my growing sympathy for deontological intuitionism in ethics, particularly in the less metaphysically structured form which I found in the writings and lectures of H. A. Prichard. It struck me as far more adequate to the complexities of moral thinking than Moore's ever so clear and distinct Ideal Utilitarianism. I was conscious, however, of being an intuitionist in a Pickwickian sense. As I put it to myself at the time, Prichard's insights would somehow have to be cashed out in naturalistic terms.

When emotivism appeared on the scene, it struck me as wrong-headed in its early insistence on the pseudo-conceptual character of ethical terms, propositions, and reasonings. And yet I also felt, from the start, that it had located one of the missing ingredients of the solution. Somehow intuitionism and emotivism would have to be *aufgehoben* into a naturalistic framework which recognized ethical concepts as genuine concepts and found a place for intersubjectivity and truth.

But before I could put these perceptions together, I would have to work out a whole new way of looking at the conceptual order. The situation was roughly the following. I had already broken with traditional empiricism by my realistic approach to the logical, causal, and deontological modalities. What was needed was a functional theory of concepts which would make their role in reasoning, rather than a supposed origin in experience, their primary feature. The influence of Kant was to play a decisive role.

I read the *Critique* with H. H. Price of New College as my tutor and began to develop in embryo the interpretation which was to become the core of *Science and Metaphysics*. It grew largely out of my increasing awareness of the importance of concepts pertaining to the intentionality of mental acts for the understanding not only of the Cartesian tradition but of British empiricism, even Hume.

I also saw, on the other hand, that by denying that sense impressions, however indispensable to cognition, were themselves cognitive, Kant made a radical break with all his predecessors, empiricists and rationalists alike. The 'of-ness' of sensation simply isn't the 'of-ness' of even the most rudimentary thought. Sense grasps no facts, not even such simple ones as something's being red and triangular. Abstractionists could think of concepts as abstracted from sense, because they thought of sensation in conceptual categories. This enabled me to appreciate that Kant wasn't attempting to prove that *in addition to* knowing facts about immediate experience, one *also* knew facts about physical objects, but rather that a skeptic who grants knowledge of even the simplest fact about an event occurring in Time is, in effect, granting knowledge of the existence of nature as a whole. I was sure he was right. But his own question haunted me. How is it *possible* that knowledge has this structure? The tension between dogmatic realism, and its appeal to self-evident truth, and transcendental idealism, in which conceptual structures hover over a non-cognitive manifold of sense, became almost intolerable. It wasn't until much later that I came to see that the solution of the puzzle lay in correctly locating the conceptual order in the causal order and correctly interpreting the causality involved.

Although this larger enterprise was never far from my thoughts, I was not even clear about the terms in which it was to be formulated. It is one thing to be convinced that any adequate philosophy of mind must take seriously the intentional structure of mental acts and quite another to make satisfactory sense of traditional formulations. Thus, while finding the act-content distinction useful, I was aware that in some sense the 'content' of different acts in different minds must be capable of being the *same,* i.e., identical. Thus, the act-content approach to the mental, with its conceptualistic overtones, threatened to turn into the act-object (or relational) theory, with a resultant commitment not only to standard platonic entities (attributes, relations, classes) but to the whole Meinongian array of objective propositions, possible worlds, possible individuals, and even possible universals. I was convinced that an adequate naturalistic philosophy of mind would have to make sense of these classical dilemmas, but it wasn't until some ten years later, when I began to *equate* thought with language, that the desired synthesis began to take shape. In the meantime, I was prepared to let the alternatives flourish, controlled only by the role that they were to play in a truly Hegelian dialectic.

In the spring of 1936, I took the examinations, and, after spending several weeks in Paris waiting for the results, during which time my chief occupation was reading *War and Peace* from cover to cover, I returned to Oxford and found that I had been placed in Class I. I was particularly pleased to learn informally that my grades had been high all across the board, from Economic History to Logic. I returned to this country in high spirits but with a growing (and sobering) awareness that an Oxford B.A. (in spite of the fact that it automatically becomes an M.A. with the help of time and a fee) was unlikely to earn me a job, particularly at a time when there were no jobs.

I returned to Oxford in the fall and embarked on the pursuit of a D.Phil., undertaking to write a dissertation on Kant under the direction of T. D. Weldon. I had no real sense of how to go about it but read extensively and made countless notes on filing cards. I knew the *sort* of thing I wanted to say and how it differed from received interpretations but simply could not get anything worthwhile down on paper. Actually, my views were so systematically different that it really *was* difficult to know where to begin; or, to put it bluntly, I would have to be clearer

about my own ideas before I could write intelligibly, let alone convincingly, about Kant. I continued to be baffled by the fact that I was so
effective at writing examinations and talking on my feet and yet so
disorganized at my desk. In spite of the growing anxiety about my
prospects for a professional career, I continued to read and discuss
philosophy with enjoyment and enthusiasm. The highlight of the year (at
least I *think* it was that year) was a seminar in C. I. Lewis' *Mind and
the World Order* led by John Austin and Isaiah Berlin.

Politically, I was still on the left. I had few illusions about the com-
munists but attributed their astonishing tactics in Germany, which
helped smooth the way for Hitler, to the ignorance and self-interest of
Moscow. It would have been difficult at the time for anyone not directly
involved to realize the extent to which Stalin had corrupted political life
in western Europe. The French Popular Front was the first encouraging
sign after years of demoralizing confusion and defeat. Although the
scene was darkened by the isolation and subsequent collapse of the
Spanish Republic, one could hope that *somewhere* the lines would be
drawn for a firm stand against fascism. It was already clear, however,
that this stand would have to be military and would involve, in all
probability, a European war.

In the fall of 1937, I went to Harvard to work for my 'trade-union
card'. I remember taking courses with D. W. Prall (Spinoza), C. I.
Lewis (Theory of Knowledge), R. B. Perry (Contemporary Philosophy), C. L. Stevenson (Hume), and W. V. Quine (Logical Positivism).
It was the last of these which I found most challenging. I had already
convinced myself that Ayer's *Language, Truth, and Logic* was a brilliant *tour de force* which led nowhere. In spite of its freshness and vigor,
it represented the end of the era initiated by Moore's "Refutation of
Idealism" and *Principia Ethica*; a *reductio* rather than a new beginning.
In Quine's course, however, the central figure was Carnap, from the
Aufbau to the *Logical Syntax of Language*. I am afraid that I got little
out of the *Aufbau*. I would, I believe, have gained a better appreciation
of the power of its technical devices if I had been able to put to one side
my violent anti-phenomenalism. Carnap was doing what can't be done,
therefore there must be something wrong about how he is doing it. It was
not until Goodman's *Structure of Appearance* that I realized my mistake. As for the *Logical Syntax of Language*, I reacted, as did many of
my contemporaries, with the idea that while a rigorous account of
syntax was clearly a *desideratum*, as far as its *philosophical* content

was concerned, Carnap was putting the cart before the horse. Surely (or so it seemed to me) the syntax of language reflects the structure of the world. And since thought deals directly with the world, *that* is where the action is. Yet a seed was planted. It might have sprouted earlier if the impact of *Syntax* had not been blunted by Carnap's own move into his semantical phase, which *seemed* to support the above reaction.

As for Lewis' increasingly ingenious attempt to salvage phenomenalism, I was most struck by his explicit use and realistic interpretation of nomological modalities. In the long run, two questions could not be avoided: (a) What was the nature of the inductive evidence for the relevant nomologicals? Could it be stated in terms of the actually given? (b) Was the form of the inductive argument *generalization* (statistical or non-statistical) or was it *hypothetico-deductive*? If the former, was it plausible to suppose that the basic laws of the physical could be stated in purely phenomenal terms? If the latter, doesn't this amount to conceding realism? Early in my reflection on phenomenalism, I had distinguished (in the spirit of the last chapter of A. C. Ewing's *Idealism*) between the thesis (a) that physical objects are tidy patterns of actually existing color expanses, *none* of which is identical with visual sense data, and the thesis (b) that physical objects are patterns—in a more abstract sense—of actual and 'possible' (i.e., conditional) sensations. The positivistic thesis that the 'given' is *subjektlos* concealed the same ambiguity. Its basic meaning was that the self which has experiences of (e.g.) color expanses is a construct out of particulars belonging to the same general category. But by itself it leaves open the question of whether color expanses exist outside this bundle. Any which did would, in *another* sense, be *subjektlos*. The thesis that *basic* laws of macrophysics could be stated in "purely phenomenal terms" was correspondingly ambiguous. I regarded the second alternative as incoherent and the first as inconsistent with our knowledge that physical objects consist of scientific objects. These ideas were to sort themselves out in the course of the next decade.

In the spring of 1938, I passed my prelims and began to look for a manageable thesis topic. At Oxford, I had come to regard ethical intuitionism as my personal property and was consequently shaken to discover how thoroughly and lucidly William Frankena (whom I had known since my days at Michigan) had mastered it. A made-to-order topic had been pre-empted. I could always fall back on Kant, but by now I had no illusions about the dimensions of the enterprise. With the spring came rumors of jobs, and, since I was to be married that summer, the idea of getting out into the real (academic) world became increasingly attractive. After all, I *had* proved myself in every dimension of academic life—except writing for publication. Surely that could come! Yet the anxiety generated by this question was to be a dark cloud on the horizon for many years to come.

I first met Herbert Feigl in 1931 at a Western Division meeting in Ann Arbor. At that time, he was (or seemed to be) a paradigm logical positivist. Indeed, it is my understanding that he invented the term. Only later did it become clear that the basic motives of his thought were the exclusive right of sense experience and science to tell us how things are, an anti-Cartesian conviction of mind-body identity, and a deep sympathy with the naturalistic realism so convincingly expounded by his teacher Moritz Schlick before the latter was converted to positivism.

Like many radical empiricists of the time, he was haunted by the challenge: How could the existence of material things 'over and above' the 'given' be anything but a hypothesis? And how could it be a hypothesis without being a 'metaphysical' hypothesis, competing, for example, with the idealism of Berkeley and the monadology of Leibniz? Positivistic phenomenalism seemed to undercut the problem, and the generic theme of Neutral Monism to provide a strategy for defending mind-body identity. Yet the situation was unstable. The development of physicalism—at first as a *methodological* thesis in the philosophy of science and, as such, presumably compatible with methodological solipsism in epistemology, which, however, soon acquired the earmarks of a substantive thesis—and the growing awareness that a "reduction" of statements about scientific objects to statements about laboratory observables could not even in principle be equated with explicit definition were forcing a choice between instrumentalism and scientific realism. Once the issue was clearly posed, Feigl's choice was never in doubt. His reflections on the nature of theoretical explanation soon led him to review his objections to construing physical realism as an hypothesis—a development which culminated in his lucid, but to my mind, unconvincing "Existential Hypotheses."[3]

But this is not an essay on the history of philosophy, and the relevant fact is that Feigl and I shared a common purpose: to formulate a scientifically oriented, naturalistic realism which would "save the appearances." He was familiar with the general outline of my father's

3. In *Philosophy of Science* 17(1950): 35-62.

Critical Realism and Evolutionary Naturalism, and when an opening occurred in the University of Iowa Department where he had been teaching since 1931, he suggested that I be invited for an interview. We hit it off immediately, although the seriousness with which I took such ideas as causal necessity, synthetic *a priori* knowledge, intentionality, ethical intuitionism, the problem of universals, etc., etc., must have jarred his empiricist sensibilities. Even when I made it clear that my aim was to map these structures into a naturalistic, even a materialistic, metaphysics, he felt, as many have, that I was going around Robin Hood's barn.

In late August 1938, my wife and I moved to Iowa City and I began my teaching career. I could scarcely have had a better opportunity. The Department consisted of Herbert Martin (the chairman), Herbert Feigl, and myself. My primary responsibility was the history of philosophy. There was a strong demand for the subject from the School of Letters (headed by Norman Foerster), and as a result it was possible to float a two-year sequence from Thales to Mill for upperclass and graduate students. I also designed a two-semester sequence, 'Philosophy of Man' and 'Philosophy in Literature', for the same clientele, of which the former introduced students to the ideas needed for the latter. Although I did not repeat the course more than once, I learned a great deal from teaching it and found it intensely interesting. I also began a rotating sequence of seminars in Theory of Knowledge, Metaphysics, Moral Philosophy, and selected figures in the history of philosophy.

During this period, I studied the whole range of the history of philosophy with a burning intensity, particularly Greek and medieval thought with which I had previously done very little. I became increasingly convinced of the importance of the subject and also came to see that much of the current literature on the subject was imperceptive and uninformed. The probing of historical ideas with current conceptual tools, a task which should be undertaken each generation, was long overdue. It will be remembered that during this period the history of philosophy was not only neglected, there was an active campaign to delete it, or at least downgrade it, as a requisite for the Ph.D.

Once again, then, I had an exhilarating new beginning. There was so much to do, and so much sense of achievement in doing it, that the tasks of finishing my dissertation, which I scarcely touched, and of publishing, moved into the background. Herbert Feigl moved to Minnesota in 1941, and Gustav Bergmann, who had come to the University as a

Research Associate with Kurt Lewin, joined the Department to teach advanced logic and philosophy of science. During his first semester he gave an excellent seminar in logical theory, based on Carnap's *Logical Syntax of Language*. It was attended by the entire Department, which, by now, included Everett Hall, who had joined us as chairman on the retirement of Herbert Martin. Bergmann became a close collaborator with Kenneth Spence, and I began to take behaviorism seriously. The idea that something like S-R-reinforcement learning theory could provide a bridge between white rat behavior and characteristically human behavior was a tempting one, but I could see no way of cashing it out in the philosophy of mind. In particular, I could not see how to relate it to the intentionality which I continued to think of as the essential trait of the mental. Bergmann at this time took a fairly orthodox positivistic position with strong overtones of Carnap and Schlick. He and I argued the whole range of "pseudo-problems." The occasion of most of these discussions was an informal seminar in current philosophical literature which met at Hall's house every week and which everybody religiously attended. The Department was still minute and highly involuted. Ideas of amazing diversity were defended and attacked with passion and intensity. It was not easy to find common ground, yet "for the sake of discussion" we stretched our imaginations. It was, I believe, a unique episode—certainly as far as my own experience is concerned. We soon had some first-rate graduate students. Among the earliest (and best) was Thomas Storer, whose death at an early age was a genuine loss to philosophy.

By the winter of 1942, my involvement in historical studies could no longer mask a growing anxiety about publication. I had made several starts, but still had not solved the problem. The war was also very much on my mind, and my draft classification gradually evolved to 1-A. Eventually, I applied for a commission in the Navy and in the spring of 1943 was commissioned Ensign in the U.S. Naval Reserves, assigned to Air Intelligence. That summer, I went to the training center at Quonset Point, Rhode Island, and, after two months of condensed courses, was posted to the Anti-Submarine Development Detachment of the Atlantic Fleet, also at Quonset Point, where I remained until the spring of 1945.

The change of environment was, once again, anxiety reducing. I plunged into my work with enthusiasm. It involved a combination of giving lectures to squadrons in training on the theory and practice of anti-submarine warfare by aircraft, running for several months a rocket range on Nantucket Island, and, later, working as liaison officer on research projects with civilian scientists. A number of other academic people were affiliated with the organization, and life was pleasant, if strenuous. My work involved a substantial amount of time in the air, sometimes under rather hazardous conditions, but I thrived on it.

I spent the final months of the war in the statistical branch of Naval Air Intelligence in Washington. The work was routine, and I began to look to the future. The sudden end of the war brought me up with a start. I had done little reading or thinking about philosophical topics for some two and a half years, and suddenly it was time to return. My wife and I realized that we simply could not pick up where we left off. She had begun to write short stories with increasing success. A conversion experience on my part was essential. We resolved on a program according to which, on our return to Iowa City, we would work up to ten hours a day, day after day, on writing, however few words we got down on paper. We put this resolve into action and stuck with it. It was a team effort, and it worked.

I began to write a paper, catch as catch can, pushing ahead, letting the argument go where it would—almost in the spirit of writing an examination. I then made marginal comments and criticisms, after which I rewrote it in the same spirit. As I remember it, the paper started out to be about names, the given, and existential quantification. Three months and ten drafts later it began to be "Realism and the New Way of Words." Rewriting large chunks of it at a time became a way of life. Some seventeen major revisions occurred before it finally appeared in print.

At last I had found a successful strategy for writing. And if, in the beginning at least, the result was a highly involuted style, I had learned that revising is a pleasure and that even the clumsiest initial draft takes on a life of its own. It took longer to put into practice the truism that a revision must simplify as well as correct and add. I soon discovered that spinning out, as I was, ideas in a vacuum, everything I wrote was idiosyncratic and had little direct connection with what others had said. Each spinning required a new web to support it, and the search for fixed points of reference became a struggle for coherence and completeness. As a result, each sentence of "Realism" is a "flower in a crannied wall." I soon came to see that a dialectical use of historical positions is the most reliable way of anchoring arguments and making them intersubjectively available. In the limiting case, this use of history is illustrated by correspondence and controversial exchanges with contemporaries. Even on paper, philosophy becomes explicitly what it has always really been, a continuing dialogue.

Until "Realism and the New Way of Words," my philosophical development took place *in foro interno,* in the classroom and in private discussion. Since that turning point, it has found a more public expression and is available for critical scrutiny.Nevertheless, as each publication moves further and further into the past (O, A-series!), there comes that time when I am moved to say, as did Carnap, "But my grandfather wrote that!"

The Structure of Knowledge*

WILFRID SELLARS
LECTURE I: PERCEPTION

I

1. There is, of course, a broad but technical sense in which even persons are 'things', though not *mere* things. There is, also, a metaphorical sense in which one can be said to treat a person as a mere thing. But this amounts to treating him, in Kant's phrase, as a means only, i.e. acting in ways which either disregard, or fail to *value* for their own sake, the traits by virtue of which we distinguish between a merely physical object and a conscious subject of purposes and intentions. In this lecture I shall be primarily concerned with our perceptual knowledge of merely material things, turning my attention in the following lecture to our knowlege of those 'things' which, however physical they may be, have, in addition, the features by virtue of which they are persons.

2. Before I zero in on my present topic, however, some remarks are in order on the broad, if technical, sense in which both merely material things and persons are 'things'. Epistemology cannot be severed from ontology as with a knife, and it is necessary to give some account of the basic categories which I shall be using, in order to provide a framework for the interpretation of what, after all, is but a fragment of a larger story.

3. The ideal aim of philosophizing is to become *reflectively* at home in the full complexity of the multi-dimensional conceptual system in terms of which we suffer, think, and act. I say 'reflectively', because there is a sense in which, by the sheer fact of leading an unexamined, but conventionally satisfying life, we are at home in this complexity. It is not until we have eaten the apple with which the serpent philosopher tempts us, that we begin to stumble on the familiar and to feel that haunting sense of alienation which is treasured by each new generation as its unique

*The Matchette Foundation Lectures for 1971 at the University of Texas.

possession. This alienation, this gap between oneself and one's world, can only be resolved by eating the apple to the core; for after the first bite there is no return to innocence. There are many anodynes, but only one cure. We may philosophize well or ill, but we must philosophize.

4. The method is easy to characterize, but difficult in the extreme to follow. One begins by constructing simple models—which are understood because we have constructed them—of fragments of this multi-dimensional framework. These initial models are inevitably over-simple and largely false. But the alternative to this path, with all its oversimplification and error, is to sketch the shifting surfaces of the functioning framework, and hope that insight comes by pasting the sketches together. This receptivity, however sensitive, and however important it may be as an *element* in philosophical method, must, by itself, fail to yield understanding. In much the same spirit, Plato warns that the poets, by concentrating on appearances, are precluded from understanding the actions and characters of men which they so contagiously depict. The real danger of oversimplified models is not that they are over-simple, but that we may be satisfied with them, and fail to compare them with regions of experience other than those which suggested them. And, indeed, the ultimate justification for system building in philosophy is the fact that no model for any region of discourse —perceptual, discursive, practical—can be ultimately satisfying unless its connection with each of the others is itself modeled. To press the metaphor to its limits, the completion of the philosophical enterprise would be a single model —the working of which, again, we would understand because we had constructed it—which would reproduce the full complexity of the framework in which we were once unreflectively at home.

II

5. The region within the encompassing framework on which I shall concentrate this evening is that of merely physical things and our knowledge of them. This knowledge is, in the first instance, perceptual or, it is better to say, *at the perceptual level*. For there is a widespread misconception, no longer as prevalent as it used to be, according to which perception—in what is often called the 'strict' or 'basic' sense of this

term—gives a knowledge of singular truths which presupposes no knowledge of general truths. According to this misconception, all knowledge of general truths at the perceptual level is inductively grounded in the deliverances of perception.

6. Now I have no objection in principle to drawing a distinction between that which we perceive *strictu sensu,* and that which we perceive 'in a looser sense of the term'. For according to the methodology which I sketched above, one is entitled to 'regiment' discourse by constructing simple models. But any such distinction must, in Plato's words, carve reality at the joints. And, as I hope to show, no way of validly making this distinction supports the idea that there is a level of perceptual knowledge of singular truths which presupposes no knowledge of general truths about material things and our perception of them.

7. In short, knowledge 'at the perceptual level' essentially involves *both* knowledge of singular matters of fact and knowledge of general truths. Neither is possible without the other.

III

8. But enough by way of anticipation and methodology. The promised sketch of basic categories remains to be drawn. I shall be making use of them throughout this series, and, while they will not loom too large this evening, it will be useful to get them out into the open, so that the larger philosophical context of these remarks can be taken into account from the beginning.

9. What is a 'merely' material thing? It is, in the first instance, an *individual,* as is, of course, a person. But what is an individual? Questions of this ontological kind arouse a strong temptation to say that one is at the level of that which must be 'shown' rather than 'said'. And the temptation is not without insight. However, as is illustrated by Wittgenstein's own work, things can be said which aid the showing, and perhaps the most useful thing to say is that the linguistic correlates of individuals are singular terms.

10. Is everything an individual? The above remarks would suggest a

negative answer, since not every linguistic expression is a singular term. It would therefore be wise to have a broader category in reserve for which we might use the word 'entity'. To do so is to countenance the idea that not all entities are individuals.[1]

11. Now some individuals are, in an important sense, 'reducible'. We feel comfortable about saying that they consist of 'simpler' individuals which are their 'parts'. One is tempted, therefore, to introduce the idea of a *basic* individual as one that has no individuals as its 'parts'.

12. Are there any basic individuals in this sense? Why might not individuals have parts, and these again, and so *ad infinitum,* as do the famous fleas which have other fleas to bite 'em. If one thinks of mathematical lines as individuals, do these not have parts, which are lines which have parts, etc.? But (1) a mathematical line is a set of points, and while sets have sub-sets which in their turn have sub-sets and so *ad infinitum,* it is doubtful whether sets are properly construed as individuals; and, in any case (2) there remain the points which, if they can be construed as individuals, and if they can be construed as 'parts', might be parts which have no parts, and, in this domain, basic individuals.

13. I mention, this, however, only to remind you of the dubious analogies which metaphysicians have often drawn between physical objects and mathematical entities. For my present purposes I shall simply stipulate that physical objects have ultimate parts. This dogma will shortly become more palatable, I hope, when I explain my use of the term 'physical object'.

14. To this I must add that it is of vital importance to distinguish between actual and potential parts. The distinction may be presented thus:

> Consider the surface of this unmarked blackboard, taken at its face value as a continuous black expanse. Construe this surface as it would be construed by one who has no inkling of microphysical theory nor of the puzzles which can lead philosophers to hold that such surfaces are 'subjective entities' which 'exist in the mind'. I draw a circle *thus.* Now I draw a diameter of this circle.

1. If the question is now pressed: are there items which are not entities?, the ontological enterprise is really under way. But that is a story for another occasion.

Where before there was one undivid*ed* but divis*ible* individual,
the circle, there are now two individuals, the semi-circles.

15. Thus an object O which has no *actual* parts may be divisible, and,
when divided, be superceded by, or, in a unique sense, become, two
individuals O_1 and O_2. These new individuals may well be qualitatively
quite different from the original object, and the composite which consists of them may be qualitatively quite different from the original
undivided object. And this not only in the trivial sense in which a
semi-circle is not a circle, but in the more puzzling sense in which a living
thing, construed in Aristotelian style as non-composite, becomes, dis-
membered, a non-living whole of non-living parts.

16. I distinguished above between *basic* individuals and *reducible*
individuals. I think that the concept of a basic individual serves as a
reasonably good explication of the traditional concept of substance. But
the above account of *reducible* individuals is much too restricted. For I
have taken as my paradigm of a reducible individual an individual
consisting of actual parts, presumably spatial. This restriction must be
removed. To begin with, we must allow for temporal parts. I do not
mean to imply that every physical object, for example, whether spatially
composite or not, has temporal parts, for, at least as I am using the term
'physical object', this is false. Rabbits do not consist of rabbit-stages nor
of rabbit-events, though the life history of a rabbit does consist of
rabbit-events, and a revisionary metaphysics can doubtless be contrived
in which doing things consists of temporally juxtaposing slabs of becoming (see [7]). I simply want to allow for such cases as that, for example,
of a regiment which at different times has different soldiers as its parts.

17. In the second place, not every reducible individual is, in any ordinary sense, a whole of parts. Thus *the average man* is a reducible
individual in the sense that statements about the average man can be
paraphrased in a way which replaces reference to the average man by a
general reference to particular men. Again *the elephant* is a reducible
individual in that statements about *the elephant* can be paraphrased in a
way which replaces reference to *the elephant* by a general reference to
particular elephants. It is in this sense, also, that *conjunctive* individuals
are, perhaps, reducible. Thus, although surface grammar obscures the
fact, in:

> Jack and Jill and Tommy are (constitute) a family,

the expression 'Jack and Jill and Tommy' functions as a singular term for the conjunctive individual *Jack and Jill and Tommy*, which the statement characterizes as a family. This example should be carefully distinguished from:

> Jack and Jill and Tommy are human,

which is short for a conjunction of three sentences sharing the same predicate. A statement about conjunctive individuals may be paraphrasable into a conjunction of statements, but not of this simple form.

18. I said above that conjunctive individuals *may* be reducible, for it turns out that, unlikely though it may seem, they pose one of the central problems in the metaphysics of persons and sentient beings generally. For to say that conjunctive individuals are reducible is to say that statements about them can be paraphrased in ways which refer only to their 'constituents' (i.e., conjuncts). Thus, presumably,

> Jack and Jill and Tommy are a family

can be paraphrased by a conjunction of statements which do not have conjunctive subjects, e.g.,

> Jack is a man
> Jack is married to Jill
> Jill gave birth to Tommy

19. When it is said that some wholes have attributes which do not consist in their parts having such and such qualities and standing in such and such relations, it is, in effect, being denied that all conjunctive individuals are reducible.

20. It might be thought that by speaking of wholes and parts, rather than of conjunctive individuals and their conjuncts, I have changed the subject. But this is not the case, for reference to a 'whole' or a 'composite' is simply reference to a conjunctive individual the elements of which are presupposed to satisfy certain qualitative and relational conditions. Thus, a regiment is a conjunctive individual which consists of soldiers who stand in certain relations to one another which constitute a military peck order. But more of this later.

IV

21. Well, given some such distinction between basic individuals (or substances) and reducible individuals, what shall we include in the former category? For the most part, I shall commit myself as I go along. But I shall begin by laying down that *some* physical objects are basic individuals, as are such quasi-physical objects as noises and flashes of lightning. More paradoxically, I shall also stipulate that persons are basic individuals.

22. What of scientific objects, the individuals postulated by micro-physical theory? Since I am usually classified as a Scientific Realist, it might be thought that in stipulating above that some physical objects are basic individuals, I was tacitly taking these basic individuals to be micro-physical particles. If so, the above claim that persons are basic individuals must have come as a surprise, for are not micro-physical particles actual parts of persons—at least if persons are not to be equated with Cartesian minds? But though I am indeed a Scientific Realist, and think that the domain of basic individuals consists of those which scientific theory will 'in the long run' find it necessary to postulate, I also regard the conceptual framework in terms of which man experienced himself and the world long before the revolution in physics was even a twinkle in the eye of Democritus, as a coherent, delicately articulated whole which it is necessary to understand in its own terms before one can be in a position to determine the precise sense in which it, or part of it, is 'replaceable' by the world-picture presented by theoretical science.

23. Thus, for methodological reasons, I shall (to borrow Husserl's useful term) 'bracket' the theoretical picture of the world and concern myself with explicating what I have called the Manifest Image. (See [8]).

24. In the Manifest Image, physical objects have perceptible qualities—roughly the proper sensibles and common sensibles of Aristotle. A dispositional property is, so to speak, an 'iffy' property; thus, water-solubility is the property of dissolving *if* placed in water. Note that for a property to be *occurrent* isn't just for it to be one that *occurs to* objects. The property of being magnetized occurs to soft iron when placed in a helix through which a current begins to pass. Nevertheless, the property of being magnetized, which occurs to the iron in these circumstances, is in our sense an 'iffy' property and is to be explicated, in first approximation, by means of the hypothetical: if an iron filing is

placed in the vicinity, then, *ceteris paribus,* it moves to the core. Whereas an occurrent property in our technical sense is one that is *not* to be explicated by a hypothetical.

25. Thus, consider, to use a favorite example of mine, a pink ice cube. Many are tempted to *identify* its pinkness with a causal property, the property of causing normal observers in standard conditions to have sensations of pink, indeed, of a pink cube. Now there may be a place for some such move when the scientific revolution is taken into account. But it is a *revisionary* proposal, and it is, in my opinion, a sheer mistake to think of it as a correct analysis of the common-sense notions of color which function in 'basic' perceptual experiences. Different conceptual strata can, and indeed do, co-exist in our ordinary experience of the world. But this co-existence, peaceful though it is (at least until philosophical issues are pressed), must not be confused with compatability in any deeper sense.

26. Only a theory-intoxicated philosopher can look at a pink ice cube in daylight and suppose that *to see it to be pink* is to see it to have the power to cause normal observers to have sensations of pink when they look at it in daylight. And it is at least as absurd—if not quite the same absurdity—to suppose that to see it to be pink is to see it to look pink to normal observers in daylight, even though it is a conceptual truth that pink things look pink to normal observers in standard conditions, which, until we become dwellers in modern caves, include daylight.

27. It should be noted that if physical objects are genuine individuals, they can scarcely have *only* iffy properties (powers, propensities, dispositional properties, and the like). They must have *some* non-dispositional or occurrent attributes. Nor, as Whitehead reminds us, will it do to limit their occurrent attributes to such 'primary' qualities as *shape* and *size;* for, to use an Aristotelian turn of phrase, geometrical qualities are 'formal' qualities and presuppose a 'content' or 'matter', thus color. Things which had 'primary' qualities without 'content' qualities would have "vacuous actuality." That Whitehead construed the occurrent content of physical objects in terms of *feeling,* rather than *color,* is a symptom of the revisionary character of his metaphysics.

V

28. Let me propose, then, as my paradigm of a physical object, a pink ice cube. It is cold, smooth, transparently pink, and cubical. In

addition to these (and other) occurrent attributes, it has, of course, many properties of the iffy type illustrated above—which it is also convenient to call 'causal properties'. Let us now bring into the picture a person who sees it.

29. In the Manifest Image, a person is a basic individual. (It should be clear that I regard Aristotle as *the* philosopher of the Manifest Image.) That which distinguishes man from merely material things and from brutes is his ability to think. Now the word 'think' is used in a number of distinguishable, but related, senses. Thus, it has a dispositional sense in which it is closely related to 'believe'. (What does *he* think about the war in Vietnam?) Thinking is often a deliberate action, as in thinking about (i.e., attempting to solve) a problem. Again, there is a sense of 'thought' in which thoughts just occur to one. We say "it suddenly occurred to me that . . .," and, we can often add, "for no reason."

30. The importance of all this is that whereas we often contrast perception with thinking, there is, nevertheless, a proper sense in which perceiving essentially is or involves *a thinking*. Roughly, seeing *this* to be a pink ice cube involves a thinking *this* to be a pink ice cube.

31. I propose that we take very seriously the view that a thought, in the sense in which thoughts occur to one, is the occurrence in the mind of sentences in the language of "inner speech," or, as I shall call it, 'Mentalese'. These sentence events, as I have pointed out elsewhere, are not to be confused with verbal imagery. Although we are able to monitor, to some extent, our thoughts and to have direct non-inferential knowledge of them, this knowledge must not be construed on the perceptual model.

VI

32. Before continuing, I must qualify the above remarks lest the animal lovers among us take them as libel and calumny. I count myself in their ranks and therefore hasten to add that of course there is a legitimate sense in which animals can be said to think and hence to be able, in something like the above sense, to see a pink ice cube and to see that it is pink. Furthermore, the point is important in its own right and not simply a rhetorical maneuver. For if one ties thinking too closely to language, the acquisition of linguistic skills by children becomes puzzling in ways which generate talk about 'innate grammatical theories'.

33. Not all 'organized behavior' is built on linguistic structures. The most that can be claimed is that what might be called 'conceptual thinking' is essentially tied to language, and that, for obvious reasons, the central or core concept of what thinking is pertains to conceptual thinking. Thus, our common-sense understanding of what sub-conceptual thinking—e.g., that of babies and animals—consists in, involves viewing them as engaged in 'rudimentary' forms of conceptual thinking. We interpret their behavior using conceptual thinking as a model but qualify this model in *ad hoc* and unsystematic ways which really amount to the introduction of a new notion which is nevertheless labeled 'thinking'. Such analogical extensions of concepts, when supported by experience, are by no means illegitimate. Indeed, it is essential to science. It is only when the negative analogies are overlooked that the danger of serious confusion and misunderstanding arises.

34. One must also take into account the sensibilities not only of animal lovers but of artists: painters, musicians, and the like. These are, of course, 'thinking beings.' But do they 'think' in the course of their distinctive creative activity?

35. One is tempted to say that the musician not only thinks *about* sound, but also 'in sound'. Thinking about sound, it might be admitted, can be construed on a linguistic model—as 'inner speech' using the vocabulary of auditory qualities and relations. Indeed, much of the thinking that a composer does is conceptual thinking about the relationships of sound patterns, and since the notion of conceptual thinking as analogous to language leaves open the question of how *precise* the analogy is, it is surely not too far-fetched to take a linguistic approach to this aspect of the composer's activity.

36. But is there not also a more intimate relationship between composition (and other forms of musicianship) and sound: the aspect I referred to above as 'thinking in sound'? And is not this aspect also a mode of *thought*? Is not a performer a 'thinking being' even while he performs? The 'linguistic model' begins to look far too narrow and specialized to capture the nature of thinking, even at the strictly human level—let alone in the sense in which animals think.

37. There is much food for reflection in these considerations. They raise questions which must be taken into account by any serious philosophy

of mind. But the fundamental problems which they pose arise already at the perceptual level. For, as we shall see, visual perception itself is not just a conceptualizing of colored objects within visual range—a 'thinking about' colored objects in a certain context—but, in a sense most difficult to analyze, a *thinking in color* about colored objects. (The point stands out most clearly with respect to visual imagination; for imagination at its best is not simply a thinking about things which are not at hand and, more generally, thinking which is not concerned with what really exists, i.e., thinking that takes the form of make-believe.) It is suffused with visual imagery and can also be said to be a 'thinking in color'.

38. What I am suggesting is that a correct theory of visual experience will throw light on the nature of visual imagination—and this, in turn, on the unique relationship between thinking and imagery which characterizes creativity in music and the other arts.

VII

39. Overt linguistic occurrences obviously involve a 'vehicle of meaning', the relevant matter-of-factual characteristics of speech which are idealized in the semanticist's concept of a 'sign design'. Once we abandon the naive idea that the vehicle of meaning in the case of inner speech is imagery, we are left with the question: What is it? Or is there, perhaps, no vehicle of meaning? In that case, the analogy between thought and speech would indeed limp.

40. Philosophers have often been tempted, in the case of overt speech, to reify the distinction between the words which are uttered and the 'meanings' which they convey. Clearly, something like this distinction must be drawn, though the crucial question would be just what sort of 'things' 'meanings' are. I have dealt with this issue in a number of places (most recently in [9], Ch. III) and will touch upon it lightly in a subsequent lecture, but for the present purposes it is sufficient to note that the analogy we are drawing between 'inner' and 'outer' speech requires that parallel questions be at least asked about inner speech. Must we not distinguish between sentence events in Mentalese and the meanings they bear? We might be inclined to say that thoughts are not, so to speak, externally related to their meanings, as are sentence events in overt speech, but rather that they embody, in a unique way, the senses of the

words in which they find expression. If so, a thinking that Nixon is President would be a mental event which *embodies,* in a unique way, the sense of 'Nixon is President'; or it is, perhaps, in a unique way, an event of the *Nixon is President* kind. Although this might seem to be a desperate attempt to preserve the analogical theory, the latter has sufficient merit to warrant strong measures. And although the formulations seem empty, it turns out, I shall argue, that they can be given empirical content.

41. I said a moment ago that *seeing* this to be a pink ice cube involves *thinking* this to be a pink ice cube. In the above terms, this means that seeing this to be a pink ice cube involves the occurrence of something like the Mentalese sentence, "This, over there, is a pink ice cube." Yet this can scarcely be all, for, we are inclined to expostulate, surely there is all the difference in the world between *seeing* something to be a pink ice cube and *merely* thinking something to be a pink ice cube.

42. Even if we take into account the fact that perception involves a causal dimension (in that, given our ability to think of something as a pink ice cube, and given that we are not blind, and given that the circumstances are propitious (daylight, unobstructed view, etc., etc.), the pink ice cube is the *cause* (in a relevant sense) of the thought that there is a pink ice cube over there), we feel that the distinctive character of seeing has not yet been captured.

43. Consider another example. I see that there is a red book in the corner. This time, since the book is not transparent, I do *not* see the other side of the book. Yet clearly I *think* of it, in the sense that in thinking of the object as a book, I think of it as something which necessarily has an opposite side, and that in thinking of the book as red, I am thinking not only of this facing side but also of the opposite side as red. Thus, we are tempted to say, most of the book is present to me as something *merely* thought of.[2] Now I am, in the circumstances, caused

2. Actually, this is the place to recognize an important role played by the imagination in perception. Must we not say that the other side of the book is *imagined*, rather than merely thought of? Fair enough! Yet, as I have already indicated, the problems involved in distinguishing between *seeing* and *merely thinking* recur when one attempts to distinguish between *imagining* the opposite side to be red and *merely thinking* of the opposite side as red. If the former distinction requires the postulation of sense impressions, the latter requires the postulation of images. Thus, the heart of our problem concerns the facing side and is the problem of understanding the difference between merely *thinking* of the facing side as red and *seeing it to be red*.

to think of the book as red and, hence, not only of the facing side but of the opposite side as red. The facing surface, on the other hand, seems to be more intimately involved. Is it merely that the facing surface is the proper cause of the *whole* experience, so that insofar as I am thinking of the facing surface as red, my thinking corresponds to the *proper* cause? Is this what makes the seeing of the facing surface more than a mere thinking of the facing surface as red? Surely not.

44. Perhaps what we should do is recognize that the propositional act, the thinking, is of a unique kind, a 'visual' thinking. This could be meant in two ways: (1) It could be claimed that the propositional act involves a unique concept which reflects in the very content of the act the element of passivity by virtue of which it is a response to visual (auditory, etc.) stimulation. But even if we grant that the thoughts involved in perception have a distinctive content, as I think they do, it is difficult to see how the addition of another conceptual item can account for the difference between *seeing* and *merely thinking of.*

45. A more promising line which might be taken is (2) that over and above its *propositional* character as the occurrence of a mental sentence, the thinking has an additional character by virtue of which it is a *seeing* as contrasted with a *mere thinking.* Although, as we shall see, this move is not incorrect, it essentially labels, rather than clarifies, the problem.

46. Notice, to begin with, that if we suppose this additional character to be that of being a *seeing,* it runs into the objection that the same difference between a perceptual experience and a mere thinking is present in cases where the experience is *not* a *seeing,* for example, that there is a red book over there, for the simple reason that there is no red book over there.

47. Superficially, at least, this objection can be overcome by referring to this additional character as that of being, not a *seeing,* but an *ostensible seeing*—a matter of something's *looking* or (visually) *appearing* to be the case. An ostensible seeing is, roughly, an experience which would be a seeing if it were veridical, just as an ostensible memory is an experience which would be a remembering, if it were *veridical.* Thus, since our problem concerns that which distinguishes seeings and ostensible seeings alike from mere thinkings, it amounts to the problem 'What

distinguishes ostensible seeings or lookings from mere thinkings?' And to answer 'the character of being an ostensible seeing' is scarcely illuminating.

48. Nevertheless, the view which we are considering is on the right track, insofar as it recognizes that the character of being an ostensible seeing or looking or (visual) appearing is a character which belongs to experiences which essentially have a propositional component, involving, as they do, the occurrence in the mind of a Mentalese sentence. On the other hand, to ascribe, as is sometimes done, the character of being an 'appearing' or ostensible seeing to the propositional act alone, as though it were an 'intrinsic' character of the act, must be a mistake. Surely the propositional act itself is an *ostensible seeing* or *looking* only in the derivative sense that it is the propositional constituent of *a total experience which is an ostensible seeing or looking.*

49. On the other hand, it is equally mistaken to ascribe the character of being an ostensible seeing to the non-propositional element in the experience. For the expressions which the contexts '. . . ostensibly sees . . .', '. . . looks . . .', '. . . appears . . .', require, to complete them, are *propositional* in character:

> Jones (ostensibly) sees there to be a red book in the corner.
> There appears to Jones to be a red book in the corner.

50. Thus, if there is a non-propositional component in the total experience, it would be incorrect to refer to it by such terms as 'looks', 'appears', etc., unless these latter are given a new and *technical* usage. And one who does so would first have to make clear *that* there is such a non-propositional component and give some account of *what* it is.

51. Now I think it clear that, phenomenologically speaking, there is such a non-propositional component. But I also think that in the absence of what amounts to relatively sophisticated theory construction, it can only be characterized in a way which raises more problems than it solves.

52. Roderick Chisholm, in his various presentations of his views on the sensible appearances of things, seems to me to race over these distinctions. The phenomenological appeal is made, but since the language of

'looks', 'seems', 'appears', is used to characterize the discriminated items, the implication that they are propositional states is never explicitly discounted, though it is clear that he thinks of his looks and appearings as non-conceptual states. But the failure to make an explicit distinction between the appearings which are propositional states and the appearings in the surreptitiously introduced new sense, in which they are not propositional states, bestows upon the latter an unearned non-problematic character with respect to the manner in which they involve the proper and common sensibles.

53. Chisholm correctly sees that the primary use of 'appears' is non-comparative. For in the comparative use we say, e.g., "This appears to be what white objects appear to be in such and such circumstances of perception." And while the whole sentence compares one appearing with others, not every sentence involving 'appears' can do so, for obvious reasons. There must be sentences to the effect that this appears to be thus and so *period,* e.g., white. But one can grant that the primary use of 'appears' is non-comparative while arguing, as I have done, that the primary use of 'appears' applies to conceptual, *but not merely* conceptual, episodes. In other words, one can grant the primacy of the non-comparative sense of 'appears', 'looks', etc. without applying these terms to the non-propositional component of the total perceptual experience.

54. I have argued in "Empiricism and the Philosophy of Mind" ([5]) that the non-propositional feature common to cases where

> One sees that the object over there is red and triangular on the facing side;
> The object over there looks to be red and triangular on the facing side;
> There looks to one to be an object which is red and triangular on the facing side in front of one,

is *primarily* identified simply as *this* common non-propositional feature. I called it the descriptive (i.e., non-propositional) core.

55. So far we would be little better off than if we simply said that *ostensibly seeing* that there is in front of one an object which is red and triangular on the facing side differs from *merely thinking that* there is an

object in front of one which is red and triangular on the facing side, by virtue of being a thinking which is *also* an ostensible seeing. But we can say more. For, phenomenologically speaking, the descriptive core consists in the fact that *something* in *some* way red and triangular is in *some* way present to the perceiver *other than as thought of.*

56. The multiple indefiniteness in this description is disconcerting and makes it clear that the concept is a problematic one, in the sense of posing problems. But then I have argued in a number of places (for example, [4]) that the 'common-sense' picture of the world, in spite of its delicate coherence, is such as to pose problems which it lacks the resources to resolve. On the other hand, the above account of the non-propositional (descriptive) core is definite in its negative aspect. The mode of presence is not that of being thought of.

57. A scholastic might say that in perception (and ostensible perception) the relevant proper and common sensibles have *being for sense* as well as *being for thought*. Thus, when I see or ostensibly see something to be a pink ice cube, a pink cube has not only being for thought but also being for sense. The *somehow* presence of the pink cube could then be referred to as its being sensed. (The problematic nature of such 'sensing' should not be forgotten.)

VIII

58. What are the boundary conditions on such a theory of the 'descriptive core' of perceptual experience? The following strike me as relevant considerations:

(1) If we are to work within the framework of the Manifest Image, we must stipulate that the proper and common sensibles involved are to be construed as qualities of physical objects (noises, flashes, etc.). We are nevertheless free to introduce new *theoretical* uses of perceptual predicates in which the latter apply to items which are not, in the ordinary sense, physical objects— though they may properly be said to be physical in an extended sense of the term.

(2) We are looking for characteristics which *actually characterize* the descriptive core. Thus, we must beware of using metaphors

which carry with them the implications of *being for thought, existence as thought-of, intentional in-existence*. For if the pink and cubical item involved in hallucinating a pink ice cube had itself merely thought-of existence, it could not do the job the theory requires. This danger is present, as we saw, in the term 'being for sense'.

59. Classical sense-datum theory, construed as a *postulational* theory rather than as a phenomenological description, would satisfy these demands, provided:

(1) Sense data are not introduced as objects of perceptual knowledge. The *objects* of perceptual knowledge are the objects referred to in the propositional component of the perceptual experience, and these are physical objects, not private, subjective (let alone theoretical) items. For this reason, the term 'sensa' would be more suitable than 'sense *data*'.

(2) Sensa are not to be taken to have 'sensible qualities' in the primary sense of this phrase in which, for example, the pinkness of physical objects is primary. This, however, permits sensa to have theoretical counterparts of these qualities. Accordingly, the *somehow* presence of an item which is *somehow* physically pink and cubical would be explained in terms of the *somehow* presence (i.e., the being sensed) of an item which is pink and cubical in an analogical sense.[3]

60. But our options are not restricted to such a revised form of sense-datum theory. Sensum theory construes sensing as a *relation* between a person and an item which is pink and cubical in an analogical sense. But once we realize that what is involved are theoretical counterparts of the proper and common sensible characteristics of physical objects, we see that the way is open to construe these items on a quite different model from the act-object model of sense-datum theory.

---

3. This is at first sight disturbing, in that what we wanted was something *physically* pink and cubical. Surely, it might be said, to offer something which actually has a *non-physical* pinkness and cubicity, even though these are the *theoretical counterparts* of physical pinkness and cubicity, is to give us a stone instead of bread. There is a bite to this objection, but the full answer involves a general account of how the impact of the scientific image of the world is to be correctly interpreted. Briefly, it turns out that the color concepts which are posterior in the (historical) order of conception—i.e., color as color of sensa—are *prior* in the order of being. Roughly, color is 'really' an attribute of sensory states of the perceiver, when these in their turn have been transposed into an adequate neuro-physiology of perception.

61. Thus, instead of saying that the non-propositional presence of a pink cube in an ostensible seeing is a matter of a *relation* of sensing between the perceiver and an item which is, in the indicated derivative sense, a pink cube, we can take the quite different tack of construing the *object* of sensing (a pink cube) as a *manner* of sensing. Sensing *a pink cube* would be interpreted as sensing *a-pink-cube-ly*.

62. This would be a cousin of what is known as the 'adverbial' theory of sensing. It differs, however, in two important respects.

> (1) The usual adverbial theory would analyze our example in terms of sensing pinkly; pink, as a feature of the non-propositional content of the ostensible seeing of a pink ice cube, being interpreted as a *manner* of sensing.

But what was to be explained was the fact that the ostensible seeing presents us, in some way, not just with 'pinkness' but with *a pink cube,* i.e., something pink and cubical. Thus, to do its job, the adverbial theory would have to construe not 'pink' but 'a pink item' as the relevant adverb. But this is not all.

> (2) Taking the preceding point fully into account, the adverb would have to be 'a pink cube', i.e., one would sense *a-pink-cube-ly*. Once we appreciate this we understand why the traditional adverbial theory limits itself to 'senses pinkly'; for it takes the sensing context to present the *primary* mode of being of colors, e.g., pink. The *esse* of blue, for example, is *sensing bluely*. Blue is a manner of sensing. But the philosophers who propound it would scarcely be happy to make the corresponding move in the case of shape. Does it make sense to say that the primary mode of being of triangularity, or, in our example, cubicity, is as a manner of sensing?

63. Thus, the virtue of the form of the adverbial theory which I am proposing is that it requires that the adverb be a phrase of the form 'a pink item' rather than 'pink', and, above all, it recognizes that the 'adverb' must take into account the *primary* qualities of perceptible things as well as the *secondary*. (The act-object or sensum theory has this advantage over the usual adverbial theory in that it can attribute to sensa not only color but shape.) Once we realize that the predicates of the theory of sensing are *theoretical* predicates, which are introduced in terms of *analogy* with predicates standing for the proper and common sensible qualities of physical objects, we see that there is no reason why

the introduced theoretical predicates should not have a quite different conceptual grammar.

64. According to this version of the adverbial theory of sensing, then, sensing a-pink-cube-ly is sensing in a way which is normally brought about by the physical presence to the senses of a pink and cubical physical object, but which can also be brought about in abnormal circumstances by objects that are neither pink nor cubical, and, finally, according to this form of the adverbial theory, the manners of sensing are analogous to the common and proper sensibles in that they have a common conceptual structure. Thus, the color manners of sensing form a family of incompatibles, where the incompatibilities involved are to be understood in terms of the incompatibilities involved in the family of ordinary physical color attributes. And, correspondingly, the shape manners of sensing would exhibit, as do physical shapes, the abstract structure of a pure geometrical system.

65. The account which I have offered is obviously but a beginning, for it leaves almost untouched the intimate relation which exists between these two aspects of visual perception. Furthermore, it leaves completely untouched the relationship between each of these aspects and the neurophysiological processes which are at least as intimately related to them as they are to each other.

66. It is some progress, however, to have a sense of what remains to be done. As I once pointed out, the evolution of philosophy is as much the evolution of philosophical questions as it is of answers to pre-existing questions. In this sense, at least, I hope to have advanced the subject this afternoon.

APPENDIX

1. One of the useful ways of emphasizing some of the points which I have been making in this lecture is to discuss an argument of Roderick Firth ([3]) to show that it makes good sense to suppose that physical redness can be defined in terms of 'looks red'.

2. It should be clear that according to the analysis which I have given, any such attempt is doomed to failure from the start—if 'looks' is taken in its ordinary sense. For 'looks' applies to experiences which contain the thought 'such and such a physical object is red', and, if my analysis is

correct, it becomes a truism that in this sense of 'looks' the concept of *being red* is logically prior to that of *looking red*.

3. Thus, if Firth's attempt is to get off the ground, he must be claiming that the non-propositional element in perceptual experience, for which he is borrowing the term 'looks', is itself red in a well-defined sense which is both other than physical redness and does not presuppose it. But, according to my analysis, the only *well-defined* sense of 'red' other than physical redness which is available is a theoretical construct which has been introduced on the analogy of physical redness and, therefore, does conceptually presuppose it.

4. Waiving this point, and granting Firth his well-defined, non-propositional sense of 'looks red and triangular', we can construe him as claiming that

> *O* looks red and triangular to me

has something like the sense of

> *O* is the cause of a red and triangular element in my perceptual experience.

Correspondingly,

> There looks to me to be a red and triangular object in front of me

would have the sense of

> There is a red and triangular element in my perceptual experience.

5. Now it should be clear that according to the view which I have been defending in this essay, one is not in a position to be perceptually aware of any fact, however minimal, unless one has a whole system of concepts which constitutes a Mentalese language of physical objects in Space and Time. But Firth, following Lewis, is willing to concede that "the *vocabulary* of 'looks'" and 'seems' expressions that we use to describe sense experience is in some sense derivative from the *vocabulary* we use to describe the physical world" ([3]: 548). On the other hand, appealing to an apparently straightforward distinction between *words* and *concepts*, Firth insists that there is a domain of *concepts* pertaining to sensible qualities which are logically independent of *concepts* pertaining to physical objects. And, in the spirit of traditional empiricism, he finds the source of these concepts to be what I have called the descriptive or non-propositional core of the perceptual experience of physical objects. Thus he writes:

. . . if a philosopher maintains that 'The apple is red' can be analyzed as meaning "The apple would look red under such and such physical conditions," he is assuming that "looks red" is logically prior to "is red," i.e., that it is at least *logically* possible to have the concept "looks red" *before* we acquire the concept "is red." But if the coherence theory of concepts is correct and we cannot fully understand "looks red" unless we possess the contrasting concept "is red," then it would seem that it is *not* logically possible to have the concept "looks red" before we have the concept "is red." This paradox might even lead us to wonder, indeed, whether the conceptual interdependence of "looks" and "is" is enough to undermine Lewis' basic assumption that we can make "expressive judgments" (e.g., "I seem to see a door knob," "It looks as if I am seeing something red") without at the same time asserting something about the nature of "objective reality." It is these expressive judgments, according to Lewis, that enable us to escape the coherence theory of justification; and if it should turn out that these judgments all make some covert reference to physical objects, then—depending, of course, on the *kind* of "covert reference"—it might no longer be possible to make the epistemological distinction that Lewis requires. ([3]: 547.)

6. In the above passage, Firth is clearly confusing the proper sense of 'looks', in which it contrasts with 'is seen to be', with the contrived sense explored in the opening paragraphs of the Appendix, in which 'looks red' contrasts with 'is red' and means something like 'causes a red item in my visual experience'.

7. But, as already noted, this is not the point I wish to press. For even more significant is the fact that the next step in his argument is simply invalid and reveals an over-simplified conception of the relation between the meaning of word and the circumstances in which it is used. He writes,

It is a genetic fact, but a fact with philosophical implications, that when a child first begins to use the word 'red' with any consistency he applies it to things that *look* red to him whether these things are, as we should say, "really red," or whether they are merely made to appear red by abnormal conditions of observation. Thus the child calls white things "red" when he sees them through red glass. In fact at this stage the child says 'red' just in those circumstances in which we, as adults, could truthfully say "looks red to me now," so that it would not be unreasonable to assert that the child is using 'red' to express a primitive form of the concept "looks red." ([3]: 547.)

He concedes that "to call this a 'primitive form' of the concept 'looks red' is to acknowledge that in some sense the child cannot *fully* understand adult usage until he is able to distinguish things that merely look red from things that really are red," but insists that "we must not suppose that the child somehow *loses* his primitive concept when he acquires a more sophisticated one." He then concludes his argument with the statement that "if we do not confuse baptismal rules with semantical rules (e.g., the semantical rule followed by the child who says 'red' when something looks red to him), the coherence theory of concepts does not seem to be incompatible with Lewis' theories of meaning and knowledge."

8. The absurdity of Firth's argument is best brought out by constructing a parallel argument which has as its conclusion,

> . . . in fact, at this stage the child says 'red' just in those circumstances in which we, as adults, could truthfully say 'electromagnetic waves of wave length λ are striking his retina', so that it would not be unreasonable to assert that the child is using 'red' to express a primitive form of the concept 'electro-magnetic waves of wave length λ striking a retina'.

LECTURE II: MINDS

I

1. In my first lecture, I was exploring the nature of our perceptual knowledge of such elementary facts as that there is a pink ice cube in front of one or that there is a red book on the shelf. I emphasized that I was 'bracketing', that is, suspending commitment to, the stratum of concepts introduced by micro-physical theory and considering perception as it might have been considered by an epistemologist who lived in the days when atomic theory was but a gleam in the Democritean eye. In short, the model with which I was working was essentially an Aristotelian one, though I was not concerned with problems of historical exegesis.

2. I was emphasizing that in this model material things are colored in a sense which is not to be *explicated* in terms of a hypothetical reference

to sensations of color. I asked you to contemplate a pink ice cube and urged the implausibility of the suggestion that to see it to be pink is to see it to have the power to cause normal observers in standard conditions to have sensations of pink or to sense pinkly. Indeed, I argued that the concept of the sensation of the pink cube is a theoretical concept, an element in a theoretical explanation, not only of how people can seem to see pink ice cubes, when no pink transparent material object is before their eyes, but how the veridical perception itself differs from a purely conceptual awareness of the pink ice cube.

3. I concluded by suggesting that the most satisfactory form of this theoretical account makes it a version of the 'adverbial' theory of sensing. According to this version, the theoretical concepts of manners of sensing are formed by analogy with concepts pertaining to the common and proper sensible attributes of physical objects as conceived in the Manifest Image of the world. Thus, the color manners of sensing form a family of incompatibles, where the incompatibilities involved are to be understood in terms of the incompatibilities within the family of ordinary physical color attributes. And, correspondingly, the shape manners of sensing would exhibit, as do physical shapes, the abstract structure of a pure geometrical system.

4. Thus, sensing a pink cube is a manner of sensing which is conceived by analogy (a transcategorial analogy!) with a pink physical cube and which, though normally caused by the presence of a pink and cubical transparent object in front of a normal perceiver's eyes, can also be brought about in abnormal circumstances by, say, a grey object illuminated by pink light or by a pink rhomboidal object viewed through a distorting medium, or in hallucination by, for example, a probing of a certain region of the brain with an electrode, or by the taking of an hallucinogenic drug after much talk of pink ice cubes.

5. I distinguished between the propositional and the non-propositional components of the visual experience. I characterized the former as a thinking that something is the case, where the thinking is construed as the occurrence, in the mind, of a sentence in Mentalese or, to use the traditional term, 'inner speech'. I said relatively little about Mentalese, save to emphasize the positive analogy between it and overt verbal behavior. I concentrated on the non-propositional aspect of visual experiences and was concerned to show that unless supplemented by theory construction, the phenomenology of perception takes us no

further than the idea that *somehow*, *something* which is in *some* sense pink and cubical is present to the perceiver when, rather than *merely thinking* that there is a pink ice cube in a certain place, he sees, or seems to see, a pink ice cube in that place.

6. In this lecture I want to explore the topic of thinking as 'inner speech' (Mentalese) and lay the groundwork for discussion of the implications of the scientific revolution for this concept. Unless one takes a purely instrumental view of scientific objects, both sensing and thinking must be correctly located in a context of neurophysiological activity. The traditional mind-body problem has two dimensions which have often been run together—or, at least, not carefully distinguished: (1) What is the relation of sensations to physical states of the body? (2) What is the relation of conceptual states (thinkings, inner speech) to physical states of the body? It should not be assumed that these two dimensions of the mind-body problem admit of the same type of solution.

II

7. How is the postulated analogy between Mentalese and overt linguistic behavior to be understood? To begin with, we must simplify our own model by abstracting from those features of language by virtue of which it is an instrument for influencing people. As Austin has emphasized, we can *do* things with words. We can inform or misinform, we can communicate our beliefs, we can make promises, etc., etc. Illocutionary and perlocutionary acts are *actions*. Like all actions, they are sometimes deliberate, sometimes unintended, sometimes thoughtless.

8. But though I am going to abstract from these features of linguistic behavior, I am not going to remove *all* reference to linguistic action from the positive analogy, for some thought processes *are* actions—that is, are the sort of things that can be *undertaken*, that one can decide to do—and, consequently, a place must be left in our model for linguistic actions proper. Roughly, I am excluding only those linguistic actions which are other-oriented and involve language as a means of communicating with, making commitments to, and influencing our fellowmen.

9. The simplified model which I propose to work with can be called 'Verbal Behaviorism'. It is not intended as an adequate account of

thinking; it is, indeed, radically oversimplified. But I believe that it will prove a useful tool which will help us understand some of the features of thinking, and of our awareness of ourselves as thinking beings, which have been a source of puzzlement since the very dawn of philosophy.

10. According to this model, 'thinking that-p', where this means 'having the thought occur to one that-p', has as its *primary* sense *saying* 'p' and a derivative sense in which it stands for a short-term proximate propensity to say 'p'. Propensities tend to be actualized (a logical point about the term). When they are not, we speak of them as, for example, 'blocked'. For the purposes of the *VB* model, the relevant inhibiting factor which keeps the saying that-p from being actualized is that of not being in a thinking-out-loud frame of mind. One might use the model of a general 'on-off' switch which gets into the 'wiring diagram' when the child learns to keep his thoughts to himself.

11. Notice that I am treating that-clauses as quoted expressions; thus;

The thought that 2 plus 2 = 4 occurred to Jones

becomes, in the Verbal Behaviorist model,

Jones said (or had a short-term proximate disposition to say) '2 plus 2 = 4'.

I shall shortly take into account the fact that non-English-speaking people are not precluded from thinking that 2 plus 2 = 4. But our initial model will be provincial.

12. Picking up some themes from the above discussion of linguistic *action*, it is essential to note that just as thinking that-p, in the sense of having the thought occur to one that-p, is not a mental *performance*, something that one does or could do voluntarily, so, in the *VB* model, saying 'p' is not to be construed as an illocutionary act. It is to be construed, as I have elsewhere put it, as candidly *thinking-out-loud-that-p* and is not to be confused with asserting (to someone) that-p, telling someone that-p, or any of the verbal performances so lovingly collected by Austin.

13. Of course, in any ordinary sense, saying 'p' *is* a performance, because the phrase permits the utterance to which it applies to be either a spontaneous thinking-out-loud-that-p or a deliberate use of words to achieve a purpose. I, on the other hand, am using the expression 'S says p' in a *contrived* sense in which these options are closed and the utterance specifically construed as a spontaneous or candid thinking-out-loud.

14. We can imagine a child to learn a rudimentary language in terms of which he can perceive, draw inferences, and act. In doing so, he begins by uttering noises which *sound like* words and sentences and ends by uttering noises which *are* words and sentences. We might use quoted words to describe what he is doing at both stages, but in the earlier stage we are classifying his utterances as *sounds* and only by courtesy and anticipation as *words*.

15. Only when the child has got the hang of how the sounds function in the language can he be properly characterized as saying 'this is a book', or 'it is not raining', or 'lightning, so shortly thunder', or 'you spanked me, so you don't love me'.

16. To say what a person says, or, more generally, to say what a kind of utterance says, is to give a functional classification of the utterance. This functional classification involves a special (illustrating) use of the expressions classified, or of synonyms—where allowance must be made for degrees of synonymy or likeness of meaning—of these expressions with which the addressee is familiar.

17. Some functional relationships are purely intra-linguistic (syntactical) and are correlated with the formation and transformation rules. Others concern language as a response to sensory stimulation by environmental objects—thus, candidly saying, or having the short-term propensity to say, 'lo! this table is red'. Still others concern the connection of practical thinking with behavior. All these dimensions of functioning recur at the metalinguistic level in the language in which we respond to verbal behavior, draw inferences about verbal behavior, and engage in practical thinking about verbal behavior—i.e., practical thinking-out-loud (or propensities to think-out-loud) about thinking-out-loud (or propensities to think-out-loud).

18. Thus, when we characterize a person's utterances by using a quotation, we are implying that the utterance is an instance of certain specific ways of functioning. For example, it would be absurd to say

> Tom said (as contrasted with 'uttered the noises') 'it is not raining' but has no propensity to avoid saying 'it is raining and not raining'.

19. In particular, to characterize a person's utterance by quoting sentences containing logical words is to imply that the corresponding sounds function properly in the Verbal Behavior in question, and is to

imply that the uniformities characteristic of these ways of functioning
are present in his sayings and proximate dispositions to say.

20. The functioning which gives the utterances of one who has learned a
language their meaning *can* exist merely at the level of uniformities, as
in the case of the fledgling speaker. Those who train him, thus, his
parents, think about these functionings and attempt to ensure that his
verbal behavior exemplifies them. In this respect, the trainer operates
not only at the level of the trainee, thinking thoughts about things, but
also at that higher level which is thinking thoughts about the functions
by virtue of which first-level language has the meaning it does. In traditional terms, the trainer knows the *rules* which govern the *correct*
functioning of language. The language learner begins by *comforming* to
these rules without grasping them himself.

21. Only subsequently does the language learner become a full-fledged
member of the linguistic community who thinks thoughts (theoretical
and practical) not only about non-linguistic items but about *linguistic*
items, i.e., from the point of view of our simple *VB* model, about
first-level thoughts. He has then developed from being the object of
training and criticism by others to the stage at which he can train and
criticize other language users, and even himself. Indeed, he has now
reached the level at which he can formulate new and sophisticated
standards in terms of which to reshape his language and develop new
modes of thought.

22. Notice that on the *VB* model of thinking, we can distinguish clearly
between the *functional* role of utterances and the *phonemic* description
of the linguistic materials which embody or are the 'vehicles' of these
functions.

23. It is a most significant fact that the classical conception of thought as
'inner speech' (Mentalese) draws no such clear distinction between the
conceptual *functions* of the Mentalese symbols and the materials which
serve as the *vehicle* of these functions. Yet, if the analogy between
thinking, classically construed, and overt linguistic behavior is to be a
reasonably positive one, the idea that there must be inner-linguistic
vehicles (materials) would seem to be a reasonable one. It is often
thought that imagery is the vehicle of Mentalese—but there doesn't
seem to be enough imagery to go round. And, indeed, the idea of
imageless thought is by no means incoherent. What might the vehicle
be?

III

24. To our *VB* model there are, in addition to the objections, considered yesterday, to any attempts to construe thinking on the model of language, three familiar objections which must be given more attention:

> (1) Surely, it will be said, thinking that-*p* isn't just saying that-*p*—even candidly saying that-*p* as you have characterized it. For thinking-out-loud that-*p* involves knowing the meaning of what one says, and surely this is no matter of producing sound!

Answer: There is all the difference in the world between parroting words and thinking-out-loud in terms of words. But the difference is not that the latter involves a non-linguistic "knowing the meaning" of what one utters; rather it is that the utterances which one makes cohere with each other and with the context in which they occur in a way which is absent in mere parroting. Furthermore, the relevant sense of 'knowing the meaning of words' (which is a form of what Ryle has called *knowing how*) must be carefully distinguished from knowing the meaning of words in the sense of being able to talk about them as a lexicographer might—thus, defining them. Mastery of the language involves the latter as well as the former ability. Indeed they are both forms of *know how*, but at different levels—the one at the 'object language' level, the other at the 'metalanguage' level.

25. I turn now to a second objection:

> (2) Surely, it will be objected, we are often thinking when we are not saying anything. Our thoughts succeed one another with lightning rapidity. How can this be reconciled with the *VB* model?

Answer: It must be remembered that according to *VB*, thinking that-*p* is saying or having a short-term proximate propensity to say '*p*'. To grasp how rapidly short-term propensities can shift, one need only think of the electromagnet in a doorbell and consider how rapidly it acquires and loses the propensity to attract the clapper.

26. A third objection runs as follows:

> (3) Thinking, as was pointed out above, does not seem to occur in words. We are often conscious that we are thinking, for example, about a certain problem, without 'any words going through our mind'.

Answer: Only a very naive person would think of the flammability of gasoline as a hidden or inner flame, or of the propensity of an electron to jump from one orbit to another as hidden jumping. Thus, the Verbal Behaviorist would point out that the short-term propensity to say "I've just missed the bus" should not be construed as an 'inner' or 'hidden' saying "I've just missed the bus." Thus, the Verbal Behaviorist believes himself in a position to account for the classical conception of thoughts as analogous to linguistic activity but as, nevertheless, involving no actual equivalents of the *words* "in the mind." He sees the classical theory as an attempt to blend into one coherent picture items belonging to the radically different categories of act and propensity.

27. Above all, the *VB* model makes it clear how we know about thoughts. For in their primary mode of being, thoughts are publicly observable episodes: *people saying things*.

28. Thus, we can know what we think, in the primary sense, by literally hearing ourselves think. When we hear ourselves say (in a candid frame of mind) "I've just missed my bus," we are literally hearing the thought occur to us that we have just missed the bus.

29. And in hearing this, we would be thinking the higher-order thought:

The thought has just occurred to me that I have missed my bus.

And this higher-order thought would be an auditory perceptual response to one's actual thinking-out-loud "I've just missed the bus."

30. But what of those cases in which we know what we think, although we are not thinking-out-loud? The answer clearly does not consist in pointing out that thoughts in this sense are propensities to think-out-loud and that the propensities of things can be known by induction.

31. We know, for example, that acid turns litmus paper red by observing the relevant sequence in a number of cases and drawing a general conclusion from these observations.

32. And in more complicated cases we can, for example, know that our dog has the propensity to go and get his leash, because he, for example, sees us start to put on our rubber boots. And, in the most relevant type of case, people who know us very well are often able to predict what we are likely to think, given what is happening to us in the circumstances in which they see us.

33. Yet in reply to all this, the expostulation is surely justified that our own knowledge of what we are thinking (when we are *not* thinking-out-

loud) is not *inductive*, is not an inference from our overt behavior, in the circumstances in which we find ourselves, to the existence of a certain propensity.

34. Yet the fact that we are able to learn the propensities of others (and ourselves) by inductive inference is the first step in the answer. But before developing it, we must consider how the account of perceptual experience sketched yesterday afternoon appears in the light of *VB*.

35. Thus, consider the case where

     Jones sees there to be a red apple in front of him.

According to the account offered in the first lecture, this experience contains as its conceptual core the thought (which Jones is caused to have)

     Here is a red apple.

36. In terms of our *VB* model, this becomes:

     Jones thinks-out-loud: Lo! Here is a red apple.

37. Now to say that this visual thinking-out-loud that something is the case is epistemically *justified* or *reasonable* or has authority is clearly *not* to say that Jones has correctly inferred from certain premises, which he has good reason to believe, that there is a red apple in front of him. For we are dealing with a *paradigm* case of non-inferential belief. *The authority of the thinking accrues to it in quite a different way. It can be traced to the fact that Jones has learned how to use the relevant words in perceptual situations.*

38. It is for this reason that, when Jones candidly says, in response to visual stimulation,

     Lo! Here is a red apple,

it is *likely to be true* that there is a red apple in front of him. I say *likely* to be true, because we all know of various ways in which things can go wrong. Jones is in front of a mirror; the supposed apple is a piece of wax; the illumination is abnormal and the object is really purple; or, there is nothing in front of him, but he has taken LSD, and people have been pounding his ears about red apples.

39. If we were to overhear him, and if we had reason to believe that none of these countervailing situations obtain, *we* would be justified in reasoning as follows,

> Jones has thought-out-loud 'Lo! Here is a red apple'
> (no countervailing conditions obtain);
> So, there is good reason to believe that there is a red apple in front of him.

Note that although this is an *inferential* justification of *our* belief that there is a red apple in front of Jones, it is a special kind of inference. It has the form:

> The thought that-*p* occurs to Jones in a certain context and manner;
> So, it is reasonable to believe that-*p*.

The same proposition, that-*p*, is mentioned in both the premise and the conclusion. But the first mention concerns the fact of its occurrence *as a propositional event* in a context to which the basic features of language learning are relevant. From this premise, the inference is drawn that the proposition in question is one which it is reasonable to believe.

40. We looked at the above example from the standpoint of an external observer. Let us now look at it from the standpoint of Jones himself. As we saw in the preceding lecture, to be fully a master of his language, *Jones must know these same facts about what is involved in learning to use perceptual sentences in perceptual contexts.* Thus, Jones too must know that other specifiable[4] things being equal, the fact that a person says 'Lo! Here is a red apple' is good reason to believe that he is indeed in the presence of a red apple. Thus, Jones, *too*, can reason:

> I just thought-out-loud 'Lo! Here is a red apple'
> (no countervailing conditions obtain);
> So, there is good reason to believe that there is a red apple in front of me.

41. Of course, the conclusion of this reasoning is not the *thinking* involved in his original perceptual experience. Like all justification argu-

---

4. Which is not to say that there are no cases in which we would not know what to say—e.g., electrode hallucinations.

ments, it is a higher-order thinking. He did not originally *infer* that there is a red apple in front of him. *Now*, however, he is inferring from the character and context of his experience that it is veridical and that there is good reason to believe that there is indeed a red apple in front of him.

42. I wish now to argue that *VB* not only throws light on non-inferential perceptual knowledge but also gives us a strategy for coping with the problems posed by the existence of non-inferential knowledge of what we are thinking when we are *not* (candidly) thinking out loud.

43. The first step in the argument consists in pointing out that part of the process of learning to use a language is learning to make autobiographical statements. And not only autobiographical statements in general, but autobiographical statements about what one is thinking.

44. Now in the case of perception, non-inferential knowledge on the *VB* model, as we just saw, involves reliably *responding* to physical objects in standard conditions with the appropriate perceptual sentences; thus:

> Lo! There is a red book over there,
> Lo! Here is a pink ice cube,

in response to a red book or a pink ice cube, where the *reliability* of the response is a function of the way in which language is learned.

45. Now the more we know about a person, the better we are able to judge what (in the circumstances as we see them to be) he would be likely to say (think-out-loud)—if he were in a thinking-out-loud frame of mind. It is obviously difficult to be accurate about this, particularly when we are dealing with sophisticated minds. But even here the difficulty is one in *practice* rather than of *principle*. And when it is children in the initial stage of learning a language who are the subjects, the difficulty in *practice* is substantially less than it becomes subsequently when they have learned to lie, deceive, and conceal their thoughts.

46. Can we not, as children, be trained by those who know us intimately (our parents), and who therefore know (*ceteris paribus*) what our short-term verbal propensities are (i.e., what we are thinking), to *respond* reliably to our own short-term propensities to say that-*p*, as well as to respond to our actual sayings of '*p*'?

47. And can not this ability be generalized in such a way that we can reliably respond to new propensities, i.e., to thoughts other than those in terms of which we have been trained? And would not the fact that such responses are *reliable* constitute the core of the explanation of non-inferential knowledge of what one is thinking (in the proximate propensity sense), as the existence of reliable verbal responses to perceptible things is the core of the explication of non-inferential perceptual knowledge?

48. Many have thought that to explicate the concept of non-inferential knowledge of 'what is going on in one's mind at the present moment', one must return to the Cartesian framework. From the point of view sketched in this lecture, the essential feature of the latter framework is that it denies that 'thinking-out-loud' makes sense save as analyzable into 'thinking *occurrent non-verbal thoughts* and giving them expression in one's verbal behavior'. In short, the Cartesian argues that the concept of thinking-out-loud *includes* the concept of thoughts as Cartesian inner episodes. According to the *VB* position, on the other hand, the concept of thinking-out-loud stands on its own feet as the *primary* concept pertaining to thought, so that if a concept *like* the Cartesian concept of thought *episodes* which are *not* propensities to think-out-loud does turn out to be needed in giving a full account of "what thinking is," those who are inclined to accept something like the *VB* position would argue that it is a concept built on a *VB* foundation and is in some sense a derivative or secondary concept. As a useful parallel, consider the case of micro-physics. Macro-objects, we say, if we are scientific realists, are *really* systems of micro-physical particles. Yet our concepts of these particles are built—not on direct observation—but on a foundation of knowledge at the perceptual level. In short, though *VB* argues that even if there is a sense in which Cartesian thoughts are prior in the order of being to thinking-out-loud, the latter is prior in the order of knowing.

IV

49. There are many delicate issues in this neighborhood, some of which can be left to slumber. Nevertheless, I introduced *VB* as a simple model, and while I have been polishing and defending it, it was introduced in order to be transcended. It correctly represents a basic

stratum in our conception of what thinking is, but it is only a part of a larger picture, to which I now turn.

50. In the case of the dispositions and propensities of material things, we distinguish between the propensities and dispositions themselves, which are iffy states definable in terms of test conditions and empirically ascertainable results, on the one hand, and the *explanation* of these dispositions and propensities, which theoretical physics has made available, on the other.

51. Consider the case of our repeatedly magnetized soft iron. The repeated onslaughts and flights of the iffy property of being such that if iron filings are present, then they cling is, from the theoretical point of view, accompanied by certain actual physical processes which are induced by the current and other physical processes which replace them when the current is discontinued.[5]

52. Can we not regard classical theories of mental acts construed as *pure* occurrents (as contrasted with short-term propensities to think-out-loud) as *theories* in a sense which is analogous to micro-physical theories? Indeed, cannot we regard our common-sense conception of thought processes as such a theory? Such a theory would be designed to *explain* propensities to think-out-loud[6] as micro-physical theory is designed to explain the powers and propensities which we know things to have at the perceptual level, sophisticated by laboratory techniques.

53. The theory of 'inner speech' or Mentalese would construe these postulated thought episodes or occurrences as items which have a strong positive analogy with the thinkings-out-loud to which the *VB* calls attention. And it is interesting to note that when we refer to the thoughts which are occurring in a person's mind, we find it quite natural to quote them—even though they are not overt sayings. Yet the negative analogy must not be neglected. They are not thought of as waggings

5. A careful formulation would distinguish between the iffy truths at the theoretical level which are correlated with the original iffy truths, and the non-iffy processes of a theoretical character which are nomologically tied to these theoretical iffy truths.

6. And it is important to note that we all grant that there is such a thing as thinking-out-loud—though Cartesians give an account of it which presupposes the concept of non-verbal conceptual episodes.

of an inner tongue. Nor, as we have seen, is the vehicle of Mentalese to be construed as imagery.

54. I shall not elaborate the theory, for this is done by classical philosophies of mind. The points I am interested in making are points *about* the theory rather than *in* it.

55. Perhaps the most important point is that what the theory postulates in the way of new entities are *processes* and *acts* rather than *individuals*. In this sense, it remains within the manifest image. Persons remain the basic individuals of the system. We have simply enlarged our conception of what persons do, as compared with the *VB* model with which we began. In addition to sayings and short-term propensities to say, we now conceive persons to be characterized by purely occurrent episodes of thinking in this analogically introduced sense. We might be tempted to refer to them as 'inner' episodes. But the spatial metaphor is misleading. They are primarily 'in' the person as *states* of the person. To be sure, they are not *perceptible*, but neither is solubility, and solubility is not in any more interesting sense 'in' the salt. It is only when we come to think that some particular part of the body (e.g., the heart or the brain) is the locus of these activities that the term 'inner' acquires richer meaning. And this is what begins to happen when the scientific revolution makes its impact on our conception of the world. But before I turn to this and other topics, let me sum up the picture of man and the world which I have been developing.

56. I introduced the manifest image of man-in-the-world as, essentially, an image which has been purged of the scientific objects postulated by physical science. The basic *individuals* which it countenances are certain merely material things, living things other than persons (about which I have had little to say), and persons.

57. The *attributes* which it ascribes to material things include, in the first instance, the proper and common sensibles. But it also allows in its universal discourse attributes which are definable in terms of sensible attributes, and of which the most interesting are the powers and propensities of material things to change in certain perceptible ways when subject to influences which are themselves definable in terms of perceptible qualities and relations.

58. Then there are persons. These individuals have perceptible characteristics and behave in perceptible ways. The behavior on which we
have concentrated is the use of language. We restricted ourselves to that
use of language which we called thinking-out-loud, and we developed a
VB model according to which the meaningfulness of verbal behavior is
to be found in the coherence which it exhibits, not only within speech
itself, but in its relation to the contexts in which it occurs and the actions
to which it leads. Here again, dispositions and propensities pertaining to
perceptible traits of individuals were taken into account—in particular,
the shifting short-term propensities to say things which, according to the
VB model, are thinkings in a secondary sense of this term.

59. But notice that this austere conception of the person has been
enriched in two important respects without introducing new individuals.
Thus, *sensings* were introduced as theoretical states involved in the
explanation, for example, of how it could seem to a person that there
is a pink ice cube in front of him when in point of fact there is not. In
both the veridical perception of a pink ice cube and a perceptual experience which *would* be veridical *if* there were such an object in front of
one, the person senses a-pink-cubely, or, in more familiar terms, has a
sensation of a pink cube (where 'of a pink cube' is to be construed
depth-grammar-wise as an adjective) so that the expression might be
parsed 'an of-a-pink-cube sensation'.

60. Again we began our account of thinking with a *VB* model but
proceeded to sketch an account of mental acts as theoretical states or
processes which provide some underpinning for the concept of Mentalese propositional episodes in terms of which the argument for sense
impressions was couched.

61. Notice, however, that I have continued to abstract from the impact
of the revolution in the physical sciences on the problem 'what is a
person?' My appeal to micro-physics has been limited to suggesting that
'classical' thoughts as pure mental episodes can be interpreted as standing to *propensities to say* as micro-physical processes stand to the
physical propensities of the familiar material things around us.

62. The *enriched* image of man-in-the-world, which includes sensings
and Mentalese thinkings, but no individuals other than common-sense

material things, living things other than persons, and persons, is what I have called the Manifest Image of man-in-the-world. Its coherence as a conceptual framework must be fully savored before one turns to the problem of assessing the impact on this Image of the scientific revolution.

63. An understandable consequence of the impact of the conceptual revolution in the physical sciences on the problem of the nature of the person was the resurgence of dualism—a dualism, however, arising from neither religious nor ethical considerations, nor from abstruse philosophical puzzles concerning the nature of knowledge, but rather from the attempt to think through the implications of science. The passage of time has intensified the problem of understanding the unity of the person (though not, of course, for those who take an instrumentalist stance toward scientific theories). The more sophisticated we get, the more intricate our puzzlement. We now await the flowering of neurophysiology, the science which is inheriting the glamor of molecular genetics.

64. The one thing we can be sure of is that we will be confronted with new ways of looking at such 'familiar' facts as that neurons 'fire' and electro-chemical impulses are transmitted through networks and around circuits in the central nervous system. Science has already presented us with new and subtle categories. I suspect that newer and still more subtle categories will be needed to solve the problem of the place of persons in the scientific image of the world. The philosopher can attempt to see the future as in a glass darkly, but essentially his role must be the (by no means unfamiliar) one of a midwife.

65. Part of this midwifery will consist in submitting existing categories to critical examination, as Berkeley, Mach, and Poincaré, to name but three, did in the case of Newtonian mechanics. Part will consist in conceptual experimentation on a cooperative basis which will parallel the free thinking in logic, mathematics, and, dare I say, ontology which provided the context in which relativity was born. Nevertheless, an essential part of the philosopher's role in the concerted attempt to understand how a person is *really* related to what his body *really* is, is to clarify what, in outline, we already know *thinking* and *sensing* to be; and it is to this task that I've addressed myself in these first two lectures.

LECTURE III: EPISTEMIC PRINCIPLES

I

1. The explication of knowledge as 'justified true belief', though it involves many pitfalls to which attention has been called in recent years, remains the orthodox or classical account and is, I believe, essentially sound. Thus, in the present lecture I shall assume that it can be formulated in such a way as to be immune from the type of counterexamples with which it has been bombarded since Gettier's pioneering paper in *Analysis* and turn my attention to another problem which has dogged its footsteps since the very beginning. This problem can be put in the form of two questions: If knowledge is justified true belief, how can there be such a thing as self-evident knowledge? And if there is no such thing as self-evident knowledge, how can *any* true belief be, in the relevant sense, justified?

2. But first let us beat about in the neighboring fields, perhaps to scare up some game, but, in any case, to refamiliarize ourselves with the terrain. Thus, are there not occasions on which a person can be said to be justified in believing something which he would not appropriately be said to know? Presumably, to be justified in believing something is to have good reasons for believing it, as contrasted with its contradictory. But *how* good? Adequate? Conclusive? If adequate, adequate for what? If conclusive, the conclusion of what is at stake?

3. We are all familiar with Austin's point concerning the performative character of 'I know'. We are also familiar with the fact that, whereas to say 'I promise to do *A*' is, other things being equal, to promise to do *A*, to say 'I know that-*p*' is not, other things being equal, to know that-*p*. Chisholm's distinction between the *strict* and the *extended* sense of "performative utterance" is helpful in this connection. According to Chisholm,

> An utterance beginning with "I want" is not performative in [the] strict sense, for it cannot be said to be an "act" of wanting. But "I want" is often used to accomplish what one might accomplish by means of the strict performative "I request." Let us say, then, that "I want" may be a "performative utterance" in an *extended sense* of the latter expression. ([1]: 16-17.)

He asks in which, if either, of these senses an utterance of "I know" may be performative. After reminding us that 'I know' is not performative in the strict sense of the term, he allows that "[it] is often used to accomplish what one may accomplish by the strict performative 'I guarantee' or 'I give you my word,'" and "hence may be performative in an extended sense of the term" ([1]: 16-17).

4. He argues, however, that 'I know' is not always a substitute for 'I guarantee', pointing out that:

> Just as an utterance of "I want" may serve *both* to say something about me and to get you to do something, an utterance of "I know" may serve both to say something about me and to provide you with guarantees. To suppose that the performance of the nondescriptive function is inconsistent with the simultaneous performance of the descriptive function might be called, therefore, an example of the *performative fallacy*. ([1]: 17.)

I think that Chisholm is quite right about this. On the other hand, it seems to me that he overlooks the possibility of a connection between 'I know' and 'I guarantee' other than the one he considers. 'I know that-*p*' might be related to 'I guarantee that-*p*' not just as an autobiographical description which on occasion performs the same role as the latter but as one which contains a reference to guaranteeing in its very meaning. Is it not possible to construe 'I know that-*p*' as essentially equivalent to '*p*, and I have reasons good enough to support a guarantee' (i.e., to say 'I guarantee' or 'You can rely on my statement')? Such an account would enable us to recognize a performative element in the very meaning of the verb 'to know' without construing 'I know' as a performative in the strict sense. It would also preserve the symmetry between first person and other person uses of the verb 'to know' which seems to be a pre-analytic datum. Thus, 'He knows that-*p*' would entail 'He has reasons good enough to support a guarantee that-*p*'.[7]

5. Furthermore, this account would enable us to appreciate the *context dependence* of the adequacy involved. Reasons which might be ade-

7. Notice that the above account of the relation of 'I know' to a performative is not quite the same as Urmson's. According to the latter, as represented by Chisholm, to say that Mr. Jones *knew* some proposition to be true is to say that Mr. Jones was "in a position in which he was entitled to say 'I know'." This account, as Chisholm points out, brings us back to the original problem of how the first person use of the verb is to be construed.

quately good to justify a guarantee on one occasion might not be adequate to justify a guarantee on another. Again, the presence of such a performative element in the very meaning of the verb 'to know' would account for the fact (if it is a fact) that we rarely think in terms of 'I know' in purely self-directed thinkings; that we rarely have thoughts of the form 'I know that-*p*' unless the question of a possible guarantee to someone other than ourselves has arisen. Of course, we *can* 'tell ourselves' that we know something, but, then, so can we be said to make promises to ourselves.

II

6. Yet even after justice has been done, perhaps along the above lines, to the performative element in the meaning of the verb 'to know', it seems to me that we must recognize a closely related use of this expression which, though it may have implications concerning action, is not in any of the above senses performative. For once the *ethical* issue of how good one's reasons for a belief must be in order to justify *giving a guarantee* is solved, there remains the problem of how good reasons must be to justify believing that-*p*, where to believe that-*p* is obviously not an *action*, let alone a performatory action in either the strict or the extended sense.

7. Confronted by this question, we are tempted to set apart a class of cases in which the reasons are not only good enough to justify believing that-*p* but good enough to make it absurd *not* to believe that-*p* (or, perhaps, to believe its contradictory). It is perhaps, some such concept as this which is (in addition to the truth condition) the non-performative core of the meaning of the verb 'to know'.

8. I think the above discussion has served its primary purpose by highlighting the concept of having good reasons for believing that-*p*. For the solution of the problem which was posed in my opening remarks hinges ultimately on a distinction between two ways in which there can be, and one can have, good reasons for believing that-*p*.[8]

8. I have called attention elsewhere to the importance of distinguishing between questions concerning the reasonableness of believing that-*p* from questions concerning the reasonableness of 'acting on the proposition that-*p*', including guaranteeing that-*p*. The concept of acting on a proposition is clear only in simple cases, as when, for example, the proposition occurs as a premise in the agent's practical reasoning. When the agent takes probabilities into account, a far more complicated story is necessary to clarify the sense in which a person can be said to have acted on a given proposition. For a discussion of these problems, see my [6].

9. Now one pattern for justifying a belief in terms of good reasons can be called *inferential*. Consider the schema:

> p;
> So, I have good reasons, all things considered, for believing q.

On reflection, this schema tends to expand into:

> I have good reasons, all things considered, for believing p;
> So, p;
> So, I have good reasons, all things considered, for believing q.

Further reflection suggests that arguments conforming to this schema have a suppressed premise. What might it be? Consider the following expanded schema:

> I have, all things considered, good reasons for believing p;
> So, p;
> p logically implies q;
> So, I have, all things considered, good reasons for believing q.

10. The line of thought thus schematically represented would seem to involve the principle,

> Logical implication transmits reasonableness.

In cases of this type, we are tempted to say, we have *derivative* good reasons, all things considered, for believing q. We say, in other words, that the reasonableness of believing q is 'inferential'.

11. Notice that the above line of thought is obviously an over-simplification, undoubtedly in several respects. In particular, it is important to note that if I have independent grounds for believing *not-q*, I may decide that I do *not* have good reasons, all things considered, for believing that-p. After all, if p implies q, *not-q* equally implies *not-p*. Yet in spite of its oversimplifications, the above train of thought takes us nearer to the distinctions necessary to solve our problem.

12. I have been considering the case where one proposition, p, logically implies another, q, and have claimed, with the above qualifications, that logical implication transmits reasonableness. Perhaps we can also take into account, with trepidation, 'probabilistic' implication, which would give us the following schema:

It is reasonable, all things considered, to believe p;
So, p;
p probabilistically implies q to a high degree;
So, all things considered, it is reasonable to believe q.

Probabilistic justification of beliefs in accordance with this pattern would, presumably, be illustrated by inductive arguments and theoretical explanations. In each case, we move from a premise of the form:

It is reasonable, all things considered, to believe E,

where 'E' formulates the evidence, to a conclusion of the form:

It is reasonable, all things considered, to believe H,

where 'H' formulates in the first case a law-like statement and in the second case a body of theoretical assumptions.

III

13. As has been pointed out since time immemorial, it is most implausible to suppose that all epistemic justification is inferential, at least in the sense of conforming to the patterns described above. Surely, it has been argued, there must be beliefs which we are justified in holding on grounds other than that they can be correctly inferred, inductively or deductively, from other beliefs which we are justified in holding. In traditional terms, if there is to be *inferential* knowledge, must there not be *non-inferential* knowledge—beliefs, that is, the reasonableness of which does not rest on the reasonableness of beliefs which logically or probabilistically imply them?

14. We are clearly in the neighborhood of what has been called the 'self-evident', the 'self-certifying', in short, of 'intuitive knowledge'. It is in this neighborhood that we find what has come to be called the *foundational* picture of human knowledge. According to this picture, beliefs which have inferential reasonableness ultimately rely for their authority on a stratum of beliefs which are, in some sense, self-certifying. The reasonableness of moves from the level of the self-evident to higher levels would involve the principles of logic (deductive and inductive) and, perhaps, certain additional principles which are *sui generis*. They would have in common the character of transmitting authoritativeness from lower-level beliefs to higher-level beliefs.

IV

15. Let us reflect on the concept of such a foundational level of knowledge. It involves the concept of beliefs which are *reasonable*, which have *epistemic authority* or *correctness*, but which are not reasonable or authoritative by virtue of the fact that they are beliefs in propositions which are implied by other propositions which it is reasonable to believe. Let us label them, for the moment, 'non-inferentially reasonable beliefs'.

16. How can there be such beliefs? For the concept of a *reason* seems so clearly tied to that of an *inference* or *argument* that the concept of non-inferential reasonableness seems to be a *contradictio in adjecto*. Surely, we are inclined to say, for a belief (or believing) to be reasonable, there must be a reason for the belief (or believing). And must not this reason be something other than the belief or believing for which it is the reason? And surely, we are inclined to say, to believe something *because* it is reasonable (to believe it) involves not only that there *be* a reason but that, in a relevant sense, one *has* or is *in possession of* the reason. Notice that I have deliberately formulated these expostulations in such a way as to highlight the ambiguities involved when one speaks of reasonable beliefs.

17. In attempting to cope with these challenges, I shall leave aside problems pertaining to inferential and non-inferential reasonableness in logic and mathematics and concentrate on the apparent need for 'self evidence' in the sphere of empirical matters of fact.

18. How might a self-justifying belief be construed? One suggestion, modified from Chisholm's *Theory of Knowledge*,[9] is to the effect that the justification of such beliefs has the form,

> What justifies me in claiming that my belief that *a* is *F* is reasonable is simply the fact that *a* is *F*.

19. But this seems to point to the existence of inferences of the form,

> It is a fact that *a* is *F*;
> So, it is reasonable to believe that *a* is *F*,

and one might begin to wonder what principle authorizes this inference.

---

9. [1]: 28. Chisholm's principle concerns 'what justifies us in counting it as evident that *a* is *F*'. But the 'evident' is defined on p. 22 as a special case of the 'reasonable'.

20. Something, clearly, has gone wrong. In order for any such argument to do the job, its premise would have to have authority; it would have to be something which it is reasonable to believe. But if we modify the schema to take this into account, it becomes:

> It is reasonable to believe it to be a fact that a is F;
> So, it is reasonable to believe that a is F,

which, in virtue of the equivalence of

> believing a to be F

with

> believing it to be a fact that a is F,

is obviously unilluminating.

V

21. Now many philosophers who have endorsed a concept of intuitive knowledge are clearly committed to the position that there is a level of *cognition* more basic than *believing*. This more basic level would consist of a sub-conceptual[10] awareness of certain facts. In terms of the framework sketched in the preceding two lectures, there would be a level of cognition more basic than *thinkings* or tokenings of sentences in Mentalese—more basic, in fact, than symbolic activity, literal *or* analogical. It would be a level of cognition unmediated by concepts; indeed it would be the very *source of* concepts in some such way as described by traditional theories of abstraction. It would be 'direct apprehension' of facts; their 'direct presence' to the mind.[11]

---

10. Where 'sub-conceptual' is far from being used as a pejorative term.

11. It is clearly some such position which is envisaged by many who explicitly reject the equation of knowledge with justified true belief. That it is *implicit* in Chisholm's position becomes clear not only when we reflect (as above, Sections 18-20) on what his principle concerning the directly evident might mean, but when we take into account his use of such phrases as "state of affairs" that " 'presents itself to him' " or that " 'is apprehended through itself' " ([1]: 28) and his general commitment to a fact ontology ([1], Chap. 7, *passim*), a 'fact', in the relevant sense, being a "state of affairs which exists" ([1]: 104). 'Exists' in this context should not be confused with the 'existential quantifier' but should be considered as a synonym for 'obtains'. It is obviously not self-contradictory to say that some states of affairs do not obtain.

22. Schematically we would have,

> It is a fact (which I directly apprehend) that a is F;
> So, it is reasonable to have the *conceptual belief* that a is F.

This multiplication of distinctions raises two serious problems: (1) What sort of entities are *facts*? Do they belong to the real (extra-conceptual) order? That 'fact' is roughly a synonym for 'truth', and 'true' is appropriately predicated of conceptual items (in overt speech or Mentalese) should give pause for thought.

23. Then there is also the question: (2) How is 'direct apprehension' to be understood? If the apprehend*ing* is distinguishable from the apprehend*ed*, is it not also 'separable'? Might not apprehending occur without any *fact* being apprehended? If so, an 'apprehending that-*p*' might not be an apprehending of the fact that-*p*. Hitting, in baseball, implies that something is hit. 'Swinging' does not. To *hit* is to *swing successfully*. Of course, 'apprehend', like 'see', is, *in its ordinary sense*, an achievement word. But does this not mean that, as in the case of 'see', there is a place for '*ostensibly* apprehending', i.e., *seeming to apprehend*, a concept which does not imply achievement?

24. Many who use the metaphor 'to see' in intellectual contexts overlook the fact that in its literal sense 'seeing' is a term for a *successful* conceptual activity which contrasts with 'seeming to see'. No piling on of additional metaphors (e.g., 'grasping', which implies an object grasped) can blunt this fact. Now the distinction between *seeing* and merely *seeming to see* implies a criterion. To rely on the metaphors of 'apprehending' or 'presence of the object' is to obscure the need of criteria for distinguishing between 'knowing' and 'seeming to know', which ultimately define what it means to speak of knowledge as a *correct* or well-founded *thinking* that something is the case.

25. If so, to know that we have apprehended a fact, we would have to know that the criteria which distinguish *apprehending* from *seeming to apprehend* were satisfied. In short, I suspect that the notion of a non-conceptual 'direct apprehension' of a 'fact' provides a merely verbal solution to our problem. The regress is stopped by an *ad hoc* regress-stopper. Indeed, the very metaphors which promised the sought-for foundation contain within themselves a dialectical moment which takes us beyond them.

VI

26. What is the alternative? I suggest that the key to our problem is provided by the Verbal Behaviorist model, developed in the preceding lecture. It is, we have seen, a simple, indeed radically over-simplified, model, but it will provide us, I believe, with the outline of a strategy for getting out of the classical labyrinth.

27. According to this model, it will be remembered, the primary sense of

> The thought occurred to Jones that snow is white

is

> Jones said 'snow is white',

where the verb 'to say' was stripped of some of its ordinary implications and roughly equated with 'to utter words candidly as one who knows the language'. In particular, it was purged of the illocutionary and perlocutionary forces which Austin and Grice find so central to their theory of meaning. 'To say', in this sense, was also equated with 'thinking-out-loud'.

28. According to the *VB*, as I described him, we must also introduce, in order to take account of those cases where one thinks silently, a *secondary* sense of

> The thought occurred to Jones that snow is white,

in which it refers to a short-term proximate propensity to think-out-loud that snow is white. When this propensity is 'uninhibited', *one thinks-out-loud*, i.e., thinks in the primary sense of this term (as construed by *VB*). There can be many reasons why, on a particular occasion, this propensity is inhibited. But, for our purposes, the most important is the general inhibition acquired in childhood when, after being taught to think-out-loud, one is trained not to be a 'babbler'. One might use the model of an on-off switch which gets into the wiring diagram when the child learns to keep his thoughts to himself.

29. In the concluding sections of the preceding lecture (cf. Lecture II, section IV), I argued that yet another concept of 'having the thought occur to one that-*p*' can be introduced which stands to the second as the theoretical concept of electronic processes stands to the acquisition (and loss) of the power to attract iron filings (or a bell clapper) by a piece of soft iron in a coil of wire attached to an electric circuit. I argued that the classical concept of thought-episodes can be construed as part of a

theoretical framework designed to explain the acquisition and loss of verbal propensities to think-out-loud. In approaching the problem of the status of non-inferential knowledge, however, I shall return to the *VB* model and concentrate, indeed, on the primary sense of having the thought occur to one that-*p*, i.e., think-out-loud that-*p*.

30. I argued in my first lecture that perceptual experience involves a sensory element which is in no way a form of thinking, however intimately it may be connected with thinking. This element consists of what I variously called 'sense impressions', 'sensations', or 'sensa'. I argued that these items, properly construed, belong in a theoretical framework designed to explain:

(a) the difference between merely thinking of (believing in the existence of) a perceptible state of affairs and *seeing* (or seeming to see) that such a state of affairs exists;

(b) how it can seem to a person that there is a pink ice cube in front of him when there isn't one—either because there is something there which is either not pink or not cubical, or because there is nothing there and he is having a realistic hallucination.

31. I've explored problems pertaining to the nature and status of this sensory element on many occasions (most recently in [9], Chapter I, and in [11], which is a reply to [2]), but further exploration of this theme would leave no time for the problem at hand.

32. What is important for our purposes is that perceptual experience also involves a conceptual or propositional component—a 'thinking' in a suitably broad sense of this accordion term. In perception, the thought is caused to occur to one that, for example, there is a pink ice cube in front of one. It is misleading to call such a thought a 'perceptual judgment'—for this implies question-answering activity of estimating, for example, the size of an object. (I judge that the room is ten feet tall.) Perhaps the best term is 'taking something to be the case'. Thus, on the occasion of sensing a certain color configuration, one takes there to be an object or situation of a certain description in one's physical environment.

33. Consider once again the case, discussed in Lecture II, sections 35-41, where

Jones sees there to be a red apple in front of him.

As we explained there, given that Jones has learned how to use the relevant words in perceptual situations, he is justified in reasoning as follows:

> I just thought-out-loud 'Lo! Here is a red apple'
> (no countervailing conditions obtain);
> So, there is good reason to believe that there is a red apple in front of me.

34. Of course, the conclusion of this reasoning is not the *thinking* involved in his original perceptual experience. Like all justification arguments, it is a higher-order thinking. He did not originally *infer* that there is a red apple in front of him. Now, however, he is inferring from the character and context of his experience that it is veridical and that there is good reason to believe that there is indeed a red apple in front of him.

35. Notice that although the justification of the belief that there is a red apple in front of (Jones) is an inferential justification, it has the peculiar character that its essential premise asserts the occurrence of the very same belief in a specific context.[12] It is this fact which gives the appearance that such beliefs are *self*-justifying and hence gives the justification the appearance of being *non-inferential*.

36. It is, as I see it, precisely this feature of the unique pattern of justification in question which, misinterpreted, leads Chisholm to formulate as his principle for the 'directly evident',

> What justifies me in counting it as evident that a is F is simply the fact that a is F. ([1]: 28.)

To be sure, Chisholm's examples of the 'directly evident' are not taken from the domain of *perceptual* beliefs, but rather, in true Cartesian spirit, from one's knowledge about what is going on in one's mind at the present moment. Indeed, he rejects the idea that particular perceptual beliefs of the kind which I illustrated by my example of the red apple are ever directly evident.

37. On the other hand, though he does think that particular perceptual beliefs of this type can at best be *indirectly evident*, he does think that

12. I called attention to this feature of the justification involved in 'non-inferential' knowledge in [10], Chapter 3. Thus, I wrote ". . . one only knows what one has a right to think to be the case. Thus, to say that one directly knows that-p is to say that his right to the conviction that-p essentially involves the fact that the idea that-p occurred to the knower in a specific way" ([10]: 88). I suggested that this "kind of credibility" be called 'trans-level credibility', and the pattern of inference involved in the reasoning which mobilizes this credibility, 'trans-level inference'. A similar point was less clearly made in Sections 32-39 of [5].

they can be *reasonable*. Should we say '*directly* reasonable'? I, of course, would answer in the affirmative. Yet it is not clear to me that Chisholm would be happy with this suggestion. If (as he should) he has at the back of his mind the reasoning;

> There (visually) appears to me to be a red apple here;
> So, it is reasonable for me (to believe) that there is a red apple here,

then he should not object to speaking of the reasonableness in question as 'direct', for the premise does not contain a predicate of epistemic evaluation. If, on the other hand (as he should not), he has at the back of his mind the following reasoning,

> It is *evident* to me that there (visually) appears to me to be a red apple here;
> So, it is *reasonable* for me (to believe) that there is a red apple here,

we could expect him to object to speaking of this reasonableness as 'direct'.

38. This tension sets the stage for a corresponding comment on Chisholm's third epistemic principle, which concerns the case where what we visually take to be the case is the presence of something having a "sensible characteristic F" (where 'F' ranges over the familiar Aristotelian list of proper and common sensibles). The principle reads as follows:

> (C) If there is a certain sensible characteristic F such that S believes that he perceives something to be F, then it is *evident* to S that he is perceiving something to have that characteristic F, and also *evident* that there is something that is F.

39. I shall not pause to quibble over such matters as whether, in the light of Chisholm's definition of 'evident', it can ever be evident to me that I am perceiving something to be pink or that something in front of me is pink—even if the claim is limited to the facing side. A high degree of reasonableness will do. The point which I wish to stress is that once again the question arises, does Chisholm think of the evidence involved in the principle as 'direct' or 'indirect'? This time it is clear that he thinks of it as *indirect*. As I see it, then, he has at the back of his mind the following reasoning:

> It is *evident* to me that there appears to me to be a pink object here;

> So, it is *evident* to me that I perceive a pink object to be here and *evident* to me that there is a pink object here.

The contrasting reasoning would be:

> There appears to me to be a pink object here;
> So, it is *evident* to me that I perceive a pink object to be here and *evident* to me that there is a pink object here.

40. Now I suspect that what has misled Chisholm is the fact that if I were to argue,

> There appears to me to be a pink cube here;
> So, it is highly reasonable for me (to believe) that there is a pink object here,

a skeptic could be expected to challenge me by asking 'What right have you to accept your conclusion, unless you have a right to accept the premise? Are you not implying that *you know* that there appears to you to be a pink object here; and must not this claim be a tacit *premise* in your argument?' But, surely, the skeptic would just be mistaken—not, indeed in asserting that in some sense I *imply* that I know that there appears to me to be a pink object here, but in asserting that this implication must be taken to be a premise in my reasoning, if it is to be *valid*, and, hence, if the corresponding epistemic principle is to be *true*. But in that case, the latter principle would be *not* Chisholm's (C), but rather:

> (C') *If it is evident to S that there is a certain sensible characteristic F...*

41. The larger import of the above reply to the skeptic will be sketched in my concluding remarks. For the moment, let me say that from my point of view something very like Chisholm's principle (C) is sound but concerns the *direct* evidence (or, better, *direct* high degree of reasonableness) of certain perceptual beliefs. Let me formulate it as follows:

> (S) If there is a certain sensible characteristic *F* such that *S* believes that he perceives something to be *F*, then it is *evident* to *S* that there is something that is *F* and, hence, that he is perceiving something to be *F*.

42. Notice that I have reversed the relative position of the two clauses in the consequent as they appear in Chisholm's principle. This is because, on my interpretation, the *core* of the principle is

> (S1) If I ostensibly see there to be an *F* object here, then it is highly reasonable for me (to believe) that there is an *F* object here.

And the move to

> (S2) If I ostensibly see there to be an *F* object here, then it is
> highly reasonable for me (to believe) *that I see* there to be
> an *F* object here

is justified by the conceptual tie between 'ostensibly see', 'see', and
truth.

VII

43. Chisholm's principle (C) and his other epistemic principles pertaining to perception and memory are themselves justified, as he sees it, by
the fact that unless they, or something like them, are true, then there
could be no such thing as perceptual knowledge to the effect, to use his
example, that there is a cat on the roof. We have here a justification of
the 'this or nothing' kind familiar to the Kantian tradition. The principles
also seem, on occasion, to be treated as candidates for the status of
synthetic *a priori* (and even, one suspects, self-evident) truth.

44. As I see it, on the other hand, these epistemic principles can be
placed in a naturalistic setting and their authority construed in terms of
the nature of concept formation and of the acquisition of relevant linguistic skills. The model which I have been using is, indeed, a very
simple one, and I have largely limited my use of it to the epistemic authority of perceptual beliefs. But if the strategy which I have suggested is
successful, it is a relatively simple matter to extend it to memory beliefs.
I have discussed the case of non-inferential knowledge of our own
mental states in some detail, using this same general strategy, on a number of occasions (most recently in [9], esp. pp. 71 ff, 151 ff).

45. But, surely, it will be urged, facts about learning languages and
acquiring linguistic skills are themselves empirical *facts*; and to know
these facts involves perception, memory, indeed, all the epistemic activities the justification of which is at stake. Must we not conclude that
any such account as I give of the principle that perceptual beliefs
occurring in perceptual contexts are *likely to be true* is circular? It must,
indeed, be granted that principles pertaining to the epistemic authority
of perceptual and memory beliefs are not the sort of thing which *could*
be arrived at by inductive reasoning from perceptual belief. But the best
way to make this point is positive. *We have to be in this framework to be
thinking and perceiving beings at all*. I suspect that it is this plain truth

which is the real underpinning of the idea that the authority of epistemic principles rests on the fact that unless they were true we could not see that a cat is on the roof.

46. I pointed out a moment ago that we have to be in the framework of these (and other) principles to be thinking, perceiving, and, I now add, acting beings at all. But surely this makes it clear that the exploration of these principles is but part and parcel of the task of explicating the concept of a rational animal or, in *VB* terms, of a language-using organism whose language is *about* the world in which it is *used*. It is only in the light of this larger task that the problem of the status of epistemic principles reveals its true meaning.

47. From the perspective of this larger task, the metaphor of 'foundation and superstructure' is seen to be a false extrapolation, to use a Deweyan turn of phrase, from specific 'problematic situations' with respect to which it *is* appropriate. And when we concern ourselves, as Philosophy ultimately demands, with *how it is* with man and his world, as contrasted with the catch-as-catch-can procedures which generate man's awareness of himself and his world, surely we can say, as I wrote some fifteen years ago in an earlier essay on this topic,

> There is clearly *some* point to the picture of human knowledge as resting on a level of propositions—observation reports—which do not rest on other propositions in the same way as other propositions rest on them. On the other hand, I do wish to insist that the metaphor of 'foundation' is misleading in that it keeps us from seeing that if there is a logical dimension in which other empirical propositions rest on observation reports, there is another logical dimension in which the latter rest on the former.
>
> *Above all,* the picture is misleading because of its static character. One seems forced to choose between the picture of an elephant which rests on a tortoise (What supports the tortoise?) and the picture of a great Hegelian serpent of knowledge with its tail in its mouth (Where did it begin?). Neither will do. For empirical knowledge, like its sophisticated extension, science, is rational, not because it has a *foundation* but because it is a self-correcting enterprise which can put *any* claim in jeopardy, though not *all* at once. ([5], section 38; quoted from [10]: 170.)

REFERENCES

[1] R. M. Chisholm, *Theory of Knowledge* (Englewood Cliffs, N. J.: Prentice-Hall, 1966).

[2] James W. Cornman, "Sellars, Scientific Realism, and Sensa," *Review of Metaphysics* 24(1970).

[3] Roderick Firth, "Coherence, Certainty, and Epistemic Priority," *Journal of Philosophy* 61(1964): 545-57.

[4] Wilfrid Sellars, "Counterfactuals, Dispositions, and the Causal Modalities," in Herbert Feigl, Michael Scriven, and Grover Maxwell, eds., *Minnesota Studies in the Philosophy of Science*, Vol. II (Minneapolis: University of Minnesota Press, 1957).

[5] _____, "Empiricism and the Philosophy of Mind," in Herbert Feigl and Michael Scriven, eds., *Minnesota Studies in the Philosophy of Science*, Vol. I (Minneapolis: University of Minnesota Press, 1956). Reprinted as Chapter V of [10].

[6] _____, "Induction as Vindication," *Philosophy of Science* 31(1964): 197-232.

[7] _____, "Metaphysics and the Concept of a Person," in Karel Lambert, ed., *The Logical Way of Doing Things* (New Haven: Yale University Press, 1969).

[8] _____, "Philosophy and the Scientific Image of Man," in Robert Colodny, ed., *Frontiers of Science and Philosophy* (Pittsburgh: University of Pittsburgh Press, 1962). Reprinted as Chapter I of [10].

[9] _____, *Science and Metaphysics* (London: Routledge and Kegan Paul, 1967).

[10] _____, *Science, Perception and Reality* (London: Routledge and Kegan Paul, and New York: Humanities Press, 1963).

[11] _____, "Science, Sense Impressions, and Sensa: A Reply to Cornman," *Review of Metaphysics* 25(1971).

WILFRID SELLARS'

Philosophical Bibliography

(Items are listed in order of composition, not in order of publication.)

1. "Pure Pragmatics and Epistemology," *Philosophy of Science* 14(1947): 181-202.
2. "Epistemology and the New Way of Words," *The Journal of Philosophy* 44(1947): 645-60.
3. "Realism and the New Way of Words," *Philosophy and Phenomenological Research* 8(1948): 601-34. Reprinted in *Readings in Philosophical Analysis*, edited by Herbert Feigl and Wilfrid Sellars (New York: Appleton-Century-Crofts, 1949).
4. "Concepts as Involving Laws and Inconceivable without Them," *Philosophy of Science* 15(1948): 287-315.
5. "Aristotelian Philosophies of Mind," in *Philosophy for the Future*, edited by Roy Wood Sellars, V. J. McGill, and Marvin Farber (New York: The Macmillan Co., 1949): 544-70.
6. "Language, Rules, and Behavior," in *John Dewey: Philosopher of Science and Freedom*, edited by Sidney Hook (New York: The Dial Press, 1949): 289-315.
7. "On the Logic of Complex Particulars," *Mind* 58(1949): 306-38.
8. "Acquaintance and Description Again," *The Journal of Philosophy* 46(1949): 496-505.
9. "Review of Ernst Cassirer, *Language and Myth*," *Philosophy and Phenomenological Research* 9(1948-49): 326-29.
10. "The Identity of Linguistic Expressions and the Paradox of Analysis," *Philosophical Studies* 1(1950): 24-31.
11. "Quotation Marks, Sentences, and Propositions," *Philosophy and Phenomenological Research* 10(1950): 515-25.
12. "Gestalt Qualities and the Paradox of Analysis," *Philosophical Studies* 1(1950): 92-94.
13. "Obligation and Motivation," *Philosophical Studies* 2(1951): 21-25.
14. "Review of Arthur Pap, *Elements of Analytic Philosophy*," *Philosophy and Phenomenological Research* 11(1950): 104-9.
15. "Obligation and Motivation," in *Readings in Ethical Theory*, edited by Wilfrid Sellars and John Hospers (New York: Appleton-Century-Crofts, 1952): 511-17. A revised and expanded version of (13).

16. "Review of C. West Churchman and Russell L. Ackoff, *Methods of Inquiry: An Introduction to Philosophy and Scientific Method,*" *Philosophy and Phenomenological Research* 12(1951): 149-50.
17. "Comments on Mr. Hempel's Theses," *Review of Metaphysics* 5(1952): 623-25.
18. "Mind, Meaning, and Behavior," *Philosophical Studies* 3(1952): 83-95.
19. "Particulars," *Philosophy and Phenomenological Research* 13(1952): 184-99.
20. "Is There a Synthetic A Priori?", *Philosophy of Science* 29(1953): 121-38. Reprinted in revised form in *American Philosophers at Work*, edited by Sidney Hook (New York: Criterion Press, 1957); also published in Italy in translation.
21. "A Semantical Solution of the Mind-Body Problem," *Methodos* 5(1953): 45-82.
22. "Inference and Meaning," *Mind* 62(1953): 313-38.
23. "Presupposing," *Philosophical Review* 63(1954): 197-215.
24. "Some Reflections on Language Games," *Philosophy of Science* 21(1954): 204-28.
25. "A Note on Popper's Argument for Dualism," *Analysis* 15(1954): 23-24.
26. "Physical Realism," *Philosophy and Phenomenological Research* 15(1954): 13-32.
27. "Putnam on Synonymity and Belief," *Analysis* 15(1955): 117-20.
28. "Vlastos and 'The Third Man'," *Philosophical Review* 64(1955): 405-37.
29. "Imperatives, Intentions, and the Logic of 'Ought'," *Methodos* 8(1956): 228-68.
30. "The Concept of Emergence" (with Paul Meehl), in *Minnesota Studies in the Philosophy of Science*, Vol. I, edited by Herbert Feigl and Michael Scriven (Minneapolis: University of Minnesota Press, 1956): 239-52.
31. "Empiricism and the Philosophy of Mind" (University of London Special Lectures in Philosophy for 1956), *ibid.*, pp. 253-329.
32. "Logical Subjects and Physical Objects," *Philosophy and Phenomenological Research* 17(1957): 458-72. Contribution to a symposium with Peter Strawson held at Duke University, November, 1955.
33. "Counterfactuals, Dispositions, and the Causal Modalities," in *Minnesota Studies in the Philosophy of Science*, Vol. II, edited by Herbert Feigl, Michael Scriven, and Grover Maxwell (Minneapolis: University of Minnesota Press, 1957): 225-308.
34. "Intentionality and the Mental," a symposium by correspondence with Roderick Chisholm, published in the same volume as (30), pp. 507-39.
35. "Substance and Form in Aristotle," *The Journal of Philosophy* 54(1957): 688-99. The opening paper in a symposium on Aristotle's conception of form held at the December, 1957, meeting of the American Philosophical Association.
36. "Empiricism and Abstract Entities," in *The Philosophy of Rudolf Carnap* (*The Library of Living Philosophers*) edited by Paul A. Schilpp (La Salle, Illinois: Open Court, 1963): 431-68.

37. "Grammar and Existence: a Preface to Ontology," *Mind* 69(1960): 499-533. Two lectures delivered at Yale University, March, 1958.
38. "Time and the World Order," in *Minnesota Studies in the Philosophy of Science*, Vol. III, edited by Herbert Feigl and Grover Maxwell (Minneapolis: University of Minnesota Press, 1963): 527-616. A Metaphysical and Epistemological Analysis of Becoming.
39. "Imperatives, Intentions, and the Logic of 'Ought'," in *Morality and the Language of Conduct*, a collection of essays in moral philosophy edited by Hector-Neri Castañeda and George Nakhnikian (Detroit: Wayne State University Press, 1963): 159-214. A radically revised and enlarged version of (29).
40. "Being and Being Known," *Proceedings of the American Catholic Philosophical Association* (1960): 28-49.
41. "The Language of Theories," in *Current Issues in the Philosophy of Science*, edited by Herbert Feigl and Grover Maxwell (New York: Holt, Rinehart, and Winston, 1961): 57-77.
42. Comments on Maxwell's "Meaning Postulates in Scientific Theories," *ibid.*, pp. 183-92.
43. "Philosophy and the Scientific Image of Man," in *Frontiers of Science and Philosophy*, edited by Robert Colodny (Pittsburgh: University of Pittsburgh Press, 1962): 35-78.
44. Comments on McMullin's "Matter as a Principle," in *The Concept of Matter*, edited by Ernan McMullin (Notre Dame: The University of Notre Dame Press, 1963): 213-17.
45. "Naming and Saying," *Philosophy of Science* 29(1962): 7-26.
46. "Truth and Correspondence," *The Journal of Philosophy* 59(1962): 29-56.
47. "Abstract Entities," *Review of Metaphysics* 16(1963): 627-71.
48. "Classes as Abstract Entities and the Russell Paradox," *Review of Metaphysics* 17(1963): 67-90.
49. "The Paradox of Analysis: A Neo-Fregean Approach," *Analysis* Supplementary Vol. 24(1964): 84-98.
50. "Theoretical Explanation," in *Philosophy of Science: The Delaware Seminar*, Vol. II (New York: John Wiley, 1963): 61-78.
51. "The Intentional Realism of Everett Hall," in *Commonsense Realism: Critical Essays on the Philosophy of Everett W. Hall*, edited by E. M. Adams, *The Southern Journal of Philosophy* 4(1966): 103-15.
52. *Science, Perception and Reality* (London: Routledge and Kegan Paul, 1963). Includes items (19), (20), (24), (31), (37), (40), (41), (43), (45), (46), and a hitherto unpublished essay, "Phenomenalism."
53. "Induction as Vindication," *Philosophy of Science* 31(1964): 197-231.
54. "Notes on Intentionality," *The Journal of Philosophy* 61(1964): 655-65. Presented in a symposium on "Intentionality" at the December, 1964, meeting of the American Philosophical Association.
55. "The Identity Approach to the Mind-Body Problem," *Review of Metaphysics* 18(1965): 430-51. Presented at the Boston Colloquium for

the Philosophy of Science, April, 1963. Reprinted in the same volume as
(57).

56. "Méditations Leibnitziennes," *American Philosophical Quarterly*
2(1965): 105-18. An expanded version of the opening paper in a
symposium on Rationalism at the May, 1958, meeting of the American Philosophical Association.

57. "Scientific Realism or Irenic Instrumentalism: A Critique of Nagel and
Feyerabend on Theoretical Explanation," *Boston Studies in the Philos-
ophy of Science*, Vol. II, edited by Robert Cohen and Marx Wartofsky
(New York: Humanities Press, 1965): 171-204.

58. "Thought and Action," in *Freedom and Determinism*, edited by Keith
Lehrer (New York: Random House, 1966): 105-39.

59. "Fatalism and Determinism," *Ibid.*, pp. 140-74.

60. *Philosophical Perspectives* (Springfield, Illinois: Charles C Thomas,
Publisher, 1967). Includes items (26), (28), (35), (44), (47), (48), (49),
(50), (51), (54), (55), (56), (57), a rejoinder to Gregory Vlastos on the
Third Man Argument (see (28)), and three previously unpublished essays: "The Soul as Craftsman" (on Plato's Idea of the Good), "Aristotle's Metaphysics: An Interpretation," and "Science and Ethics."

61. *Science and Metaphysics: Variations on Kantian Themes*, The John Locke
Lectures for 1965–66 (London: Routledge and Kegan Paul, 1967).

62. "Phenomenalism," in *Intentionality, Minds, and Perception*, edited by
Hector-Neri Castañeda (Detroit: Wayne State University Press, 1967):
215-74. An abbreviated version of the essay referred to in (52) above.

63. "Reply to Aune," *ibid.*, pp. 286-300.

64. *Form and Content in Ethical Theory*, The Lindley Lecture for 1967
(Lawrence, Kansas: Department of Philosophy, University of Kansas,
1967).

65. "Some Remarks on Kant's Theory of Experience," *The Journal of
Philosophy* 64(1967): 633-47. Presented in a symposium on Kant at the
December, 1967, meeting of the American Philosophical Association.

66. "Metaphysics and the Concept of a Person," in *The Logical Way of Doing
Things*, edited by Karel Lambert (New Haven: Yale University Press,
1969): 219-52.

67. "Some Reflections on Thoughts and Things," *Noûs* 1(1967): 97-121. Reprinted as Chapter III of (61).

68. "Reflections on Contrary to Duty Imperatives," *Noûs* 1(1967): 303-44.

69. "Kant's Views on Sensibility and Understanding," *Monist* 51(1967):
463-91. Reprinted as Chapter I of (61). The first of the six John Locke
Lectures.

70. "Some Problems About Belief," in *Philosophical Logic*, edited by J. W.
Davis, D. T. Hockney, and W. K. Wilson (Dordrecht: D. Reidel, 1969):
46-65. Reprinted in *Words and Objections, Essays on the Work of
W. V. Quine*, edited by D. Davidson and J. Hintikka (Dordrecht:
D. Reidel, 1969): 186-205.

71. "Are There Non-deductive Logics?," in *Essays in Honor of C. G.
Hempel*, Synthese Library (Dordrecht: D. Reidel, 1970): 83-103.

72. "Language as Thought and as Communication," *Philosophy and Phenomenological Research* 29(1969): 506-27.

73. "On Knowing the Better and Doing the Worse," *International Philosophical Quarterly* 10(1970): 5-19. The 1969 Suarez Philosophy Lecture delivered at Fordham University.

74. "Science, Sense Impressions, and Sensa: A Reply to Cornman," *Review of Metaphysics* 25(1971): 391-447.

75. "Towards a Theory of the Categories," in *Experience and Theory*, edited by L. Foster and J. W. Swanson (Amherst: University of Massachusetts Press, 1970): 55-78.

76. "Actions and Events," *Noûs* 7(1973): 179-202. Contribution to a symposium on the topic at the University of North Carolina, November, 1969.

77. "The Structure of Knowledge: (1) Perception; (2) Minds; (3) Epistemic Principles," The Matchette Foundation Lectures for 1971 at the University of Texas. Published for the first time in this volume.

78. "Reason and the Art of Living in Plato," in *Essays in Honor of Marvin Farber* (Buffalo: The University of Buffalo Press, 1973).

79. ". . . this I or he or it (the thing) which thinks," the presidential address, American Philosophical Association (Eastern Division), for 1970, *Proceedings of the American Philosophical Association* 44(1972).

80. "Reply to Donagan," *Philosophical Studies* 26(1975).

81. "Ontology and the Philosophy of Mind in Russell," in *Bertrand Russell's Philosophy*, edited by George Nakhnikian; (London: Duckworth; New York: Barnes and Noble, 1974): 57-100.

82. "Reply to Marras," *Canadian Journal of Philosophy* 2(1973): 485-93.

83. "Conceptual Change," in *Conceptual Change*, edited by P. Maynard and G. Pearce (Dordrecht, Holland: D. Reidel, 1973).

84. "Reply to Quine," *Synthese* 26(1973): 122-45.

85. "Autobiographical Reflections" (February, 1973). Published for the first time in this volume.

86. "Double-Knowledge Approach to the Mind-Body Problem," *New Scholasticism* 45(1971): 269-89.

87. "Meaning as Functional Classification (A Perspective on the Relation of Syntax to Semantics)." To appear in the proceedings of the University of Connecticut Conference on Semantics (1973), along with replies to Daniel Dennett and Hilary Putnam.

88. "On the Introduction of Abstract Entities," a paper read at the University of Wisconsin at Milwaukee conference on ontology, April, 1972. To be published in an anthology on the philosophy of logic, edited by members of the philosophy department at the University of Western Ontario.

89. "Givenness and Explanatory Coherence," (Presented at a symposium on Foundations of Knowledge at the December 1973, meeting of the American Philosophical Association). An abbreviated version was printed in the *Journal of Philosophy* 70 (1973).

90. "Seeing, Seeming, and Sensing," in *The Ontological Turn: Studies in the Philosophy of Gustav Bergmann*, ed. by M. S. Gram and E. D. Klemke (Iowa City: University of Iowa Press, 1974).

INDEX